FOOD
POLICY
ANALYSIS

A WORLD BANK PUBLICATION

FOOD
POLICY
ANALYSIS

C. Peter Timmer
Walter P. Falcon
Scott R. Pearson

Published for The World Bank
The Johns Hopkins University Press
Baltimore and London

First printing June 1983
All rights reserved
Manufactured in the United States of America

The Johns Hopkins University Press
Baltimore, Maryland 21218, U.S.A.

The views and interpretations in this book are those
of the authors and should not be attributed to the
World Bank, to its affiliated organizations, or to any
individual acting on their behalf.

Figures Pensri Kimpitak
Binding design Joyce Eisen

Library of Congress Cataloging in Publication Data

Timmer, C. Peter
  Food policy analysis.

  "Published for the World Bank."
  Bibliography: p.
  Includes index.
  1. Food supply—Government policy.   2. Underdeveloped
areas—Food supply—Government policy.   I. Falcon,
Walter P., 1936–   II. Pearson, Scott R.
III. Title.
HD9000.6.T48   1983   338.1'9   83–4389
ISBN 0–8018–3072–9
ISBN 0–8018–3073–7 (pbk.)

HD9000
.6
.T48
1983

Contents

Preface

Food policy will be of paramount concern to economic development efforts for at least the next two decades. Governments are trying to confront their food problems, and they need good analysis and good analysts to do so. This book attempts to show that food problems are immersed in the broader problems of economic development and that solving food problems is a complex task involving a long-run vision of how food systems evolve under alternative policy environments. Our goal is to establish for the reader a sense of that vision.

The book presents the tools and analytical frameworks for doing the sectoral analyses that are the foundation of a consistent domestic food policy. Both the vision of the system and the analytical steps needed to understand it have been fermenting in our minds for the past several years, partly because we have been doing food policy analysis in various settings, partly because we have been trying to teach a variety of audiences how to do it. Indeed, in many ways this book has emerged from the exhilaration and frustration of teaching food policy analysis to diverse groups of students scattered around the world.

The students provided a major stimulus to write this book and also a complex, composite image of our ideal audience. Our classes on food policy analysis have been attended by students from a wide variety of backgrounds. Economics students, along with students in the allied fields of agricultural economics, economic development, and economic history, are interested in applying the theory and tools of economics to real-world settings. The nature of the topic—the problems of food and agriculture—also draws a range of specialists, from public health professionals to political scientists, who find parts of the approach to these problems relevant to their own disciplines. Civil servants from developing countries have enriched the classes with their experience and insights. What brings all these students, plus a sprinkling of urban planners, art history majors, and divinity students, is a desire to know more about the problems of the world, especially the pressing and urgent problems of poverty and hunger.

Once the expectation is raised that problems of this magnitude will be dealt with, it then becomes difficult to narrow the investigative focus. Temptation and pressures are great to consider all the relevant factors—sociological, political, anthropological, demographic, economic, historical, biological, and medical—so that nothing will be missed. It is especially difficult to talk about poverty and hunger without including the myriad of political factors that so influence the basic choices a society makes, which result, in many countries, in large, dispossessed classes of people.

It was beyond the scope of this book to structure meaningfully the political issues of food policy. The interests of different groups may range from those of competing factions within a bureaucracy to those of revolutionaries trying to bring down a government. A reminder to students that a course in food policy analysis is not a course in revolution brings knowing smiles from foreign students, for they are keenly aware of the crucial role of politics and the limitations of incremental change designed to reduce hunger within a particular political context. Political factors, however, do not necessarily dominate the formation of effective food policies. For example, three Asian countries mentioned in this book—China, Indonesia, and Sri Lanka—have vastly different political climates, yet each has a core of government and university people genuinely committed to solving the pressing problems of hunger and poverty in their societies. Nearly all countries have a few such people. In many countries they do not form a critical mass or have sufficient access to political power to have an influence on policy.

The confidence to proceed with this book draws from experience with these committed individuals and with students around the world, deeply concerned about food problems in their societies, who come to our classes, test the simple models against their own experiences, and depart, they say, with a better understanding of the complex forces at work in their own countries. This book focuses on analysis, its power and its limits for improving food policy. Analysis has an important role in policy design, but it cannot solve all the problems that fall within its vision and grasp. Its most effective contribution is the analytical process itself: the careful thinking through of complex problems within a consistent framework.

So it was with this modest and limited approach—building a framework using the theory and tools of economics and applying it to the problems of hunger and poverty—that we set out in 1979 to write a book that would show how to analyze food policies. The most difficult task—which has bedeviled us for three years—was identifying the audience we wanted to reach.

Who is this "food policy analyst" who figures so prominently in the book? In a narrow sense, the food policy analyst is the staff member of a food ministry, such as the Indonesian Food Logistics Agency (BULOG). The three authors teach a three-week training course to BULOG staff, most of whom return to provincial centers where defending the "floor price" to farmers and the "ceiling price" to consumers has a very real immediacy. These people are involved in the day-to-day management of a food policy. BULOG staff in larger centers and the capital contribute directly to making policy, a responsibility shared by the staffs of the Indonesian National Planning Agency, ministries of agriculture and finance, and the central bank.

But in a broader sense, the analyst is all of our students. The audience includes students who ultimately fan out around the world to staff agriculture ministries, planning agencies, bilateral donor agencies, international voluntary organizations, foundations, research institutes, the World Bank, and the International Monetary Fund. In many countries, former students teach in colleges and universities where they in turn train students to staff government posts and an equally wide variety of positions. Some in this diverse group join international organizations that provide development assistance to poor countries.

The diversity of our audience encouraged us to use an unconventional (some colleagues might say bizarre) approach in writing this book. There are few econometric techniques presented and virtually no recipes to follow that will assure success. Rather, the book relies on simple models to organize the complexity of an interdependent food system and to develop a way of thinking about food and agriculture, and the associated poverty and hunger, that will facilitate solving these problems.

By the standards of the economics profession, the analytical techniques seem overly simple. But the book is not meant to train specialists. The book's purpose is to make food policy analysts stop and think about what is happening and what is driving the system. It encourages the analyst to make tentative, rough calculations at first, and then, if the analysis seems to be getting somewhere, to pursue the topic with more sophisticated techniques. The book should help policy analysts know when the skills of a specialist—an economist to analyze data on price formation or do benefit-cost studies, a nutritionist, or an agriculural scientist—can effectively be used in dealing with the problems at hand.

The substantive theme of the book grows out of four separate streams of development policy analysis as approaches to the problems of poverty and hunger: agricultural production and rural development, food consumption and nutrition, macro policy and planning, and comparative advantage through international trade. We have attempted to incorporate all four approaches into a "macro food policy framework" that specifically seeks to reconcile the short-run tradeoffs between producers and consumers in the context of efficient and secure patterns of international trade and a healthy macroeconomic environment.

A variety of specific acknowledgments are in order. Four institutions played important roles in providing the resources to write and revise this book. The World Bank provided both financing and substantive encouragement (and discouragement where necessary) for the book, although it is not clear that Graham Donaldson, chief of the Economics and Policies Division of the Agricultural and Rural Development Department, got what he thought he was going to get when the first conversations were held. BULOG provided a laboratory for our substantive ideas and pedagogical approaches. It is fair to say that without the several training sessions, so generously sponsored by Generals Bustanil Arifin and Sukriya Atmadja (the chairman and vice-chairman of BULOG, respectively), and the intellectual and strategic counseling by the late Drs. Sidik Moelyono, head of the Expert Staff, that the book would not look anything like it does, and it probably would not exist at all. Both the Food Research Institute at Stanford University and the Division of Research at the Harvard Business School provided resources and, significantly, time for the coauthors to think about the issues and to write down their ideas.

Our intellectual debt is obviously large, and the annotated chapter bibliographies contain extensive references to many other works that were crucial in the development of the ideas here. We also incurred some more specific intellectual debts, as our colleagues have read and considered our drafts, pleaded, and then bullied us into appropriate responses. Bruce Johnston, Bill Jones, and Tim Josling at Stanford played this role, as did David Cole, Malcolm Gillis, Ray Goldberg, Kathy Hartford, Michael Reich, and Rob Schwartz at Harvard. A special thanks goes to Nick Eberstadt, who read repeated drafts and bled over each of them with his red pencil. To Nick we are indebted for our understanding of the special problems of reaching the very poor in both urban and rural societies.

The World Bank solicited a set of external reviews before making up its mind about the fate of the manuscript. After pondering the reviewers' extensive comments, ultimately their wisdom and sense sank in, and we hope they all see a personal, albeit anonymous, contribution to an improved and more effective book. Others in the Bank also provided reviews of specific topics. John Cleave, Jim Goering, Cliff Lewis, Gerald O'Mara, and Pasquale Scandizzo all deserve thanks for being willing to wade through a four-inch manuscript in their "spare" time.

Lastly, the book is truly the result of Carol Timmer's organizational and editorial skills and her ability to juggle 600 pages of manuscript not only in her head, but on a cumbersome computer as well. It is a fine line between improving how a substantive point is made and the substance itself. That line never bothered Carol; she simply crossed back and forth at will as if she had full diplomatic immunity. She claims she would be uncomfortable to be named a coauthor, but all three of us feel her presence has vastly enhanced the quality of the book.

C. PETER TIMMER
WALTER P. FALCON
SCOTT R. PEARSON

June 1983

FOOD
POLICY
ANALYSIS

1

Introduction to Food Policy Analysis

Anyone who examines the world's annual output of basic grains—rice, wheat, corn, and other coarse grains—and compares it with the world's total population will make a startling discovery. If the grain is converted into calories and protein available on a daily per capita basis, the total is significantly greater than the amount of nutrients needed for human survival. Further, over the past three decades the world has produced more grain per capita, not less. And yet in any given year of that recent history several million people have died from hunger-related causes. On any given day perhaps a billion individuals are restricted by their economic circumstances to consume less food than they would like, and hundreds of millions have their growth and physical activity limited by inadequate food consumption.

The juxtaposition of global food adequacy with widespread hunger raises a perplexing question. Because food is so basic to our physiological and emotional well-being, why do societies not work out mechanisms to distribute food more equally? Why must a food policy be more complicated than a set of international arrangements to move food from surplus to deficit countries and domestic programs to funnel the food to the needy?

Answering these questions requires an understanding of the nature and causes of hunger. Such an understanding reveals two separate but linked problems. One involves global grain markets, international trade, and price formation. The second problem is at the human level of chronic food deficits and the accompanying impairment of people's lives. The global market and the human problems may seem only loosely linked, but the connections dictate the nature of domestic food policy interventions needed to alleviate hunger.

The Global Food Problem

Whatever a reasonable estimate of daily calorie requirements might be, the world has almost always produced more, and usually significantly more. The contrast between "bad" and "good" harvest years is particularly revealing. In the recent past, 1972 was the worst year, and its poor harvest contributed to the "world food crisis" of 1973 and 1974. Good weather and strong incentives to farmers to increase food production were factors in making 1978, in per capita terms, the best harvest year in history, even better than the bumper harvests of 1981 and 1982.

The difference between 1972 and 1978, however, was less than 12 percent in per capita daily calories available from basic grains alone, a calculation that makes no adjustment for grain stocks carried into and consumed in 1972 or for nonconsumption of grain stocks accumulated in 1978 which were available for future consumption. Relative to an arbitrary average energy requirement of 2,500 calories per day, 1972 grain production was 128 percent of requirements while 1978 production was 143 percent. Even discounting nutrients available from such nonstaples as pulses, sugar, fats and oils, range-fed meat, and fruits and vegetables, it is apparent that any global food problem is obscured by, not revealed in, the global food *production* statistics. For example, knowing that in recent years about 40 percent of world grain was fed to livestock helps explain these puzzling numbers.

A very different picture emerges by looking at food *price* statistics. In the span of a decade, wheat prices have risen more than threefold, fallen back to less than half their peak, nearly regained it, and under the influence of good harvests in the United States and weak demand abroad, have fallen to new lows. After accounting for inflation, 1982 grain prices were lower than at any time since the 1930s. World grain markets are highly competitive, and because prices determined in reasonably competitive markets measure the scarcity of a commodity, the extreme volatility of basic grain prices over the past few decades is troubling. Despite enough food each year to meet human needs, the sharply fluctuating prices indicate periods of significant surplus and scarcity of food available for purchase in the residual international grain market. Countries dependent on this market for even a minor proportion of their consumption needs find these extreme fluctuations in world market prices unsettling and threatening to their domestic food security.

Perhaps the most important aspect of the global perspective on the world food problem cannot readily be captured in price or trade statistics. The world's food economy is now intimately and probably inextricably interdependent. The linkages among countries and commodities are provided through international trade in grains that are highly substitutable both in origin and in consumption—corn and low-quality wheat are equally satisfactory to cattle, for example. Trade in agricultural inputs, especially the petroleum-based inputs, such as fertilizers, diesel fuel, and pesticides, also connects the agricultural and industrial economies of many countries. Mirroring these physical flows are a set of international financial transactions whose ramifications ripple through domestic economies in a remarkably pervasive manner. The effect of foreign exchange transactions and the foreign exchange rate on the entire macroeconomic climate of a country strongly conditions the set of possibilities for a domestic food policy.

Global interdependence in the world's food economy makes analysis of food policies more difficult. Feedback mechanisms in an interdependent world sometimes amplify and sometimes dampen the welfare impact of an initial shock. But interdependence also has the potential to spread risks and stabilize the welfare costs of agricultural fluctuations, as long as large trading countries do not attempt to dump the burden of adjustment outside their own national economies, thus leaving small countries especially vulnerable to instability. Interdependence can enhance international specialization and promote higher productivity for all participants, but the distribution of the gains may be sharply skewed. The global market aspects of the world food problem are caused partly by the increasing interdependence in the world food economy over the past few decades. Solutions are likely to be found not by attempts to dismantle this new interdependence but by a better understanding and utilization of its positive potential at the national level.

The Human Problem of Hunger

In contrast to the sharp fluctuations in the global problem, the human problem of hunger is chronic and grinding. The number of people whose daily existence revolves around the source of their next meal increases somewhat in years of poor harvests and decreases to some extent with good harvests, but the number is quite insensitive to the factors that influence the global situation.

The great majority of the world's hungry people are the very poor, the landless and nearly landless, the vulnerable groups of young children, pregnant and lactating women, and the elderly, and they live mostly in Asia. Although problems of poverty and quality of life certainly affect many of the world's small, semisubsistence farmers, the worst problems of hunger in the developing world are not found on small farms. Even if all the small farmers were well fed, many of the hungry people on the globe would be untouched, and it is not even clear whether the *process* of raising small farmers to that level would help or hurt the hungry in the short run.

The Asian focus of the hunger problem is obvious. More than half the world's population lives in Asia, and most of these people are very poor relative to average incomes for the other half, even including Africa and Latin America. Two-thirds of the world's serious hunger exists in nine countries, six of which are Asian, and these statistics exclude the 100–200 million in China recently said "not to get enough to eat." Only Zaire and Ethiopia in Africa and Brazil in Latin America have large enough numbers (*not* percentages) of hungry people to join India, Bangladesh, Indonesia, Pakistan, the Philippines, and Cambodia in accounting for two-thirds of the world's hunger. In relative terms other countries have more hungry people: for example, Haiti or the countries of the Sahel. But eliminating hunger in the first nine countries would radically transform the human dimensions of the problem.

In searching for the causes of hunger, it must be recognized that hunger is not a disease or a single biological state, but an individual problem caused by inadequate food intake. For purposes of food policy, which deals with the decisions made by food consumers and producers, inadequate food intake is defined relative to the individual's own perception of the food needed to maintain good health, provide for growth, and allow a choice of physical activity levels, including work levels. Hunger among children too small to make food intake decisions for themselves is obviously a more complicated question that must be treated in a general household decisionmaking framework. Hunger as discussed in this book encompasses the entire range of conditions related to food deficits—from acute starvation during famines, to elevated morbidity and debilitation, and to milder forms of energy deficits.

From this view, hunger is caused by restricted choices of basic food quantities available to individual consumers. Solving hunger involves expanding the available choices, which are a function of incomes, food prices, food supplies, and consumer knowledge. Although the hunger of any particular individual can be solved fairly easily by providing more income or more food directly, solving the problem of hunger for a whole society is much more complicated because the direct approach is either too expensive or too disruptive to the rest of the economy in which hungry people function.

The more general problem of hunger is enmeshed in the set of processes that produce (and consume) agricultural commodities on farms, transform these commodities into food in the marketing sector, and sell the food to consumers to satisfy nutritional as well as esthetic and social needs. These processes make up the food system. The actual functioning of this system frequently leaves many poor people inadequately fed because of a network of connections that determine their employment and income status, the prices they must pay for food and other goods and services, and their ability to move in search of better opportunities. The same food system, however, offers vehicles for the policy interventions that reach poor people with sustainable improvements in their access to food.

Policy interventions can touch the food system along its entire dimension, from agricultural inputs to nutritional supplementation. The connections between these food system components are illustrated in figure 1-1, which distinguishes agricultural, food, and nutrition sector issues. It identifies the primary linkages affecting the design of policy interventions intended to reduce hunger while preserving a viable food and agricultural economy. Understanding these connections in the food system enables food policy analysts to avoid isolating specific and apparently simple problems from the context in which they occur.

Hunger is one of those apparently simple problems, for it is caused by inadequate energy intake from basic foods. A food system that contains many hungry people is a failure in at least one dimension. But is it a failure to produce enough food, to produce the right kinds of food, to generate enough income to buy that food, or to educate families about what foods to eat? Each of these factors can contribute to the food problem; what must be identified are the direct and indirect causes of hunger.

Few people willingly go hungry, and most hungry people know what to eat. These simple facts focus the search for the causes of hunger and lead to an equally simple answer. Most hunger is caused by a failure to gain access to the locally available supplies of food or to the means to produce food directly. The link between poverty and hunger reflects an individual's access to food, what A. K. Sen calls the "exchange entitlement." The main groups of people with low or insecure access are the very poor, the landless and near-landless, the disadvantaged groups of young children, pregnant and lactating women, and the elderly who have lost a productive role in their societies.

Even in normal circumstances these groups exist in the nutritional margin where daily food intake restricts activity levels, growth, and resistance to disease. But they are also subject to sharp deterioration in their economic circumstances, through a failed crop, a lost job, an additional infant in the family, or higher food prices in the market. This vulnerability is already extreme for subsistence households combatting the vagaries of monsoons, droughts, and pests. Participation in the market activities of the food system, however, as a food buyer or seller or as a wage laborer, adds to the uncertainties and the vulnerability because market forces are as far beyond the household's control as are the whims of the weather and locusts.

Market forces can bring both good news and bad news. Markets can open up new employment opportunities and more secure incomes and can bring food supplies into an area experiencing a poor harvest. Alternatively, however, market competition can drive local employers out of business, eliminating many jobs and the incomes they provide, or crop failures miles and even oceans away can drive up local food prices. Poor people are especially vulnerable to misfortune. Market connections simultaneously extend the range of misfortunes that might befall them, while bringing opportunities to end their poverty or cushion their local misfortunes. The tensions between

Figure 1-1. Linkages among Agriculture (A), Food (F), and Nutrition (N)

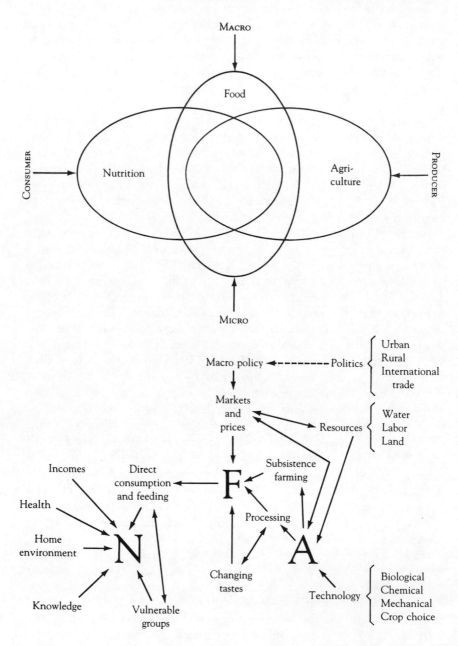

these two effects explain much of the controversy over the impact of market penetration by the world economy. A domestic food policy can protect poor people from being further disadvantaged *by* markets while it improves their access *to* markets and the economic opportunities generated by trade.

Market connections provide the most important links between the world grain economy, with its price instability and periods of gluts and shortages, and the extent of the hunger problem within individual countries. The market connections between the two are not direct, because most countries attempt to buffer their own food consumers and producers from the vicissitudes of world grain prices. To the extent such policies are successful, the price link between international grain markets and domestic food markets is weakened. Even where the efforts are successful, however, they require large administrative and financial resources—resources with an opportunity cost in terms of the policies and programs that could otherwise be directed at the domestic hunger problem. Also, few countries are able to isolate completely their domestic food prices from international prices. Either their economies are too porous (someone looking at Indonesia's coastline once remarked, "God meant Indonesia for free trade"), or the foreign exchange and budgetary resources are inadequate for the task of full isolation.

Can a country hope to solve its food problems while the global problems of periodic shortages and price volatility remain? Does domestic economic policy have the potential to reduce poverty and hunger, or must the international economic system be reformed before progress can be made within poor countries? The debate over these questions is important to food policy analysts because world grain markets are integral components of the global economy. More important, the connections between domestic problems of hunger and the global food problem condition the range of choices open to domestic policymakers and influence the extent of the hunger problem itself.

Food Policy

Food policy encompasses the collective efforts of governments to influence the decisionmaking environment of food producers, food consumers, and food marketing agents in order to further social objectives. These objectives nearly always include improved nutrition for inadequately nourished citizens and more rapid growth in domestic food production. Many countries also seek more equal income-earning opportunities and security against famines and other food shortages. Food policy analysis is the process of research and thinking designed to discover the complementarities and tradeoffs among food policy objectives and to identify government initiatives in the project, program, and policy arenas that can best achieve these objectives.

Food policy analysis is concerned with all food-related issues, ranging from agricultural performance to the distribution of nutrient intake, and with the mechanisms available to address these issues. The price paid for this breadth of scope and range of potential policy levers is the resulting complexity of analysis, as is apparent in a simple example. In many developing countries the primary protection for poor consumers against high food prices comes from an overvalued exchange rate, which at the same time is an important factor in keeping those consumers poor. Overvalued exchange rates slow economic growth and lower incentives for agricultural production; the combination reduces the demand for unskilled labor.

This surprising dual role of a single variable, apparently far removed from the reality of hunger and poverty, is just one example of the complexities that extend food policy analysis beyond the traditional boundaries of agricultural or nutritional policy. When successful, the analysis offers important insights for solving food problems in individual countries. Precisely because the analysis is complicated, however, analysts need a framework to help organize their research and thinking, nurture the analysis, and bring it to bear on the design and implementation of an effective national food policy.

In this book, the task of building a food policy perspective is separated into three components: an analytical focus on micro behavior of food consumer and producer households; a trade perspective on the role of markets, both domestic and international, in linking the micro sector and its household issues to the macro sector and its policy issues; and an understanding of the effects of macroeconomic policies on the performance of the food system. The flow of the argument is from micro through trade to macro, and the book is structured accordingly. Separate chapters examine food consumption, food production, domestic food marketing and price formation in an international setting, macroeconomics and the food system, and a macro perspective on food policy.

The micro-oriented chapters (chapters 2, 3, and 4) review and restate basic economic models of consumption and production from the decision-making viewpoint of food consumers and food producers, who frequently live in the same household. The goal is to understand why these participants in the food system behave as they do and how that behavior can be changed. Food consumption decisions are influenced by a household's income, the prices for food and other commodities, and a host of social and individual factors which may or may not be susceptible to government influence. Similarly, farm households allocate their resources to food and cash crop production in the context of their own knowledge, access to productive inputs and prices of output, and attitudes about what factors will best contribute to improved individual or family welfare.

Food consumers and food producers react to food prices in opposite ways. For consumers, higher food prices restrict the range of foods and other commodities and services that can be purchased, while lower food prices permit greater food intake, a wider variety of foodstuffs, and a higher quality diet, as well as an occasional new shirt or a radio. Food prices are especially important to the very poor, for they spend much of their incomes on starchy food staples. For these households, survival itself may hinge on low food prices.

Farm households see food prices as a major factor determining their incomes. For a particular harvest, if the input costs are already paid and the yields are already in, the price received for the output is virtually the sole determinant of farm income. In the longer run, the output price signals the incentives to the farmer to use purchased inputs, new technology, and household labor and managerial skills, which directly affect the level of output. Food prices reflect relative scarcity and abundance. They communicate to both governments and farmers the collective desire and ability of consumers to provide adequate incentives to maintain food supplies, either from domestic production or imports.

The dual role of food prices—determining food consumption levels, especially among poor people, and the adequacy of food supplies through incentives to farmers—raises an obvious dilemma for food policy analysts. Indeed, the dilemma runs deeper than is first apparent. The incomes of the poor depend on their employment opportunities, many of which are created by a healthy and dynamic rural sector. Incentive food prices for farmers are, in the long run, important in generating such dynamism and the jobs that flow from it. But poor people do not live in the long run. They must eat in the short run, or the prospect of long-run job creation will be a useless promise. This food price dilemma provides one major theme for the book. The microanalytical focus of food policy analysis directs attention to the decisionmaking environment that creates the dilemma and to the potential interventions that can bridge the short-run and long-run effects.

The emphasis on trade recognizes the critical role played by specialization and exchange in raising labor productivity—the only long-run solution to poverty. Trade begins at the farm household, which, even though it relies heavily on home production for family consumption needs, usually also purchases inputs, markets output, and buys a range of items for home consumption from suppliers outside the household. Such trade communicates price signals to farm decisionmakers, but the markets in which trade takes place also provide the arena for price formation itself. Markets thus have a dual role which significantly conditions the potential of government policy to influence price formation for traded foodstuffs.

In a world of free trade there would be no need to discuss domestic food price formation separately from international food price formation. In a world of trade barriers, however, the two are quite different, and the analytical discussion of domestic price formation in chapter 4 must be extended to international commodity markets. This approach permits the design of an appropriate relationship between domestic and international prices and helps analysts know how international trade in cash and food crops can be used to further domestic policy objectives.

One aspect of the food price dilemma for domestic food policymakers is how tightly to link their country's food system to world commodity markets. The economic efficiency and potentially rapid growth generated by an open economy and relatively free trade offer wider choices for both today's and tomorrow's consumers. But the instability of world markets threatens to upset urban consumers when supplies are short and may prove ruinous to domestic farmers during periods of glut. The future trends in grain market prices are obscure, which makes current agricultural investment decisions appear risky. Policymakers can respond by increasing their domestic financial flexibility to deal with short-run price fluctuations and by following international price trends in the longer run.

The trade policies that separate domestic prices from international commodity prices in the short run are implemented in the macroeconomic context of foreign exchange rates and budget policies, which is described in chapter 5. The entire food system, and not just pricing policy, has broad connections to the two primary components of macroeconomic policy: the macro price policy that includes interest and wage rates as well as foreign exchange rates; and the more traditional macro policy that includes fiscal, monetary, and budget policy. Neither component of macroeconomic policy can be addressed primarily to food policy concerns, for the interests of the entire economy must be incorporated in the design of macro policy. But food policy analysts can contribute effectively to the macro policy debate when they understand both the sectoral issues and their important connections to macroeconomic forces.

The links between macro policy and the food system work in both directions. Macro policy and the macroeconomic environment exert powerful influence over the performance of the food sector and the options available to improve it. But in most developing countries the forces in the other direction are also important; macroeconomic performance, and especially macroeconomic stability, depend significantly on production, consumption, and prices in the food sector. For this reason, food price policy is treated as an important element of both trade policy and macro price policy.

The macroeconomic approach is extended in chapter 6 to a political economy framework for the design and implementation of food policy. The macro perspective is especially useful in understanding how the various constraints facing food policymakers interact to stymie policy initiatives aimed directly at reaching food policy objectives. The objectives often conflict with each other in subtle, complicated, but ultimately powerful ways. These conflicts are at the heart of the food price dilemma—the short-run welfare consequences for the poor of rural price incentives that have the long-run potential to lift them from their poverty. Many tensions between politics and economics in rich and poor countries alike flow from this dilemma. Resolving it involves identifying policies for the food sector that deal with the dilemma and understanding their capacity to produce desirable effects in both the short run and the long run.

Why a Food Policy Approach?

The motivation for placing traditional agricultural or nutritional policy analysis in a broader macro context, despite the major complications such food policy analysis encounters, is the failure of alternative approaches to establish a strong connection between levels and changes in food supplies available and the reduction of hunger. The failure of government policies to deal more effectively with hunger—despite trends showing greater availability of food—reflects a lack of understanding of the direct and indirect causes of hunger and its relationship to a country's food system.

All food systems must accomplish similar tasks. By organizing the production or provision of food, its marketing, and its consumption by the citizens of the society, food systems around the world end up having much in common. The choices a society faces in organizing these tasks are completely analogous to the larger economic choices faced by any society whether socialist or capitalist: what to produce, how to produce it, and for whom. Different societies make fundamentally different choices in each area and yet have food systems that are understandable within a common methodology of food policy analysis.

The macro perspective places the food system squarely in the context of economic growth and efforts to alleviate poverty. These efforts involve strategies for raising productivity in the agricultural sector, for it is there that much poverty is found. A healthy and dynamic rural sector is essential to reducing hunger, but the policies that create such rural dynamism do not all emanate from agricultural planning offices. Most of the economic environment required to stimulate efficient resource allocation, labor productivity, and more jobs is created by macroeconomic policy.

Using macro policies to alleviate poverty in the long run is only part of an effective food policy. Reaching the poor in the short run is always difficult because of their weak link to the food system and the rest of the economy. Poor consumers have different diets from those who are better-off, and their income sources are usually much less secure. Similarly, very small farmers often do not control adequate resources in the form of land, water, or credit to participate fully in the potential of new agricultural technology. The task is to find interventions in the micro environment that can protect their welfare while the macro forces strengthen their links to the economy in the long run. A primary function of the disaggregated food consumption analysis discussed in chapter 2 is to find these links that will permit the careful targeting of food subsidies to the poor.

A major role of the food policy analyst is to design a bridge between the problems at the micro level and the macro environment that leads to more rapid growth. Understanding the role of trade and markets provides the supports for that bridge, but closing the gap between short-run and long-run effects of macro policy requires job creation, rural development strategies that reach small producers, effective use of food price policy, and carefully targeted food subsidies.

Most countries start from a food price policy environment that uses food imports and budget subsidies for across-the-board consumer protection, while a host of production-oriented government projects attempts to increase food output. One of the primary lessons that comes from understanding the complexity of hunger and its connections to the food system suggests that such a price policy/project orientation is backwards. Governments can more effectively meet the full range of food policy objectives by using price policy, not to keep food prices low for consumers, but as part of the incentive package that induces greater food production from millions of small farmers. Programs and projects can then provide targeted food subsidies to protect the very poor until they find jobs and higher incomes that result from the new policy environment.

Reversing the prevailing policy/project orientation toward dealing with hunger does not mean a new emphasis on production while food consumption problems are quietly ignored. Such a strategy would fail on both political and humanitarian grounds. The reversal of policy and project roles does mean dealing with *both* production and consumption issues in a manner that creates fewer—not more—problems of poverty and hunger for the future.

Starting the Analysis

Developing an effective domestic food policy depends on creating an environment in which alleviating poverty is a major function of the economy. Within this environment, an understanding of the causes of hunger and their connections to the food system provides a starting point for the design of programs and policies that will balance the conflicts universally encountered in a government's objectives. Although the weights will vary by country and over time, most societies have four basic objectives for a national food policy:

- Efficient growth in the food and agricultural sectors
- Improved income distribution, primarily through efficient employment creation
- Satisfactory nutritional status for the entire population through provision of a minimum subsistence floor
- Adequate food security to insure against bad harvests, natural disasters, or uncertain world food supplies and prices.

Because of their direct contribution to a nation's health and welfare and, implicitly, to its political stability, these four broad goals for the food and agricultural sectors are held by most policymakers in poor and rich countries alike. Growth, jobs, a decent minimum standard of living, and security against famine or extreme food shortages encompass most of what might be achieved by a successful food policy. The problem is not in defining objectives but in getting from here to there. For policymakers to influence the process of change, they must understand the environments and behavior of food producers and consumers. This insight helps identify the policy instruments that can alter household decisionmaking so that society's objectives are realized.

Parts of this book are applicable to the full range of countries sharing the globe, but the chief concerns are the food problems of developing countries. Analysts in the United States, Japan, Germany, and Hungary, for example, may find the discussion relevant to their own concerns because development is a continuum, and all food systems must solve some common problems. But food problems are more pressing at the bottom end of the development spectrum, where the scarcity of resources limits flexibility in reconciling the interests of producers and consumers.

A country's food policy is formed at several levels of government, and each level has a different analytical focus and need for food policy analysis. Parts of the book are intended to help policymakers organize their thinking about food problems. Far from offering answers, this approach concentrates on the issues that need to appear on the agenda. An old political adage holds that whoever controls the policy agenda controls policy. This book seeks to provide policymakers with the data and arguments needed to help set the agenda.

Once the policy debate is focused, policy analysts can illuminate it in a genuinely impartial and technically sound fashion. Providing the framework for that analysis and the useful techniques for carrying it out is an important rationale for this book. Analytical technique is helpful, however, only when it addresses the relevant questions; therefore the discussion here deals with the agenda and the analysis simultaneously.

The three micro-oriented chapters of the book are designed to help analysts, and ultimately policymakers, understand the decisions of millions of individuals and households in the food system. The diverse decisionmaking environments of food consumers, food producers, and the marketing agents who connect them are examined in chapters 2, 3, and 4. Each of these chapters has a similar structure: the nature of the problem in the sector; the understanding that economic theory offers of how decisionmakers react within their environments and to policy-induced changes; the sources of data and the analytical techniques to develop policy-relevant insights; and the nature of potential policy interventions that address both specific sectoral problems and the full set of food policy objectives.

Analysts will gain an understanding of the importance of a broader macroeconomic approach to food policy analysis in chapter 5, which seeks to widen the analyst's training to include macroeconomic concepts particularly relevant to food policy. The chapter may prove helpful as well to those macro economists or macro policy analysts who have little understanding of the role of food and agriculture in the macro economy. Much macro policy is designed in ignorance of any ramifications for the food system. Chapter 5 begins the two-way educational process that can incorporate these ramifications into the policy debate.

Because of the two-way nature of the macro food policy debate, parts of the book, especially chapters 4, 5, and 6, are directed to a wider audience than analysts and policymakers in food-related agencies. Many important food policy decisions are made not in agriculture or food ministries but in ministries of finance or planning or in the central bank. These agencies dictate the environment in which decisionmakers in the food system operate. They are also the agencies that negotiate with the International Monetary Fund and the World Bank over conditional assistance. The structural and financial reforms required for such assistance frequently have severe repercussions on the welfare of poor people, primarily through their access to food. One purpose of this book is to enable senior domestic policymakers to bring a food policy perspective to these discussions.

The book has two time frames. One deals with the long-run process of equitable and rapid economic development in which the needs and contributions of the food system are part of the strategic design. The other focuses on the more immediate day-to-day management of food policy and programs. Food policy analysis seeks to bridge the gap between the two time frames by designing programs to cope with the short-run consequences of policy while retaining a consistent long-run vision of economic transformation.

Analysts will find the book's main lessons about programs and the elements of a consistent and workable macro food policy in chapter 6. This chapter explains the desirable attributes of several ideal solutions, such as land redistribution, lump-sum income transfers, and neutral technical change leading to lower food prices. These solutions are best when they can be had. However, they are not generally available to food policy analysts, who typically search for incremental improvements in an untidy world. Some environments offer no scope for such marginalist skills. But even after the revolution, a poor country discovers that it is still poor, and this book's analytical perspective becomes relevant.

Some "solutions" seem not to work. Their failure is not the accident of history, but rather is deeply rooted in the nature of the problem and the political and economic mechanisms available to change it. But policy can be pointed in the right direction by focusing on job creation, incentives to increase food production, and greater investment in agricultural infrastructure. Economic efficiency and rising productivity are of prime importance in poor countries. They cannot afford mismanagement, waste, and inefficiencies caused by bad policies if their economies are to grow, mature, and ultimately provide a wider range of choices to their citizens. But poor people cannot be excluded from a share of current economic output if they are to survive to share in the larger pie. Their survival hinges on access to adequate amounts of food to grow, live, and work. At least in the short run, that access is likely to depend on a food policy that designs and implements targeted food subsidies. With political commitment, good analysis, and careful implementation, food policy offers developing countries an important vehicle for reconciling short-run equity with long-run growth and efficiency. This is no modest claim, of course. The analysis that makes it possible lies ahead.

Bibliographical Note

Food policy analysis is part of the evolving debate over the role of agriculture in economic development. Some of the mileposts in that literature are still important reading: W. Arthur Lewis, "Economic Development with Unlimited Supplies of Labor," *Manchester School of Economic and Social Studies*, vol. 22 (May 1954), pp. 139–91; Carl E. Eicher and Lawrence Witt, eds., *Agriculture in Economic Development* (New York: McGraw-Hill, 1964); Theodore W. Schultz, *Transforming Traditional Agriculture* (New Haven, Conn.: Yale University Press, 1964); John W. Mellor, *The Economics of Agricultural Development* (Ithaca, N.Y.: Cornell University Press, 1966); Herman M. Southworth and Bruce F. Johnston, eds., *Agricultural Development and Economic Growth* (Ithaca, N.Y.: Cornell University Press, 1967); Clifton R. Wharton, Jr., ed., *Subsistence Agriculture and Economic Growth* (Chicago: Aldine, 1969); Yujiro Hayami and Vernon Ruttan, *Agricultural Development: An International Perspective* (Baltimore, Md.: Johns Hopkins University Press, 1972); Keith Griffin, *The Political Economy of Agrarian Change* (Cambridge, Mass.: Harvard University Press, 1974); Bruce F. Johnston and Peter Kilby, *Agriculture and Structural Transformation: Economic Strategies in Late-Developing Countries* (New York: Oxford University Press, 1975); Lloyd G. Reynolds, ed., *Agriculture in Development Theory* (New Haven, Conn.: Yale University Press, 1975); Radha Sinha, *Food and Poverty* (New York: Holmes and Meier, 1976); Michael Lipton, *Why Poor People Stay Poor: Urban Bias in World Development* (Cambridge, Mass.: Harvard University Press, 1977); John W. Mellor, *The New Economics of Growth* (Baltimore, Md.: Johns Hopkins University Press, 1978); and Theodore W. Schultz, ed., *Distortions of Agricultural Incentives* (Bloomington: Indiana University Press, 1978).

These volumes trace the idea that agriculture in developing countries is more than a source of surpluses to spur industrialization. Agriculture can be a dynamic source of growth, but it requires investment in research, infrastructure, human capital, and producer incentives to play a positive role relative to its large and frequently impoverished population.

Missing from the agricultural development literature is any serious attempt to deal with the short-run consumption consequences of an incentives-led production strategy. John R. Tarrant, *Food Policies* (New York: Wiley, 1980), does deal with food consumption issues but not as they relate to production strategies. The macro perspective of this book has no known precursors in the agricultural development literature. Lance Taylor approaches the same issues with a different analytical perspective by building macro models with disaggregated food sectors, as in F. Desmond McCarthy and Lance Taylor, "Macro Food Policy Planning: A General Equilibrium Model for Pakistan," *Review of Economics and Statistics*, vol. 62, no. 1 (1980), pp. 107–21.

Five useful and varied assessments of the world food economy can be found in Radha Sinha, ed., *The World Food Problem: Consensus and Conflict* (Oxford: Pergamon Press, 1977); Lester R. Brown, *Food or Fuel: New Competition for the World's Cropland*, Worldwatch Paper no. 35 (Washington, D.C.: Worldwatch Institute, 1980); D. Gale Johnson, ed., *The Politics of Food: Producing and Distributing the World's Food Supply* (Chicago: Chicago Council on Foreign Relations, 1980); International Food Policy Research Institute, *Investment and Input Requirements for Accelerating Food Production in Low Income Countries by 1990* (Washington, D.C., 1979); and Food and Agriculture Organization of the United Nations, *Agriculture to the Year 2000* (Rome, 1979).

The treatment of the world food problem and the human problem of hunger is influenced by Shlomo Reutlinger and Marcelo Selowsky, *Malnutrition and Poverty: Magnitude and Policy Options*, World Bank Occasional Paper no. 23 (Baltimore, Md.: Johns Hopkins University Press, 1976). The international dimensions are treated in D. Gale Johnson, *World Food Problems and Prospects* (Washington, D.C.: American Enterprise Institute, 1975); and in Gordon O. Nelson and others, *Food Aid and Development* (New York: Agricultural Development Council, 1981).

Two books provide useful analytical assistance with the techniques and perspective offered here. The first, Edith Stokey and Richard Zeckhauser, *A Primer for Policy Analysis* (New York: Norton, 1978), is an extremely helpful guide to using complicated analytical methodologies in policy settings. It is an appropriate companion volume to *Food Policy Analysis*. The second, Hollis Chenery and others, *Redistribution with Growth* (London: Oxford University Press, 1974), is a technically sophisticated treatment at the level of the whole economy of the equity-efficiency dilemma that is discussed in this book from the perspective of the food system.

2

Analysis of Food Consumption and Nutrition

This chapter has two broad tasks. The first is to outline a definition of hunger that is relevant for policy purposes. The second task is to introduce the very different approaches by which a society can and does intervene to alter the number of hungry individuals and the severity with which their lives are affected. A recurring theme in the book is that the most important interventions are frequently not specifically aimed at reducing hunger, and some that are so aimed fail to have a fully satisfactory impact when many other, negative forces are at work. This chapter's intent is to improve understanding of the context and causes of hunger and to identify sustainable policy interventions that work to eliminate it.

To address these microeconomic issues, this chapter, like chapters 3 and 4, is structured according to a sequence of analytical questions. What are the right issues? What principles or theory can organize the analysis? What data and analytical techniques are required? How can the results be interpreted in a policy context? The chapter ends with a review of specific government initiatives that increase food intake of the poor.

Understanding the Hunger Problem

During the 1970s concern over the short-run and long-run consequences of hunger and malnutrition mobilized international development agencies and many national governments to devote new attention and resources to improving the nutritional status of their populations. Countries as rich as the United States and Sweden and as poor as Bangladesh, the Philippines, Mexico, and Senegal developed plans and interventions designed by nutritional scientists and based on modern understanding of human nutrient requirements.

The new attention to nutritional status is due in part to scientific evidence, accumulated over the past two decades, which points to the heavy personal and social costs of malnutrition, especially inadequate energy intake. Much of the new concern, however, stems from the concreteness of hunger as a measure of poverty and deprivation and from the strong emotional response of planners and donors when confronted with stark evidence of a hungry population. In short, the nutrition issue has increasingly been used as a lever for mobilizing development efforts to deal with poverty and the basic needs of the poor.

Unfortunately, the approaches used to improve nutritional status have frequently been simplistic and oriented to very short-run, palliative interventions; thus they divert attention and resources from broader strategies with a better chance of effecting long-term improvements in the nutritional status of the poor. This book presents a framework for analyzing a country's development efforts in the context of nutritional (and other) objectives. This chapter identifies the questions to be answered before a sensible food and nutrition intervention program can be designed and implemented.

A government program to deal specifically and effectively with hunger requires an understanding of (1) who the hungry are; (2) how food intake changes when people's circumstances change; (3) the program interventions that will raise food intake; and (4) how programs can be linked to policy.

1. Who are the individuals most vulnerable to inadequate food intake, where are they located geographically, and during what seasons does hunger occur? Much of this information will be available from household budget surveys, nutrition surveys, or even reports from regional hospitals and clinics. This information reveals the nature and prevalence of hunger and, to some extent, the functional significance of the problem. How important is intervention to the individual, to the family, to society? The evidence will almost certainly suggest that certain vulnerable groups (infants, children, and pregnant or lactating women) are more likely to suffer than adult men or women in the formal work force. The extent to which this is true will strongly condition the nature and cost of alternative interventions. If adequate food resources exist at the household level but significant malnutrition occurs among some household members, the intervention strategies employed will be quite different from those used when poor households simply do not have access to enough food to meet their nutritional requirements.

2. How do the poor change their food consumption patterns when basic decision parameters change? Answering the previous questions requires descriptive evidence. This question requires analysis of that evidence to understand how food intake changes when incomes change, when food commodity prices change relative to nonfood prices or to each other, or when family size, place of residence, health, or season of the year changes. Much of this chapter is devoted to such disaggregated food consumption analysis because the resulting parameters are essential to further food policy analysis. The

analysis tends to be complicated, but there is significant potential for borrowing and carefully adapting basic food consumption parameters from other societies.

This analysis proceeds from two assumptions rooted in comparative experience. First, there is significant substitutability between various starchy staples (for example, between rice and cassava or wheat and corn) in the diets of the poor in societies where market availabilities make substitution possible between staple foods with markedly different prices. Indeed, where such substitution is possible but not demonstrated, a strong case can be made that the poor in that society do not suffer from serious calorie shortages. Other nutritional problems may still be serious, and small children may have energy deficits because of the bulkiness of the starchy staple. General hunger, however, is unlikely to be a priority for government intervention if poor people are not consuming "inferior" starchy staples where they are available at low cost.

The second assumption is that food consumers are rational; that is, they logically weigh alternative ways to improve their welfare and pick the one that uses the fewest resources. Studies of decisionmaking and time allocation of adults within households have shown that consumers exhibit a strong rationality in allocating scarce resources to meet household objectives. Evidence of rationality permits the use of powerful economic models of household decisionmaking with respect to food consumption choices. This chapter shows how to use (and how not to abuse) those models in a research setting constrained by poor data, inadequate computer facilities, and limited time for analysis. The expectation of rationality in consumer decisionmaking also justifies the search for some rough rules of thumb about plausible results from the consumption analysis.

3. How does a government program intervene in food consumption decisions to change nutritional outcomes? This chapter outlines the efforts that have been tried in various countries, from food stamp programs to fair-price shops, from child-feeding programs to amino acid fortification of basic cereals. The range of possible interventions is enormous. Their efficacy is little studied or understood. Potential problems and costs of each type of program or policy are considered in this chapter. Whether the costs will be worth paying will depend on the results of each program in a particular circumstance.

4. How are various consumption programs and government policies linked? How are the consumption programs linked to the rest of the food sector? Consumption analysis deals with the ramifications of these programs for food production, the marketing sector, and even the macro economy and international trade.

To address these four issues, data on the related topics of food consumption patterns, nutrition patterns, and family food security must be assembled and interpreted to provide an adequate base of knowledge about a country's hunger problem. The connection between food consumption and the resulting nutritional status is not straightforward. Many variables intervene between the two, and opportunities for intervention are apparent along the entire chain of causation. For nonfarm households the chain begins with household purchasing power. Rural households, even those with only small household plots, have other options for securing their food. Once variations in food consumption patterns and the sources of access to the food are understood, points of potential vulnerability of poor people and opportunities for government interventions to improve and stabilize their food intake begin to emerge. Further analysis can then sharpen those points and provide insight into how to target the interventions so that budget subsidies and secondary effects on the rest of the food system can be minimized.

Food Consumption Patterns

Assembling food consumption data could provide a scholar a lifetime's work, but most food policy analysts will think in terms of days or weeks. Shortcuts are inevitably necessary, and fortunately most countries have a surprising wealth of information about food consumption patterns scattered among various ministries. Food is not the province of any single sector or government agency. It is important to statistical bureaus which calculate cost of living indices, to commerce bureaus which monitor and regulate trade, to agricultural departments which project food requirements to justify agricultural investments and intensification programs, and to health departments which frequently establish a relationship between the size and character of their patient load and the diets of those patients. Nurses in clinics dealing with sick children often know a great deal about what those children eat.

THE FOOD BALANCE SHEET. The starting point is usually a food balance sheet, which most countries now publish on an annual basis. A condensed example from Indonesia is shown in table 2-1. Great commodity detail is usually available from files or original publications. The food balance sheet is the primary device for showing average food consumption levels. It can also be used to determine the representativeness of sample surveys. If the per capita intakes measured by sample surveys, when "blown up" to national levels by multiplying by total population, do not correspond to food balance sheet data, then something is amiss. In the past, food balance sheets tended to understate the average level of food consumption because of biases against full measurement of food production for household use and the tendency to tax farmers on the basis of output. But with recent heavy pressures on government agencies to increase domestic food production, it is no longer clear that all the biases in reported food production statistics are downward. Some upward biases, especially for basic food grains which supply the bulk of calories in most developing countries, might also be present as local officials try to show positive results from government agricultural development efforts.

The Indonesian food balance sheet is a useful example because of its commodity complexity. The version published in the official statistical handbook lists seventy commodities, and the worksheet contains many times more than that. And yet fourteen commodities provide 96 percent of the total calories consumed. The starchy staples (this excludes sugar) provide 77 percent, and a single staple, rice (plus rice bran), contributes 54 percent of the energy in the average Indonesian's food intake.

This pattern is fairly typical of developing countries, especially those in Asia, and three aspects are important. First, one preferred starchy staple dominates the food consumption picture. It is usually rice or wheat, but it can be corn, cassava, or yams.

Second, the other starchy staples as a group are quite important on average. In the Indonesia example they account for about half as many calories as the single preferred staple. Since they are not preferred foods, they will probably be consumed primarily by the poor, but the food balance sheet says nothing about distribution. Whenever inferior staples make up a significant fraction of the calories a society consumes, however, differences in food consumption patterns between less advantaged and more privileged consumers are likely to be pronounced.

Third, despite the great array of food commodities available in the society, only a few are important for food policy. The Indonesian food balance sheet shows that entire categories of commodities—fruits, vegetables, fish, meat, milk, eggs, and animal fats—are virtually irrelevant to calorie intake on average. Only bananas in that entire list supply more than 20 calories per capita per day. More surprising is the fact that the same list is almost as irrelevant to protein intake, for less than 13 percent of total daily protein consumed is contributed by all those categories combined. Of course, *all* the animal protein is in that list, but Indonesia is not unusual among developing countries in having animal protein contribute only 10 percent of average total protein intake. For both protein and calories, basic food crops (especially the starchy staples) will command the major attention of food policy analysts. Livestock projects for producing meat, eggs, or milk should be justified primarily on the basis of their contribution to farm income rather than their alleviation of nutritional problems. Exceptions occur, of course, but they should be treated as exceptions, to be specifically defended against the normal expectation.

FOOD BALANCE SHEETS BY INCOME CLASS. The information in food balance sheets identifies the general priorities for consumption analysis and overall food policy attention. Disaggregation by income class sharpens these priorities and brings the hunger problem into clearer focus, primarily because the poor are so much more sensitive to changes in incomes and prices than are the better-off groups in the society.

Constructing the equivalent of food balance sheets by income class is the

Table 2-1. Summary Food Balance Sheet, Indonesia, 1976
(thousands of tons)

Commodity	Production	Changes in stocks[a]	Imports	Exports	Total domestic supply
Cereals					
Wheat			964.53		964.53
Wheat flour	694.46	+21.88	1.93		674.51
Rough rice	23,300.94		10.21		23,311.15
Milled rice	14,737.89	+183.58	1,290.98		15,845.29
Rice bran	1,733.87			162.64	1,571.23
Shelled corn	2,572.14		54.38	3.51	2,623.01
Fresh corn	299.38				299.38
Subtotal					
Starchy foods					
Sweet potatoes	2,381.21				2,381.21
Cassava	12,190.73		239.37	413.06	12,017.04
Tapioca	118.15				118.15
Sago flour	97.30				97.30
Subtotal					
Sugar					
Refined sugar	1,318.55	+186.23	201.55		1,333.87
Other	284.00		3.80	169.08	118.72
Subtotal					
Pulses, nuts, seeds					
Peanuts	324.26		6.11	1.57	328.80
Soybeans	521.78		171.75	0.55	692.98
Fresh coconut	13,974.97				13,974.97
Subtotal					
Fruits					
(Bananas)					
Vegetables					
Meat					
Eggs					
Milk					
Fish					
Fats and oils					
(Coconut oil)					
Total					
Vegetable					
Animal					

Note: Mid-year population was 133.65 million.
a. When stocks increase (+), quantities available for consumption are reduced.

Domestic use					Per capita consumption		
Animal feed	Seed	Milling and processing	Waste	Total consumed	Kilograms per year	Kilo-calories[b] per day	Grams of protein per day
		964.53					
				674.51	5.05	48	1.57
466.23	9.10	21,673.37	932.45				
			316.91	15,528.38	116.19	1,165	20.37
840.61				730.62	5.47	41	1.99
52.46	66.35		52.46	2,451.74	18.34	175	4.51
				299.38	2.24	22	0.56
						1,451	29.06
			238.12	2,143.09	16.04	42	0.40
240.34		421.96	1,201.70	10,153.04	75.97	204	1.46
				118.15	0.88	9	0.03
				97.30	0.73	7	0.03
						262	1.92
				1,333.87	9.98	96	0
				118.72	0.89	9	0.03
						105	0.03
	30.16	19.73		278.91	2.09	31	1.34
	29.48		34.65	628.85	4.70	52	4.52
		8,669.97	1,397.50	3,907.50	29.24	120	1.20
						203	7.06
						39	0.48
						(26)	(0.33)
						10	0.66
					3.38	19	1.22
					0.84	4	0.26
					2.90	5	0.27
					8.60	15	2.76
					4.86	118	0
					(4.51)	(109)	0
						2,231	43.72
						2,186	39.21
						45	4.51

b. "Kilocalorie" is the precise term for what is commonly known as a "calorie." For simplicity, this book uses "calorie" rather than "kilocalorie" as a unit of measure stipulating the energy value in food, but the reader should bear in mind that 1 kilocalorie = 1,000 calories = 1 Calorie.

Source: Central Bureau of Statistics, Statistik Indikator, 1978/79, Jakarta, Indonesia.

next step. Household budget surveys are the main source of information. In recent years they have used improved methodologies and field techniques to measure expenditures more accurately. Thomas Poleman's paper contains a useful discussion of the uses and abuses of household budget surveys. Their specific relevance to food policy analysis is summarized here.

The very best of the household budget surveys, for purposes of food policy, actually merge with the nutrition surveys discussed below. They collect detailed information on household characteristics, income, expenditures on specific commodities, quantities consumed, and, for a subsample of the survey, anthropometric measurements of the household members. Such anthropometric measurements (age, weight, height, sometimes arm or thigh circumference) can be made quickly and can provide reasonably accurate indicators of both short-term and long-term energy deficits. Their collection in the same survey with data on household income and food commodity expenditures will help establish the connection between the level of food resources available to households and individual nutritional status relative to growth standards.

If budget surveys collect only expenditure data, it is hazardous to interpolate quantities of individual commodities consumed by the household during the period of the survey (typically a week). If all the households faced the same prices for the various commodities, no problem would arise, and expenditures on a particular commodity could be divided by its average price to yield the quantity purchased. Three factors, however, intervene in such a calculation:

- *Regional price differences*. Prices in different regions of a country can differ significantly, especially for those commodities for which transportation costs tend to be a large proportion of total value, as is true for many staple foods. Region-specific commodity prices are needed.
- *Seasonal price differences*. Prices vary during the year for most food commodities because of the seasonality of production and positive storage costs. Since most household budget surveys are conducted over an extensive period of time (frequently an entire year), while each household is surveyed for a particular day or week of that period, time-specific food commodity prices are needed to convert the expenditure data accurately into quantities.
- *Quality differences*. Prices for a given commodity vary with the quality of the commodity. Although in principle each variety and grade of rice, for example, could be identified in a food expenditure questionnaire as a separate commodity, such detail is not common because of the time required to administer each questionnaire and the unreliability of results. The quality effect for even a relatively homogeneous commodity, such as wheat or rice, can be quite significant. Upper-income households may spend on average twice as much for each calorie of food energy as very low-income households even for starchy staples. The quality effect becomes even more important for broader commodity groupings—cereals, starchy staples, carbohydrates.

Spot surveys can often be used to make ad hoc adjustments for quality in surveys reporting only expenditure data. Much information can be gained from such surveys when appropriate exogenous data are added to the analysis. The solution to all three problems, however, is to have the original budget survey itself collect data on both food expenditures *and* quantities bought (or average prices paid), plus home-produced amounts and gifts. Such information permits a much more accurate picture to be drawn of the distribution of food calories by commodity, income class, region, and sometimes season. Such disaggregated pictures permit a comparison of food consumption patterns of the poor with those of the national average and with other income groups.

A particularly picturesque summary of how nutrient intake patterns change by income class was prepared from a review of the food balance sheets of many countries by J. Périssé, F. Sizaret, and P. François (figure 2-1). The figure shows roughly 75 percent of total calories coming from starchy staples at the lowest income levels. The figure for Indonesia was 77 percent. This proportion declines rapidly to only 30 percent at high income levels, with separated edible fats (butter and lard) and unseparated animal fats in meat, milk, fish, and eggs accounting for more than half the change. Increased sugar intake accounts for most of the rest. Somewhat surprisingly, total protein intake as a percentage of calories remains virtually constant with a noticeable substitution of animal for vegetable protein. Total protein intake does rise with income because total calorie intake rises with income, at least to a middle-income plateau.

The Périssé figure is even more revealing in terms of specific commodities for individual countries or regions. Data from the 1969–70 Indonesian Socioeconomic Survey IV can be rearranged into this format, as shown in figure 2-2. The commodities that loom large in the diets of the poor are readily apparent.

To devise programs that increase food energy intake, policymakers do not need to know exactly what the poor eat or what they switch to with higher incomes, if the costs of the programs are of no concern. The poor are quite willing to eat the foods of the rich if available to them. What analysts learn from studying food consumption patterns is which foods the poor eat that the rich do not. This permits targeted interventions to be designed specifically to raise food intake of the poor, and these will be more efficient—more food energy consumed by the poor per program dollar—because the intervention commodities are consumed primarily by the target group. In addition, the analysis identifies the likely impact on the poor (in nutritional terms) of changes in their incomes or in the prices of food they consume.

Nutrition Patterns

Determining a society's patterns of hunger and malnutrition is quite a different task from understanding its food consumption patterns, although

Figure 2-1. The Effect of Income on Diet Schematized: Percentage of Total Calories Derived from Fats, Carbohydrates, and Proteins, by Annual per Capita GNP

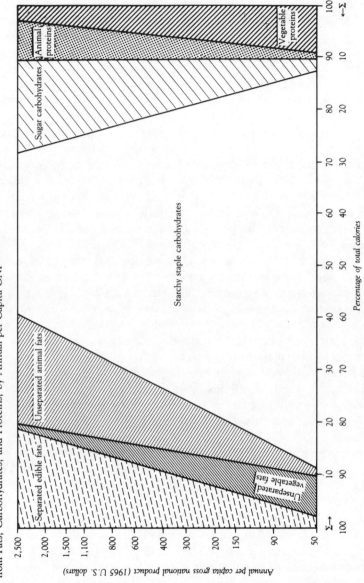

Note: The figure is drawn in semi-logarithmic scale.
Source: J. Périssé, F. Sizaret, and P. François, "The Effect of Income on the Structure of the Diet," (FAO) *Nutrition Newsletter,* vol. 7, no. 3 (July-September 1969), p. 2.

Figure 2-2. The Effect of Income on the Commodity Composition of Diet: Rural Indonesia, 1969–70

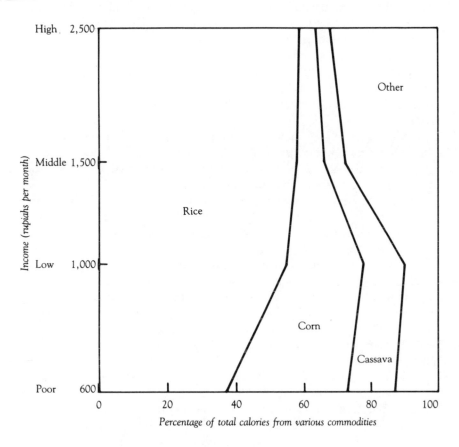

Note: The income axis is drawn in logarithmic scale.
Source: Indonesian Socioeconomic Survey IV.

some of the same data are used. All individuals have certain fundamental knowledge about food consumption. It is fairly easy to interpret statistics about availabilities of different commodities or to talk with people at different levels of society about what and how much they eat. Evaluating nutritional status, however, is a task for specialists familiar with the broad array of methodologies available and for those who can judge the biomedical evidence for human significance. Nutritional status is an outcome of a complicated biological process in which food intake is but one of many important variables. The untrained outsider can spot gross malnutrition and incipient starvation, but most of the subclinical hunger and its consequences are invisible except to trained observers.

NUTRITION SURVEYS. Food policy analysts should not expect to carry out nutrition surveys that use medical examinations to determine nutritional status along with questions on socioeconomic status. They should be prepared to interpret their findings and translate the results into a rough matrix relating nutritional problems to fundamental causes. It is the role of hospitals and clinics to deal with acute nutritional disorders. Food policy analysis tries to understand the causes and to find effective interventions, sometimes at the level of basic causes, sometimes further up the chain where palliatives are necessary.

If a nutrition survey shows an insignificant incidence of stunted growth and health problems directly attributable to inadequate food intake, the food policy analyst could shift attention to the other objectives of the food system—efficient economic growth, more equitable income distribution, and food security. Very few societies fit this description, however. Even countries as rich as the United States would have a significant number of people suffering from chronic hunger if there were no specific programs, such as food stamps, to improve poor people's access to food.

Poor societies almost inevitably have many citizens who suffer from a range of environmental deprivations, most notably inadequate access to food. Surveys that fail to identify these people may not have looked in the right places or at the right times. Food policy analysts in poor countries should be skeptical of nutrition surveys that show no significant food-related malnutrition (as opposed to nutritional diseases caused by shortages of specific micronutrients, such as iron or vitamin A) unless some type of food intervention program is already in place. Some food programs may not have been originally designed to further nutritional objectives, but they in fact have major nutritional effects. The food ration in Sri Lanka, maintained primarily for political reasons, seems to have been very successful in eliminating the worst manifestations of inadequate food intake. A survey showing little severe hunger in such a society might not be surprising.

By interpreting nutrition surveys, food policy analysts can form a set of expectations, drawn primarily from knowledge of disaggregated food consumption patterns, about the probable causes of chronic hunger, slow growth, and poor health measured by nutrition surveys. Because of the wide variety of important factors other than household food consumption influencing nutritional status, such expectations may well be off the mark. The task is then to find out why the disaggregated food consumption patterns seem inconsistent with the information provided by nutrition surveys, for the answer affects the nature of potential interventions.

In a world where social benefit-cost analysis is taken as the paradigm of modern, efficient government, evidence of malnutrition is apt to elicit a response of "so what?" This question must be faced directly. A typical nutrition survey will report three categories of malnutrition classified according to the Gomez scale of expected weight for age. Third degree malnutrition, the severe category, is reserved for individuals whose weight is less than 60 percent of the expected weight for that age. Between 60 and 75 percent is the moderate category, or second degree malnutrition. First degree, or mild, malnutrition is reported for individuals between 75 and 90 percent of expected weight, and 90 to 110 percent is considered normal. Such weight-for-age statistics are used to interpret current nutritional status, while height-for-age statistics are taken as indicators of more chronic nutritional problems. Heights less than 90 percent of height-for-age standards indicate stunting associated with long-standing food deficits.

The World Health Organization suggests that among children five years old or younger in developing countries, perhaps 3 percent suffer from third degree malnutrition, 25 percent from second degree malnutrition, and as many as 40 to 45 percent from mild, or first degree, malnutrition. What is the functional significance of such statistics? How do various degrees of severity affect the welfare of the individual? What is society's stake in reducing hunger? What are the social benefits to be matched against the governmental costs of programs that shift children from third degree to second degree malnutrition, from second to first, and from first to normal?

Unfortunately, no very clear answers to these questions exist. Some evidence suggests the social costs are enormous and the effects of malnutrition extend several generations into the future, but other evidence indicates that virtually all the impact of even severe malnutrition can be quickly and permanently reversed, except for body stature. In a heavily populated, poor society with many claims on its scarce governmental revenues, this uncertainty about the functional significance of malnutrition tends to immobilize careful attempts to address the benefit-cost issue. Marginal government revenues are directed by default to projects with more apparent or more calculable benefits.

The significance to the individual of stunted growth and poor health because of malnutrition is somewhat easier to document. In most societies small individuals are at a competitive disadvantage relative to larger ones. The severity of malnutrition is also strongly correlated with the extent and severity of illness—upper respiratory infections, gastrointestinal infections, measles, and many others. While such diseases are a nuisance to the well-nourished, they can be fatal to the malnourished.

Society clearly has some stake in these statistics. Costs for treating such health problems can skyrocket if a curative approach is taken seriously. The work capacity and productivity of individuals severely stunted and underfed are limited. Perhaps the greatest social concern, and the one with the least satisfactory evidence, is over the potential mental impairment of generations of citizens because of significant malnutrition in their formative early years.

Scientific evidence will probably never be sufficiently clear-cut to enable a budget analyst to make a distinct choice among building a steel rolling mill, implementing a child-feeding program, or maintaining a two-tiered pricing system for wheat. Building commitment to implement food consumption interventions is only partly the responsibility of the food policy analyst. If a government shows a willingness to examine alternative interventions designed to reduce hunger, however, the food policy analyst can accept a wide mantle of responsibility for demonstrating the range of effectiveness of different interventions and the associated costs of each. Such analysis can be compelling. In a surprising number of circumstances it will speak for itself. Food policy analysis cannot create the environment for effective government action against hunger, but within such an environment it can mobilize the effort effectively.

FOOD AVAILABILITY AT THE HOUSEHOLD LEVEL. Food consumption can be improved in two ways. The first is to increase household income or resources so that current mechanisms of access to food can be used more effectively. Altering incomes is fundamentally a task of price and income policies. The second way is to change the mechanisms themselves. In contrast to urban households, which have few options but to buy their food, most rural households have some potential, and sometimes a very large potential, to improve the quantity and quality of food consumption. Farm families can adopt different cropping patterns that provide nutrient diversity and more stability of output from month to month and year to year. For villagers and landless laborers with small homesteads, who must buy most of their basic food staples, a home garden can offer an important nutritional margin. Properly managed, even 100 square meters of intensively cultivated garden in a tropical setting can provide a family of four with all its vitamins and minerals, one-third of its protein, and 10 to 20 percent of its calories. Such yields require great skill, adequate inputs of labor, water, seeds, and fertilizer, and a conducive village environment. Families cannot survive on 100 square meters of land, but a family that is able to buy only 75 percent of its staple food needs and has little income left over for variety or nonfood items might find a well-tended garden plot the difference between chronic hunger, stunted growth, and wretched lives and a life of comparative security and modest well-being.

Beyond household gardens, small farmers have several options for diversifying their cropping patterns to improve the quality and security of their household food supply. Typically, farm households use their land wisely in relation to their opportunities and needs. Agricultural researchers, however, have not always developed new biological technology that matches the full range of the farmers' needs (including nutritional needs). Heavy emphasis on research to improve basic cereals has yielded impressive results. The new high-yielding varieties significantly increase the relative profitability of growing cereals in monoculture stands, particularly when package programs of fertilizer and other inputs are available with subsidized credit. In the face of such technical change most farmers would be foolish to adopt multiple crop-ping and intercropping of a wide variety of food crops that would provide a balanced spectrum of nutrients and a more even seasonal distribution. With some redirection, researchers could make such a farming system an objective of their research. Making such systems economically competitive with mono-culture cereal growing could have significant nutritional dividends.

The seasonal aspects of food availability also deserve attention. Early ob-servations of the effects of the preharvest "hungry season" in Africa suggested that adults tolerated the food deficits and resulting weight loss without undue effects on productivity. Current evidence, especially from Bangladesh, sug-gests that the seasonal effects are more subtle. Illness rates among small children tend to be significantly higher during the "short season" preceding the harvest, and the death rates from those illnesses are also elevated. Sea-sonal hunger translates into higher rates of infant mortality rather than adult starvation. Stabilizing the seasonal availability of cereal grains, or even root crop substitutes, will have significant effects on nutritional welfare, partic-ularly of children, in addition to the consumer surplus effects normally used to justify price stabilization schemes.

Food Consumption versus Nutrition as a Focus for Analysis

Food policy uses household food consumption as the primary variable to improve the nutritional status of individuals within the household. This policy perspective is based on a hierarchical division of malnutrition into two broad and overlapping stages. In the first stage, the entire household suffers from inadequate food intake, although the distribution of the energy deficit among individuals in the family may be quite uneven. In the second stage, chronic calorie deficits at the household level have been eliminated, but nutrient imbalances such as vitamin and mineral deficiencies remain and vulnerable groups within the household may still not receive adequate food to meet their special nutrient requirements for pregnancy, lactation, or growth. Both types of households may be seriously affected by endemic disease and parasites or poor public health environments, especially with respect to water and sanitation.

Strategies for improving nutritional status are likely to be quite different depending on whether a household is classified primarily as stage one or stage two. Stage one households, those suffering significant energy deficits, gen-erally respond somewhat to efforts designed to improve the efficiency of the connection between food available at the household level and the resulting nutritional status of individual family members—problems associated with stage two households. However, the fundamental problem of the level of food resources will dominate such environments. The variables that intervene between food consumption and nutritional status are just as important as for stage two households, but interventions to improve water supply, sanitation, and health are not likely to be effective in improving nutritional status until the basic issue of caloric adequacy is addressed.

The situation for stage two families is quite distinct (although the two stages are clearly just points along a continuous spectrum). With adequate food within the household to meet the daily energy needs of all family members, nutritional concern shifts to a complex of synergistic variables that simultaneously condition the nutritional well-being of each individual.

These variables make up what is now commonly called the "basic needs package": clean and abundant water supplies, proper waste disposal and sanitation facilities, housing sufficient to provide protection from the local climate, local health care facilities to treat infections and provide midwife services along with family planning materials and information, and education programs designed to achieve functional literacy. The overall relationship between a basic needs package and improved nutritional status is obvious, but the actual connections are quite complicated when it comes to quantifying the variables and precisely determining the effects.

The more obvious connections among these variables include: the relationship between the extent of gastrointestinal infections and the efficiency with which food is digested and made available to the body for work and growth; the connection between water and sanitation standards and the extent of such gastrointestinal infections; the role of functional literacy in mothers' knowing the food requirements of their children when sick and well; and the overall role of an accessible clinic in maintaining health levels of the community.

Improving any one of these factors for a household would permit a higher nutritional standard for any given level of food availability. Providing a package of such services will undoubtedly improve the connection between food availability and nutritional status. The total effect of a package will probably be greater than the sum of individual contributions. But nobody knows the extent to which these statements hold or their quantitative dimensions. There is only the loosest sense of what the tradeoffs might be within the package. The debate over a package of basic needs is productive when it focuses on the role of the poor in an economy—"why poor people stay poor," to use Michael Lipton's phrase. For this reason, food policy analysts are likely to find it more productive to deal with stage one of the malnutrition problem rather than with the more household-specific stage two problem.

Nutrition education programs may be useful at stage two, once adequate amounts of food are available at the household level. Programs to improve the mothers' nutritional knowledge—what foods to buy, how to prepare them to retain maximum nutritional value, what to feed a sick child, the efficacy of breast-feeding—almost certainly can have a high payoff in certain village environments. The situation is similar to farmer extension programs which find a wide variation in the skills farmers have in growing crops. In both cases the program must have something to extend. Through painful experience development specialists have learned that "bad" farmers frequently are behaving quite rationally for their own environment, and many apparently irrational food customs turn out to have a similar wisdom behind them. Other ways may certainly be better, but understanding why a mother behaves the way she does is just as important as understanding why a farmer applies only half the recommended fertilizer.

Food policy analysis of nutrition and consumption issues can be seen as a task of establishing priorities. In particular, the descriptive data from food balance sheets and household budget surveys, when linked to available nutrition survey data, will indicate whether the nutrition problems are primarily stage one (chronic energy deficits at the household level) or stage two (nutrient imbalance or maldistribution within the household). The food policy perspective presented here is designed mostly for stage one environments. When a country's nutrition problems are primarily of the stage two type, the nutrition task can be assumed by the public health and education specialists. Until then, much of the specialists' efforts will be ineffective. Consequently, the analytical focus of most of this chapter is on understanding food consumption patterns as the major connection between nutrition problems (and interventions to address them) and macro food policy.

Food Consumption Analysis

For the food policy analyst, the analysis of food consumption data serves two specific functions. First, the analysis provides the parameters to understand consumption adjustments in the macro food economy. What happens to total cereal demand when prices fall or incomes rise? If cereal availability changes, what will happen to prices? Second, the analysis helps determine the likely nutritional impact of changes in the economic circumstances of the poor. What happens to the consumption bundle of the poor when their incomes change and prices fluctuate for the commodities they consume?

Theoretical Perspective

Empirical investigation of food consumption data provides some answers to these questions. Economic theory can be of great assistance in the empirical research by establishing a rational decisionmaking framework in which to organize the range of potential consumer choices and by providing some simple and plausible assumptions about what constitutes rational behavior. Both the framework and the assumptions are subject to verification from actual performance. During the past fifty years the framework has withstood exposure to the real world remarkably well, and the basic assumptions about rationality and the importance of prices and income have been repeatedly confirmed.

CONSUMER CHOICE. The consumer brings to the marketplace a certain purchasing power and some sense of preference for different goods. In the marketplace an often bewildering array is available—various commodities, qualities, and amounts. The consumer decisionmaking framework presented here relates choices available to choices desired. Typically, a unique bundle of purchased commodities maximizes the consumer's satisfaction.

This framework can be illustrated by the choices available to a consumer between two inclusive commodities, for example, "food" and "nonfood." Figure 2-3 shows increasing quantities of food available along the vertical axis and increasing quantities of nonfood along the horizontal axis. Point A represents a particular bundle including both food and nonfood, amounts F_A and NF_A, respectively. Point B represents a different bundle of food and nonfood, with more of each commodity. Consumer theory assumes that rational consumers will always choose bundle B over bundle A if given a free, unconstrained choice because more goods to consume are better than fewer goods. On any smoothly increasing ray from the origin, for example OAB, points farther from the origin are always preferred over points closer to the origin.

Figure 2-3. Choices of Food and Nonfood Available to a Consumer

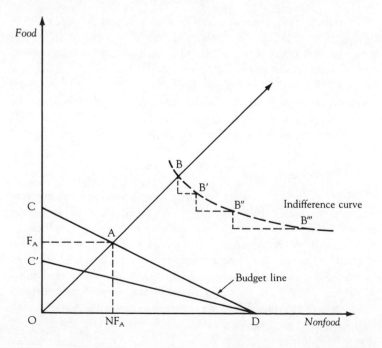

What of the choice between B and B'? There is no unambiguous answer to this question. Only the individual consumer can say which of the two commodity bundles is preferred. Bundle B has more food than B', but B' has more nonfood. Within a reasonable range and for small changes, consumer theory assumes that some quantity of nonfood can substitute for a small loss of food and still leave the consumer feeling equally well off. Thus the dashed "indifference curve" connecting B, B', B'', B''' . . . shows combinations of food and nonfood that the consumer finds equally satisfactory to the starting point B.

This curve is drawn with a particular shape that reflects the increasing difficulty of substituting one commodity for another as more and more of the first commodity is taken away. Thus one unit of nonfood will substitute for one unit of food (from B to B'), but two units of nonfood are required for the consumer to be willing to give up a second unit of food (B' to B''). Four units of nonfood are required if yet another unit of food is given up (from B' to B'''). This decreasing rate of commodity substitution is quite characteristic of most consumption circumstances and is very important when the theoretical framework combines choices available with choices desired.

THE BUDGET CONSTRAINT. The choices *desired* are indicated by the location and shape of the indifference curves. In principle there is one indifference curve passing through every possible combination of commodities. The choices *available* to the consumer are dictated by the money income of the consumer—the budget line—and the prices of the commodities available for purchase. If the consumer spends the entire income available on food and nonfood, a reasonable assumption if savings are part of nonfood, then line CD (the budget line) passing through point A reflects two separate constraints on the consumer: the total income available to be spent *and* the relative prices of the commodities that can be purchased.

If the consumer spent the entire income on food, amount OC could be purchased, but no nonfood. Similarly, if the entire budget were devoted to nonfood, OD could be purchased, but no food. The straight line CD reflects all linear combinations of food and nonfood starting with amount OC of food and OD of nonfood as extremes. Point A is one such possible combination for the consumer whose overall purchasing power is reflected by CD. Thus CD is the outer boundary of choices available to this particular consumer in the face of the relative price of food to nonfood. Points on the interior of CD do not use the entire budget available. An implicit assumption is that no household scale economies exist in the consumption of goods, which is probably reasonable for food consumption in poor households.

If the relative food price changes, the choices available to the consumer change. For example, if the consumer's money income remains constant while the price of food doubles, the choice set available is restricted to C'D instead of CD. With food prices doubled, the given amount of money will buy only half as much, OC' instead of OC. For any amount of nonfood purchased, only half as much food will be available. Only consumers who were buying exclusively nonfood find their range of choice as large as before the price rise. All consumers who purchased some food will find their potential purchases restricted by the food price increase. No economic theory is involved in this result. As most consumers know, it is a matter of simple arithmetic.

Maximizing satisfaction. The contribution of economic theory is in explaining how desired choices (indifferences curves) and available choices (budget lines) are reconciled through rational decisionmaking. Figure 2-4 illustrates the framework in the same context as the above discussion. In this example the consumer has income equal to CD reflecting the initial relative price of food to nonfood. The consumer's preferences are revealed in the shape of the indifference curve I, along which any combination of food and nonfood is equally satisfactory. In seeking to maximize the degree of satisfaction from consuming food and nonfood within the constraint of the budget CD, the consumer will seek the highest indifference curve possible. The maximum satisfaction possible for this consumer is represented at the point of tangency, shown in figure 2-4 at point A. By choosing to purchase and consume quantities F_A of food and NF_A of nonfood, the consumer just reaches indifference curve I. No higher indifference curve can be reached from budget

Figure 2-4. Matching Consumer Desires with Available Consumer Choices

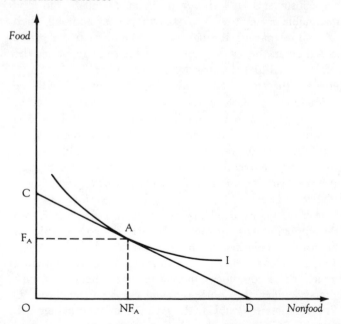

line CD. Any lower indifference curve yields less consumer satisfaction. Theory suggests that the consumer chooses to consume F_A of food and NF_A of nonfood when income is CD and relative prices are reflected by OC/OD, the negative of the slope of the budget line.

This is a powerful result. It *"explains" each purchase of a commodity as a function of the consumer's income, the prices of the commodities, and individual preference.* The uniqueness of the individual preferences is a critical component of consumer theory. Each consumer, even with identical income and facing the same prices as other consumers, can have a unique consumption bundle of food and nonfood. Such diversity is expected by economic theory, not inconsistent with it. The food policy analyst should expect great diversity in how different individuals will respond to changes in the variables—incomes and prices—that drive the consumer theory framework. In particular, poor consumers typically behave differently (but still rationally) from middle- and upper-income consumers with respect to food consumption as incomes and prices vary. The rationale for disaggregating food consumption analysis draws on this reality—a reality entirely consistent with economic theory of the consumer.

IMPLICATIONS OF THE FREE-CHOICE MODEL. Freedom of consumer choice in the face of a budget constraint is one of several ways commodities can be allocated among consumers. The market orientation implied by such a model of consumer choice has two extremely important policy implications, even before the model is used to understand consumer behavior when prices and income change.

First, this model of equilibrium between budget lines and indifference curves implies that *all* consumers (who actually consume both commodities) have the same rate of substitution between commodities. Although each indifference curve is unique to the individual, and the same is true of income level, all consumers face the same relative prices and hence have the same *slope* to their budget lines. At equilibrium, where consumers have just reached their highest indifference curves and the budget line and indifference curves are tangent (just touching so that the slopes are equal), all consumers have the same rate of commodity substitution. The rate is the same as the relative price of the two commodities. For small changes, one commodity substitutes for another at the same physical rate as their relative prices for physical quantities. For larger substitution shifts, the degree of curvature of the indifference curve is important. Should the question arise, for example, as to how much an additional ton of wheat flour will substitute for an existing ton of rice being consumed, the relative prices in the market provide the appropriate starting point for analysis (despite the fact that a ton of rice and a ton of wheat flour are roughly equivalent in nutritional terms).

The second important implication of the free-choice model of consumer behavior is the welfare implications of individual choice as opposed to rationing. Providing each citizen with an equal or "fair" share of society's economic output is certainly a legitimate way to divide the pie, a fundamental decision all societies must make. Figure 2-5 shows a society that provides each of its two citizens with equal rations of food and nonfood, labeled A and B. Thus citizen A receives a bundle with F_A of food and NF_A of nonfood, and citizen B receives exactly the same bundle, F_B and NF_B. If both citizens have identical tastes and preferences, they will be content with their rations because both would be on the same indifference curve passing through A,B.

Suppose, as figure 2-5 illustrates in an exaggerated fashion, that A and B have significantly different tastes and preferences, which are reflected in their respective indifference curves I_A and I_B. Both indifference curves must pass through the commodity bundle A,B, for that point indicates the initial endowment or ration of the consumers. If no trading among consumers is permitted, then both A and B are restricted to I_A and I_B, respectively. However, citizen A may discover that citizen B is fed up with so much food in his ration and craves more nonfood. Citizen A finds, to her delight, that more food would be welcome and parting with some nonfood a minor in-

Figure 2-5. Gains in Consumer Welfare from Trade as Opposed to Rationing

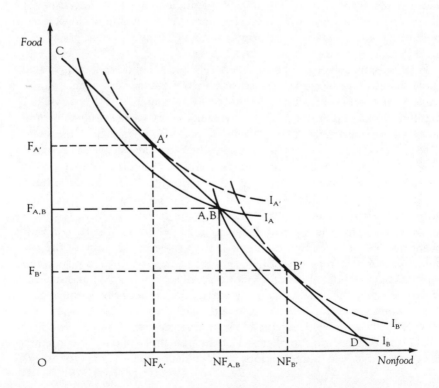

convenience. If some ratio can be worked out, A and B have discovered they would *both* be better off by trading part of their rations to each other, with A giving up nonfood for more food and B receiving the nonfood in return for the food.

Many trading ratios are possible in such a bilateral situation, depending on whether A or B is the better bargainer, but the line CD reflects one plausible trading ratio that splits the gains of the trade fairly equally. Along this trading line citizen A gives up an amount of nonfood equal to (NF_A − $NF_{A'}$) to citizen B, who thus gains ($NF_{B'}$ − NF_B); the two amounts must be equal. In return, B gives up (F_B − $F_{B'}$) to A whose food consumption increases by the same amount ($F_{A'}$ − F_A).

The remarkable fact is that after this trade, both A and B find themselves on higher indifference curves, $I_{A'}$ and $I_{B'}$, respectively, than was possible by consuming the rationed commodity bundles A,B directly. The possibility of trading makes both consumers better off. In a world of rationing, the trading line must be discovered or negotiated between each pair of consumers. Although time-consuming and probably inefficient, the many examples of such trading in places where rations are used suggest that it is well worth doing.

Is there an easier and more efficient way to do the trading? A *market* does it automatically. The line CD is no more than the price ratio between food and nonfood—a price ratio at which all consumers can trade to maximize their own personal satisfactions from an initial endowment of goods or income. A system of free choice in open markets allows consumers to capture all the welfare gains to trade that are possible. The market paradigm is used widely even in those societies that profess otherwise. Where a government actively suppresses the open market, black markets tend to spring up as consumers attempt to improve their positions by trading goods surreptitiously.

Why does rationing remain such a popular government intervention? The answer lies not in the gains or losses from trading or nontrading but in the transfer of real purchasing power to consumers by distributing evenly or fairly a limited supply of an important commodity. Poor people with little purchasing power would be unable to purchase adequate supplies of such a scarce commodity if high market prices were used to allocate it instead of per capita rations.

Basic grain is such a commodity in a number of poor societies. The government frequently has no effective mechanisms, other than physical distributions on an equal basis, to ensure that poor people receive adequate amounts of food. Permitting free trading of such rationed food grains would still permit the gains to trade illustrated in figure 2-5. It might, however, undermine the government's distribution mechanisms or control of grain markets, and it might tempt poor families to sell grain that they "should" consume for nutritional reasons. Implementing food ration schemes will obviously be difficult, but they should not be dismissed out of hand simply because economic theory says they are "inefficient." If they are one of the few mechanisms available to the government to implement income distribution or nutritional goals, their costs and benefits need to be analyzed with careful attention to who will actually benefit and to the long-run impact on the rest of the food system and on the macro economy.

INCOME ELASTICITIES. The analysis of the costs and benefits of food consumption interventions requires fairly detailed understanding of food consumption parameters. Economic theory helps condition expectations about whether such parameters of change in commodity consumption will be positive or negative when incomes and prices change, but theory is of little help in predicting the quantitative magnitudes of consumer reactions. This is the task of empirical analysis. Whether the results of such analysis are sensible can be judged relative to theoretical expectations and comparative experience. Empirical research provides the real world parameters for further food policy analysis.

What are the theoretical expectations? Two changes are important and can be analyzed sequentially. First, figure 2-6 shows what happens when the

Figure 2-6. Effect of Increasing Available Choices
on Consumer Decisionmaking

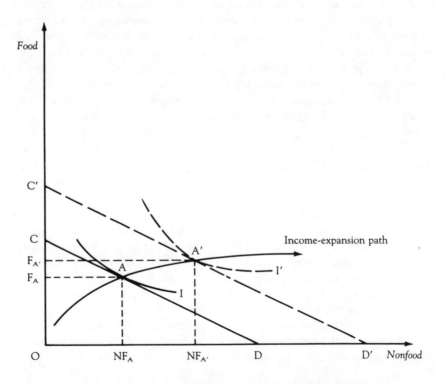

consumer's income is raised from CD to C'D', a neutral 50 percent increase in money income. The size of the income increase can be determined by comparing OC with OC' or OD with OD'. Since the new food and nonfood availabilities are 50 percent larger than the initial availabilities, the consumer's purchasing power, or income, is 50 percent larger.

The extended range of potential commodity purchases is reflected in a higher available indifference curve than I. Of course, it is still possible to choose a bundle of food and nonfood that lies on I, but such a bundle is no longer the best choice available. As figure 2-6 indicates, the new equilibrium is where I' is tangent to C'D', at A'. In this particular illustration the new commodity bundle contains both more food and more nonfood. This is not a necessary result. Some commodities—"inferior" goods such as potatoes or cassava—become less desirable at higher incomes, and indifference curves can easily be drawn to reflect this.

By connecting the points of consumer choice between food and nonfood at increasing income levels, it is possible to construct an "income-expansion path" similar to the one shown in figure 2-6. In this case food purchases increase rapidly at low income levels but level off at higher income levels, thus reflecting the smaller proportion of income spent on food at higher incomes—a phenomenon generally characterized as Engel's law. The relative degree of food consumption increases, compared with income increases, is frequently quantified as an income elasticity for food. In this example an income increase of 50 percent generated a food consumption increase of 20 percent ($OF_{A'}/OF_A = 1.2$), and so the income elasticity is (roughly, because of the large size of the change) 0.4 (20 percent divided by 50 percent).

Consumer theory indicates two important properties of income elasticities. First, since they are derived from the income-expansion path, such income elasticities can be unique to each individual consumer and, in particular, are likely to vary systematically with the income of the consumer. Second, each income-expansion path is drawn for a particular set of relative prices that is maintained during this example showing increasing incomes. If those prices change as well, the income-expansion pathway may change also. The lesson is that income elasticities are not likely to be constant, either from one consumer to another or from one price environment to another. It is sometimes convenient to use a single income elasticity of demand for food for an average or representative consumer when trying to understand how entire economies will adjust to new policies, foreign exchange rates, or changed prices. But much diversity has gone into the aggregate parameter, diversity which could be important in judging the desirability or reliability of a predicted outcome.

PRICE ELASTICITIES. Economic theory also provides expectations about the impact on consumers and their choices of commodities when prices change while money income remains constant. Figure 2-3 showed that a food price increase leaves consumers with reduced consumption opportunities. Figure 2-7 shows how consumers adjust to those reduced consumption opportunities when food prices rise.

The starting point is the familiar consumer income of CD that permits reaching indifference curve I with commodity bundle A, containing F_A of food. The nonfood results are straightforward in this two-commodity world and are not analyzed separately. If food prices double while nonfood prices and money income remain constant, the new budget constraint is C'D, showing the reduced consumption possibilities for the consumer—OC' is just half of OC.

How will the consumer react to the new higher food price? The analytics of choice remain the same as those that produced the initial choice of A. The consumer will seek a combination of food and nonfood that yields the highest indifference curve subject to the new purchasing power constraint C'D. In the illustration this is achieved by A' where I' is just tangent to C'D. Food consumption is reduced from F_A to $F_{A'}$ because of the higher food price. In this particular illustration, a doubling of food prices reduces food purchases to less than half their original value.

Figure 2-7. Effect of a Food Price Increase on Consumer Decisionmaking

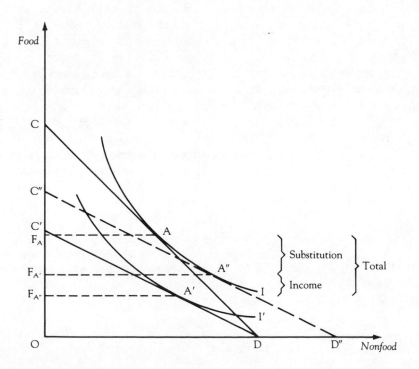

INCOME AND SUBSTITUTION EFFECTS. Two separate factors can be seen to
cause the overall drop in food purchases. First, higher prices cause real purchasing power to fall when money incomes stay constant. This drop in real
incomes will cause consumption of most commodities to fall although inferior
goods will be an exception. Second, even if the consumer were to receive
compensation for the reduction in real income caused by the higher food
price, the change in *relative* price would still cause most consumers to adjust
the composition of their commodity bundle against the commodity that has
become relatively more expensive.

Both the income and the substitution effects are illustrated in figure 2-7.
When the price of food changed the consumer's budget line from CD to
C′D, the overall or total consumption adjustment was from A, on I, to A′,
on I′. Suppose the consumer received a small income supplement (for example, the government granted a pay increase when it raised the price of
food) just sufficient for the consumer to reach the old indifference curve I
but from the new relative price relationship. This new income is shown as
C″D″, which is parallel to C′D but tangent to I at A″. With C″D″ the
consumer is not worse off after the price change because the original indifference curve I is still available.

The consumer, however, does *not* purchase the original commodity bundle
when prices are reflected by the slope of CD. In fact, the higher price of
food causes the consumer to substitute nonfood for food along indifference
curve I until the new equilibrium is reached at A″. That is, after a compensated price increase for food that leaves the consumer identically as well off
as at the beginning, food purchases drop from F_A to $F_{A''}$. This compensated
price adjustment is known as the pure substitution effect, and it is always
the opposite sign of the price change if indifference curves have their normal
shape. Economic theory can "prove" this, but the proof is based on plausible
assumptions noted above and has been amply demonstrated by years of empirical experience.

Most price changes are not compensated by government or anyone else.
In such cases the "income effect" of the price change must also be added to
the negative substitution effect to see the total change in consumption that
will be reflected in actual consumer behavior. In figure 2-7, the income effect
is shown as the change from A″ to A′, a further drop in food purchases from
$F_{A''}$ to $F_{A'}$. For normal goods, the income effect reinforces the negative
substitution effect, as lower real incomes lead to reduced consumption.

Inferior goods—commodities such as potatoes, cassava, whole grain flour,
or cornmeal consumed primarily by the poor—are the exceptions. For these
commodities the income effect works in the opposite direction of the substitution effect because lower real incomes caused by higher prices lead to
increased consumption of inferior goods. It is logically possible for such an
opposite income effect to be larger than the substitution effect if the inferior

good requires a very large proportion of the consumer's budget, as potatoes did in nineteenth-century Ireland. At that time Parson Giffen thought he observed a paradox: poor consumers were forced to buy more potatoes when potato prices rose because the income effect was so powerful.

Understanding the logic of the Giffen paradox is a good measure of ability to understand the economic theory of consumer behavior. No satisfactory statistical evidence for the paradox, however, has ever been presented from real-world examples. Food policy analysts are justified in expecting that consumers will react to price increases with reduced purchases, and vice versa, in the absence of other factors not included in the basic theory explained here.

ADDING REALISM TO THE THEORY. Some of those other factors can be important in the short run. Changing expectations, in particular, can upset the theoretical model. If sugar prices rise, many consumers rush out to buy more sugar, not less, for they fear even sharper price rises in the future. Such anticipatory hoarding usually makes the expected price rises actually result. The expectations are self-fulfilling. Such behavior does not invalidate economic theory. It simply reinforces the necessity for analysts to use actually perceived decision variables, in this case expected prices, rather than current market prices.

Expectations and anticipatory hoarding are extremely important for food policy. Very small shortages in a relative sense, 3 to 5 percent of normal consumption, frequently lead to panic buying and price increases of several *hundred* percent. Preventing such shortages is obviously the best strategy for food policy, but, failing that, finding mechanisms to prevent panic buying can have extremely large welfare effects for poor consumers who purchase much of their food from open markets. Rationing schemes or market injections of grain can be quite effective in the short run in preventing such panic buying.

Quality effects can also lead to an apparent rejection of the normally negative relationship between quantities purchased and price. If consumers judge the quality of the product by its price (but without any "real" quality difference to justify the higher price), higher prices may well lead to greater consumption. Understanding the potential role of the quality effect is very important when analyzing household food consumption data gathered from cross-section surveys. The role of quality variations by income class in food consumed is frequently critical to understanding the true impact of income and price differentials on actual nutrient intake as opposed to monetary value of food consumed.

THE SLUTSKY EQUATION. The theoretical perspective on food consumption is conveniently summarized by the Slutsky equation, which relates the total change in consumption of a commodity to the change in price of any commodity, including but not restricted to the commodity whose change is being observed. Consumption of substitutes will rise when a commodity's price rises; consumption of complements will decline. Rice consumption will change when rice prices change (relative to all other prices), but it might also change when wheat flour or cassava prices change. Indeed, from the perspective of the Slutsky equation, any price change, even for flashlight batteries, may affect rice consumption. Empirically, of course, such cross-price effects could be too small to measure because the effects are swamped by errors in the data. Over time, however, the cumulative impact of some cross-price effects can be quite significant. The cross-price linkages among commodities suggested by consumer theory are an important element in understanding how the food system adjusts to both exogenous forces and policy changes.

The elasticity version of the Slutsky equation shown below is convenient to interpret and use, where for small changes elasticities refer to relative percentage changes.

$$e_{ij} = \varepsilon_{ij} - E_i\alpha_j$$

where e_{ij} = overall demand elasticity for commodity i when the price of commodity j changes

ε_{ij} = the pure substitution elasticity for commodity i when the price of commodity j changes

E_i = the income elasticity for commodity i

α_j = the budget share of commodity j in the consumer's total expenditures on all commodities.

This equation is usually discussed in an empirical context for the same representative consumer in a society depicted in figure 2-7, which illustrated the same changes graphically. Economic theory requires that each consumer potentially have a unique Slutsky equation. It is already well recognized that E_i and α_j (income elasticity and budget share) tend to vary systematically by income class. Most low-income consumers devote a large share of their budgets to food (60 to 80 percent is not uncommon). They also buy significantly more food when incomes increase. Income elasticities for food for very low-income consumers sometimes approach one.

These factors alone suggest that e_{ij}, the overall demand elasticity, will also tend to vary systematically by income class, with low-income consumers likely to make larger (in absolute values) adjustments in commodity purchases than better-off consumers. Further evidence, to be discussed below, suggests that ε_{ij}, the pure substitution term, also varies by income class.

The combined effects provide an important insight for food policy analysts. Low-income consumers are likely to be far more sensitive in adjusting the quantities of food they consume to changes in prices than either the representative consumer in the society, who reflects average data, or the upper-income groups. Empirical analysis is needed to say how much more, but the theoretical framework does provide an important set of expectations about the patterns the empirical data should reveal.

Estimating Consumption Parameters

The quantitative impact on food prices (and on the food energy intake of various population groups) of changes occurring in the production, marketing, macro, or international arenas can be specified with confidence only if empirical food consumption parameters for the society are available. Such parameters, in the form of income elasticities, own-price elasticities, and cross-price elasticities, are needed at the macro level to link aggregate food consumption to production levels, food imports, and food exports. For example, if per capita incomes are projected to rise by 4 percent, but domestic grain production will increase by only 2 percent, how many tons of grain will have to be imported to keep prices stable? If imports do not increase, how much will grain prices rise? Aggregate income and price elasticities are needed to answer such questions.

At the micro level consumption parameters are used to determine the implications of price and income changes on nutritional status, especially among the poor. This time the parameters must reflect the specific behavior of the target group. The poor are very flexible in their food purchase decisions when their economic environment changes. To know how their nutritional status might be affected by the grain price increase calculated in the aggregate example just discussed, the analyst needs to estimate disaggregated income and price elasticities. These parameters are also needed for program design to improve the efficiency with which targeted subsidies actually reach the intended population. Commodities with high aggregate income elasticities, for example, are not efficient vehicles for subsidization because upper-income households consume more, and hence receive more of the subsidy, than low-income households.

Finally, short-run and long-run parameters are likely to be significantly different. Consumers require time to adjust, and parameters estimated from data that reflect full adjustment to changes in prices and incomes will be larger than the actual adjustment that is likely to take place in the short run.

The types of data available and the particular parameters sought determine the approach used to estimate these parameters. Several texts provide step-by-step details for both time series and cross-section analysis, and such details are inappropriate here. But it is useful to know how to frame the question, organize the data, and interpret the statistical results. These points are covered here. Specific examples of analysis can be very helpful as case studies to follow from beginning to end, and several are listed in the annotated bibliography to this chapter.

TYPES OF DATA. The food balance sheet and the disaggregated household food consumption data will indicate what commodities are important enough to justify detailed consumption analysis. The primary starchy staples are always important. They provide the bulk of both calories and protein, especially to the poor. The choice of other commodities to include in the analysis depends on the nature of the nutrition problems, on existing production and trade patterns, and on how sharply the consumption patterns differ by income class.

Table 2-2 shows the usual sources of information and data for obtaining consumption parameters. The table shows that national aggregate data on consumption, production, trade, and prices are almost never suitable sources for estimating micro consumption parameters, that is, the consumption elasticities for specific income groups. The reason is fairly obvious. Information about which individual household consumes which commodities is lost in the aggregation. Without this information, estimation is impossible. Only household budget data that retain such household-specific characteristics are usually adequate for such estimation and then primarily for long-run parameters. Such long-run parameters capture the full adjustment process to a change in income or price. Typically, a five- to ten-year period is assumed necessary for full adjustment by consumers to take place.

Even for macro consumption parameters—those that reflect the overall aggregate response of all consumers to a change in average per capita income or in prices—household budget data are usually necessary to find the long-run adjustment coefficients. The short-run parameters are typically estimated

Table 2-2. Usefulness of Various Data Sources for Obtaining Consumption Parameters

Source of data or information	Consumption parameters			
	Micro		Macro	
	Short-run	Long-run	Short-run	Long-run
National production, consumption, trade, and price data	N	N	U	S
Household budget survey data	S	U	S	U
Marketing and food trade sources	S	N	S	S
International comparisons	S/N	S	S	S

U = Usual source.
S = Secondary source.
N = Not likely to be a useful source.

from the aggregate data directly. However, many confounding influences condition the usefulness of aggregate data for any sensible consumption analysis. Typically only one data point per year is available, and fifteen to twenty years of data are needed for reliable statistical estimation. With changes in tastes, expectations, structure of the economy, and even statistical reporting procedures, such lengthy time series of consumption data for most developing countries are justifiably viewed with some skepticism. Useful information, sometimes even reliably estimated parameters, can be gleaned from such data. The analyst will discover, however, that the gleaning process is labor intensive and not successfully mechanized.

Unfortunately, no good sources of information or data exist for finding short-run micro consumption parameters. Micro parameters estimated from cross-section data tend to reflect long-run adjustment processes. Unless panel data—consumption statistics collected from the same households at regular times, frequently quarterly—over reasonably long periods of time are available, no direct estimates of short-run coefficients are possible. Panel data are extremely expensive to collect and are especially difficult to gather for the very poor, who tend to have less fixed places of residence, to be illiterate, and often do not want to cooperate with investigators who pry into their lives but offer nothing in return. Few sources of panel data for developing countries exist.

Short-run micro parameters must, of necessity, be pieced together from various sources. The skill and intuitive feel of the investigator, acquired through experience with formal statistical estimation on a variety of data sources and through widespread discussions with knowledgeable people in the food marketing arena, are essential for achieving sensible results. Clearly, what is sensible is in the eye of the beholder. Theory and international comparisons provide guidelines at the outset; the final test is the reliability of predictions.

FRAMING THE QUESTION. Numbers become data only when organized into some coherent framework for analysis, and the questions asked always dictate the analytical technique. Food consumption analysis seeks primarily to explain patterns of food purchases and intake, and the forces causing change in those patterns. Statistical analysis does not reveal these important causal connections; causality is inferred by the analyst on the basis of the underlying analytical framework from consumer theory. Merely estimating significant correlations between variables is of little help in a policy context. Because of the complexity of basic economic structures, many correlations between variables are produced indirectly. Knowledge of the structure and of indirect causal mechanisms helps analysts predict accurately the effects of policy changes.

For understanding food consumption, some causal mechanisms are obvious and direct (higher incomes permit larger food purchases, for example). Others

can be quite subtle and indirect. For example, higher incomes for middle-
and upper-income households may increase demand for livestock products
and ultimately reduce food intake of the poor. The large conversion factor
between feed grain and meat, coupled with high income elasticities of demand
for meat in middle- and upper-income households, means that societies with
highly skewed income distributions have the potential for very rapid increases
in grain demand. Indeed, a skewed income growth path can increase grain
demand faster than income growth targeted to the poor even with their
higher income elasticities for basic food grains. Such indirect and roundabout
mechanisms indicate the complexity of most food systems.

The framework for analysis at the micro level is provided by household
consumer theory. What factors will the food buyer be considering during the
purchase decision process? The list of factors provides the starting point for
the list of variables that must be organized for the analysis to proceed. Household income and various food prices are the first items on the list, but when
actual household level data are being used, many other variables may also
be important, such as size and composition of the family, location, and season
of the year. Education levels, occupation, and exposure to life outside a
traditional village could be other factors that influence the decision.

Many of these factors have no obvious policy significance. The analyst
might be tempted to ignore them in the pressure to produce results. However,
their inclusion helps reduce any bias in the estimated coefficients of the more
directly policy-relevant variables. Price coefficients could be the main parameters sought in a particular instance for policy purposes, but it will still
be necessary to understand to what extent the price coefficients reflect seasonal or locational factors rather than short-run response to variations in day-
to-day market prices. The more carefully the relationship is specified before
estimation, the more likely it is to provide the desired parameters of change.

GRAPHICAL ANALYSIS. Organizing the data graphically is frequently a revealing exercise. Although the two dimensions of a sheet of paper cannot
capture subtle relationships among several variables, graphical presentation
of the data forces the analyst to decide what variables relate to each other.
Frequently it helps specify the shape of the relationship—linear, logarithmic,
or more complex. Complex statistical techniques often overpower the modest
information available from typical data sets from developing countries. Ex-
tracting the information actually contained in the data set, but not more
than is contained therein, is sometimes easier with simple graphical techniques than with computers.

Figure 2-8 illustrates the usefulness of graphical analysis. Per capita rice
consumption in rural Java during each trimester of 1976 is plotted against
per capita income for the consuming households. Each axis is scaled in
logarithms so that the slope of the relationship between rice consumed and
per capita income can be read directly in elasticity terms. The slope of the

line at any point indicates the income elasticity of demand for rice, that is, the percentage increase in rice demand for a 1 percent increase in income, at any income level. The household budget survey data shown in figure 2-8 were collected during calendar year 1976 and were reported separately for each trimester, January–April, May–August, and September–December. These periods correspond roughly to seasonal patterns of rice cultivation and harvesting, and significant seasonal variations in rice prices occur between time periods. The lowest average prices occur during the main harvest period, May–August, while the highest prices are reached in September–December. If monthly data were available, a somewhat more accurate division into harvest, preharvest, and cultivation periods could be made, but the existing division does reflect a uniform seasonal movement of rice prices.

Two patterns leap at the analyst from figure 2-8. First, the elasticity relationship between income and rice consumption is not constant. It would

Figure 2-8. Rice Consumption Related to Income, Rural Java, 1976

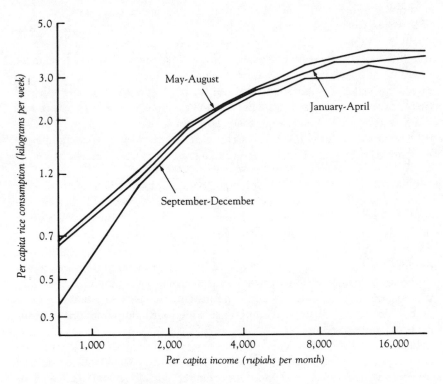

Note: The figure is drawn in logarithmic scale.
Source: Indonesia, Central Bureau of Statistics, National Socioeconomic Survey V (Jakarta, 1976).

be difficult or, to be blunt, simply wrong to fit a single straight line to the data plotted in the figure. The curvature of the relationship is very regular and strong. What functional form fits the data best is a question for statistical estimation and a little trial and error, but certainly a log-linear function with a constant income elasticity will be inappropriate. Simple examination of figure 2-8 shows that the income elasticity for rice is nearly one for low-income households. It is zero or possibly slightly negative for very high-income households. Since it is already known that rice plays a dominant role in overall caloric intake in Indonesia, this pattern is both plausible and indicative of broader nutrient intake patterns (although the low-income households are likely to be consuming substantial quantities of other, cheaper starchy staples in addition to the relatively expensive rice).

The second powerful pattern is the uniform shift of the entire income-rice consumption relationship from period to period. The overall graphical relationship is quite smooth because the data from many households are averaged together to form "cell means" for each income class. In some cases more than a thousand households are averaged to show a single data point. Such averaging tends to yield fairly smooth graphical relationships. The uniform shifting of the relationship, however, is an entirely separate matter. It is possible to stop with the obvious explanation that there is a seasonal shift in rice consumption for each income class, but a more satisfactory explanation suggests that the seasonal movements in rice prices cause the consumption shifts.

A very rough price elasticity of demand for rice can be calculated from figure 2-8 by measuring the relative shifts from the low-price months (May–August) to the high-price months (September–December) and comparing this consumption shift with the relative movements in rice prices themselves. Since the rice prices are roughly 10 percent different and the consumption is about 6 percent different in the opposite direction, a crude overall price elasticity of − 0.6 is indicated. This number can be greatly refined and made income-class specific with computer analysis, but the preliminary graphical analysis has already produced the main results needed for understanding the dynamics of rice consumption. Naturally, the world is not always so neat as figure 2-8 might suggest, and more subtle analytical techniques are needed. Graphical analysis, however, can guide the search for appropriate analytical procedures.

ECONOMETRIC ANALYSIS. At some point in consumption analysis, resort to econometrics becomes inevitable. Discussion of econometric techniques has been delayed here solely to block the instinct to move directly from numbers to computer printout. All the earlier steps need to be taken so that the analyst feels quite comfortable with how the consumption data were gathered and what they look like for several different plausible two-dimensional plots. Formal statistical analysis can then be extraordinarily powerful in refining expectations formed in the primary stages and in revealing subtle patterns and relationships that are invisible in raw data.

Although both time series aggregate data and cross-section household-specific data are generated by the same decisions within the household, econometric analysis of the two types of data is quite different. First, the number of observations, and consequently the degrees of freedom for analysis, is usually very large for cross-section data sources (if raw household data rather than cell means are being used) but highly constraining for most time series sources (if annual data are used). Time series analysis is usually deemed quite successful if it yields reasonably robust estimates of price and income coefficients, with attention given to major structural changes during the observation period. Frequently incomes and time are so strongly correlated that no separate coefficients are possible, and it takes a great deal of faith to attribute all time-related changes solely to income causation. But attributing it all to time is a profound expression of ignorance of the causal mechanisms at work.

Cross-section data, especially in their raw form, are far richer in information than time series data but specifically do not reflect how a household changes its consumption decisions when incomes and prices change. The cross-section survey, by definition, collects data from different households, which have different incomes and which sometimes face different prices because of temporal, spatial, or quality differences. These households differ in many other subtle ways as well. The common practice is to interpret income and price coefficients estimated from cross-section data as long-run adjustment parameters that reflect the adjustment of all variables causing households to be different, including education levels and traditional expectations about what constitutes normal consumer behavior. Both psychological evidence and economic theory suggest that adjustments are normally much more flexible as decisionmaking gradually adapts to a new income or price environment. Consequently, cross-section consumption parameters for individual commodities are expected to be significantly larger, in absolute terms, than the short-run responses revealed by actual purchase decisions. (The short-run versus long-run behavior of total consumption and savings is a separate and different story.)

Care in specifying consumption equations is an essential step in estimating sensible parameters (assuming adequate information is contained in the data in the first place). Specification—determining what variables and what functional form will best suit the regression estimated—is an art. Like all art, elements of technique can be taught, and competence comes with experience as an apprentice. As with other artistic endeavors, flair and creativity may be inborn. Some simple guidelines help at the beginning:

- *Real or deflated values.* Consistency is important with respect to whether absolute values, deflated values, or relative values of incomes and prices are being used. Over a long time in inflationary settings the subtle effects of relative price changes may be lost in the wash of general price increases. Deflating prices and incomes by cost of living indices sometimes works, but such deflation often adds biases because of peculiarities of the weights used and the commodities included in the index.

• *Functional forms.* Economic theory provides general guidelines as to reasonable functional forms for consumption analysis, but it offers little insight into which form is preferred for regression analysis of food consumption data. For the purposes of food policy analysis the most important criterion for choosing among functional forms that make sense and are stable over time is goodness of fit, especially for the domain of low-income consumers. Additional considerations include ease of estimation and interpretation and the potential for specifying an overall regression form with income-class-specific coefficients.

• *Tests of significance.* Experimentation by including and excluding variables and by using different functional forms is essential to understand the patterns of variance in any given data set. But even modest experimentation, using a single set of data for the dependent variable, calls into question all normal statistical tests of significance. Consequently, the specification for the *first* run should not be regarded as merely one of many plausible specifications. Careful attention should be given in advance to the form and content of the equation most likely to give significant and plausible results. The statistical tests of significance for this first regression and the coefficients in it can be taken quite seriously. All other variations yield additional insight, and seeing the pattern of changing (indicated) significance is often helpful. The first results, however, should be held as the standard of comparison. This purist concern can be ignored if no a priori reasons exist for preferring one specification over another, but it remains important to think carefully about specification *first.*

• *Interpretation of results.* If specification is the artistic part of consumption analysis, interpreting the results often seems to call for magic. Sometimes apparently implausible coefficients remain statistically significant despite careful efforts at respecification. Analysts frequently go through great contortions to explain such results. The attempt is important, for only through efforts to explain awkward results does the analyst finally come to understand the patterns of variance in the data. Ultimately it may be legitimate simply to throw up one's hands and say "it's crazy," but not until a genuine effort has been made to find a plausible explanation for the result. The analyst tests a possible explanation by trying a different specification, which should yield a predictable change in the result.

Interpretation is not always so difficult. Indeed, with skill and luck the original specification of a functional relationship, before major complications and disaggregation are introduced, will be entirely straightforward. Negative price coefficients and positive income coefficients will appear, all in some plausible range. That is a starting point. A basic rule of empirical research is to extend the complexity of the analysis until the results begin to lose statistical significance and the data will no longer support the subtlety and disaggregation of the specification. Art and magic coalesce at this point where the entire analysis begins to come apart at the seams but the patterns are still apparent.

Guidelines to Econometric Results

What should the empirical results look like? Are there any empirical regularities to guide the analyst? Fortunately, an enormous history of food consumption analysis stretches back well over a century. Several regularities have been sufficiently observed to be classified as the economic equivalent of laws.

Engel's law states that the proportion of a family's budget devoted to food declines as the family's income increases. Frequently attributed to "the limited capacity of the human stomach," Engel's law does not in fact refer to the quantity of food ingested but to expenditures, which continue to rise well after calorie intake has stabilized. One common interpretation of the law is that the income elasticity of demand for food is less than one. Although this seems to be universally true for all aggregate income elasticities for entire societies, individual low-income consumers may actually have income elasticities for food of one or greater. On average, Engel's law is perhaps the best-established empirical relationship in all of economics. It is not, however, a necessary guide to individual family behavior in low-income households.

Bennett's law states that the "starchy staple ratio" declines as household incomes increase. The proportion of calories that an individual derives from the basic starchy staples (mostly grains and root crops)—the starchy staple ratio—falls with rising income as the consumer diversifies the food consumption bundle to include higher-priced calories. The Périssé illustration (figure 2-1) showed this diversification by nutrient classification. Figure 2-2 showed that considerable substitution *within* the starchy staple category takes place before any tendency is seen to reduce the relative importance of starchy staples in the total diet.

Bennett's law is well documented for changes in national diets over time as average incomes increase as well as for cross-country comparisons of diets at different income levels. As with Engel's law, the relationship is not a reliable guide to individual family behavior. Especially for international comparisons, both relationships are conditioned by other factors, particularly basic food prices relative to prices of industrial and light consumer goods.

A logical corollary of Engel's law is that the income elasticity of demand for food—less than one on average for a society—is likely to be relatively large for low-income consumers and to decline to very small levels for upper-income consumers. Bennett's law suggests that such a pattern will be much sharper for the starchy staples for two reasons. First, Bennett's law refers to sources of calories, the intake of which is limited by human physiology (for given activity levels and stable weight). Second, Bennett's law reflects the seemingly universal desire for variety in the diet and for high-quality protein and refined sugar.

Figure 2-9 illustrates these relationships via the simple but useful distinction between food quantity and food quality. Although food quality is a vague term at best, economists can be very precise about its definition in this context: food quality is measured by the average price paid for calories. Hence it can be seen that Engel's law refers to observed patterns of food expenditure

Figure 2-9. Various Measures of Food Consumption Relative to Household Income Level

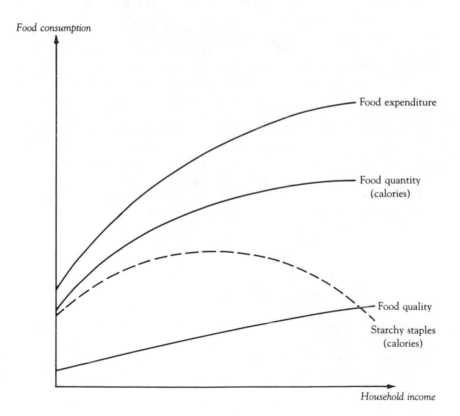

Note: The figure is drawn in logarithms to illustrate elasticities.

(log) Food quality = (log) food expenditure − (log) food quantity.

relative to income, while Bennett's law refers to food quantities (or more specifically, sources of food calories) relative to income. The regular relationship between the two—that the average quality of food calories, measured by prices, rises with incomes—should probably be called Houthakker's law.

Strong empirical evidence demonstrates that consumers respond to commodity price changes by appropriate, that is, inverse, adjustments in commodity purchases and consumption. Abstracting from expectations, speculative behavior, and the snob effects of higher prices, which can clearly influence any specific empirical test of the relationship between commodity price and quantity consumed, the negativity of the own-price elasticity is almost as firmly established as Engel's law. The downward slope to the demand curve should probably be named Slutsky's law in honor of the Russian theoretician who first showed how to decompose the observed demand curve relationship into its substitution and income components.

Much of the empirical validity of Slutsky's law derives from the income term in the Slutsky equation previously given. The empirical regularities driving this income term, which is the negative of the income elasticity times the budget share, derive mostly from Engel's law. At least for low-income societies, the budget share devoted to basic food commodities is likely to be large and the income elasticity significantly greater than zero. Consequently, the income component alone of the Slutsky equation normally leads to observed negative price elasticities. Since the pure substitution term is always negative (but of unknown size from either theory or any known empirical relationship), Slutsky's law almost always holds in a static world.

Price elasticities, like income elasticities, vary by income. But it is much more difficult to relate the *change* in price elasticity to income-class changes than it is to find the similar relationship for income elasticities. The Slutsky equation again offers a convenient framework for forming empirical expectations about how price elasticities for basic foods change with incomes. First, the income term of the Slutsky equation is clearly a function of income class, via variants of Engel's and Bennett's laws. The proportion of the household budget devoted to food falls as incomes rise (Engel's law), and the income elasticity also declines (Bennett's and Engel's laws combined). Even if the pure substitution term is constant for all income classes, the overall price elasticity for basic foodstuffs should be larger in absolute terms for poor households in a society than for the better-off. A poor household spending 85 percent of its budget on food, with an income elasticity for food of 0.8, would have an own-price elasticity of demand for food of -0.68, even if the substitution effect were zero. A family spending only 25 percent of its budget on food, with an income elasticity of 0.1, would have a price elasticity of only -0.025 (again ignoring the substitution effect).

The pure substitution effect also depends on income. Preliminary empirical evidence from several countries relates the change in the absolute size of the pure substitution elasticity by income class to the rate of change of income elasticities. Although economic theory seems to provide no insight what-soever into this relationship, the pure substitution elasticity for each com-modity tends to decline in absolute size, as incomes rise, at about half the rate of decline in income elasticities. It is premature to call this a "law," but the relationship does offer a mechanism by which aggregate demand param-eters estimated from time series or combined cross-section/time series data can be modified to become income-class specific. Income elasticities by in-come class and commodity are needed in this calculation. These can fre-quently be estimated from cross-section data using log-quadratic or semi-log demand functions.

A simple example might work as follows. Suppose the price elasticity of demand for rice, the basic staple, is estimated from time series data to be -0.40, a reasonable value for a food staple in a poor society with a multi-staple food economy. Table 2-3 shows the necessary data and steps for cal-culating the own-price elasticity for rice for three—low, average, and high—income groups in this society. The income elasticity is estimated from a log-quadratic function, and so the pure substitution term becomes a declining (in absolute values) function of the log of per capita income, taken to be $100, $300, and $600, respectively, for each income class.

The results are quite dramatic. Although the overall price elasticity of demand for rice, as estimated from time series data for the society, is only

Table 2-3. Calculation of Price Elasticity by Income Class

Income class	Annual per capita income (dollars)	Budget share to rice	Income elasticity for rice[a]	Pure substitution elasticity[b]	Total price elasticity[c]
Low	100	0.60	0.96	-0.41	-0.99
Average	300	0.40	0.52	-0.19	-0.40
High	600	0.20	0.24	-0.05	-0.10

a. Calculated from the following Engel function·

$$\text{Log rice consumption} = 2.80 \log Y - 0.20 (\log Y)^2$$
$$\text{Rice income elasticity} = 2.80 - 0.40 (\log Y)$$

b. Calculated from the Slutsky equation and "Timmer Curvature" relationship in the fol-lowing fashion:

$$\text{Average pure substitution} = \varepsilon = (E)(\alpha) + e$$
$$\bar{\varepsilon} = (0.52)(0.40) - 0.40 = -0.19$$

The "Timmer Curvature" relationship is: Income-class-specific pure substitution term, ε_Y = Intercept (I) + half the income elasticity coefficient times log of income. $\varepsilon_Y = -1.33 + 0.20 (\log Y)$. The intercept term (-1.33) was calculated from the average relationship $-0.19 = I + (0.20)(5.70)$, where $5.70 = \log 300$.

c. Calculated using the basic Slutsky equation for each income class.

−0.40, the price elasticity for the low-income group is −0.99, more than twice as large. The price elasticity for the high-income group is only −0.10. The steps involved in calculating these elasticities are lengthy, somewhat complicated, and draw on a mixture of theoretical and empirical regularities. The results, however, are plausible, are sufficiently different from the overall average to be well worth the effort, and provide a convenient shortcut to the expensive and time-consuming consumption analysis needed to estimate such parameters directly.

The full-blown consumption analysis should be conducted whenever possible to refine the parameters further and provide additional insight into the "empirical regularities" used to create the results in table 2-3. Such an analysis, however, is not likely to be high on the list of priorities for food policy analysts. They will be forced to borrow, to adjust, and to interpolate from other studies and settings. The rules and guidelines provided here are intended to make that ad hoc process as easy and successful as possible. At the same time, the limits to what these estimated and borrowed parameters can tell the analyst should be recognized. At best, they capture the reactions of consumers who participate in markets, have measurable incomes, and live at fixed residences where interviewers from statistical bureaus can find them. The parameters do not capture, nor is very much known about, the consumption behavior of the very poor—the destitute who subsist below the relative safety of mere poverty. It is not clear that policy can reach these people, for the same reasons that interviewers cannot. Their hope lies in a dynamic economy that creates ready jobs for unskilled workers and in the compassion of their society for the truly unfortunate.

Using Consumption Parameters

Food policy analysis focuses major analytical attention on food consumption patterns because of the relationship between the quantity of food consumed and hunger. The market demand parameters for basic foodstuffs that are an early product of food policy analysis are used to answer several important questions. When average per capita GNP rises, how much is market demand for rice likely to increase? What will be the effect on market demand for wheat? How will demand for cassava, corn, or meat change? How much meat is grain-fed, and what will growing meat demand do to grain demand? How sensitive is market demand to absolute and relative food prices? If all food grain prices rise relative to nonfood prices, how much does demand drop? When rice prices rise, does wheat consumption rise while rice consumption falls?

Answering these questions is important because the resulting income, own-price, and cross-price elasticities provide necessary linkages from macro price policy and macroeconomic performance to food consumption and, through the food marketing sector, to incentives for agricultural production. Estimating these aggregate market demand parameters with any real confidence is seldom easy. Time series data are frequently short and of dubious accuracy when domestic food grain production makes up a significant part of total consumption. Mechanical regression analysis seldom gives plausible parameters. A combination of intuitive judgment, talking to traders, evidence from household surveys, simple graphical and statistical analysis of available data, and familiarity with similar parameters in other countries is frequently the best that can be achieved.

The second step in food consumption analysis disaggregates the first step. The motivation for this step is quite different from the need to know aggregate market demand parameters to understand the macro linkages in the food sector. The disaggregated consumption understanding is needed to trace the effects of various price and income policies on the food intake of the poor. For designing programs that target food subsidies efficiently, knowledge of how the consumption parameters of the poor differ from those of the middle- and upper-income households is essential.

The starting point is to discover what the poor actually eat. Everyone knows that they eat *less* than the rich eat. But in virtually all societies the *composition* of foods the poor eat is also significantly different from the diets of middle-income and wealthy consumers. The point can usually be demonstrated and suitably quantified by preparing separate food balance sheets for three or four income classes in a society and comparing them with the aggregate food balance sheet published by the government. The information needed to do this is normally available from household expenditure surveys.

Food policy analysts should always go this far in understanding disaggregated food consumption patterns. It is critical to get the commodities and the amounts right. Whether it is then possible to disaggregate the demand parameters by income class will depend on data availability, computer facilities, and analytical capacity. The results of the few such analyses that have been conducted are both satisfying and exciting. Intuitive prior judgments that the poor, in their food consumption decisions, are significantly more responsive to economic signals—both income and price signals—have been strongly borne out in the analysis.

The ultimate goal of food consumption analysis is to improve the potential for and efficiency of government interventions to increase staple food intake among the very poor. Such interventions have two effects: the changed food intake among the target population; and secondary and usually unintended ramifications for food production, marketing, and even for the rest of the economy. For example, generalized food subsidies through low food prices have potentially negative effects on food production. The mechanisms by which subsidies and food price policies are implemented usually have an enormous impact on the food marketing sector. An overvalued exchange rate that is maintained partly to hold food costs down can have very widespread ramifications for overall economic growth. Likewise, policies and interventions in the rest of the economy, including but not limited to the food system, frequently have unintended consequences for food consumption among the poor. The disaggregated food consumption parameters permit analysts to predict, if only roughly, how important this impact might be.

From Commodity Consumption Functions to Individual Nutrient Intakes

Commodity consumption functions, even those estimated for specific income classes, have two important limitations. First, because virtually all food consumption data are gathered at the household level, few consumption functions address the question of distribution of food within the household despite the greater extent of malnutrition among young children and pregnant and lactating women. Second, information on foods consumed is not the same as information on nutrients consumed. The body uses nutrients to provide energy for work and growth and the raw materials for healthy metabolism and body development. Individual food commodities carry a variety of nutrients, and often nutrient analysis is a helpful additional step in consumption analysis.

NUTRIENT ANALYSIS. Nutritional status depends heavily on nutrient intake. While such nutrients come from food, the body is more or less indifferent to the source of specific nutrients, whether calories, amino acids, vitamins, or minerals. Carrots and papaya both provide vitamin A; the eye can hardly tell the difference at the level of blood chemistry. Individual commodity analysis is extremely important to understanding actual consumer decision-making, for people buy and consume foods, not nutrients. Most foods, however, contain many different nutrients, and not all important nutrients are completely supplied by normal amounts of one particular food. Hence, an important distinction exists between food commodity analysis and nutrient analysis, and some understanding of overall changes in nutrient intake is necessary to complement the individual commodity results.

Separate analysis of individual nutrients (such as calories, protein, iron, calcium, and vitamin A) can be made as if they were commodities. With information from nutritional scientists and dietitians the quantity of food consumed can be converted into nutrients actually available to the body. Few such consumption analyses have been conducted, especially for disaggregated income classes, and all have focused on income effects. Except for studies in the United States (by Anne Thomson), Indonesia (by C. Peter Timmer and Harold Alderman), and Bangladesh (by Mark Pitt), no price effects for basic nutrients by income class have been directly estimated. Per Pinstrup-Anderson and others have generated such parameters for urban households in Cali, Colombia, using a mixture of empirical and theoretical modeling. Knowledge of disaggregated food commodity consumption parameters is just beginning to accumulate, and knowledge of the overall nutrient effects is well behind even this modest level.

The impact of income change on nutrient intake can also be built up from individual commodity functions if enough commodities have been analyzed. A fairly satisfactory understanding of protein and calorie intake, the important nutrients for food policy analysis, can usually be generated from a half dozen commodities. The same is not true of the micronutrients (vitamins, minerals, and trace elements) since they tend to be supplied from secondary foods that need not be consumed in large quantities to provide significant amounts of a particular micronutrient. A very small quantity of red palm oil, for instance, can supply several months' requirements of vitamin A.

Price effects on overall protein and calorie intake cannot be aggregated easily from individual commodity functions. Cross-price effects tend to dampen significantly the overall protein and calorie adjustments to a change in a single commodity price. Since these cross-price effects are quite difficult to estimate reliably when several commodity prices are changing simultaneously, the prediction of a calorie or protein change becomes very inexact. More satisfactory results may be obtainable by estimating directly how calorie or protein intake changes as a function of some weighted price of calories or protein. Large changes in consumption patterns create difficulties in choosing appropriate weights for the prices, but the problem is not significant for fairly small changes.

FOOD DISTRIBUTION IN THE HOUSEHOLD. All the food and nutrient consumption analysis discussed so far has been conducted at the household level. The nutrition survey data, however, usually identify certain vulnerable groups in low-income households. Infants, small children, and pregnant or lactating women suffer from hunger and malnutrition far more frequently and severely than the population as a whole. The elderly are often severely affected. How can food distribution within the family be determined?

Despite the importance of the questions, there are no answers. Even the descriptive data available on food consumption by income class of households seldom contain accurate information on distribution within the family. With data on household size and composition by age, sex, and occupation it is sometimes possible to estimate roughly the distribution of food to family members and the long-run parameters of change in food intake by individual family members in response to income or price change. Since the short-run change coefficients have never been estimated successfully, only anthropological insights are helpful with this problem. Because of such data and analytical problems, food policy analysis focuses at the household level rather than on members within it. Nutrition interventions frequently try to target their inputs more precisely, but consumption interventions normally treat the household as the basic decisionmaking unit.

Food and Nutrition Interventions

Food and nutrition interventions are available over a wide range of categories and approaches. For example, an overvalued exchange rate for a food-importing country provides a significant subsidy to all food consumers in the society. Given the tendency for many poor, food-deficit countries to maintain overvalued exchange rates, the most prevalent and probably the most important food consumption intervention in terms of aggregate impact on food energy intake is precisely via this macro price, the foreign exchange rate. This is the broadest and least targeted food consumption intervention.

At the extreme opposite end of the spectrum is hyperalimentation through intravenous feeding. Hospital patients can be kept alive, even healthy, for months and even years while entirely bypassing their digestive systems. All required nutrients for maintenance and growth can be supplied directly to the bloodstream without prior eating or digestion. This is certainly the ultimate in targeted nutrition intervention.

Table 2-4 attempts to break this wide spectrum of potential interventions into a 2 by 2 matrix of categories: food versus nutrition interventions and

Table 2-4. Categories of Food and Nutrition Interventions

	Food	*Nutrition*
Targeted	Food stamps with means test Fair-price shops with means test and geographic or commodity targeting Targeted ration programs Supplementary feeding programs for women, children, or other vulnerable groups Price subsidies for inferior food commodities Food-for-work programs	Maternal and child health clinics with means tests or geographic targeting Targeted nutrition education Targeted weaning foods Vitamin and mineral supplements for deficit populations Malnutrition wards in hospitals for severe cases
Nontargeted	*Direct (program)* General food ration schemes Fair-price shops for primary foodstuffs and unrestricted access *Indirect (policy)* Overvalued exchange rate for imported food General food price policy or subsidy Food production input subsidies (fertilizer, water, credit, seed, machinery)	Nutrition education on radio and television and through other general media General fortification schemes (for example, iodized salt) Basic policies encouraging breastfeeding or discouraging infant formula Public health interventions (water, sanitation, innoculations)

targeted versus nontargeted interventions. Both distinctions are blurred at best, but they do provide ends of spectrums along two important dimensions. The matrix provides a starting point in the effort to understand a country's existing or potential food and nutrition interventions.

FOOD VERSUS NUTRITION INTERVENTIONS. The first important distinction is between food interventions and nutrition interventions. Many nutrition planners consider all interventions that ultimately might have an impact on nutritional status as nutrition interventions, but a much narrower view is taken here. Specifically, nutrition intervention projects, as discussed here, are restricted to activities that achieve nutritional objectives without using the changed intake of staple foods as the primary cause of the nutritional change. Nutrition education, development of calorie-dense weaning foods, vitamin and mineral supplementation or fortification, encouragement of breast-feeding, and public health measures all can have significant impact on nutritional status without significant changes in the consumption of staple foods.

The other major category, food interventions, includes the possibilities for improving the distribution of intake of food staples, hence reducing the extent and severity of chronic hunger. This category of interventions is the main focus of food policy analysis, not because nutrition interventions are unimportant but because they can be much more efficient and effective where significant food energy deficits have been eliminated. This assessment is controversial, especially when broad-scale food interventions are set against broad-scale public health interventions that attempt to improve nutritional status by capturing the synergistic impact of clean water, adequate sanitation facilities, and simple treatment of infections and gastrointestinal disease.

However this debate is resolved in any particular empirical setting, it should be made clear what the debate is *not* about. In the context of widespread food energy deficits, nutrition interventions in the narrow sense—nutrition education, malnutrition wards in hospitals, food fortification, even child-feeding or school lunch programs—have not been very successful at improving the nutritional status of the recipients. Such narrowly focused nutrition intervention projects usually can be effective only when household food intake is sufficiently above a threshold at which all family members have access to adequate protein and calories for growth and body maintenance.

TARGETED VERSUS NONTARGETED INTERVENTIONS. The second major distinction is between targeted and nontargeted interventions. Targeting directs the benefits to a specific group of recipients. If an intervention is designed so that virtually all the benefits are broadly distributed among an entire population, the program is untargeted. Since targeting is not an all-or-nothing proposition, the intent of the program must be clearly distinguished from the actual distribution of its benefits. On the one hand, for example, a food stamp program might be intended to be highly targeted because of an income test for qualification; but if no independent data can be used to verify a person's reported income, the program can actually be relatively untargeted. On the other hand, a shop selling subsidized food in the center of a very poor section of town could be freely accessible to all buyers, but because of the targeted location (and perhaps restrictions on the quantity that may be purchased at one time, for example, no truckload lots), the food subsidy in fact accrues almost entirely to food-deficit households.

Targeting can be judged only by result, not by intent. Disaggregated food consumption analysis provides the descriptive and analytical understanding of the food consumption patterns of the poor necessary for predicting actual results. Knowing what the poor eat and why and how those patterns will change when the external environment changes is essential to designing food interventions that target in fact as well as in intent. Since most food interventions take the form of an implicit or explicit subsidy, either altering the price facing the consumer or transferring real income, the need to have disaggregated price and income elasticities for important food staples is obvious.

Why is targeting such an important topic? Why not use fairly simple international trade instruments, such as imports with subsidies, to provide cheap food to the entire population? Although quite effective if implemented widely and with vigor, as in Egypt and Sri Lanka until 1979, such broad subsidies are extremely expensive and can have powerful disincentive effects on the agricultural sector. Targeting consumer subsidies to just the households in greatest need provides most of the nutritional gains of the broader subsidies without the enormous fiscal burden or the production disincentives.

Food consumption interventions can be targeted in a variety of ways, but all require substantial knowledge about food consumption patterns of the poor, both descriptive (including who the poor are and where they are located) and analytical (how the poor will change their food consumption patterns when their incomes or prices change).

Targeting Mechanisms

Targeting refers simply to getting more food to the identified group and not to others. The success of any targeting mechanism depends on limiting the leakage of program benefits to nonprogram families. Such leakages tend to be a function of the size of the program benefits. Small benefits provide little incentive to cheat or to participate contrary to the intent or regulations of the program. However, small benefits do little to alleviate hunger, which requires the transfer of adequate resources to generate a significant increase in food intake. Programs with relatively large program benefits for target families—those with food energy deficits—tend to encounter large leakages (some would say hemorrhages, on the basis of historical efforts to target food subsidies). One of two things must happen for ambitious food interventions to succeed. Either the program will become more expensive and the fiscal burden greater, or the targeting mechanisms must be more carefully designed and implemented.

MEANS TEST. Targeting is a tricky concept for program design. The most obvious mechanism for targeting food interventions to the poor is to implement a means test, that is, to have an income threshold above which individuals or families do not qualify for the program. By design, a means test can be graduated, with benefits declining as incomes rise, so that the implicit tax on earned income is not so high as to create a strong disincentive to work. Means tests are expensive to administer, however, and tend to become tainted with fraud and abuse because of bureaucratic inability to monitor closely every participant's income. Moreover, although the work disincentive effects of such subsidy programs on recipient families can be cushioned and made gradual, they cannot be eliminated altogether.

Means tests are used fairly successfully in industrialized countries with extensive income tax records and computerized social security files. In societies with less extensive accounting information about individuals, the record of bureaucratic implementation of means tests is quite dismal. Limiting food program subsidies to low-income families by having government civil servants approve or disapprove applications on the basis of income information submitted by each family can in principle lower food subsidy costs relative to general subsidy costs. But such a bureaucratic approach to food intervention targeting is not likely to lower the costs enough for the fiscal burden to be manageable without extensive outside financing. In addition to the high costs of bureaucratic targeting, a means test frequently leaves out the most needy, who are unable or unwilling to face a government officer in such a procedure. Other forms of targeting need to be investigated.

Beyond the income-related means test, targeting mechanisms for the various programs listed in table 2-4 are identified by studying the results of a country's food consumption analysis. The goal is to find effective targeting mechanisms that can extend the range of possible interventions in other dimensions of policy. Some of these mechanisms are fairly obvious; others have surprising twists. In addition to income targeting by a direct bureaucratic means test, five other forms can be considered for targeting the food and nutrition interventions in table 2-4 more precisely to the intended beneficiaries: geographic, temporal, sex and age, "roundabout" carrier, and commodity targeting.

GEOGRAPHIC TARGETING. Geographic targeting requires fairly precise identification of urban or rural areas that have a uniformly high proportion of poor people suffering from inadequate food energy intake. Government fair-price shops located in the center of such areas selling heavily subsidized foods in retail quantities—for example, up to five kilograms of wheat flour or rice—

are sometimes an efficient mechanism for targeting the food subsidy to the poor.

TEMPORAL TARGETING. Temporal targeting is less well recognized but is done fairly frequently. If high food prices shortly before a main harvest cause significant hunger, the government can dampen the seasonal price peak by market injections of food and thereby reduce energy deficits and lower seasonal morbidity and mortality. Such temporal targeting of food subsidies is not costless in a broader sense, however, because the private marketing sector will drop out of transportation and marketing activity unless adequate price margins are provided to generate normal profits.

A government that decrees uniform prices for the entire year usually finds itself handling the entire marketed surplus rather than just a small margin sufficient to dampen high prices. The benefits to such a drastic policy might be positive but only if the government is fully prepared for the new task, has the financial capacity to carry it out, and manages the marketing functions as efficiently as the private sector. With successful temporal targeting of food subsidies, the significant welfare gains from improving the seasonal distribution of food consumption have both economic and nutritional components. With realistic demand curves for low-income food consumers, price stabilization can be shown to increase consumer surplus, the economic measure of a consumer's welfare. The gains in health and productivity which arise from the improved nutritional status can be added to the economic gains, thus providing further impetus to policy efforts to remove sharp seasonal fluctuations in the availability and prices of basic foodstuffs. At the same time, holding grain stocks is expensive, and managing those stocks as part of a price stabilization policy is a complicated undertaking. Chapters 4 and 6 return to these issues.

SEX AND AGE TARGETING. Sex and age targeting is possible because much of the serious hunger and malnutrition, resulting from inadequate food intake at the household level, is concentrated among small children and pregnant and lactating women. Programs that direct food to these groups may be very efficient in nutritional impact per dollar of program subsidy. But finding mechanisms that target specifically to the vulnerable groups is very complicated. For instance, providing a child a free, nutritious meal at a school or day-care center would seem to be very precise targeting. However, if the child receives 800 calories extra in the school lunch but 200 calories less at home for breakfast and 400 calories less for dinner because the parents know the child was well fed at school, three-quarters of the food has leaked away from the target recipient.

The available evidence, especially as reviewed by James Austin and Marian Zeitlin, suggests that such indirect leakages are pervasive and that age and sex targeting tends to be translated into family-wide income supplements. Such supplements are not necessarily bad, of course, but nutritional impact on the target individual is significantly diluted unless the programs specifically provide sufficient food resources for the entire family. If this is done, however, the program is no longer an age-targeted program but a roundabout carrier, which uses one vulnerable family member as the vehicle for reaching an entire poor family. Some form of target criteria must still identify the child or mother in need, and so the targeting requirement remains.

ROUNDABOUT CARRIERS. Roundabout carriers sometimes transfer significant resources to poor families. Finding such carriers involves knowing how the poor spend their money and locating an efficient commodity or service that can be subsidized specifically for the poor. In 1981 the kerosene subsidy in Indonesia, for example, provided the equivalent of about forty kilograms of rice per year for families in the bottom third of the income distribution. The kerosene subsidy caused serious distortions in the rest of the economy, but the example suggests that food subsidies are not the only feasible way of increasing food consumption. Subsidized bus passes, water, or education can have similar consequences for food consumption. The disaggregated consumption analysis helps determine whether they do have such effects and whether new policy and program opportunities have been revealed.

COMMODITY TARGETING. Commodity targeting can be used to focus and enforce geographic or age and sex targeting, for example, but it also has considerable potential as a direct targeting mechanism. Knowledge of food consumption patterns and of the entire food system is essential to commodity targeting. If a food is consumed primarily by the poor, that commodity can serve as an efficient vehicle for a subsidy intended to increase food intake among the deficit population.

Figure 2-10 shows stylized food consumption patterns as a function of income. Three sources of calories (rice, dried cassava, and "other") and their consumption relative to income are shown in the figure along with the total calorie intake as a function of income. C^* indicates the recommended calorie intake for the representative consumer, and Y^* indicates the income level at which such a calorie intake is normally consumed. Rice and dried cassava are used as generic names for convenience; the commodities could be wheat and millet or even white flour and brown flour. Indeed, one of the challenges of the commodity targeting approach is to create new food commodities with desired characteristics for efficiently carrying food subsidies to the poor.

It can be seen from figure 2-10 that subsidizing rice is not a very efficient mechanism for targeting subsidies to the poor. Rice has a high income elasticity, and its consumption rises sharply with income. Consequently, most of the subsidy accrues to upper-income groups in the absence of further

Figure 2-10. Stylized Food Consumption Patterns as a Function of Income

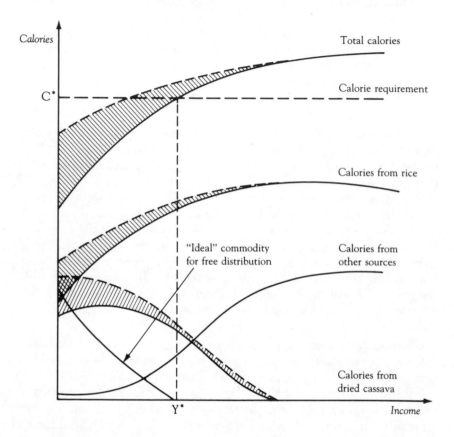

Note: Solid lines indicate consumption patterns before a subsidy on dried cassava; dotted lines indicate consumption patterns after a subsidy on dried cassava. The shaded areas indicate increases in calorie intake after the subsidy.

targeting mechanisms. But the consumption of dried cassava behaves very differently, rising with income among the very poor but then becoming a sharply inferior good with negative income elasticities for income classes on both sides of Y^*. Dried cassava ultimately becomes a negligible factor in calorie intake for middle- and upper-income households.

The dotted lines indicate a plausible result of a hefty subsidy on dried cassava for consumption in nonproducing households. (The effects are more complicated for producer-consumer households, and implementing a commodity price subsidy that affects only consumers requires careful attention to the marketing issues discussed in chapter 4.) With the subsidy, dried cassava consumption increases fairly sharply for the very poor, with relatively small increases for those with incomes over Y^*, until eventually the price subsidy has no impact at all on higher-income households. Next, some of the income effect of the subsidy is used to increase rice consumption, a superior food for low-income households. Since this income effect depends on the amount of cassava in the overall household budget, it drops off very sharply as Y^* is approached. This income effect might be offset and even made negative by a significant cross-price effect between rice and cassava. Empirical evidence by income class for such cross-price effects between starchy staples is virtually nonexistent. Cassava consumption in Indonesia seems to fall when rice prices fall and rise when rice prices rise. This reflects normal substitution. Current statistical estimates do not show a significant impact on rice consumption when cassava price changes, however, perhaps because the budget share of cassava is small even for poor households. Figure 2-10 shows rice consumption as complementary to cassava consumption as a basic calorie source because of a positive income effect.

The combined effect of increased dried cassava and rice consumption on total calorie intake shows up as a dramatic shift in the calorie-income relationship in favor of people below C^*. Of course, this is a stylized example designed to make precisely that point, but the consumption patterns shown are not atypical. The potential for using self-targeting commodities justifies a fairly intensive analysis of food consumption patterns in search of commodities that behave like cassava. In fact, figure 2-10 also shows what an "ideal" commodity might look like. It is the mirror image of the calorie-income curve "reflected" from C^*. If such a commodity were available (or could be invented by food technologists) and distributed free to any consumer who wanted it, the entire calorie deficit would be precisely and exactly eliminated. Such precision is not possible in the real world, but the concept of an efficient carrier of food subsidies to poor people is quite sound. A gruel made from dried cassava with some vegetable oil (for caloric density), a small amount of soy or peanut meal (for protein), and red peppers (so the chickens won't eat it) might actually improve protein-calorie intake more cheaply and efficiently than any existing alternative.

Keeping the chickens (and hogs, cows, goats, or pets) from eating a subsidized food is important. Most inferior foodstuffs, such as corn, sorghum, or millet, are high-quality animal feeds. Poor countries typically feed little grain (or even rootcrops, except to pigs in China) to livestock because it is too expensive. Subsidizing such grains can fairly quickly transfer subsidies to a grain-intensive livestock industry, distributing benefits by income class exactly opposite to the intention of the original targeting scheme. Bread carried by truckloads to feed poultry on the outskirts of Cairo indicates the potential problem can be quite real. Those concerned with commodity targeting must look in two very different directions: at the consumption patterns of the poor, and at livestock-feeding patterns and the potential for a shift to a subsidized inferior foodstuff. Ways to reach one group without benefiting the other are essential if commodity targeting is to be effective. Table 2-4 provides the categories of interventions available for this purpose.

Linkages among Food and Nutrition Interventions

Program linkages complicate the design and implementation of food and nutrition interventions. Several factors raise or lower the efficiency and effectiveness of any single intervention when others are introduced simultaneously or sequentially. Integrating the conceptual design of food and nutrition interventions will probably pay high dividends through greater cost-effectiveness of individual programs and greater opportunities to sense and capture program synergies. The possible range of food and nutrition interventions is extremely wide, from subsidized food imports to malnutrition wards in hospitals. A main task of food policy analysis is to identify all the interventions under way, whether advertised as such or not, and to quantify, however roughly, their actual impact on energy deficits.

With the understanding gained from the consumption analysis and resulting income and price elasticities, the analyst will be in a position to identify proposed targeting mechanisms that will not work effectively and to suggest others that will perform better. Much of the improved performance will come from intersecting targeting, for example, by geographic region at particular times of the year with specific commodities consumed primarily by the poor. Significant synergy might also be expected from programs that intersect. Maternal and child health clinics that provide staple foods and birth control information and devices along with their maternal and child health care might raise the effectiveness of all three programs. Integrating the delivery of such diverse services is not without cost, however. The managerial and organizational complexity of such integrated programs increases as more of the tasks must be simultaneously and efficiently performed. Managerial and organizational talent is not a free good. The true costs and actual ability to deliver through such integrated schemes must be considered relative to the potential synergistic gains from integration.

This chapter has attempted to demonstrate both descriptively and analytically how the food consumption sector of an economy can be understood from the perspective of public policy aimed at reducing calorie deficits. The public policies that ultimately achieve that result will almost certainly not be restricted to narrow sectoral interventions designed to deliver more food to hungry people. It is more likely that hunger will be eliminated by a coordinated effort involving many sectors and a complicated array of policies with partially conflicting objectives and effects. Food policy analysis identifies these relationships and seeks ways to reduce the conflicts and enhance the nutritional effects. Understanding food consumption patterns is the first step in such analysis.

Bibliographical Note

No single source or even collection of source materials provides the perspective on food consumption and nutrition presented here. This chapter deviates substantially from much of the nutrition planning literature in its concern for policy levers as opposed to program elements. It is radically different from much of the consumption literature in economics in its lack of concern for estimating systems of equations and its antiquarian insistence on thorough inspection of data, careful specification, and concern for what question is being asked in the first place. Consequently, the literature listed here will help fill in the nooks and crannies of the perspective presented in this chapter, but none of the works expands on the theme. In fact, many of the sources listed contradict some of what is presented here. The reader is forewarned!

The household decisionmaking perspective used throughout the chapter draws its logic from the "new household economics" which is conveniently summarized in Robert T. Michael and Gary Becker, "On the New Theory of Consumer Behavior," *Swedish Journal of Economics*, vol. 75, no. 4 (1973), pp. 378–96. The classical model of consumer behavior used to explain the Slutsky equation perspective on the impact of price changes is explained intuitively in Robert Dorfman, *The Price System* (Englewood Cliffs, N.J.: Prentice-Hall, 1964), and a full mathematical statement in an econometric context is contained in Louis Phlips, *Applied Consumption Analysis* (New York: North-Holland/American Elsevier, 1974). Many useful graphical techniques are presented in the basic volume by Frederick V. Waugh, *Demand and Price Analysis*, Technical Bulletin no. 1316 (Washington, D.C.: Economic Research Service, U.S. Department of Agriculture, 1964). The best review of techniques for analyzing cross-section data is in W. J. Thomas, ed., *The Demand for Food* (Manchester, England: Manchester University Press, 1972).

The perspective on disaggregated food consumption analysis draws on an initial paper by Per Pinstrup-Anderson and others, "The Impact of Increasing Food Supply on Human Nutrition: Implications for Commodity Priorities in Agricultural Research and Policy," *American Journal of Agricultural Economics*, vol. 58, no. 2 (May 1976), which used a methodology by Ragner Frisch that requires separability among commodities in the utility function. Concern over the restrictiveness of such a commodity "system" approach led to a series of papers and dissertations employing direct estimation techniques on very large data sets. The work can be traced sequentially in the following sources: C. Peter Timmer, "Food Prices and Food Policy Analysis: Issues and Methodology" (Boston, Mass.: Harvard Business School, 1979; processed); C.

Peter Timmer and Harold Alderman, "Estimating Consumption Parameters for Food Policy Analysis," *American Journal of Agricultural Economics*, vol. 61, no. 5 (December 1979), pp. 982–87; Anne Thomson, "Nutrition, Food Demand, and Policy," Ph.D. dissertation, Food Research Institute, Stanford University, 1979; Prasarn Trairatvorakul, "Food Demand and the Structure of [the] Thai Food System," D.B.A. dissertation, Harvard Business School, 1981; and Cheryl Williamson Gray, *Food Consumption Parameters for Brazil and Their Application to Food Policy*, IFPRI Research Report no. 32 (Washington, D.C.: International Food Policy Research Institute, September 1982). Attempts to merge the disaggregated and the "system" approaches have recently been partially successful, especially Mark M. Pitt, "Food Preferences and Nutrition in Rural Bangladesh," *Review of Economics and Statistics*, vol. 64, no. 1 (February 1983), pp. 105–14; and John Strauss, "Determinants of Food Consumption in Rural Sierra Leone: Application of the Quadratic Expenditure System to the Consumption-Leisure Component of a Household-Firm Model," *Journal of Development Economics*, vol. 11, no. 3 (December 1982), pp. 327–53. The possible relationship between changes in income elasticities and pure substitution price elasticities for basic foodstuffs as income levels change is explored in C. Peter Timmer, "Is There 'Curvature' in the Slutsky Matrix?" *Review of Economics and Statistics*, vol. 62, no. 3 (August 1981), pp. 395–402.

The nutrition literature is far too extensive to summarize here. The major paper by Thomas T. Poleman, "Quantifying the Nutrition Situation in Developing Countries," *Food Research Institute Studies*, vol. 18, no. 1 (1981), is an excellent introduction to the difficulties in measuring hunger and malnutrition. A framework for relating national statistics to the degree of hunger is developed by Roger W. Hay, "The Statistics of Hunger," *Food Policy*, vol. 3, no. 4 (1978), pp. 243–55. The classic book that raised policy awareness of nutrition as an issue for development planners is Alan Berg, *The Nutrition Factor* (Washington, D.C.: Brookings Institution, 1973). Current thinking about nutrition policy is reflected in Alan Berg, *Malnourished People: A Policy View* (Washington, D.C.: World Bank, June 1981).

A major survey of nutrition intervention programs has recently been completed by James E. Austin and his collaborators at the Harvard Institute for International Development. The overview, edited by James E. Austin and Marian F. Zeitlin, *Nutrition Intervention in Developing Countries* (Cambridge, Mass.: OG&H Publishers, 1981), summarizes the seven supplemental studies published in paperback by OG&H Publishers in five volumes. These studies, by a variety of collaborators, are as follows: vol. 1, *Supplemental Feeding*; vol. 2, *Nutrition Education*; vol. 3, *Fortification*; vol. 4, *Formulated Foods*; vol. 5, *Consumer Price Subsidies*; vol. 6, *Agricultural Production, Technical Change, and Nutritional Goals*; and vol. 7, *Integrated Nutrition and Primary Health Care Programs*. A survey by Lance Taylor and Sue Horton, "Food Subsidy Programs: A Survey" (New York: Ford Foundation, December 1980; processed), provides a thorough review of subsidy economics as well as a discussion of empirical experience with food subsidies in several countries. A persuasive argument for integrating nutrition, health, and family planning interventions is contained in Bruce F. Johnston and William C. Clark, *Redesigning Rural Development: A Strategic Perspective* (Baltimore, Md.: Johns Hopkins University Press, 1982).

A recent book attempts to pull together a wide range of issues affecting the design and implementation of nutrition plans and policies: Nevin S. Scrimshaw and Mitchell B. Wallerstein, eds., *Nutrition Policy Implementation: Issues and Experience* (New York: Plenum Press, 1982). The "Summary Comments" by Sol H. Chafkin are particularly insightful. The nutrition planning literature received its impetus from a paper by Leonard Joy, "Food and Nutrition Planning," *Journal of Agricultural Economics*, vol. 24, no. 1 (1973), pp. 165–97. The connections to agriculture quickly become apparent. Nevin S. Scrimshaw and Moises Behar, eds., *Nutrition and Agricultural Development* (New York: Plenum Press, 1976), contains several useful papers that relate to this connection. Three papers in particular provide policy analysts with a helpful perspective on some of the human biological issues that underlie the nutrition component of food policy: Joaquin Cravioto and E. R. DeLicardie, "Microenvironment Factors in Severe Protein-Calorie Malnutrition"; Michael C. Latham, "Nutritional Problems in the Labor Force and Their Relation to Economic Development"; and Fernando Mönckeberg, "Definition of the Nutrition Problem—Poverty and Malnutrition in Mother and Child." The seasonal connection between agriculture and malnutrition is one of the topics explored in Robert Chambers, Richard Longhurst, and Arnold Pacey, eds., *Seasonal Dimensions to Rural Poverty* (Totowa, N.J.: Allanheld-Osmun, 1981). The more general connection between malnutrition and food crises is reviewed in A. K. M. A. Chowdhury and Lincoln Chen, "Interaction of Nutrition, Infection, and Mortality during Recent Food Crises in Bangladesh," *Food Research Institute Studies*, vol. 16, no. 2 (1977), pp. 47–62.

Two works have attempted a general integration of food price policy with food consumption and nutrition: C. Peter Timmer, "Food Prices and Food Policy Analysis in LDC's," *Food Policy*, vol. 5, no. 3 (August 1980), pp. 188–99, and Giorgio Solimano and Lance Taylor, eds., *Food Price Policies and Nutrition in Latin America* (Tokyo: United Nations University Press, 1980). In addition, a series of IFPRI Research Reports have examined the food consumption consequences of food pricing, distribution, and ration policies in several countries with serious food problems. See Shubh K. Kumar, *Impact of Subsidized Rice on Food Consumption and Nutrition in Kerala*, IFPRI Research Report no. 5 (Washington, D.C.: International Food Policy Research Institute, January 1979); P. S. George, *Public Distribution of Foodgrains in Kerala—Income Distribution Implications and Effectiveness*, IFPRI Research Report no. 7 (March 1979); Raisuddin Ahmed, *Foodgrain Supply, Distribution, and Consumption Policies within a Dual Pricing Mechanism: A Case Study of*

Bangladesh, IFPRI Research Report no. 8 (May 1979); James D. Gavan and Indrani Sri Chandrasekera, *The Impact of Public Foodgrain Distribution on Food Consumption and Welfare in Sri Lanka*, IFPRI Research Report no. 13 (December 1979); Raisuddin Ahmed, *Agricultural Price Policies under Complex Socioeconomic and Natural Constraints: The Case of Bangladesh*, IFPRI Research Report no. 27 (October 1981); and Grant M. Scobie, *Government Policy and Food Imports: The Case of Wheat in Egypt*, IFPRI Research Report no. 29 (December 1981).

3

Analysis of Food Production Systems

Agriculture is the basic source of food, and farmers are the basic food producers. Farmers are remarkably diverse people, ranging from near-subsistence peasants in India and Guatemala to corporate businessmen in California and São Paulo. Nevertheless, private agriculture is a markedly homogeneous industry in the kinds of decisions that must be made day in and day out and in the kinds of uncertainties that condition those decisions. The corporate soybean farm in São Paulo or the rice farm in California has more in common with the wheat-growing peasant operation in the Punjab than with U.S. Steel or Volkswagen of Brazil.

In a substantial part of the world, agricultural decisions are made within a collective environment—from North Korea through China to Vietnam and in Eastern Europe and the U.S.S.R. Perhaps half the world's farm households are part of collectivized or communal agriculture, and yet these households, like their private counterparts, must still make many decisions that are not made by higher authorities. Much of farmers' daily work is done at their own initiative, and the incentives that induce them to work in a timely and careful fashion strongly influence the quality and quantity of agricultural output. In both private and collective agricultures the decisionmaking environment is conditioned by incentives to work. Identifying the factors that influence the size and composition of agricultural output is impossible without an understanding of the decisionmaking environment of the farm household.

This chapter addresses four questions about the food production system. First, what are the objectives for the sector itself, as opposed to the broader objective of providing food to meet consumption requirements? Answering this question involves understanding why the agricultural sector is different from the steel or transportation industry and what the social and analytical issues are that flow from these important differences.

Second, how do farmers make decisions? Only with a decisionmaking framework that incorporates the full range of factors influencing farm households is it possible to address the behavior and performance of the food sector as a whole. Most farm households are characterized by joint consumption-production decisions, but not in a tightly defined subsistence setting. Farm households base their consumption and production decisions on farm input prices, cash and food crop output prices, the prices of consumer goods from the market, the opportunity cost of their members' time either in outside labor markets or on farm production (including household work), and demand for leisure. The full context of household decisionmaking is essential to understanding how food production will change when external circumstances change.

Third, what government interventions are available to change household decisionmaking and thereby change the performance of the food producing sector? Understanding how interventions will affect decisionmaking is more important for agriculture than for any other sector, for the government has very few interventions available that can directly alter domestic food production. State-run farms and public exhortations to farmers to step up output still must deal with the reality of millions of day-to-day decisions in planting, tending, and bringing in the crops. An old saying holds that governments do not grow food; only farmers grow food. But governments can import food, subsidize fertilizer, make agricultural research a priority, or "purchase" food surpluses at gunpoint. For better or worse, the farmer's fate is tied to government policy, and the government's fate, or at least the success of its food production plans, hinges on the willingness of farmers to go along.

Fourth, what are the elements of a successful agricultural development strategy? Of the wide variety of possible government interventions, what combination will reinforce the achievement of sectoral goals and simultaneously serve the broader set of food policy objectives? This question raises somewhat different issues from those of traditional output-oriented agricultural development literature, for the food policy analyst is concerned with the intersectoral and consumption consequences of a production strategy as well as the impact on yields.

Understanding Food Production Issues

What does society want from its food producing sector? The answers used to be cheap food and cheap labor to foster industrial development and the earning of foreign exchange to buy the capital machinery to make it possible. A host of new complexities, however, has been added. A concern for rural poverty, unstable world markets, and the importance of efficient growth in the rural economy as well as in industry now make the question much more difficult to answer. A major lesson of postwar development experience is that agriculture is site specific. What works in one location may not work in another, even in the same country, because the ecological setting is different or because farm households face different constraints on their decisionmaking. The food production issues important to the policy analyst begin with understanding why agriculture as a sector is so different from other industries and why agriculture itself is so heterogeneous from farm to farm and even from field to field.

Five features set apart the agricultural sector from other productive sectors of an economy: its large contribution to national income, the large number of participants, the peculiarities of the agricultural production function, the role of the agricultural sector as a resource reservoir, and the importance of home consumption of output. These features are more evident in traditional societies, and their distinctiveness tends to erode during the process of economic modernization. Indeed, perhaps the most striking characteristic of agriculture is its almost universal tendency to diminish in importance relative to other, more rapidly growing sectors of the economy. There are healthy and unhealthy declines, however. An urban-biased development strategy that neglects agricultural investments and incentives can force an agricultural decline. The alternative path—rapid growth in both agricultural and industrial sectors—leads to a relative shift in the agricultural sector's importance because citizens with higher incomes consume relatively less agricultural produce. Finding the path that fosters growth in agriculture and industry is the goal of the analysis here.

The Size of Agriculture in Gross National Product

A large proportion of economic activity is provided by agriculture in most poor societies. The agricultural sector contributes as much as 70 percent of national product in a few countries just emerging from centuries of traditional economic organization. Half the output in many developing countries is still produced in agriculture. If related industries are also counted in, as these develop rapidly in the course of modernizing agriculture itself, the share of this broader agribusiness sector seldom declines to less than one-quarter of national economic output, even in advanced industrial societies. In very few societies do consumers spend less than one-fifth of their incomes on food alone. If other agricultural activities—the input industries and the production of industrial raw materials—are also added in, the continued importance of agriculture is obvious.

When agriculture contributes half or more of gross national product, rapid growth in average per capita incomes is very difficult to achieve unless rural incomes are rising. From a macroeconomic perspective in poor countries, rapid and efficient increases in agricultural output will be essential to meeting overall growth goals. From a growth perspective, simple arithmetic makes agriculture more important than other sectors.

Number of Participants

In many countries, 60 to 80 percent of the population still lives in rural
areas, earning a livelihood directly or indirectly from agriculture. In industrially advanced economies many of these people move to the industrial sector
while still engaged in agriculturally related jobs—producing fertilizer, canning
tomatoes, or stocking supermarket shelves. But in nearly all developing countries a majority of the population lives in the countryside. The overwhelming
predominance of the rural population has three important consequences for
understanding agricultural decisionmaking: most farms will be small because
large numbers of people must share the arable land; millions of individuals
will each behave according to particular decisionmaking environments; and
much of the world's poverty and its human welfare costs will be in rural areas.

SIZE OF OPERATIONS. In most countries, if the available arable land were
divided equally among the farm population, the resulting average farm size
would be small by comparison with U.S. or European standards. Farms of
less than a hectare would characterize China, Bangladesh, and Java, and
even Japanese farms average only slightly more than a hectare. The average
in India would be about 1 to 2 hectares, and in Africa and Latin America
farms would tend to be less than 20 hectares. Average farm size is well over
100 hectares in the United States and well over 50 hectares in the United
Kingdom.

The available farmland, of course, is usually not divided equally among
all the potential farmers. The conditions of land tenure and the size distribution of farms are important characteristics of a country's agricultural decisionmaking environment. Although exact farm-size distribution is a subject
for analysis in each country, its general pattern is important in judging the
likely degree of poverty and the income distribution consequences of growth
strategies for the rural sector.

A country with a unimodal distribution of farm sizes—a large number of
small, family-operated farms capable of supporting the family members above
a subsistence level, with only a fringe of smaller and larger farms around this
modal norm—has the potential to use agricultural development strategy to
reduce rural poverty at the same time that it increases food production.
Countries with bimodal distributions of farm sizes—many very small farms
on a minority of the land with a few very large, estate-like farms that occupy
most of the arable land and produce most of the food surplus available for
urban markets—face much more difficult dilemmas in reducing rural poverty
while using traditional output-increasing strategies of agricultural development. Such land tenure patterns are common in Latin America and are one
reason that land reform issues are so much more prominent there than in
Africa or Asia.

The circumstances under which farm households have access to land for growing crops have many ramifications beyond the obvious insecurity and commonly weak bargaining position of tenants and renters. Landownership provides an asset which farmers can use to obtain credit for inputs or investments in farm capital. It provides greater incentives to save from household income. The conditions of tenure frequently affect the willingness of landlords to invest in land improvements and the willingness of tenants to use yield-increasing inputs at socially efficient levels. The discussion of food production strategies engages this issue in the context of the broader objectives of food policy.

DECENTRALIZED DECISIONMAKERS. Growing food is a decision-intensive undertaking. What crops to plant, what inputs to use, when to plow, to seed, to cultivate, to irrigate, to harvest, how much to keep for home consumption, how much to sell and how much to store for later sale are the decisions that occupy the daily routine of most farmers. Agriculture is truly unique in that literally millions of individuals and households are making these decisions themselves or in consultation with relatively small numbers of neighbors, friends, or partners. In Brazil, India, Indonesia, Nigeria, and even China, influencing agricultural production decisions to increase food output is an entirely different process from changing decisions about how much steel or cement to produce. In each of the countries—indeed, in most countries—a dozen or so individuals could take direct action which would lead to a 10 percent increase in steel output in a year or so. Their decisions would be decisive.

Nowhere, not even in socialist countries, can a similar small group of individuals decide to raise food production by 10 percent. To be sure, a small group of planners or the president and the cabinet can decide they *want* food production to rise by 10 percent. They can tell the food logistics agency, the ministry of agriculture, the newspapers, and agriculture extension agents that they want food production to rise by 10 percent. But they cannot increase food production 10 percent by themselves. They must also convince the millions of farmers in their country to want to increase food production by 10 percent, *and make it in their self-interest to do so.*

Here is the true importance of the vast number of agricultural decisionmakers. There are simply too many of them to reach directly either with pleas for cooperation or with police power. Farmers must see the benefits of higher yields for themselves; there are too many opportunities to let high yields slip beneath the hoe or in a late fertilizer application, even under the watchful eyes of a guardian. Farming is a subtle combination of skilled craft and brute force. Brute force alone will not achieve high yields.

Farmers' decisions are likely to be altered only when they perceive the incentives to be favorable to the change. A heated and frequently sterile debate has been waged over the incentives needed to induce change in farmers. The elements range from pretty ribbons to raising political consciousness, from basic literacy to the availability of consumer goods for purchase in rural markets. The debate is nearly dead now, for the answer is largely in. Most farmers respond to opportunities to improve their economic and material well-being.

The evidence is overwhelming that farmers make economic calculations in considering their agricultural decisions. When the economic environment changes, their calculations change in directions predicted by economic models of producer behavior. Collective ownership of land and other implements, and collective decisionmaking with respect to basic cropping patterns and investments, can alter sharply the perception of risk from farming. If the returns are also shared collectively, the perception of reward for individual work and initiative is altered as well. To produce agricultural output efficiently, most socialist agricultural systems have found it necessary to maintain personal or household incentives that link farming effort to rewards.

The tendency toward economic rationality in farm household decisionmaking justifies the use of basic economic models to help analysts judge the efficacy of policy interventions designed to change the decisionmaking environment of rural households. Just as models of consumer decisionmaking with respect to food help organize analysts' research and policy design, so do producer models help organize the complexity of the farm environment into several issues that are central to food policy.

Of these policy issues, some are of special importance: the efficiency with which farmers allocate the resources at their disposal to produce crops, relative to alternative uses of these resources; the technical ability of farmers to achieve the maximum output from a given set of inputs; and the impact of alternative forms of land tenure on both the allocative and the technical performance of farmers. Each of these issues conditions the scope for effective government intervention. One of the policy levers most susceptible to effective government control is price policy for food crops and agricultural inputs. The role of prices in influencing the behavior of farmers is extremely important and depends on farmers' allocative and technical efficiency and on the form of tenure for the land they farm.

Characteristics of Agricultural Production Functions

The only way to produce output is to combine the necessary ingredients—the inputs or factors of production—in suitable proportions so that the overall process yields the desired product. One unusual feature of the agricultural production function—the technical relationship that specifies how much output will be produced from any particular combination of inputs—is the joint combination of labor and management. Knowing what the right inputs are, how to combine them, and how to tend the process is the major function of management. In farming, this management skill is frequently combined with the farm household's own labor power, which is also an important ingredient in growing food. Several other features contribute to the uniqueness of agricultural production functions. The most important are seasonality, geographical dispersion, risk and uncertainty, and sources of technical change.

SEASONALITY. No agricultural region of the world has an absolutely constant year-round climate. Winter and summer create distinct growing seasons in the temperate zones. Wet and dry seasons and monsoons create conditions in which planting is appropriate, harvesting is difficult, or some crops simply do not thrive. Climatic variations cause agricultural production to follow distinct seasonal patterns even in most tropical areas, but seasonality is not a fixed and rigid constraint. Rice will grow in the dry season if irrigation water is provided, and tomatoes will grow in Siberia in January under artificial lights in a warm greenhouse.

Seasonality is important to farmers because it is generally cheaper to let Mother Nature provide many of the essential inputs for agricultural production—solar energy, water, carbon dioxide, temperature control, and essential nutrients from natural soils. But it is not always economical to let nature dictate the agronomic environment. One of the major tasks of government policy is to invest in socially profitable interventions, such as irrigation and drainage, that increase farmers' control over the crops that can be grown in particular regions and seasons.

Seasonality also tends to place high premiums on the timely performance of such critical agricultural tasks as plowing, planting, cultivating, and harvesting. Even though the available labor pool may seem more than adequate to provide the required number of man-days per hectare over an entire year for all the crops being grown, significant labor bottlenecks may occur if certain tasks must be performed very quickly at specific times to ensure maximum yields. Such bottlenecks frequently induce individual farmers to mechanize specific tasks—plowing or harvesting—even when much rural unemployment exists over the course of the year. Furthermore, a tractor that pays for itself by timely plowing then has a very low marginal cost of operation for other tasks as well, and labor displacement can be much more widespread than would be indicated by the removal of the plowing bottleneck alone.

Three lessons are apparent. First, seasonal aspects of agricultural production frequently constrain yields because of input bottlenecks. Labor is most often the constraining factor, but fertilizer, seeds, credit, or irrigation water must also be available at specific times. When fertilizer reaches the village godown a month after the proper application time, it may as well not have arrived at all. Government authorities responsible for managing the distribution of agricultural inputs are frequently unaware of or insensitive to the extreme importance of the timely availability of inputs. Suppliers whose incomes depend on providing appropriate inputs to farmers when and where needed are much more responsive to shifts in weather, cropping patterns, and new technologies than are government agencies trying to allocate inputs available from a planned industrial sector. Modern agriculture that uses industrial inputs as the basis for high yields is a dynamic enterprise quite unlike factories. It requires smoothly functioning input and output markets for production in the sector to grow rapidly and efficiently.

Second, there are often very high private economic returns to eliminating seasonal bottlenecks in production. When these private returns are generated at least partly by higher and more stable yields of agricultural products, society is also likely to gain. But if the private gains come from displacing hired labor that has few alternative jobs, the social gains may be small or even negative.

The third lesson is the importance of viewing agricultural production in a seasonal context. Most agricultural data are published on an annual basis, and there is an inevitable tendency to think about the sector in terms of the same criteria used to evaluate the annual performance of the steel or cotton textile industry. Such an annual approach, characteristic of five-year plans, hides two important roles for government analysis and intervention—the appropriate provision of inputs when and where they are needed and the full analysis of the social impact of private investments to reduce seasonal bottlenecks in agricultural production.

GEOGRAPHICALLY DISPERSED PRODUCTION. Agriculture is the only major sector that uses the land surface as an essential input into its production function. Like seasonality, this widespread use of land is due to the largesse of nature. It is simply cheaper to let farms capture the free solar energy and rain than to stack a hundred hydroponic "fields" on top of each other and provide the light, nutrients, and water from industrial sources. This wide geographical dispersion of agricultural production has an important economic consequence. Transportation becomes essential if any output is going to leave the farm for consumption by others or if inputs, such as modern seeds, fertilizer, pesticides, or machinery, are to be used on the farm to raise output.

In combination, seasonality and geographical dispersion create the need for a marketing system that can store the product from a short harvest period to the much longer consumption period and can move the commodity from the farm where it was grown to the many households where it will be consumed. Both functions require that the commodity change hands and that ownership be exchanged. This transaction can happen only when both parties agree on the terms of the exchange, that is, the price, for the commodity at the point of sale. In socialist economies the terms of exchange are usually set by the state, but all other marketing services must still be provided if the food grown by farmers is to be eaten by consumers. The role of marketing in price formation and the provision of food to consumers is the subject of the next chapter.

RISK AND UNCERTAINTY. Farmers the world over talk primarily about two topics, the weather and prices. On these two variables ride the rewards for the whole year's effort in farming. A failed monsoon, a flood, or a hailstorm can wipe out the crop. A bumper harvest can cause large losses if the price falls too low. No other industry depends on the whims of nature and volatile markets as much as farming does. Farmers who repeatedly make good decisions in response to rapid changes in their economic environment tend to survive and thrive. Those who do not, frequently fail and move to urban areas in search of jobs. Or they become impoverished landless laborers dependent on the rural economy for their incomes and access to food. Socialist-managed agricultures can cushion much of the welfare shock to individuals by sharing risks, but rapid and effective decisionmaking remains the key to dynamic efficiency in agricultural systems.

The fact that weather is uncertain causes farmers to behave differently than they would if weather were always known. This general uncertainty usually leads farmers to choose crops that will resist the extremes of weather, particularly crop varieties that are more tolerant of weather variations, and lower levels of inputs than would be optimal in a predictable world because of the risk of losing the investment altogether. These individual farmer reactions to uncertainty spill over into the arena of policy concern, for the resulting crop mix and aggregate output might be quite unsatisfactory for meeting government goals.

Equally important, farmers' reactions to weather variations have consequences for aggregate output. A late monsoon may cause millet instead of wheat to be planted, good rains may permit a second or third rice crop, and high temperatures and humidity can bring pests and diseases that force farmers to change crop rotations. As each farmer reacts, the adjustments can spill over into rural labor markets and cause serious shortages if planting must be done suddenly when the weather breaks or the harvest brought in before a flood. A particularly "dry" dry season may mean the second crop is not planted or harvested, and an important, perhaps critical, source of wage income is eliminated for many rural workers. The reduced harvest may not be the most important consequence of such a crop failure. A famine could result because of the failed income opportunities.

At an aggregate level, weather-induced variations for staple crop output are frequently 5 percent above or below normal. For countries so small that erratic weather patterns affect all farming regions simultaneously, as in Sahelian Africa and Central America, variations of more than 20 percent from one year to the next have been recorded. Because food demand tends to be quite inelastic in the short run as people shift other budget expenditures to maintain adequate levels of food intake, even small variations in basic food output can cause large fluctuations in market prices unless governments have substantial buffer stocks available for price stabilization or can arrange for additional imports in a timely fashion. In socialist economies, the availability of food rations can be sharply curtailed if a crop fails and planners have not anticipated the need for additional supplies from alternative sources.

In addition, fluctuations in aggregate production are magnified at the level of marketings (produce available for consumption by nonfarm households) because farm household consumption tends to vary somewhat less than production. Consequently, marketings vary considerably more than production in economies where a significant share of food production is consumed directly by the farm household. In years of poor weather, net marketings decline proportionately more than production. Similarly, in good years the percentage increase in marketings is usually substantially larger than the percentage increase in production. These wide fluctuations simply add to the government's difficulty in stabilizing domestic food prices and provisioning urban areas. A tendency to use food imports for these purposes is certainly understandable, but it frequently discriminates against food producers.

Price uncertainty also adds to the farmer's difficulty in deciding what crops to grow and how many inputs to use in growing them. Unlike the handful of manufacturers in large-scale industries, farmers are unable to set their output prices and then adjust production and inventory levels to meet the price targets. Unlike consumers, who know with near certainty the price they must pay for a given quantity and quality of a commodity at the time they buy it, farmers must make major input purchase decisions well in advance of knowing what prices their resulting output will bring. At the time many key farming decisions are made—the allocation of land to various crops, fertilizer applications, hiring labor for weeding—the farmer can only guess at the prices for the output.

Reducing weather and price uncertainties is an important task for food policy interventions. Dams and drainage ditches can reduce the impact of rainfall variations, crop insurance can provide a guaranteed income floor even if heavy investments are wiped out, and research on more adaptable but still high-yielding plant varieties can reduce the risks of new technology. Similarly, a government can reduce price uncertainty by providing better price forecasting information, by using import and export policy to provide a band of prices within which domestic price formation can take place, or by implementing a more aggressive floor and ceiling price policy with a government-operated buffer stock program. But these efforts to stabilize prices must be visible in market operations, not just in press releases and legislative actions. Most farmers have learned by painful experience that simple statements of government *intentions* to stabilize prices—or even to require them by law—are ineffective.

SOURCES AND DYNAMICS OF TECHNICAL CHANGE. Technical change is the source of most productivity growth in the long run, as continued investment in traditional technology very quickly faces low marginal returns. Most farmers are inveterate experimenters and tinkerers, always on the lookout for a slightly better way of doing things, whether a different seed spacing or a modified shape to the plow. As late as the 1920s most of the agricultural innovations in Europe and the United States arose on the farm and were gradually diffused by word of mouth and by agricultural colleges. Such on-farm innovation continues, but the scientific revolution in agriculture has made the process of technical innovation much more knowledge- and capital-intensive. Very few farmers even in the United States have the resources to carry out significant agricultural research, and most of it is now conducted by publicly funded agricultural research centers and by a handful of large agribusiness concerns, which are involved primarily in developing hybrid seed technology, chemical technology (herbicides and insecticides), and agricultural machinery. The small scale of most farms and limited financial resources mean little important agricultural research is conducted by farmers.

Technical change in agriculture shares many of the characteristics of technical change in other sectors, especially the tendency for individual inventors to be unable to capture the full economic rents from their inventions. The economic returns to innovation are small from the private inventor's point of view unless the new agricultural technology can be restricted for sale by its inventor or approved licensees. But the social returns to innovation may well be very large. Both the sheer scale of investment required for modern agricultural research and the inability of private research companies to capture the full return to their inventions mean that public agencies should play a leading role in funding and in carrying out agricultural research.

Diffusion of new technology is also a matter of policy concern, especially because not all farm households have equal access either to the knowledge to use new technology or to the agricultural and financial resources needed to make it productive on their own farms. Credit programs designed to improve the access of farmers, especially small farmers, to modern inputs are an essential component of the input programs themselves. Some inputs are "lumpy" and cannot be used efficiently on farms of even average size in many parts of the world. Large-scale tubewells and tractors might contribute significantly to higher productivity even on small farms if institutional arrangements can be found to separate the ownership of the assets from the service flows that such inputs can provide.

This public role can be overemphasized; the evidence suggests that truly profitable innovations spread quickly no matter what the government does. Where the entrepreneurship exists and the economic environment permits, rental arrangements and tractor-hire services frequently emerge spontaneously. But the location-specific nature of much new agricultural technology, especially seed technology, means that large areas of a country may be bypassed by the diffusion process unless government research and extension workers are actively engaged in the on-farm testing and evaluation of new technology. Adapting a general agricultural technology to a specific seed strain or technique that fits individual farming environments is a major responsibility of local research and extension stations.

An important policy concern is the impact of technical change on agricultural employment and rural income distribution. Historical evidence shows enormous variation in both the short-run and long-run impacts of innovations. The issues cannot be addressed satisfactorily by looking only at an individual farm. Because agricultural innovations tend to be embodied in inputs that must be provided through markets, they have complicated effects on the entire rural economy and eventually on the urban economy as well.

Most technical changes alter the biological processes of plants and animals to increase yield or they improve the efficiency of the mechanical functions needed to tend those biological processes. Primitive agriculture uses natural biological materials and processes in combination with human labor and management to bring in a food crop or livestock product. Modern agriculture uses scientific knowledge to reshape the biological materials so that each plant and animal is more productive, and it increasingly substitutes machines for human labor. Biological-chemical innovations, such as hybrid seeds, fertilizers, and pesticides, tend to increase yields and save land. Mechanical technology can also have a yield effect when it permits heavy soils to be cultivated or water to be pumped to dry lands, but most mechanical technology is designed to make agricultural work physically less burdensome and to save on the labor needed to produce a unit of output.

Yujiro Hayami and Vernon Ruttan have shown that biological-chemical innovations have tended to be discovered and introduced in land-scarce, labor-rich societies, such as Japan and Western Europe, whereas mechanical innovations were developed and used in land-rich, labor-scarce societies, such as the United States, Canada, and Australia. Such "induced innovation" suggests that each society develops an agricultural technology appropriate to its resource endowments and agricultural needs. Whether such society-specific innovation will continue to yield appropriate results in the context of a much more interdependent international agricultural system is a prime question for the rest of the century.

Because most new agricultural technology is embodied in a physical input— a bag of fertilizer, a new seed variety, a tractor, or an irrigation pump—it can be effective in a farmer's field only if a purchase (or rental arrangement) is made. Several consequences flow from this simple fact. For small farmers to participate in the benefits of technical change, they must be able not only to use the input on their farms (combines, for instance, usually are too large), but also to purchase the input that carries the new technology. Where a new seed-fertilizer package has a 200 percent rate of return, even borrowing from a village moneylender at 10 percent per month may be profitable. But for the full benefits of modern technology to reach small farmers, a credit program accessible to the farm household with only half a hectare or less may be essential.

Equally important, since new technology is embodied in inputs, a marketing and distribution system will be essential for both socialist and capitalist farmers to be able to purchase the inputs. Many traditional agricultural societies have a long history of small-scale marketing of surplus output to urban regions in exchange for consumer items, such as cloth, kerosene, or pots and pans, needed by farm households. There is no similar experience with large-scale movements of inputs, such as fertilizer or modern seeds, to those same dispersed farm households. The embodied nature of agricultural technology means that farmers cannot just be told about it. The marketing system must also deliver the inputs when needed.

Complementary fixed capital investments are often required to achieve the maximum benefits from the innovation. Usually this investment takes the form of better water control, land leveling, and drainage. Better control of seed bed preparation may sometimes require tractors with modern implements. Combines or threshers may be needed for faster and more sensitive harvesting techniques to avoid shattering and other harvesting losses. Shorter-maturity cereal varieties are often ready to harvest while the rainy season is still under way and solar drying is difficult or impossible. In such cases mechanical dryers and added storage capacity are essential.

The Farm Household as Both Producer and Consumer

Truly subsistence households produce to meet their own consumption needs and do not use the market for either buying or selling. To such households price signals are not only irrelevant, they are unseen. Few such households remain in today's world, not because farm families no longer consume produce from their own fields but because most farm families now buy and sell inputs and output in rural markets. They are aware of and react to market prices in making a wide variety of household decisions. But most farm households still retain some or most of their farm production for home consumption, which is a further distinguishing feature of the agricultural sector. Few steelworkers or even textile workers take their products home for household use.

The need to make connected production and consumption decisions within a single household obviously complicates life for the farm household, for the value of additional time spent in food preparation or tending the children must be balanced against the productivity of an additional hour weeding the rice, driving the ducks, or tending the home garden. The opportunity to spend some of that time working for cash on a neighbor's farm or in a rural wage-labor market places a lower bound on the value of household-farm time, and the value of leisure ultimately places a limit on the willingness to work, especially at low-productivity tasks. But for households with inadequate land to grow surplus crops for sale and with limited outside employment opportunities, the marginal value of leisure time may be low indeed, and possibly near zero. Even tiny increments to output can be valuable for very poor households.

The importance of joint household-farm decisionmaking also raises complex questions for analysts in search of ways to organize data and research issues into manageable and comprehensible frameworks for analysis. These complex questions have recently become the focus of a revived interest in models of household economies. At one level, the "new household economics" provides a powerful insight into joint decisionmaking about food production, food consumption, investment in human capital, and even fertility and other demographic factors. By showing how all these decisions are related to each other and to the economic environment surrounding the household, the household economics models provide analysts with a conceptual understanding of the complicated lives that rural people live.

At the level of full empirical specification, however, the household economics models have so far not been able to provide more than a hint of the quantitative significance of the internal decisionmaking relationships. This shortcoming is partly because precise data on actual time allocations within households are difficult to obtain, just as food distribution among family members is difficult to determine without having the observer bias the distribution itself. More important, judging the real opportunity cost of time is both conceptually and empirically difficult because the true value lies within the mind of the decisionmaker. Knowing whether the possibility of entering the wage labor market really influences the amount of time a mother allocates to raising children or the time family members spend in the fields and gardens is critical to using household economics models. But such knowledge may not be attainable. This question of the real opportunity cost of time arises several times in this chapter because of household labor's important role in agricultural production; it is a main factor in understanding how farm households respond to economic incentives and what their costs of production are when responding.

Agriculture as a Resource Reservoir

Much of the early literature on agricultural development was based on strategies that saw modern industry as the cutting edge of the economic growth process. In this context, agriculture served a relatively passive role of resource reservoir to be tapped as industrial needs required. Virtually all early models identified agriculture as the traditional sector that housed surplus labor which could be moved to higher-productivity industrial jobs at constant real wages as capital investment created a demand for their services. More sophisticated and historical models looked to agriculture to provide food surpluses for urban workers, capital surpluses to be siphoned into industrial investment, and an "expenditure" surplus that permitted purchases of output from the industrial sector. Open economy models also focused on agriculture's role in earning foreign exchange so that the modern sector could import capital goods.

These images of agricultural surpluses to be used by the industrial sector die hard. In a dynamic setting, where the agricultural sector itself is participating in rapid and efficient growth, many of the transfers are possible and desirable. But in the context of a static and traditional agriculture, such exploitation models lead to both agricultural and industrial stagnation. Arthur Lewis argued that agricultural and industrial revolutions always go together. From that perspective agriculture does play a unique role in providing resources for economic development. A healthy rural economy creates productive employment for a large population that might otherwise seek jobs in the overcrowded cities, while it provides opportunities for investing in new technology with some of the highest returns available in any sector.

Food Production Analysis

Because of agriculture's extraordinary diversity and heterogeneity of decisions required daily from farm to farm and in the entire marketing system, the sector is unique among major productive activities. This diversity places a heavy premium on decentralized decisionmaking. Planning agencies are simply incapable of making the necessary decisions efficiently and rapidly. Attempts to do so have stifled agricultural productivity in a number of countries, especially the socialist economies that have attempted to incorporate their agricultural sectors into the framework of central planning. As noted earlier, collective ownership and decisionmaking offer important gains in some areas of rural life, especially reduction of risk for individual households and more equal distribution of assets and incomes. In both socialist and market systems, however, many decisions that affect farm yields and the productivity of inputs must be made on the spot, day in and day out, by the individuals actually performing the work. The pressures and incentives these farmers face to make the decisions efficiently vary widely according to the type of economic and social structure and the agricultural policies pursued. Given that wide variation, it is important for analysts and policymakers to understand how farm-level decisions are likely to be made in a given context and how they will change when the structure and policies change. This section explains the nature of the production decisions that need to be made and the choices of individuals in the agricultural sector as they work to improve their personal or household returns from farming.

Theoretical Perspectives

With an understanding of the features that make agriculture a unique sector, analysts are ready to address the basic production decisions farmers must make to function effectively year in and year out: what crops to produce, what combination of inputs to use to produce them, and what total output

to produce. These decisions are related to each other in an economic decisionmaking framework that provides a rationale for farmer response to changed
incentives. This section focuses on each of the decisions individually and
then combines all three to relate output decisions to changes in output (or
input) prices in order to construct a supply curve. The supply curve is a very
convenient conceptual and empirical tool which summarizes a great deal of
complicated producer decisionmaking in a simple two-dimensional diagram.
In combination with the consumer demand curve for the same commodity,
the supply curve is an essential tool in economists' understanding of price
formation in market economies, one of the topics dealt with in chapter 4.

PRODUCT-PRODUCT DECISIONS. From an often wide array of possible crops,
farmers must decide what commodities to produce. Except for perennial tree
crops and pastoral livestock systems, these choices about which products to
grow—often called product-product decisions—are faced annually, sometimes
even monthly, by farmers. To make such choices in a rational fashion, farmers
must assess the opportunity cost of growing more of one crop at the expense
of another.

The production possibilities available to a farmer are depicted graphically
in figure 3-1. A production possibility curve, LGFA, is drawn to show the
various combinations of two crops that are technically possible for a farm
household to grow using its available resources on a given plot of land in a
single season. In this example, a farmer could choose to grow only beans
(OA kilograms) and no corn. At the other extreme the choice could be to
grow only corn (OL kilograms) and no beans. Point F represents a farmer's
decision to grow some of each, OD kilograms of beans and OE kilograms of
corn.

A rational and knowledgeable farmer would consider only points actually
on the production possibility curve. A point such as K, which is inside the
curve, represents an output level substantially less than the available farm
resources could produce. It is not uncommon, however, to observe a farmer
operating at an interior point such as K. The reasons might include bad
weather or a pest infestation, lack of knowledge about appropriate production
techniques, or an experimental new technique that failed. Understanding
why some farmers are not on the production frontier is one step in determining
the constraints on expanding output.

The production possibilities are shown as a curve, rather than a straight
line, because the farm household's resources cannot produce corn and beans
equally well. If the two crops were perfect substitutes, the production possibility curve would be a straight line. The greater the curvature, the less
easy it is to substitute one crop for another. Nearly all crops are substitutable
for others to some degree if suitable investments are made in providing an
appropriate growing environment. Whether such investments should be made
for a particular crop is a crucial issue for agricultural policy. If self-sufficiency

Figure 3-1. Product-Product Relationship

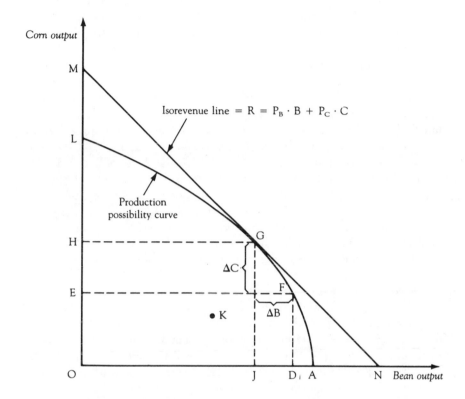

in corn is an important objective, it is possible to tear out rubber trees or tea bushes and plant corn. The decision to do so is only partly an agronomic issue. Policy and economic incentives are often the determining factors.

A farmer represented in figure 3-1 who wants to increase the production of corn, from point F to G, that is, by ΔC, must give up ΔB units of beans. This opportunity cost is shown by the slope of the production possibility curve. As drawn in the figure, this slope is measured in physical units (such as bags, bushels, or kilograms). But farmers want to know the relative values they gain and give up, not weights. For this comparison, they need to know unit prices for the output. Whether the farmer's decision to grow more corn and fewer beans produces greater revenue can be determined only by comparing the value of bean output forgone ($\Delta B \cdot P_B$) with the additional revenue expected by growing more corn ($\Delta C \cdot P_C$), where P_B and P_C are the sale prices of beans and corn, respectively. If the gain exceeds the loss (if $P_C \cdot \Delta C > P_B \cdot \Delta B$), the farmer will find point G more profitable.

The combination of corn and bean output that maximizes revenue is tangent to the highest possible isorevenue line. This line is shown as MN in figure 3-1. It represents the combined value of output of both corn and beans ($P_B \cdot B + B_C \cdot C$). Along this isorevenue line the total revenue is constant. The farmer prefers higher isorevenue lines to lower ones but is equally content with any position along a particular line (in the absence of differing variable costs and assuming the same risks for each crop).

The slope of this isorevenue line is $-P_B/P_C$ and represents the rate at which corn can be exchanged for beans in the market. This property is identical to the price relationship facing consumers with a given income, or budget, constraint. In fact, for the simple decisionmaking environment illustrated here, line MN is the farm household's budget constraint as well as its maximum revenue possibility. When this isorevenue line and the production possibility frontier are tangent, as at G, the slopes of both lines are equal. The production possibility frontier represents the physical tradeoff between corn and beans, or $\Delta C/\Delta B$, and the isorevenue line represents the monetary tradeoff, or $-P_B/P_C$. These two ratios must be equal when the two lines are tangent. At this point, G in figure 3-1, the revenue of the production lost is just equal to the revenue gained because $P_C \cdot \Delta C = P_B \cdot \Delta B$. The marginal cost equals the marginal revenue, the standard economic criterion for maximizing profit.

The equality of the two slopes also has implications for consumer welfare. If the farm household were to choose between corn and beans for its home consumption, the highest indifference curve it could reach would be tangent to MN, its income constraint. The rate of commodity substitution in consumer decisionmaking is thus exactly the same as the rate of substitution in production (if marketing costs are ignored). No reallocation of resources in production or consumption can improve on this result without lowering output or welfare in some other part of the economy. Such a result is said to be a Pareto Optimum.

Relative prices are clearly a major factor determining important decisions of both consumers and producers. Since government policy frequently uses import or export controls to alter relative commodity prices, as well as exchange rate policy to alter the level of prices, it is apparent that farm-level decisions about how much of which crops to grow can be directly influenced by such indirect government interventions. Extension agents may be urging farmers to grow more corn, but if government price policy favors beans, many farmers will ignore the advice.

FACTOR-FACTOR DECISIONS. When the farmer has decided which crops to grow, the next decision is how to grow them. To a significant extent farmers can use varying combinations of factors of production, or inputs, to produce a given crop. When the inputs are labor and capital, these factor-factor decisions have important consequences for employment and income distribution in rural areas. The extent to which labor and capital might substitute for each other in the agricultural production process is represented graphically in figure 3-2. The curved line DGBA represents all the different combinations of labor and capital that could be used to produce, for example, 100 kilograms of output. Point A would be a relatively capital-intensive technique. Point D would use more labor to produce the same amount of product.

An infinite number of input combinations is theoretically possible on the 100 kilogram isoquant that shows equal quantities of output. In practice, however, only a limited number of combinations are likely to be important to farmers. Figure 3-2 illustrates four alternative techniques: hand labor (point D), oxen (point G), a small tractor (point B), and large mechanized equipment (point A). The isoquant connecting these points portrays the possible technical alternatives for growing 100 kilograms of rice.

The appropriate combination of labor and capital is determined by the prices of the inputs. A farmer cultivating with human labor, who contemplates using oxen, wants to know how much labor is saved and how much

Figure 3-2. Factor-Factor Relationships for Growing Rice

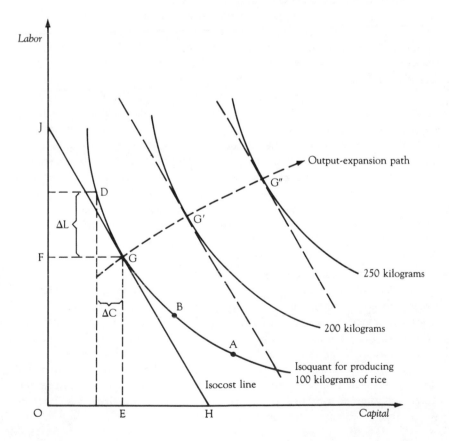

oxen time is needed. Schematically, this is shown as a move along the isoquant from point D to G, to represent a change in the combination of inputs, with ΔL less labor and ΔC more capital. If labor and capital were priced so that the cost of the labor given up were greater than the cost of the additional capital used, that is, if $\Delta L \cdot P_L > \Delta C \cdot P_C$, where P_L and P_C represent the prices of labor and capital, respectively, the farmer would find the switch to the more capital-intensive combination profitable.

With the prices for the two inputs known, it is possible to construct an isocost line connecting points of equal costs. This line represents the various possible combinations of labor and capital that have the same cost. Like the slope of the isorevenue line, the slope of an isocost line is the negative of the price ratio of the two inputs. In figure 3-2, where the isocost line is tangent to the 100 kilogram isoquant, at point G, the farmer has determined the least-cost combination of labor and capital that will produce 100 kilograms of output. At any other point on the same isoquant, it will cost more to produce that amount of output. When marginal costs equal marginal revenue ($\Delta L \cdot P_L = \Delta C \cdot P_C$), a farmer is using the least-cost combination of inputs to produce a given level of output.

To produce any more output, the farmer would have to use more capital, more labor, or both. Each level of output has its own isoquant, represented in figure 3-2 by isoquants labeled 200 kilograms and 250 kilograms. A dashed isocost line is shown parallel to the first (the price ratio of labor and capital is the same) and tangent to the 200 kilogram isoquant. The point of tangency at G' represents the least-cost combination of labor and capital to produce 200 kilograms of output. In this example a farmer using the least-cost combination to produce 200 kilograms would employ relatively more units of capital than labor in expanding output from 100 kilograms to 200 kilograms.

Farmers make decisions about their techniques of production—their factor-factor choices—according to the price relationships that prevail for the factors relative to their productivity. Whether those choices are "appropriate" in a broader social sense depends on whether the prices and available technology that led to the decision reflect the total costs to society of the techniques chosen. If capital is subsidized, either directly or indirectly, farmers are likely to choose techniques that use more capital than otherwise. If labor policy tries to push up wages, fewer workers will be hired.

The actual prices for factors of production faced by rural decisionmakers—wages, the cost of capital and imported equipment—are influenced significantly by macro policy. Such policy is often made by government officials who have little knowledge of whether the resulting rural decisions produce appropriate or inappropriate technology choices in agriculture. In many developing countries macro policy is designed to keep capital cheap to favor investment, to raise wages to increase incomes of workers, and to provide direct or indirect subsidies to imported capital machinery, such as tractors or combines, to raise productivity in agriculture.

If unskilled labor is widely available in both rural and urban areas, however, these policies often have exactly the opposite effect from that intended. The number of jobs created for each dollar of capital invested is low, wages outside the large-scale, formal sector are depressed, and mechanized farming exists side by side with rural unemployment and extreme poverty. The economic incentives determined by macro policy influence thousands of decisions about how to plant, cultivate, and harvest crops. These decisions in turn influence how many workers can find productive jobs directly. The breadth of rural purchasing power, largely a function of agricultural prices and the choice of technology in agricultural production and processing, determines the indirect and second-round employment effects. Together, the direct and indirect employment effects reflect how dynamic the rural economy is and how widely shared are the benefits of growth.

FACTOR-PRODUCT DECISIONS. Agricultural performance is linked to macro policy not only through farm-level decisions about which crops to grow and how to grow them, but also through the overall response of total farm output to the economic environment that determines the profitability of more intensive agricultural effort. Policymakers are concerned about the outcome of farmers' decisions, for they determine the level of food grain supplies, the availability of foreign exchange earnings from the agricultural sector, and incomes in rural areas. To understand how these decisions are made and how they affect such important variables of policy concern, a production function relating inputs to output is a convenient conceptual tool.

Various technical relationships, the prices of inputs, and the output price the farmer expects are all weighed in the decision of how intensively to use factors to produce output—the factor-product decision. The production function is the basic technical relationship used to analyze these issues, and it is illustrated by curve GEMH in figure 3-3. This simplified one-factor function shows the yield of rice per hectare which could be expected from applying different amounts of fertilizer. This function assumes that other factors of production (such as land) are fixed and that all increases in output are due to fertilizer, the variable input shown on the horizontal axis. The figure is drawn to show diminishing marginal returns, that is, each additional unit of fertilizer results in a smaller increment in output. If no fertilizer were applied, a yield of OG would be obtained. The physical maximum yield of OD would be attained with OB application of fertilizer. Informal talks in the countryside with farm households and agricultural research workers can give the analyst some insight into what these values might be.

Curve GEMH shows the rate at which fertilizer can be converted into rice at varying levels of fertilizer input. This conversion is nature's exchange relationship between rice and fertilizer. The exchange can also be made in the other direction, from rice to fertilizer. When farmers take rice to the market and return with fertilizer, they are carrying out a market exchange even if they use money as an intermediary for convenience. The rate at which farmers can exchange rice for fertilizer is also shown in figure 3-3 as the line OP. It reflects the ratio of the price of fertilizer to the price of rice. When fertilizer prices rise, the line becomes steeper, reflecting the fact that more rice is required to buy a unit of fertilizer. Inversely, if rice prices rise, the line becomes flatter as each bag of rice buys more fertilizer.

For most farmers the price line is more or less straight. Except for quantity discounts for large purchases and price premiums for very small purchases, rice and fertilizer prices are little affected by individual farmer decisions. Because prices are nearly the same whatever the level of use, the line OP can also be thought of as a total cost curve in this example, for fertilizer is the only input. (The generalization to many inputs provides similar insights but with more complicated mathematics.) Here costs are measured in the same units as output, and so any excess of output over input costs for a given level of input use means the farmer is earning a profit. When the cost curve is above the production function, net revenues are negative and losses occur.

Figure 3-3. A Production Function Illustrating
the Factor-Product Relationship

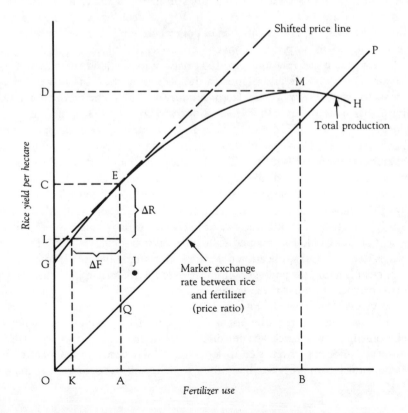

In a riskless world where farmers maximize profits, figure 3-3 can be used to determine how much fertilizer a farmer should use and how much output would result. The maximum profit occurs when the distance between output and input costs is the greatest. This point can be found by shifting the price line OP upward in a parallel fashion until it is just tangent to the production function. The dashed line shows this point of tangency at point E, where total rice production is OC and fertilizer use is OA. An amount of rice equal to AQ must be exchanged for the fertilizer used (OA), thus leaving an amount of rice equal to QE left over to repay the farmer's labor and use of land. AQ plus QE add up to OC, which is total output.

Of course, the degree of risk faced by farmers varies enormously—collective agricultural systems often significantly cushion individuals against risk, while market systems expose small farmers to substantial risks that affect their use of inputs. Also, pure profit maximization is an extreme case of rational behavior not likely to be found in the complicated world in which farm households make decisions. But an alternative formulation of the decision-making framework of profit maximization can illustrate how farmers adjust their fertilizer use and output decisions in response to inappropriate starting points or changes in prices or technology: the farmer simply seeks to move in a direction that increases net revenue. By comparing the additional revenue any increased yield will bring with the cost of the additional fertilizer required to produce that output, the farmer can decide whether additional fertilizer is profitable. If the marginal cost of the fertilizer is less than the marginal revenue (if $\Delta F \cdot P_f < \Delta R \cdot P_r$) the additional fertilizer is profitable. The farmer will continue to use fertilizer up to the point where the slope of the production function equals the slope of the ratio of the price of fertilizer to the price of rice ($\Delta R/\Delta F = P_f/P_r$), which is reached at E in figure 3-3.

This is the same point found by maximizing profits in a single, all-knowing decision, but this time the farmer arrives at E by a more plausible route of incremental trial and error. When farmers compare additional costs with the expected additional benefits, a natural and rational way to make choices, their behavior approximates that predicted by these simple economic models. Consequently, thinking about how farmers will respond to changed economic or technical circumstances with this basic production function model is likely to provide analysts with considerable insight into what will actually happen.

Figure 3-4 shows how this framework can help in understanding likely farmer reactions to significant changes in the underlying technology available for rice production. The development of modern fertilizer-responsive seed varieties shifts the entire production function up, allowing more output to be produced even with the same fertilizer input. But something else has happened in the shift as well, for even at the same fertilizer-to-rice price ratio a larger application of fertilizer is now profitable. The optimal point is E″ where OK fertilizer is used to produce OC″ rice.

The increase in output is composed of two separate effects of the technical change. As figure 3-4 shows, there is a neutral increase in yields from C to

Figure 3-4. Effect of Technical Change on Fertilizer Use and Yields

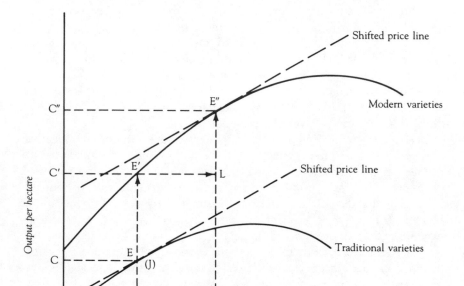

C' even when fertilizer use stays constant at the previously optimal level OA. This increase occurs because the production function has shifted upward from E to E'. Second, because of the fertilizer-using nature of the technical change, optimal fertilizer input shifts from E' to E'' even though the price relationship between rice and fertilizer remains the same. Fertilizer use expands from OA to OK (for those farmers who can afford it), and output reaches its new optimal level of OC''. A shift can also occur through simple learning. As they observe other farmers' results with fertilizer or experiment with small amounts themselves, farmers gradually shift their own production function and demand for fertilizer upward.

The availability of different technologies may also explain why some farmers appear to be "inside" the production function, as at point J in figure 3-3. As figure 3-4 indicates, such farmers may be using the traditional seed varieties either for lack of knowledge or for lack of access to the appropriate inputs needed to use the modern varieties efficiently.

OUTPUT-PRICE RELATIONSHIP. The second major factor influencing the farmer's decisionmaking environment shown in figure 3-4 is the relative price of fertilizer to rice, for this relationship determines the economic incentives to use more fertilizer. In most countries these prices are heavily influenced by government policy. Figure 3-5 illustrates what happens when the price of rice increases or the price of fertilizer falls (the two are equivalent in this two-dimensional world, and hence only the price ratio is important here). As fewer units of rice must be exchanged for a unit of fertilizer, the farmer is encouraged to use more fertilizer to grow more rice.

As long as the farmer can convert one unit of fertilizer into enough rice to buy more than that unit of fertilizer, it makes sense to expand fertilizer use. When an additional unit of fertilizer fails to produce enough rice to pay for itself, the farmer has gone too far. The appropriate stopping point is where

Figure 3-5. Effect of Relative Price Change on Fertilizer Use and Yields

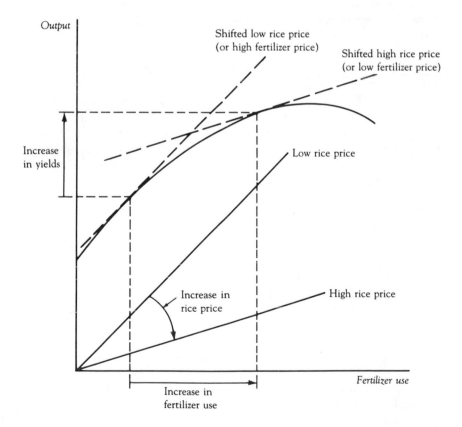

the exchange ratios are the same, a lesson already learned. Lowering the amount of rice needed to buy fertilizer—lowering the price ratio—normally leads to increased fertilizer use and higher yields (and vice versa). According to the theoretical model, farmers are expected to apply inputs more intensively in order to increase their output of a commodity when its price goes up, if other prices remain constant. This positive supply response can also be illustrated within this framework, and the result is shown in figure 3-6.

The upper part of figure 3-6 is constructed from the technical relationship between inputs and resulting output that is shown in the production function in figure 3-3. Because the price of rice in this example does not depend on quantities sold, the total revenue line for the farmer is a straight line, where the angle indicates the rice price itself. At higher prices the angle is steeper, indicating more revenue per unit of output. The total cost curve is constructed from the production function and a given price of fertilizer. At each level of output a particular level of fertilizer is required. The cost of purchasing this fertilizer determines the cost of producing that output. As in figure 3-3, the optimal output is at point E, where the excess of total revenue over total cost is maximized, that is, where profits are greatest. As noted before, this point is also where the slopes of the two curves are equal, or where marginal revenue (equal to the price of output) equals marginal cost (the slope of the total cost curve).

The lower part of figure 3-6 shows these marginal conditions directly as they relate to total output. The vertical axis now measures cost per unit, as well as the price per unit of output. Since the price at which the farmer can sell output is constant for all output levels, it can be represented by the horizontal line at P_0. Both the average cost curve and the marginal cost curve rise as output rises because inputs are being used more intensively with lower marginal productivity. The higher marginal costs then pull up average costs. Because output greater than D is impossible from this particular farm with its available technology, marginal and average costs become infinite at that point.

The farmer's choice of output level in the lower part of figure 3-6 corresponds to the choice in the upper part (and to the choice in figure 3-3). This point is again E, where the marginal cost of increasing output equals the marginal revenue gained by producing it. This marginal revenue is the price of output—each additional unit of output sold by the farmer brings in revenue equal to the price of output—and so the farmer's best choice is where the marginal cost curve intersects the market price of output. This is an extremely important result. If market demand or government policy caused the price of output to rise from P_0 to P_1, the optimal decision point for the farmer would change from E to E', and output on the farm would rise from OC to OC'. The farmer's supply response to higher price incentives—the relationship between output supplied and output price—is simply the farmer's marginal cost curve for producing additional output.

Figure 3-6. The Relationship between Farm Output of Rice Supplies and the Price of Rice

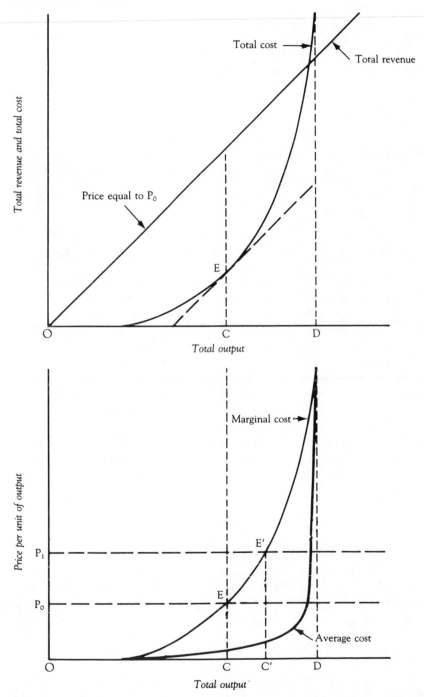

Note: The farm area planted in rice is held constant.

With all the provisos noted about the simplified nature of these two-dimensional diagrams, the farmer's supply curve is the same thing as the marginal cost curve. Anything that shifts the marginal cost curve, for example, new technology, access to new irrigation facilities, or even the weather, will also shift the supply curve. Many of these shifts result directly or indirectly from government policy or investments, and so the interest of analysts in farmers' responses is clear. Because the supply curve summarizes so much of farmer decisionmaking in terms of two variables of great relevance to the rest of food policy—output and price—knowing more about the elasticity of supply for important commodities is the next step for food policy analysts.

Estimating Farmer Supply Response

Government policy influences the location of the supply curve through investments that lower marginal costs of agricultural production (or through unintended actions that raise costs). Policy also influences where on the supply curve farmers choose to be, as price policies alter the incentives to use more intensive techniques of farming to produce more output. "Cheap food" policies can suppress growth in farm production while increasing consumption, often requiring subsidized food imports to be effective. As governments look at the costs and benefits of such policies, an immediate question is whether farmers will respond with greater output if better incentives are provided or with less output in the face of reduced incentives. The answer will vary for the short run as opposed to the long run, as well as for areas where additional land can be brought into cultivation. Some environments, especially in Asia, must rely on yield increases as the primary means of raising output. In addition, the supply response for individual crops, where, for example, corn can substitute for beans, differs from that for aggregate agricultural production, where substitutions do not alter total output significantly and response must come through changed intensity of input use, including labor.

These concerns are empirical, not theoretical. They can be addressed only by careful attention to exactly which question is being asked, coupled with specific statistical analysis of country or regional data. The empirical estimation of supply response functions is an enormous and complicated topic and can be surveyed only briefly here. Just as with sophisticated food consumption function estimation, the food policy analyst is likely to be less concerned with actual estimation techniques than with a solid sense of what the important issues are, when to distrust econometric razzle-dazzle, and how to interpret representative empirical results.

ISSUES FOR ESTIMATION. The lower part of figure 3-6 shows a positive relationship between price and quantity of output. A natural inclination might be to look for a series of observations on a commodity's price and its output and to plot them graphically or even to estimate a regression with output as a function of price. Sometimes this technique actually works, but often the result is merely a confusing cluster of data points or, even worse, a perceptible negative relationship between price and output. Does this mean that farmers are perverse and have a backward-bending supply curve and produce less as prices rise? Usually it means the analyst has identified a curve with elements of both a demand curve and a supply curve. This "identification problem" has a famous history in economics, and although the theoretical issues are resolved, it continues to bedevil empirical investigators. Without additional information about whether the supply curve or the demand curve, or both, are shifting, any estimation results are unclear. If no additional information is available, the identification problem is simply insoluble.

The most common approach in the empirical literature is to assume that consumers react to actual prices in their purchase decisions and that farmers react to expected prices in their planting and cultivating decisions. As argued earlier, this distinction is an important characteristic of agriculture because of the time between the farmer's input decisions and the output results. If a way can be found to approximate the price the farmer expects when making input decisions, most of the identification problem is resolved. Many models simply assume the farmer reacts to the previous price received, with a time lag of one year or one season. The results of estimating these models with time series data are surprisingly useful, for they indicate how responsive farmers actually are to short-run changes in price signals. Naturally, they may adjust much more as time passes, but the simple one-year lag model captures their immediate response.

The longer-run response can be captured only with more sophisticated models of formation of expected prices or of lags in responding to changed environments. An innovative methodology for doing this modeling was first used in an agricultural setting by Marc Nerlove and is appropriately called Nerlovian distributed lag analysis. Reproducing the complicated algebra needed to derive an appropriate estimating equation is not necessary because the results are intuitively plausible.

A farmer's output is a function of the previous price of output and of output the previous year. This lagged output term serves as a proxy for all previous adjustments to prices (and even to other excluded variables). The short-run supply response to price continues to be estimated by the coefficient attached to lagged price, but the long-run adjustment is larger by a factor determined by the coefficient estimated for the lagged output variable. (The actual formula is: long-run supply response = short-run supply response ÷ [1 − the coefficient of lagged output].) In a typical case, if the short-run supply elasticity is 0.1 and the coefficient attached to (log) lagged output is 0.6, then the long-run elasticity is 0.25, that is, 0.1/(1 − 0.6). A very common result of this type of analysis is that the long-run supply elasticity is roughly twice as large as the short-run elasticity.

This methodology for direct estimation of supply curves requires time series data with enough observations to provide reliable statistical results at the same time that significant structural change or technological innovation is minimal. Most developing countries have undergone both in their relatively short histories, and most supply curve estimation is confounded by these likely but difficult-to-measure shifts in the supply curve itself. As figure 3-7 shows, rapid shifts in the supply curve mean that both an apparently positive or a negative estimated supply response could be consistent with actual positive and quite inelastic short-run supply curves.

One approach to dealing with this problem, and other aspects of the identification problem as well, is to use cross-section data to estimate supply functions. As with the use of cross-section data for consumption analysis, this approach requires that the decisionmakers face reasonably comparable environments if the results are to have any direct policy relevance. At the

Figure 3-7. Effects of Technical Change on Estimation of Supply Curves

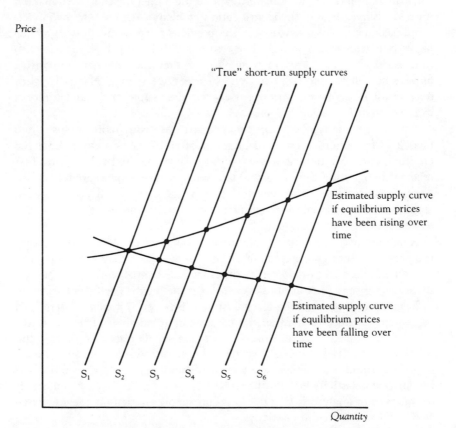

same time, the decisionmakers must face different prices that cause measurable differences in output if the statistical analysis is to succeed in estimating an accurate supply response to price. Multiple regression analysis can be used to control roughly for differences in environments, but many factors that decisionmakers consider are extremely difficult to measure.

Cross-section estimates are frequently made across states, provinces, and even countries in order to find significant price variation. With such cross-section estimates, the argument is usually made that the resulting supply response parameters reflect full and long-run adjustment in all aspects of the environment that are related to price, not just the short-run response of farmers to price when that environment is held constant. Since this includes such important variables as farmer knowledge, irrigation facilities, and well-adapted seed varieties, this distinction is quite important. In fact, several researchers have discovered very high supply responses to agricultural prices by using this methodology. Work by Willis Peterson, in particular, shows an aggregate agricultural supply elasticity of about 1.2, but the countries in the sample that generated this result are probably a century or more apart in their economic development and hence in the full adjustment of the environments facing their farmers.

An alternative approach to direct estimation of farmer supply response uses technical or engineering data to estimate the agricultural production function, specifying an appropriate functional form and then using conditions of profit maximization to trace out the marginal cost function and hence the short-run supply response. Either time series or cross-section data can be used for this indirect approach, and each presents its own set of difficulties. The obvious general problem with estimating production functions to derive supply response functions is that the approach assumes what was the object of the search, that is, the extent to which farmers actually respond to price changes. Such "normative" supply curves are useful for placing upper bounds on plausible farmer responsiveness, and they sometimes show that farmers are already using inputs such as fertilizer about as intensively as is profitable. They are a relatively poor basis, however, for making predictions about the impact of changed prices on aggregate supply unless no other information is available. Then, of course, the one-eyed man is king.

A SYNTHESIS OF SUPPLY ELASTICITIES FOR CEREAL GRAINS. A recent volume by Hossein Askari and John Cummings surveyed agricultural supply response estimates available in the mid-1970s. The book has an extensive review of the Nerlovian supply response model and of many of the studies around the world that tried to use it to estimate supply elasticities for a wide variety of crops. Table 3-1 is extracted from their summary table and shows the short-run supply elasticities for rice, wheat, and corn, by approximate numerical range, for the regions and countries for which reasonably reliable estimates could be located.

Table 3-1. Supply Elasticities for Rice, Wheat, and Corn for Various
Regions, by Approximate Numerical Range

Grain	Range of supply elasticities and region
	Less than zero
Rice	Uttar Pradesh,[a] Himachal Pradesh,[b] Gujarat,[b] Maharashtra,[b] Madras,[b,c] Kerala,[b] Egypt[b,c]
Wheat	Uttar Pradesh,[a,c] Madhya Pradesh-Berar,[b,c] Bombay-Sind,[b,c] Iraq[b]
Corn	Jordan,[b] Egypt[b,c]
	Zero to one-third
Rice	Assam,[b] Bihar,[a] Mysore,[b] Punjab, West Bengal,[b] Tripura,[b] Pakistan,[b] Bangladesh,[b] Thailand, West Malaysia, Japan,[b] Philippines, Egypt[b,d]
Wheat	Mysore, Punjab,[b] Rajasthan,[b] West Bengal,[b] Maharashtra,[b] Himachal Pradesh,[b] Pakistan,[b] Hungary, Jordan,[b] Lebanon, Egypt,[b,c] United States
Corn	Punjab, Egypt,[b,d] Lebanon,[b] Sudan, Philippines, United States
	One-third to two-thirds
Rice	Punjab,[a] Bihar-Orissa,[a] Peru,[b] Java, Iraq
Wheat	Uttar Pradesh,[a,d] Bihar,[a] Egypt,[a,d] Syria, Lebanon,[a] New South Wales, United Kingdom,[b] France, Argentina, Chile
Corn	Punjab, Hungary, Sudan[a]
	Two-thirds to one
Wheat	Gujarat,[b] Egypt,[a] New South Wales,[a] New Zealand, United States,[a] Canada[b]
	More than one
Rice	West Malaysia,[a] Iraq[a]
Wheat	Syria,[a] New Zealand,[a] Chile[a]
Corn	Thailand,[b] Syria[b]

Note: Unless otherwise noted, elasticities are short run.
a. Long-run elasticity.
b. Short- and long-run elasticity.
c. Pre–World War II.
d. Post–World War II.
Source: Assembled from Hossein Askari and John T. Cummings, *Agricultural Supply Response: A Survey of the Econometric Evidence* (New York: Praeger, 1976).

Askari and Cummings note that their summary table was prepared by
weighting different, sometimes conflicting, results for the same crop and
region and by using their own judgments about the reliability of alternative
estimating procedures or the particular time series data employed. Table 3-
1 gives only a hint of the full array of evidence gathered by Askari and
Cummings; indeed, nearly 500 separate supply elasticities are presented in
their appendix!

Two points are important. First, most of the supply elasticities reported
for basic cereal grains are positive, with a median value likely to be near the
top of the zero to one-third range. Although it is preferable to determine

grain supply elasticities on the basis of local conditions and data, sometimes this is not possible. If forced at gunpoint to pick a number from comparative experience, the analyst will not be far from the mark with an elasticity of 0.2 to 0.3.

Second, there is a noticeable tendency for the supply elasticity to be larger in more-developed countries and in regions with longer commercial histories. This larger supply response is partly because farmers are more economically minded, but also because purchased inputs have a greater role in farm production. The decision to purchase inputs instead of relying on traditional household resources inevitably reflects a willingness to calculate costs and benefits. In such circumstances the actual supply response begins to approach the normative supply response predicted by the economic models used here to understand farmer behavior. As the role of modern agricultural technology widens, the supply responsiveness of farmers around the world is likely to increase.

The neoclassical decisionmaking approach outlined in this section can be very helpful to analysts in illuminating the underlying factors that explain trends in output of particular crops, in input use, and to some extent in incomes in farming areas. Lagging productivity growth in corn production might be traced to low fertilizer use. This could be explained by poor technology available to farmers or to poor incentives to use inputs intensively. The answers have direct relevance to agricultural policies, whether for budgetary resource allocations to research stations or for improved price incentives for important crops. A sense of the responsiveness of farmers to policy changes is needed to pursue the issue from identification of problems to appropriate policy responses. In the early stages of agricultural development when one or two primary food crops dominate both traditional farm production and policy interests, fairly simple supply response analysis can provide many of the needed insights. As agriculture becomes more commercialized and more complicated, a broader approach that examines the full decisionmaking environment of the farm household is likely to offer important additional insights.

Understanding Farming Systems

Neoclassical production theory is very helpful for understanding the direction of likely farmer response to a changed economic environment at the farm level. This approach is crop-specific, and the empirical estimates of farmer supply responsiveness have concentrated almost exclusively on single commodities, as table 3-1 illustrated. Useful as this focus and the accompanying supply elasticities are to policymakers in contemplating either pricing changes or the macro connections between agriculture and the rest of the

economy, several critical farm-level and broader rural issues are neither identified nor analyzed within this framework.

Commodity substitution, land and labor allocations to alternative crops
and farm household tasks, and potential income-earning opportunities for
farm labor in rural off-farm jobs are broad and important issues. They influence
the income and welfare of the farm household directly while contributing
indirectly to the commodity supply responsiveness of immediate concern to
policymakers. These issues can be understood by analyzing the entire set of
farming activities and important nonfarm activities within a decisionmaking
framework that specifically accounts for the connections and opportunity
costs across both crop and other income-earning activities.

Activity analysis, or linear programming, is a technique for analyzing entire
farming systems. Based on the construction of a farming system tableau, it
is a helpful and ultimately powerful technique for understanding these broader
farm decisionmaking issues. The tableau can help analysts identify the aspects
of farming systems that need much more careful attention and more rigorous
analysis. Specialists or outside consultants can then be brought in for this
work, and their efforts made productive and relevant by specific terms of
reference based on the preliminary assessments from the tableau analysis.

Describing the Agricultural Sector

Describing the agricultural sector in statistical terms is complicated by
agriculture's unique characteristics that set it apart from the rest of the economy. Annual production statistics by crop for the entire country are very
important for describing overall crop balance, aggregate supplies relative to
domestic demand and import needs, and gross input requirements to maintain
aggregate rates of growth in agricultural output. Since ministries of agriculture, planning agencies, and central banks need these aggregate estimates to
plan investment and foreign exchange allocations, their gathering and analysis has dominated the statistical description of the rural sector.

The individual farm household decisions that generate these aggregate
results are made from a very different perspective, however. Each farm sits
within a particular ecological setting (sometimes more than one) and faces
an economic environment dictated by the technological opportunities for
crop production in that setting and by the input and output markets nearby.
To understand how farm households will react when new technology is
developed, input prices are subsidized, or output prices are raised, policy
analysts need much more specific information about these individual decisionmaking environments than can be gleaned from national aggregate data.
Such information usually must be collected from relatively homogeneous
agroclimatic zones at the farm level. The descriptions of representative farming systems, the variations in yield and prices across those farms, and the
distribution of farm sizes within each zone will provide the analyst with

sufficient information to understand how various farm households are likely to react to policy or exogenous changes in rural conditions and how these changes together provide an aggregate view of farmer responsiveness to economic incentives.

AGROCLIMATIC ZONES. The ecological setting in which crops are grown strongly conditions the farmer's choice of crops, the techniques used to grow them, the resulting yields, and how much is available for sale in outside markets. Every field has a unique ecological setting, and each farm is different from neighboring ones. Too acute an awareness of this ecological diversity is immobilizing to policy analysts attempting to define agroclimatic zones, however, because central tendencies and representative settings are swamped in the local detail. Finding an appropriate balance between aggregate national data and the specific crops grown in individual fields and farms is necessary to bring any sense of order to the chaos of nature. It is good enough to know in principle that every farm is different. In practice, finding a half dozen or so representative agroclimatic zones that are reasonably consistent internally and have significantly different cropping patterns from zone to zone will capture all the diversity the analyst can hope to cope with and still retain an overall sense of how the pieces add up to form the nation's agricultural output.

When the analyst has time to conduct original survey research or has access to raw data from village-level surveys, boundaries around agroclimatic zones can be drawn on the basis of uniform ecological settings. Most analysts will have to settle for less precise boundaries, however, and will use district or provincial agricultural data that have already been collected. These administrative units are usually responsible for collecting agricultural data. When the administrative borders correspond, even roughly, to agroclimatic zones, the analyst can shortcut the data-gathering process significantly. In most cases, major compromises over the definition of a true agroclimatic zone are worthwhile to make it fit the existing data.

Just such a compromise has been made in the example used throughout the discussion of data gathering and food production analysis. East Java, a major province of Indonesia, is a diverse region with a larger population (more than 30 million people in 1981) than most countries. It is not a single agroclimatic zone, yet its representative farming systems are significantly different from those of neighboring Central Java or Bali. Certainly much can be learned by looking at individual districts or even villages within East Java, for they vary considerably. But in view of the difficulty of trying to understand Indonesian agriculture and its production responsiveness on the basis of individual farm households or the thousands of districts or hundreds of thousands of villages, a focus on representative decisions and production patterns in East Java is an appropriate compromise.

Even when provincial data correspond fairly closely to agroclimatic zones, as they do in East Java, the data most useful to analysts may not be available from government agricultural offices. Because government departments and programs are often organized around single crops (for example, a rice improvement program), agricultural ministries tend to collect new information mainly on individual commodities. Having data on typical farms, however, is likely to be much more important for understanding how farmers react to policy changes. Since most key farming decisions involve tradeoffs and opportunity costs as farmers seek to increase their incomes, information is needed about alternative farm activities, not just about individual crop productivity and response.

Farm-level data can be limited to the major crops or they can include garden, household, livestock, and off-farm employment activities. Where land is abundant and labor is relatively expensive, as in much of Africa, data limited initially to crop activities should suffice, for most income tradeoffs will revolve around crop choice. If labor is abundant and land is relatively much more scarce, as in parts of Asia, off-farm employment activities are likely to be more significant in determining household incomes and consequently in assessing farmer response to agricultural policies.

Data from representative farms in a half dozen different agroclimatic zones provide the descriptive basis for setting up a farming system tableau. The analyst begins with the main crop activities for the zone and adds other components, such as livestock or off-farm employment, when they are needed to understand farmers' responses to agricultural policies. The tableau serves to organize the analysis of important rural issues. To link the tableau analysis to policy issues, the analyst also needs farm size distribution and price and yield data. Some of these data can be found in published sources. Others will require discussions with farmers and agricultural field staffs. First-hand knowledge gained while spending time in the countryside gathering data imparts a sense of the diversity from field to field and the actual environment in which farmers must make their decisions and is thus as important for the analyst as the tabulations themselves.

FARMING SYSTEMS DATA. The combination and sequences of crops grown by representative farmers make up a farming system, and usually only a few different types are dominant in an agroclimatic zone. As with the zones themselves, any definition of dominant farming systems is somewhat arbitrary. Cropping patterns vary among farms because of differences in soils, irrigation, prices, and proximity to markets. Still, policy analysts can usually pick a few primary cropping arrangements within a zone and resist the temptation to describe a large number of farming systems in hopes of representing all the various patterns within the countryside. Too many data tend to obscure rather than clarify the issues before policymakers, who need to understand how decisionmakers in a few representative farming systems are likely to respond to alternative policy initiatives that will affect the farming environment.

The cropping system diagram shown in figure 3-8 is an efficient way to visualize farming systems. To capture the seasonality that is important in agricultural production, the horizontal axis is divided into time periods. The three-season agriculture of East Java is shown over a one-year period, broken down by month. Systems involving tree crops might cover a longer period. A temperate agriculture that is limited by the number of frost-free days would cover a much shorter time.

Each rectangle in figure 3-8 represents the percentage of total arable land

Figure 3-8. Illustrative Cropping System for East Java, Indonesia

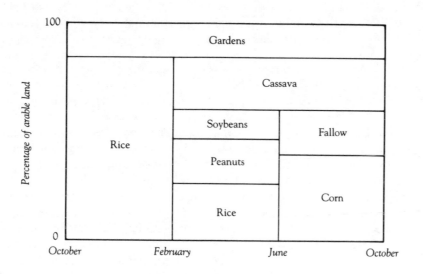

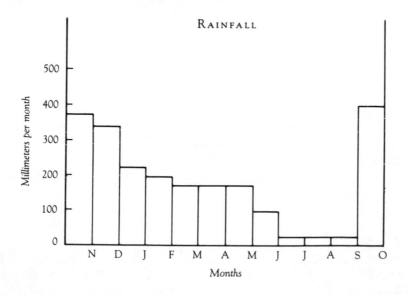

that a given crop occupies in the region over three major seasons. The height of the rectangle is calibrated to show the relative area planted to a crop, thus indicating the importance of the commodity in the region. Such a visual picture of the farming system is simple and readily understandable and helps identify important decision options and tradeoffs faced by farm households. Other useful seasonal data, such as rainfall, irrigation flows, temperature, or intensity of sunlight, can be charted similarly to the rainfall graph in the lower part of figure 3-8.

This simple presentation of a farming system reveals important crop competitions and complementarities within seasons. The interactions between weather and cropping systems are also highlighted and may indicate potential benefits of irrigation or drainage investments. Several charts of this type can readily present the broad dimensions of farming operations within a region.

FARM SIZE DISTRIBUTION. Table 3-2 illustrates data on farm size distribution for the province of East Java. Many of the numbers in this table and the other examples are approximations rather than actual data, and the farming systems have been greatly simplified to illustrate the concepts more easily.

From table 3-2 it is apparent that more than half (54 percent) of the farmers have landholdings of less than 0.3 hectares, yet they occupy a total of only 18 percent of the land. In terms of production, the 30 percent of farmers with 0.3 to 0.5 hectares are more representative than the smaller farmers because they cultivate more than one-quarter of the land. Because farm-size distribution data identify different types of "representative" farmers—most representative in total number or in area farmed—the information in table 3-2 helps organize field visits. To think about the implications of policy changes for agricultural production, analysts need to understand the likely reactions of several representative farmers. The table identifies their characteristics; field visits then permit analysts to talk with these farmers about their decisionmaking.

Table 3-2. Size Distribution of Farm Operating Units in East Java

Size of farm (hectares)	Number (millions)	Percentage of farmers	Area (millions of hectares)	Percentage of land
0.05–0.1	2.0	20.0	0.15	3.2
0.1–0.3	3.4	34.0	0.68	14.5
0.3–0.5	3.0	30.0	1.20	25.6
0.5–1.0	1.0	10.0	0.75	16.0
1.0–2.0	0.3	3.0	0.45	9.6
2.0–5.0	0.2	2.0	0.70	15.0
5.0+	0.1	1.0	0.75	16.0
Total	10.0	100.0	4.68	100.0

Note: The numbers illustrate general trends; they are not specific data representing actual conditions.

A simple farm-size distribution table can also indicate a great deal about the income distribution of a rural region and the numbers of farmers whose net marketings are likely to be significant. Information on respective yields by farm size can also be added, although this is complicated by different cropping patterns and by differential access to inputs. For example, small farmers often use multiple cropping systems that are much more labor intensive than the cultivation of uniform stands of cereals. Further, they often achieve higher yields per hectare for a given level of fertilizer use, but credit constraints cause them to use less fertilizer per hectare than larger farmers.

A rough estimate of the number of people likely to be affected by hunger if off-farm employment is unobtainable can be made by adding the number of landless and near-landless laborers to the table. In the East Java example an additional 2 million families would be included. In areas where large landowners split their holdings among several tenants, a table showing ownership rather than operating patterns would reveal something of the role of landlords in the countryside. Accurate ownership data are usually difficult to assemble, but they are particularly important for assessing policy changes affecting tenancy or landlord-tenant relations.

PRICE AND YIELD DATA. Information on farm prices and yields actually paid and received by farmers brings the analyst face to face with the decisionmaking environment in which rural households operate. By talking with a range of farmers and with experiment station workers, the analyst can draw a rough picture of the relationship between input use and crop yields. With input and output price data added, the profitability of intensifying crop production can be estimated. In combination, the input, yield, and profitability data provide the analyst with a sense of potential gains in production from available technology or changes in the structure of costs and prices and of the importance of developing new technology.

PRICE COMPARISONS. Prices actually received and paid by farmers in the region are essential to calculating several price ratios that reflect the economic environment facing farm decisionmakers. In particular, the ratio of commodity prices received by farmers to the price paid for a key input such as fertilizer provides a rough assessment of how tightly the agricultural sector is being squeezed by low economic incentives relative to other regions and countries.

A second calculation compares regional prices with international market prices for each commodity. The comparison between rice prices in Bangkok and in East Java shown in table 3-3, for example, cannot be made with any precision without careful attention to quality differentials and possible exchange rate biases. But product and factor prices often vary enormously from country to country relative to the import or export price. These wide price variations can alert analysts to local price environments that are greatly distorted. In the Indonesian example in table 3-3, local corn prices may be

Table 3-3. Illustrative Data on Agricultural Technology
and Prices for East Java, Indonesia

| | Tons per hectare per crop | |
| | Shelled corn | Paddy rice |
Technology		
Experimental yields per hectare per crop		
International	10	15
East Java	3.5	10
Ratio of international to East Java	2.9:1.0	1.5:1.0
"Progressive" farm yield per hectare per crop		
(East Java)	2.5	6
Average farm yield per hectare per crop		
(East Java)	1.5	3.5

| | Dollars per ton (rupiahs converted at Rp 625 per US$1) | |
| | Shelled corn | Milled rice |
Prices		
World price, October 1980	$145[a]	$445[b]
East Java farm price, October 1980	145	280[c]
Ratio of world price to East Java price	1.0:1.0	1.6:1.0
World price of urea, October 1980	250[d]	250[d]
East Java farm price of urea, October 1980	115[e]	115[e]
Ratio of world price to East Java price	2.2:1.0	2.2:1.0
East Java commodity price ÷ East Java urea price, October 1980	1.26	1.78
World commodity price ÷ world urea price, October 1980	0.58	2.43

a. F.o.b. U.S. Gulf port (no. 2 yellow).
b. F.o.b. Bangkok (25 percent brokens).
c. Rice equivalent at farm gate.
d. F.o.b. Near East (bagged).
e. Subsidized rate of Rp 72 per kilogram.

somewhat high if corn must be imported from the United States; rice prices seem significantly lower than the potential cost of landing Thai rice in Indonesia. Urea prices are less than half the world price, indicating very large subsidies.

Wide deviations in local prices from international market quotations reveal the potential for significant economic distortion and waste through misallocation of resources. Some of this distortion may be planned to advance other government objectives, such as food security or income transfers to farmers or consumers, but frequently the distortions and wasted resources are an unforeseen byproduct of government policies for the nonagricultural sectors. By identifying the magnitude and potential impact of these price distortions in the countryside, analysts can bring to planning sessions a much more informed and persuasive case for showing how government policies affect agricultural performance.

The exact calibration of yield and price data for a region requires fieldwork plus a bit of desk research to fit the data together. They can be assembled rather quickly, however, into the type of information in table 3-3. This table illustrates how much variation can occur across commodities even within the same region and for different types of farmers. It is especially important to be on the lookout for factors that create an adverse economic climate for small farmers. When appropriate allowance is made for credit arrangements with suppliers, village moneylenders, and purchasing agents, small farmers often pay higher input prices and receive lower output prices than do large farmers.

YIELD COMPARISONS. In the East Java example, the ratio of local to international experimental yields indicates that the development of appropriate varieties is much further advanced for rice than for corn. International experimental rice yields are only half again as high as East Javan experimental yields. In contrast, international experimental corn yields are nearly three times as high as in East Java, despite the fact that the ratio of domestic to international prices is much more favorable for corn than for rice.

If farmers are obtaining low yields for the major food crop in a country, there is a reason. Perhaps farmers do not have a technological package capable of producing high yields reliably in their ecological setting. Perhaps farmers do not judge the economic returns from high yields to be worth the costs, efforts, or risks of producing them. Or they may not know how to use the available (and accessible) technology in such a way as to make a reasonable profit by producing high yields. No doubt any one of these reasons is important in many circumstances, and maybe all are relevant on occasion. A constraints framework developed by Arthur Mosher helps analysts organize these factors and identify the constraints on farmer behavior under existing circumstances.

THE CONSTRAINTS FRAMEWORK. For a particular agroclimatic zone, the Mosher framework organizes farm households according to their output per hectare for the dominant crop in the region. In figure 3-9, the horizontal axis represents the percentage distribution of all arable land within an agroclimatic zone, and the vertical axis measures yield per hectare for the dominant commodity, usually one of the cereal grains. The achievement distribution, denoted *a*, indicates the distribution of yields actually obtained by farmers, ranked left to right from the highest to the lowest. The slope and location of the *a* curve is determined empirically from the yield data. If all farmers had the same yields, the achievement distribution would be horizontal. Analysts would expect farmers' yields to vary because not all farm households have equally good managers, land quality varies, and not all

Figure 3-9. Agricultural Development Activities Appropriate to Raising
Technical and Economic Ceilings and Achievement Distributions

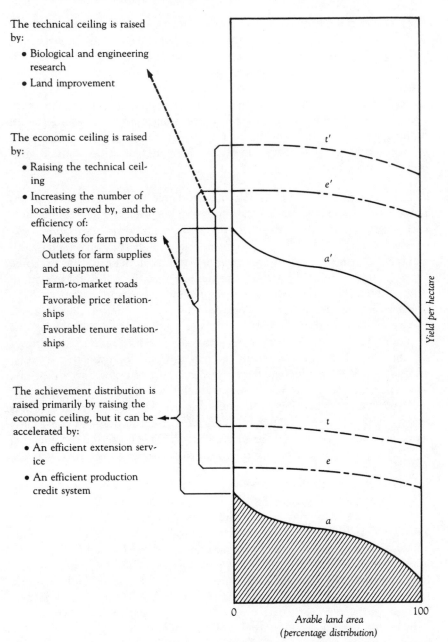

The technical ceiling is raised
by:
- Biological and engineering
  research
- Land improvement

The economic ceiling is raised
by:
- Raising the technical ceiling
- Increasing the number of
  localities served by, and the
  efficiency of:

  Markets for farm products
  Outlets for farm supplies
  and equipment
  Farm-to-market roads
  Favorable price relation-
  ships
  Favorable tenure relation-
  ships

The achievement distribution is
raised primarily by raising the
economic ceiling, but it can be
accelerated by:
- An efficient extension service
- An efficient production
  credit system

Yield per hectare

0   100

Arable land area
(percentage distribution)

Source: Arthur T. Mosher, *An Introduction to Agricultural Extension* (Singapore: Agricultural
Development Council, Singapore University Press, 1978), p. 73.

farmers have access to specific knowledge about how to raise their yields. Thus the *a* curve slopes downward. When the height of the achievement distribution measures the yield and the base reflects the land area achieving each yield, the area beneath the curve represents the total production of the crop, shown as the shaded area in the diagram.

The technical ceiling, the *t* curve, indicates the biological maximum yield for that crop, the yield an experiment station could achieve in the region. (Yields technically possible elsewhere in the world can be above a region's *t* curve within a zone.) The technical ceiling curve probably also slopes downward somewhat because of varying soils or other biological reasons.

The economic ceiling, shown by the *e* curve, reflects the yield constraint imposed on farmers by various price and technical relationships, and by definition it lies below the technical ceiling. The economic ceiling represents the yield achieved when all inputs are used at their most profitable levels on average. Most farmers are risk-averse in the face of uncertain weather, many face credit constraints on how many inputs they can purchase, and only a few are likely to know with any precision what the profit-maximizing levels will be. For these reasons, the economic ceiling cannot be directly observed in the field.

Still some simple calculations can help the observer determine the yields that reflect the current economic ceiling. If an additional unit of fertilizer will produce five units of grain, but the grain-to-fertilizer price ratio is only 1:6, the rational farmer will not use additional fertilizer to raise yields. The marginal response of grain to fertilizer can be determined accurately only by estimating fertilizer response functions with farm-level data, but it can be readily approximated by asking farmers about their own experience with fertilizer and by comparing different farmers' fertilizer use and resulting yields. Local experiment stations also frequently have guidelines on fertilizer responsiveness in their locale.

With price data and information on farm-level yields relative to experimental yields in several representative regions, the analyst is in a position to plot the achievement distribution quite roughly and determine whether the economic and technical ceilings are tightly constraining or not. A wide variety of possibilities might result, of course, but figure 3-10 shows four quite different environments which capture much of the diversity of agricultural settings in developing countries.

A farming system with low productivity, tightly constrained by technology, is depicted in Area A. Since the achievement distribution is near the economic ceiling, most farm households are doing as well as can be expected, and little increase in output can result from changes in economic policy or from more aggressive extension agents. For food production to be increased, biological and engineering research and investments in land improvement would be needed to raise the technical ceiling. A large number of ecological zones characterized by marginal rainfall and poor soils fit this pattern. In

Figure 3-10. Various Relationships between Technical
and Economic Ceilings and the Achievement Distribution

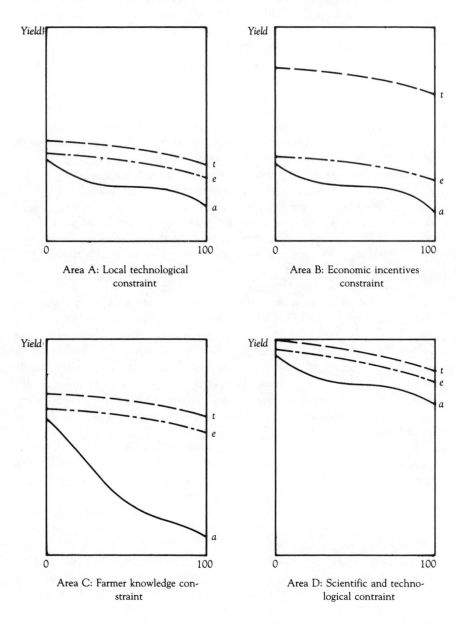

Area A: Local technological
constraint

Area B: Economic incentives
constraint

Area C: Farmer knowledge constraint

Area D: Scientific and technological contraint

such areas high-yielding crop technology does not yet exist. In other, more hospitable areas which look like Area A, adaptive research has been neglected, and efforts to borrow appropriate technology from other regions have not been made.

Area B represents rational and knowledgeable farmers whose output levels are constrained by economic policies, especially those affecting prices for inputs and output. When the economic ceiling is far below the technical ceiling, policies affecting input and output prices, international trade, the marketing system, and land tenure are preventing rapid increases in productivity and higher yields.

In Area C a few farm households are taking advantage of the available technology, but many are not. When at least parts of the achievement distribution are well below the economic ceiling, efforts to provide education, credit, and extension services are likely to be important parts of a production strategy to raise the achievement distribution.

A high technology dilemma is represented in Area D. In parts of China and Japan rice yields are currently pushing against the technical ceiling on rice production. Raising the technical ceiling requires long-run investments to increase biological potential and is not a source of rapid growth in the short run. To raise rural incomes more rapidly, it might be necessary to diversify the farming system into higher-valued crops.

Policy analysts can use the Mosher framework to determine the position of a country's agricultural sector with regard to the technical and economic ceilings and the actual achievement distribution. Because the framework is crop-specific, it is much more helpful in identifying issues for campaigns to raise the output of wheat or rice, for instance, than it is for dealing with the complexity of multicommodity farming systems. At the early stages of agricultural development this commodity focus is not a serious shortcoming because major productivity gains from new technology tend to be commodity-specific, and most agricultural development plans are already organized around particular commodities. At later stages in development, however, efforts to raise agricultural productivity usually encounter complicated tradeoffs among commodities as well as competition for farm labor from wage labor markets. Then other analytical techniques, particularly the tableau discussed below, illuminate these more complex decisions made by most farm households.

Modeling Farmer Response with a Farming System Tableau

The broad picture of a farming system shown in figure 3-8 illustrates the alternative crops grown in each season, but it does not explain why farmers chose to grow these crops. To understand these choices more fully, farming systems data can be organized into a tableau of information for economic analysis. The concept of a tableau is derived from early attempts to organize the activities of an economy into a consistent framework to show how national output was generated. The literature on mathematical programming and activity analysis has developed the tableau into a formal tool which can be used to calculate optimal solutions to farming or policy problems. Even without the formal analysis, however, organizing information according to the conceptual elements of a tableau is an effective way to portray the array of decisions that farmers face.

The basic elements of a tableau are presented in table 3-4. Each component is identified in a farming system context and is linked to its analogous relationship in a linear programming framework. The core of a linear programming model is the input-output coefficient matrix—the a_{ij} matrix which indicates the amount of input i (for example, fertilizer) needed to operate activity j (for example, a hectare of rice) that will produce, say, 2.5 tons of output. The inputs are listed in rows on the left, the possible crop activities are shown in columns in the center, and the availability of inputs is indicated on the right-hand side of the tableau. Each crop activity produces a net revenue, and simple programming models have as their objective the maximization of the sum of all crop revenues. This happens when at least one input is fully utilized and output cannot be increased further.

The analyst need not (perhaps even should not) be a linear programming specialist to use this tableau framework successfully. The importance of the linear programming technique is its insistence on consistency and accurate specification of variables and data. In short, the tableau helps develop a logical and consistent approach to the full range of farm decisionmaking.

CROP ACTIVITIES. In a tableau as shown in table 3-5, the crops a repre-

Table 3-4. Elements of a Tableau

Inputs	Crop activities (crop production techniques)						Constraints
	1	2	3	4	5	...	
List of inputs needed for all activities (often called the input vector); not all activities require all inputs.	Input-output coefficient matrix (the a_{ij} coefficients that indicate the amount a of input i needed to operate activity j on a unit, or hectare, of land. The coefficients are linear and constant).						Input availabilities or resources available to the farmer (often called the constraints vector or the right-hand side)

Maximize → the objective function = net revenue

The objective function is the sum of the output for each crop activity times the net revenue per unit of output for producing it. If no cash costs are incurred, net revenue per unit is equal to the price of output.

Table 3-5. Inputs for an Illustrative Farming System in East Java, Indonesia

Inputs	Crop activities							
	1	2	3	4	5	6	7	8
	Paddy rice				Soybeans	Peanuts	Cassava	Corn
	Technique 1	Technique 2	Technique 3	Technique 2				
Land (hectares)								
Season I	1	1	1	1	1	1	1	
Season II								
Season III							1	1
Labor (days per hectare)								
Season I	340	400	435					
Season II		500		400	200	175	100	
Season III							150	120
Fertilizer (kilograms per hectare)								
Season I	0	500	1,000	500	0	0		
Season II							500	
Season III								0
Yield (tons per hectare)	2	3	3.5	2.5	0.5	0.4	20	1.0

sentative farmer in a region could grow during a year are listed along with the inputs required to produce each crop on one hectare of land in each season. The major commodity grown in the area usually can be produced with several alternative techniques, and each is listed as a separate potential farm choice. Multiple cropping and seasonality are built into the tableau by indicating various crops and inputs separately for each distinct growing season, denoted in this example as Seasons I, II, and III.

Each alternative crop and cropping technique is a potential *activity*, and table 3-5 illustrates the alternative activities available to a representative farmer in East Java. The labor inputs, in days per hectare, required for each activity are recorded in the appropriate time periods for the three growing seasons in the year. Similarly, the fertilizer rows list fertilizer inputs for each crop and cropping technique (that is, for each activity). Since the input data for growing these crops have been standardized for one hectare, the coefficient 1 in the land rows refers to the particular season a given crop occupies that one hectare of land.

The tableau represents the technical relationship between inputs and the resulting output, and hence it is a numerical approximation of the production function. In this example paddy grown on one hectare using 340 days of labor and no fertilizer yields 2 tons of rice (Activity 1). With 400 days and 500 kilograms of fertilizer, a yield of 3 tons can be produced on that same hectare of land (Activity 2). By increasing fertilizer input to 1,000 kilograms and labor to 435 days, the farmer can produce 3.5 tons of rice using Activity 3. These three data points (fertilizer input, labor input, and resulting rice output) lie on a multifactor production function analogous to the one-factor continuous function depicted in figure 3-3.

RESOURCE AVAILABILITY. Farm households must make their cropping decisions in the context of their land, labor, and capital resources available for crop production. To reflect these constraints, the total number of hectares of land, days of labor the family can provide, and capital resources in the form of cash, oxen, irrigation water, or other inputs, are entered along the right-hand side of the tableau, as in table 3-6. The constraints, however, are not necessarily fixed. Family labor may supply 400 days of labor in a year, but if the family had sufficient capital resources and if there were a market for agricultural labor, the farm household could hire additional laborers and alter the labor constraint. Similarly, a credit constraint could be altered if borrowing were a possibility.

The simple tableau in table 3-6 does not capture all possible constraints, particularly biological and behavioral constraints. For example, if nematodes infest the soil, such crops as tomatoes must be rotated from field to field to break the cycle of nematode reproduction. Planting a crop in only one year out of three in a particular field presents a planting constraint. Behavioral constraints can also be important to the actual outcome. If a farm household

Table 3-6. An Illustrative Farming System Tableau for East Java, Indonesia

				Crop activities					
	1	2	3	4	5	6	7	8	
		Paddy rice							
Inputs	Technique 1	Technique 2	Technique 3	Technique 2	Soybeans	Peanuts	Cassava	Corn	Resource availabilities
Land (hectares)									
Season I	1	1	1						2 hectares
Season II				1	1	1			2 hectares
Season III							1	1	2 hectares
Labor (days per hectare)									
Season I	340	400	435						400 days ⎫ Price of labor:
Season II				400	200	175	100	120	400 days ⎬ $1 per day
Season III							150		400 days ⎭
Fertilizer (kilograms per hectare)									
Season I	0	500	1,000						$1,000 ⎫ Price of urea fer-
Season II				500	0	0	500		$1,000 ⎬ tilizer: $0.25 per
Season III								0	$1,000 ⎭ kilogram
Yield (tons per hectare)	2	3	3.5	2.5	0.5	0.4	20	1.0	
Price per ton	$200	$200	$200	$200	$500	$600	$35	$160	
Gross revenues per hectare	$400	$600	$700	$500	$250	$240	$700	$160	
Net revenue per hectare	$60	$75	$15	−$25	$50	$65	$325	$40	

intends to produce enough grain for the family's consumption before engaging in other production alternatives, a home consumption constraint must be added to the farming system tableau to reflect such behavior.

PRICES. The prices farmers face for both inputs and output complete the picture of the decisionmaking environment of a farming system. Actual input prices paid and output prices received by farmers in the region—for each activity—are used to calculate the gross and net revenues shown at the bottom of table 3-6. Gross revenue per hectare is simply the yield in tons for each activity multiplied by unit values (prices per ton) for output. Cost data for inputs used in each activity, for example, seed, fertilizer, and pesticide prices, are needed to determine net revenue per hectare for each crop or cropping technique.

With these calculations made and the tableau complete, comparisons among various crop activities can readily be made. The economic conditions faced by farm households, their responses to them, and the structure of incentives are all revealed by the tableau, even in this simple version. Analysts can gauge the impact of alternative output prices for various crops, of fertilizer prices, availability of credit, and so on, and thus identify opportunities for policy initiatives that will reflect both the resource constraints facing farmers and their likely behavior in response to various economic alternatives.

GUIDELINES TO PROGRAMMING SOLUTIONS. In the simplified tableau shown in table 3-6, the rational farmer's decision of what crops to grow can be found by inspection and a little arithmetic. In Season I paddy rice grown with Technique 2 yields $75 per hectare in net revenue, the highest of the three possibilities. In Season II peanuts yield $65 per hectare, but cassava returns $325 per hectare if it is left in the ground for both Season II and Season III. Since corn is the only Season III alternative, its $40 net revenue per hectare can be added to the $65 from peanuts in Season II for comparison with cassava's returns. The $325 cassava returns far exceed the $105 joint returns from peanuts and corn. The net-revenue-maximizing farmer thus grows 3 tons of rice in Season I, making $75 per hectare, and 20 tons of cassava in Seasons II and III, making $325 per hectare, for a total net revenue of $800 from the two hectares of land on the farm.

With somewhat more time and effort this solution could have been obtained from a linear programming model run on a computer. For this simple but still quite interesting and revealing example, the back of an envelope is easier and faster than the computer. As complexities are added, however, or other issues need to be addressed, recourse to formal programming models and solutions may be inevitable.

Formal programming models are necessary when the tableau includes more than about ten activities and ten inputs, counting different techniques and seasons. Such complexity arises when a wide variety of potential crops can be grown, as in warm regions with year-round irrigation, and when the timing of planting, cultivating, and harvesting is intimately connected with the mix of other crops being grown and with seasonal fluctuations in labor availability and in product prices. Full programming solutions can be very helpful in understanding how farmers are likely to react to changed circumstances in such complicated environments.

A second setting that requires formal solutions is the prevalence of buying and selling activities for intermediate inputs, such as fodder or feed grains, or for labor in different seasons. Modeling these activities efficiently requires knowing some tricks of the trade, most of which are presented in the volume by Raymond Beneke and Ronald Winterboer listed in the bibliography. "Grow or purchase" decisions and on-farm versus off-farm work are not merely issues for highly commercialized agriculture, however. Chinese agricultural planners are interested in simple linear programming models that would address such questions at the commune level (and even lower).

More complicated models also become important when the simple linear relationships presumed in the tableau begin to break down. Diminishing returns to fertilizer were captured in table 3-6 by using three separate production techniques for rice cultivation. The farmer is forced, however, to choose one technique or another rather than use each over its efficient, but limited, range. Similarly, all purchased inputs are available at a fixed price, and all output can be sold for a constant price. This fixed-price environment is probably a fair representation of the individual farmer's perspective, but analysts who worry about how the results look when aggregated into market totals need to know whether strong demand for fertilizer will raise its price or whether the market price for cassava will fall below $35 per ton if every farmer grows 40 tons of it.

For the analyst, formal programming techniques have two important uses which the simple techniques in the next section cannot address. The first is the opportunity to ask whether the full set of constraints facing the farmer is actually incorporated in the tableau being used by the analyst. As additional biological and behavioral constraints are imposed on the farmer's decision-making, the simple maximization of net revenue outlined above will no longer give the "right" answer. While some analysts view the outcome of this simple maximization as a test of the farmer's "rationality," it is closer to a test of the analyst's ability to see the world through the farmer's eyes and to model what the farmer sees.

Part of the farmer's perception involves the aggregation problems raised above. Most farmers know that the market prices for many specialty crops— fruits and vegetables—are very sensitive to the quantities supplied. Through years of trial and error farmers have learned not to overplant these crops despite their apparent high profitability per hectare. Programming models that have all of India growing watermelons are not unheard of, and they measure the modeler's rationality, not the farmer's.

The second major role for formal programming solutions is the insight they provide into the value of additional units of the inputs available in fixed amounts. Linear programming solutions calculate how much net revenue will increase for a one-unit increase in each constrained input. Because these values are like implicit prices that allocate among the various fixed inputs the total net revenue produced by the optimal solution, they are often called shadow prices. These implicit input prices generate the same optimal solution using cost minimization (with costs equal to shadow prices times input use) as would the original revenue maximization solution. Since the revenue maximization procedure is normally done first, it is called the "primal solution." The shadow prices attached to the fixed inputs constitute "the dual solution."

Shadow prices from dual solutions provide important insight into the scarcity values of the inputs available in fixed or partially fixed supply at the farm level. These inputs include land or fixed capital, rationed inputs such as irrigation water for which the farmer may pay a price but still desire more, and family labor, which may not have easy access to jobs in rural markets. The shadow price attached to each of these inputs (the dual of the amount of input used in the optimal solution) indicates the value at the farm level of increasing the availability of the input by one unit. Inputs in surplus supply—for example, farm household labor in Season II on the representative farm shown in table 3-6, where only 200 of the available 400 days are utilized growing cassava—will not contribute any additional revenue if more is available. In the absence of outside hiring activities, the shadow price of such labor is zero. Conversely, in Season I the shadow price of family labor would be positive if the 400 days of labor hired from the rural labor market were not available to this farm. In fact, the shadow price of labor in Season I is about $1.17 for Technique 1 and $1.13 for Techniques 2 and 3 (assuming family labor is not paid an internal wage in calculating costs).

Shadow prices are also helpful in determining the value of added water supplies since an appropriate specification of water constraints at the farm level can provide planners with a full picture of how the dual solution changes when water constraints are varied. Sometimes it is necessary to distinguish between social and private costs and benefits in this exercise, a proviso that is equally appropriate for determining the marginal value of labor. These dual values also provide insight into farmers' behavior, especially their ability to allocate highly productive fixed inputs to appropriate uses. Additional constraints may also be revealed. If fertilizer has a much higher shadow price for a particular farm than the apparent market price, when actual use is inserted as a constraint, then the farm household has insufficient capital to purchase it, the fertilizer market price is not actually applicable at the farm level, or the risks of using larger quantities are perceived as being very great. Determining which answer is the relevant one requires some field investigation, but the programming results have raised the right questions.

DATA FOR A TABLEAU. In collecting the data appropriate to the particular farming system, the first step is to select the number of seasons or time periods to include, and the appropriate number obviously depends on the possible crop activities for a region. Two or three seasons are frequently sufficient to capture the major elements of seasonality in the system, but in irrigated areas where farmers have substantial flexibility in choosing planting dates for key crops, inputs may have to be broken down on a monthly basis to reflect the full options open to the farmer. A breakdown into shorter time periods is rarely necessary.

Eight to ten cropping activities are usually adequate, including different techniques for growing the most important commodities. Interplanted crops can be specified as a single activity; for example, corn or rice as an early intercrop with cassava represents a single activity. The input requirements, yields, and revenue would pertain to the entire mixture. Despite the importance of home gardens for improving incomes and nutrition, they cannot be modeled satisfactorily without introducing extreme complexity in the tableau design.

Input requirements can be quickly estimated from a few published sources and later verified and modified by talking to farmers in the countryside. Having the right input coefficients—the values for a_{ij} that indicate the amount a of input i into activity j—is clearly critical to using the tableau successfully to represent farmer behavior. To ensure that the input data are representative, interviews in a region should focus on variables such as irrigation, soils, and farm size, that determine the dominant crop activities and farming techniques. A series of group interviews will enable the analyst to inquire about the expected range and representative values for the input coefficients. Large farmers tend to dominate group meetings, and the answers will be biased unless the analyst is careful to sound out small farmers as well.

Input coefficients can also be obtained from farm management surveys, but since such studies tend to be village censuses, policy analysts can be swamped with irrelevant data. In addition, many tabulations average across discrete activities, rather than treat them separately. For example, if half the farms use oxen and half use tractors in growing cereals, separate data are needed for each activity, not an average coefficient for both.

Synthetic activities can be constructed to reflect crops or crop techniques that might be used by a farmer but currently are not. For example, to explore the implications of introducing a power tiller when no tillers are used in a region, it will be necessary to develop synthetic data on the productivity of tillers from other areas. Similarly, investment in an irrigation system could radically alter cropping possibilities. These synthetic activities are simply added to existing crop and input activities to assess likely farmer reaction to agricultural production programs based on new technology or infrastructure. Great care must be taken in this procedure, however, not to assume the answer by using a highly optimistic coefficient of input productivity or actual on-farm availability. The trick is to see the innovation from the farmer's viewpoint and to include it in the tableau in a realistic fashion.

Defining the appropriate geographic area to be covered by a resource constraint is sometimes an issue for policy analysts. Since the tableau is used for policy planning, not for planning an individual farm, the resources or constraints might plausibly apply to the entire agroclimatic zone. While some resource constraints, such as irrigation supplies, are more clear-cut at the regional level than at the farm level, no regional decisionmaker actually chooses particular crop activities and then invests time, effort, and resources in growing them. Socialist economies frequently plan allocations of area to various crops and inputs to the respective areas, but such plans are not self-fulfilling. Farmers must still receive the inputs and the information from the plan on how, when, and where to use them. If a late monsoon delays the planting of wheat, then corn or sorghum may be more appropriate. The tableau is built not to help planners *make* these types of decisions, but to analyze how farm households make day-to-day decisions. For this reason, it is preferable to design the tableau to reflect decision activities of typical farms.

Cost data for the inputs, such as fertilizer, pesticides, irrigation water, and seed, are straightforward entries which can be determined by talking with farmers or farm supply depot managers in rural areas. Cost data for the primary factors, such as labor, are more difficult to collect. Even though many farms rely primarily on family labor, opportunities may exist both to hire additional farm labor if needs are great and for family members to work off the farm for wages if they are not needed (or are not very productive) on the farm. Because of these alternative opportunities, wage rates in nearby markets are needed to evaluate farmer response to new technology, altered price policy, or investments in infrastructure. Questions with regard to wage rates by season, differential wages between sexes (and children), and forms of payment need to be noted as part of the early field interviews.

Input costs can be incorporated in the tableau in several different ways. For many purposes, supplemental side listings of price and cost data, as shown in table 3-6, and solutions by inspection of the tableau for the farmer's maximum revenue choices will be adequate. But when separate activities that show purchases, sales, and transfers are added to the tableau, the farmer's best choices of activities can no longer be found by simple inspection of the various alternatives. Mathematical programming techniques are then needed to find optimal solutions to particular farming system or policy problems. Using such techniques requires expertise and practical experience if the results are not to be mechanical or trivial.

Using a Farming System Tableau for Policy Analysis

Aggregate farm output for any crop is defined by two variables: yield per hectare and area harvested. Both variables are partially under the farmer's control and partially determined by weather and other exogenous factors. The opportunities available to the farmer in both dimensions are illustrated in the tableau in table 3-6.

INPUT USE. The important decision for the farmer in Season I is not what crop to grow but how to grow rice since no other crop is competitive enough even to enter the tableau. The three alternative techniques shown are representative of a wider, perhaps infinite, set of possibilities. Technique 1 uses traditional technology with no fertilizer to produce 2 tons of rice per hectare. To grow two hectares of rice using this technique, the farm household must hire 280 days of outside labor, at $1 per day, to assist the 400 days of household labor available. The 680 days of total labor cost $680, assuming the household labor is paid the market wage. The gross revenue is $400 per hectare, or $800 in total, from which the $680 in labor costs must be deducted, leaving a net revenue of $120 for the farm, or $60 per hectare as the return to management and land during Season I if Technique 1 is used.

Techniques 2 and 3 use more modern technology with moderate and large applications of fertilizer, respectively. The added fertilizer, in combination with greater labor inputs, raises yields to 3 tons per hectare with 500 kilograms of urea per hectare and to 3.5 tons with 1,000 kilograms per hectare. With urea fertilizer prices at $0.25 per kilogram and labor costs at $1 per day, the added yields from Technique 2 more than repay the added costs, and net revenue rises to $75 per hectare or $150 for the farm. But the additional yield from Technique 3 is not worthwhile, and net revenues fall to only $15 per hectare. The fully rational farmer will choose Technique 2 to maximize net revenue, but the additional $60 in labor costs and $125 in fertilizer costs per hectare to earn an extra $15 in net revenue may look like a risky investment to some farmers who would thus choose Technique 1 because of its smaller cash outlays.

CROPPING PATTERNS. In Seasons II and III the farmer must choose among several potential crops. Rice can still be grown using Technique 2, but the yield will be only 2.5 tons rather than 3 because less water is available. Soybean and peanut yields are very small, but they bring high prices. Cassava can be planted in Season II, but it produces no revenue then because it occupies the land for two full seasons, thus displacing any further crop in Season III. As noted earlier, the farmer must compare the two-season cassava revenues with the combined revenues from a single Season II crop and a single Season III crop. In this example, only corn can be grown successfully in Season III, but the cassava revenues dominate all possible combinations of corn with other Season II crops. Consequently, the farmer represented in the table 3-6 tableau chooses to grow cassava over the second two seasons, earning a net revenue of $325 per hectare.

The total income for the farming system is $800, not including the $900 earned by family labor during the three seasons ($400 in Season I, when family labor supplies were exhausted and 400 days of hired labor were required; $200 in Season II working on cassava; and $300 in Season III working on cassava). No additional labor income is earned when family labor is in surplus supply on the farm. This $800 net revenue is the basis for calculation of shadow prices for the fixed factors of production, and it thus serves as return to the farm household's land and management skills. This amount may seem like a satisfactory return for the family, depending on alternative uses of their land and management skills (and whether they could get jobs paying $900 per year off the farm). For example, if land of similar quality were selling for $2,000 per hectare, the $800 net return to land and management represents a 20 percent rate of return on the value of land alone.

MARKETING OUTPUT. One decision not represented in the tableau but which is important both to farm households and to policy analysts is how much of the rice and cassava produced will be retained for home consumption and how much will be sold to market intermediaries to become available for off-farm consumption or export. The additional steps needed to incorporate this decision into the tableau make it sufficiently complicated that formal solution techniques are needed to find the optimal answer, but the analyst's intuition can provide an estimate even without formal models. If the farmer can raise cheaper food crops for home consumption while offering more of the expensive crops for sale, the retained net revenue for the household will be greater. This topic is treated in more detail in chapter 4.

Modeling the farmer's static choices of cropping patterns and input use is more a test of the analyst's ability to calibrate the tableau properly than a test of the farmer's rationality, although the two must be decided jointly. The usefulness of the tableau becomes apparent when parameters influencing the farmer's decision-making environment begin to change. How do farmers respond when output or input prices vary or technical change occurs? The tableau is designed to help analysts address these questions.

OUTPUT PRICES. Most governments have the potential to influence the prices for basic food crops with import and export controls, floor and ceiling price policies implemented with buffer stocks, or even special foreign exchange rates. Such price policies are closely examined in chapter 4. Needed here is some sense of how farmers might react to them.

The tableau in table 3-6 can be used to address this question. If labor and fertilizer costs are held constant and rice prices are raised progressively by a policy intervention from $180 per ton to $325 per ton, the farm household represented in the tableau will change rice production decisions according to each new net revenue calculation. At $180 per ton, the farmer uses Technique 1 to produce 4 tons of rice. From $185 to $320 per ton, the farmer uses Technique 2 and produces 6 tons of rice. At $320 per ton, the farmer switches to Technique 3 and produces 7 tons of rice. All of this supply response comes during Season I from higher yields achieved by more intensive labor and fertilizer use, an intensity made profitable by higher rice prices.

If rice prices continue to climb, the farmer begins to look at Season II.

Growing rice in this season had been absolutely unprofitable at $200 per ton, and it was even less desirable relative to the large income-earning potential of two-season cassava. If rice prices exceed $324 per ton, however, the farmer will switch to growing rice in Season II and produce an additional 5 tons of output from the entire farm, making a total of 12 tons of rice produced for the year. In addition, 2 tons of corn will be grown in Season III, and 40 tons of cassava output will be lost. This supply response can be plotted as a "normative" supply curve, as in figure 3-11.

This supply curve, with its abrupt jumps in output at critical price levels, does not look much like the smooth supply curve drawn in figure 3-6 in correspondence to the short-run marginal cost curve. The jagged supply curve generated from the tableau shows what farmers "should" do if they make precise calculations whenever prices change and then switch immediately to

Figure 3-11. Rice Supply Curve for the Two-hectare Farm Described in Table 3-6

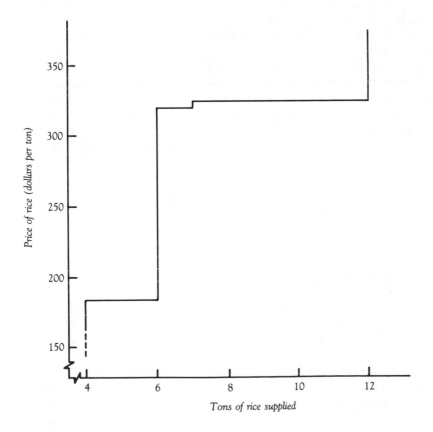

Tons of rice supplied

the newly profitable technique and level of input use. Risk aversion and an understandable desire to experiment on a small plot or with partial changes in input use, behavior which is not formally incorporated in the tableau, will make *observed* supply changes in the face of rice price changes less abrupt and, no doubt, somewhat less elastic in the short run. However, the supply function in figure 3-11 is a good indicator of the likely direction of change when the farm household's environment is altered, and it provides an upper bound to the potential magnitude of the response.

Several features should be noted about such a normative supply curve generated from a farming system tableau. The illustrated supply curve is for one cropping system only. To obtain a national supply curve, two steps are needed: aggregation of individual farms represented by several tableaux into a regional total, and aggregation of regional totals into a national level. For example, if there are four representative farms per agroclimatic zone and six zones in the country, an assessment would be required of twenty-four different farming systems. This is a sizable number although many systems might show similar responses. In table 3-6, increases in rice output in response to rice prices are caused primarily by increased fertilizer use. The area planted to rice and other crops in the system is affected only after a substantial rise in rice prices. Knowing the general mechanisms that lead to supply response and the relative weights of the various farming systems in national farm production is usually sufficient for policy analysts to form rough judgments about farmer responses to output price changes.

The farmer response to higher rice prices also illustrates the concept of cross-elasticities of supply, which are analogous to cross-elasticities of demand. In the tableau example, increasing the supply of rice from 7 to 12 tons by raising the price of rice above $324 per ton is done at the expense of cassava output. Cassava is also an important starchy staple, especially among the poor in East Java, and the expanded rice output might have negative nutritional consequences despite the larger supply of rice available. If the expansion of rice production increased hiring of rural labor and wages rose, the poor who eat cassava might be better off, because of their higher incomes, despite the smaller supply of cassava available. If most of the added labor comes from the farm family household in Season II, the rural landless poor could then be significantly worse-off. At rice prices above $324 per ton, corn production in Season III expands and is thus complementary with rice production in Season II.

A third complication not reflected in the supply curve in figure 3-11 is the potential interaction between quantities and prices. In the example, the increase in rice supply generated by the higher prices does not cause rice prices to fall because government policy determines the rice price. This assumption might be reasonable for small changes in quantity or for very well-managed policies. In some instances, however, increased supplies may depress prices and cause farmers to reevaluate their production decisions.

INPUT PRICES AND SUBSIDIES. Purchased inputs produced in the modern industrial sector contribute to higher yields on farms that have appropriate environments to use them. Differential use of purchased inputs, especially fertilizer, explains much of the differential yields for important food crops around the world. Average rice yields for countries in Asia, for example, are highly correlated with fertilizer applications. These applications in turn are directly related to the farm price of rice relative to the price of fertilizer. Countries not wishing to use higher output prices as a means of stimulating food crop production understandably turn to lower prices for fertilizer and other inputs as a way to increase food supplies.

The farming system tableau in table 3-6 can be used to examine the farmer's response to changed input prices just as to changed output prices. If rice prices are $200 per ton and the price of urea is $0.125 rather than $0.25 per kilogram, the rational farmer would switch to Technique 3 from Technique 2. More rice is produced with the lower fertilizer price, and the farmer's net income increases from $75 to $140 per hectare in Season I. Both income to the farmer and production of rice increase. This distinction is very important, for although subsidies can be used to lower input costs in order to raise production, their main effect might be to transfer income to farm households. Subsidizing farmer incomes can be entirely legitimate when it is intended, but the analyst should understand the distinction between the effects of subsidies on production and effects on income transfers.

This distinction becomes even more important when assessing the relative merits of product price supports as opposed to input subsidies. Within the assumptions of the simplified tableau of table 3-6, the rational farmer will use the same quantity of fertilizer in Season I whether the price of paddy is $200 per ton and the price of urea is $0.125 per kilogram or the price of paddy is $400 per ton and the price of urea is $0.25 per kilogram. In both instances the ratio of input to output prices is the same. As shown in figure 3-5, this price ratio determines optimal fertilizer use and rice yields per hectare in a simple production function model. But the income effects of the two price regimes are vastly different. In the $400/$0.25 example, the net revenue per hectare for the farm is $715 in Season I, but in the $200/$0.125 example, the net income is only $140 per hectare. The more than fivefold difference in net income is likely to change farmers' notions of risk, their capacity to make investments in subsequent seasons, and their entire consumption bundle. Analysis of which price policy pays greater social returns requires tracing the employment effects of such sharply different income streams. This effort requires the macro perspective of chapter 5 to complement the farm-level analysis here.

TECHNICAL CHANGE. Farmers react to input and output prices within the technical environment of their farms. Changing that technical environment by providing more effective water control, new biological technology, or better mechanical equipment can change crop output significantly even within a stable price environment. For example, if the farm household in the tableau in table 3-6 were suddenly to have access to free irrigation water in Season II, rice yields from Technique 2 might rise from 2.5 to more than 4 tons per hectare (with other inputs remaining constant) because of the reduced cloud cover and greater solar energy available in the dry season. Growing a second crop of rice thus becomes profitable in combination with corn in Season III, despite the low price of rice and high price of fertilizer. Such changes in crop productivity are the major justification for investing in irrigation facilities or more rapid technical change. The farming system tableau provides a quantitative framework for examining these productivity effects.

Analysts can also make rough estimates of the production impact of other investments in rural infrastructure. For example, the effects of a new rural road, which might significantly influence farm-gate prices (especially for perishables), can be assessed by calculating existing transportation costs and estimating the costs that would prevail with a new road. With an estimate of how much marketing margins will be reduced as a result of lower transportation costs, analysts can translate the lower marketing costs into higher output prices for farmers as well as lower input prices. The new prices facing farmers are inserted in the tableau, and the analyst solves for new net revenue. If the lower marketing costs are all passed on to consumers through lower retail prices while farm-gate prices remain the same, no production impact will be felt although consumer welfare may increase significantly.

These rather simple calculations are obviously no substitute for detailed investment project reports or for the sophisticated benefit-cost procedures developed by the World Bank, and others. With a general familiarity with farming systems in the region, however, a policy analyst using these techniques is likely to be much more creative (and demanding) in the use of consultants to identify fruitful development projects.

COSTS OF PRODUCTION. Farmers usually argue that they are "losing money" and that government price supports should cover "costs of production." Policy analysts are frequently asked to calculate these costs as a basis for price policy. It is important to understand, however, that even an individual farmer does not have a unique cost of production and that the full array of a country's farmers have widely different costs. A tableau can be used to calculate production costs and to illustrate the nature of the serious conceptual and empirical problems with such cost-of-production calculations.

The out-of-pocket costs a farmer incurs are calculated directly from the tableau. For each activity, the costs of production divided by total yield result in unit costs, that is, the average cost per ton of output. These costs specifically do not include a return for the farm household's land or managerial skills, but some assumptions about family labor costs are usually included. These family labor cost assumptions may not accurately reflect the actual opportunity cost of that labor in its next-best employment possibility unless great care has been taken to understand the dynamics of the rural labor market when the tableau was being constructed. Depending on the inputs used and the crop activities chosen, each farmer's costs of production can vary significantly.

The supply curve in figure 3-11 (or its smooth theoretical equivalent in figure 3-6) illustrates that there is no single cost of production, even for one crop produced by one farmer. At a price of paddy of $180 per ton, the cost of paddy production is $170 per ton for producing 4 tons of paddy on the two-hectare farm. With the output price at $320 per ton of paddy, the production cost per ton is $196 for the 7 tons produced, and at $325 per ton the production cost rises to $202 per ton for 12 tons produced.

The supply curve for a farm crop is directly related to its marginal cost curve, that is, the additional cost of producing additional units of output. The point at which a rational farmer chooses to be on the cost curve (or the supply function) depends not only on the price of inputs but also on the absolute and relative prices of the various crop outputs. Even for a single crop on a given farm, *the* cost of production is a fiction; there is only a schedule of costs and outputs. These schedules vary by farm and by agroclimatic zone. Both conceptually and empirically, therefore, the search for a single cost of production is fruitless, despite the tendency of government procurement agencies and price control boards to justify their prices on just such a basis. Various estimates over a wide range can all be correct even if the numbers are generated from reliable farm surveys. There cannot be one right answer even with perfect measurements.

Even for a single farm household growing a single crop in the context of a given price environment, calculating the cost of producing that crop is difficult when the value of family labor (or land) is included in the cost analysis. When family labor must be supplemented in peak seasons with hired labor, using the market price for labor in calculating net revenues is appropriate. But how is labor to be valued when there is surplus labor in the labor market or when family labor availability generally exceeds labor requirements?

Very high implied costs of production result from using government-set minimum wage rates to value farm labor. But smallholder agriculture is rarely affected by minimum wage laws, although plantations often comply. Since minimum wages often bear little relation to labor productivity in agriculture and are almost always higher than market wages for unskilled rural labor, market wage rates are likely to be much closer to a correct value for labor, especially from the perception of the farmer needing to hire additional workers. Market wages often vary considerably by season, being relatively higher in the planting and harvesting seasons and relatively lower when crops are growing or when meager rainfall prevents intensive agriculture. Although the tableau example uses a constant wage rate across seasons, seasonal wage rates would more accurately reflect labor costs.

Even local market wages might overstate the actual opportunity cost to the economy of hiring an additional worker or of a family member's working an additional day on the farm. In regions with surplus labor, a farmer hiring additional labor will have to pay a wage, even if it is low. More people may be seeking jobs at this low rate than can be hired, but the market wage falls only so far because no one is willing to work for zero wages or for less than some traditional level that covers subsistence costs. In such situations, the opportunity cost of labor—what labor is worth in its next-best occupation, such as petty trading—will be less than the market wage. Thus, the market rate will overstate the true labor cost to the economy, the shadow price of labor in the programming terminology discussed earlier, even though the market rate must be paid by an employer.

It is important for policy analysts to understand the logic of shadow prices for analysis of the macro implications of farmer decisionmaking, but their relevance to what farmers actually do in the countryside is limited. Farm households make decisions on the basis of their perceived opportunity costs. Market wage rates are a reasonable approximation for valuing both family and hired labor if the analyst has good data on wage variations by season and knows whether rural workers can find jobs at these wage levels. If they can, the labor market provides a reasonable basis for valuation. If family workers cannot find jobs, the marginal value of a family member's time may be near zero. This situation commonly occurs when the costs of migration to find part-time or seasonal work outweigh any potential earnings.

If wage labor opportunities are near zero, it is rational for farmers to exclude labor costs in making their production decisions and to calculate their return to the combined resources of land, management, and labor. The cost data calculated in such circumstances then have considerable meaning for price policy because they cover only cash costs incurred in crop production. Crop prices that are below these direct cash costs will indeed cause losses.

Social Profitability Analysis

Farmers make decisions that are privately profitable, basing their calculations on the prices they actually pay. From a macroeconomic perspective these prices may be distorted for a number of reasons, including surplus labor conditions, tariff barriers, and government subsidies or taxes. Net social profitability analysis reveals how the calculations would change if all the price distortions were removed.

If rice prices are held down by trade policy, more intensive rice production will show greater profitability in social terms than in the private calculations of farmers. Alternatively, a fertilizer subsidy will make rice production (and other fertilizer-intensive crops) appear more profitable to individual farmers than to society as a whole. Net social profitability analysis weighs all such positive and negative effects to arrive at an overall judgment on the social desirability of carrying out a particular project.

Private profitability calculations are unlikely to result in a nation's best use of its resources when monopoly elements in marketing or segmentation in the labor market give price signals to farmers that cause them to misallocate resources. In addition, price distortions induced by government policies frequently cause farm prices to diverge from the opportunity costs of inputs or output. Government subsidized credit to farmers, for example, may encourage them to purchase capital equipment, thereby displacing labor even in a labor surplus economy. Various government trade policies, including taxes, subsidies, and bans on imports and exports, can cause domestic food prices to be vastly different from those prevailing internationally. Subsidy and trade policies intended to protect domestic industry raise prices of many consumer and producer goods used by farm households, thereby reducing their incomes and distorting their allocation of resources.

ADJUSTING PRICES. To measure net social profitability, the price data in a tableau such as table 3-6 are adjusted in two ways. First, output and the inputs that are traded in international markets are valued in world prices to eliminate the transfer effects caused by government policies. Output is valued at the price a country must pay for imports of a commodity (or can receive for its exports) instead of the actual market price that prevails domestically. Similarly, an input, such as fertilizer, that can be purchased or sold abroad is valued at its international cost rather than at a subsidized (or taxed) market price. International prices measure the opportunity costs of growing various crops because countries have the option of purchasing or selling goods abroad, whether or not these international markets are competitive. Identifying the international price that is relevant for the comparison is not always straightforward, however, because of short-run fluctuations in many important world commodity markets. Rough guidelines for finding appropriate opportunity costs are provided in chapters 4 and 6.

The second adjustment to the price data requires that domestic resources, such as labor, capital, and land, be valued to reflect their social opportunity costs within the country—at the value of the output forgone from not using these resources in their next-best alternative employment. If farmers receive subsidized credit at an interest rate of 6 percent when the government could otherwise have used the capital in a development project yielding a 15 percent social rate of return, the social, or shadow, price of capital would be 15 percent.

COMPARING PRIVATE AND SOCIAL PROFITABILITY. After the two price adjustments are made, social benefits—the value of the output for each activity at the adjusted prices—can be compared with the social costs—the opportunity costs to society of using the inputs. Whether the commodity is a desirable good for consumption is a separate social question that depends on the distribution of purchasing power and a society's attempt to provide a minimum consumption floor for basic goods and services. Once consumption of any commodity is contemplated or under way, society has an obvious need to obtain the supplies as efficiently as possible. If social profitability is positive (if benefits exceed costs), it is efficient to produce the commodity instead of trading for it. The calculation of social profitability can be done for different commodities, different techniques of production, and different regions by using the data in the tableau format of table 3-6.

At the private market prices for inputs and output shown in table 3-6, the farm household grew 3 tons of rice per hectare in Season I using Technique 2 and 20 tons of cassava per hectare in Seasons II and III. Suppose, however, that those private market prices resulted from two government policy actions that subsidized rice imports by keeping the domestic price at $200 per ton while import prices were $250 per ton, and that subsidized cassava exports by keeping internal prices at $35 per ton while the export price was only $20 per ton (the cassava example especially is hypothetical). What would farmer decisionmaking be in the absence of these government policies?

This is equivalent to asking whether the two activities chosen by the farmers are socially profitable as well as privately profitable. In fact, when the social prices are inserted in the tableau and the new calculations performed, rice production increases from 3 tons to 5.5 tons per hectare as the farmer shifts to Technique 2 for growing rice in Season II, corn production increases from zero to 1.0 tons per hectare in Season III, and cassava production drops to zero, for its social profitability is negative. Although simple, the example shows clearly how government policies that influence market prices can significantly affect total food supplies, the composition of output, and even employment in the rural area.

Social profitability can diverge from private profitability in dimensions other than output prices. Table 3-7 shows the calculations of social profitability if private wage rates are different from social wage rates and if fertilizer is subsidized, thus causing private costs to diverge from international opportunity costs. By combining the total effects of each divergence, the analyst can judge the overall social profitability of each activity. Equally important, table 3-7 shows the contribution of each component of the divergence—output price policy, wage policy, input subsidy policy—to actual social profitability (or loss).

The difference between the private and social calculations in table 3-7 is striking. In this example, cassava, which was the main income-earner under private prices, would have a negative social profitability because the decline in private profitability from a lowered product price (−$300) and from the additional cost of fertilizer (−$125) is not offset by savings on labor (+$62). Rice would be much more profitable under social prices, even though less

Table 3-7. An Illustration of Private versus Social Profitability
(dollars)

Crop activity	Private profitability (1)	Commodity price effect (2)	Fertilizer subsidy effect (3)	Wage effect (4)	Social profitability (5)
Rice					
Technique 1	60	100	0	85	245
Technique 2	75	150	− 125	100	200
Technique 3	15	175	− 250	109	49
Technique 2					
(Season II)	− 25	125	− 125	100	75
Soybeans	50	0	0	50	100
Peanuts	65	0	0	44	109
Cassava	325	− 300	− 125	62	− 38
Corn	40	0	0	30	70

Notes:
Column 1: Private profitability per hectare as shown in table 3-6.
Column 2: Commodity price effect, assuming the social opportunity price of rice (paddy) equals $250 per ton and the cassava price equals $20 per ton.
Column 3: Fertilizer subsidy effect, assuming an international price of $0.50 per kilogram of fertilizer as opposed to a domestic price of $0.25 per kilogram.
Column 4: Wage effect, assuming an opportunity wage of $0.75 per day as opposed to a market rate of $1.00 per day.
Column 5: Social profitability per hectare, assuming social prices and the physical coefficients of table 3-6.

fertilizer would be used in rice production. Rational farmers facing social rather than private prices would also have a very different combination of crop activities with peanuts and corn replacing cassava. Rice production in Season II is no longer the most profitable crop after the fertilizer subsidy is dropped. Employment would increase under social prices from 1,300 to 1,720 days. In short, government policies can have a large impact, and using social prices in a farming system tableau permits these effects to be identified and quantified.

Forming a Production Strategy

A strategy for agricultural development within a food policy framework is broader than a simple concern for expanding farm production, important as that is for other elements to be effective. Growth in other sectors, job creation, income growth and distribution, access of poor people to food, and household and national food security are also integral components of a production strategy. The vast literature on agricultural development strategies and more recent analysis of rural development strategies have devoted considerable attention to such issues. Food policy incorporates these sectoral perspectives into a macro policy context while addressing consumption concerns.

Among the most difficult issues for agricultural sector planners are those of food self-sufficiency and comparative advantage, which inherently deal with international markets, appropriate border price policies, and foreign exchange rate management. These issues raise many of the topics treated in this book, and an integrated discussion is not possible until the last chapter. But social profitability analysis is the primary conceptual tool available to analysts to address these questions. Its ability to illuminate the issues raised by concerns for food security, self-sufficiency, rapid economic growth, and reduction of hunger is instructive at this stage.

Improving the Social Profitability of Agriculture

A major role of agricultural production policy is to reconcile differences between private and social profitability, for farmers make their decisions on the basis of the market signals they actually perceive, not those used by analysts in a planning agency. The desirability of reorienting a nation's farming systems toward socially profitable patterns is obvious. By definition, such patterns lead to more efficient resource allocation and faster growth in output. They do not, however, necessarily solve short-run problems of unemployment, poverty, and hunger. Some of these problems were addressed by the consumption interventions outlined in chapter 2, and some must await the appropriate macroeconomic environment to be discussed in chapter 5. However, the production strategy itself has some potential for alleviating these short-run problems.

To start, policy analysts need to understand what to do if social and private profitability calculations show substantial divergence. As shown in table 3-7, farm activities can have positive or negative social profits, even before a return to land is included. In some cases, private profitability greatly exceeds social profitability because a set of government policies promotes the inefficient use of domestic resources. Then crops are being grown for which a country does not have a current cost advantage. In countries especially worried about self-sufficiency in food production, governments might wish to absorb small resource costs in the interest of increasing food production at the expense of other crops. Such a decision involves assessing the tradeoffs between greater food self-sufficiency, the budgetary costs required to achieve it, the transfer of incomes from consumers to producers because of higher prices, and the efficiency losses that occur because of misallocation of resources in a narrow economic sense.

FOOD SELF-SUFFICIENCY. One of the most important roles of government is to ensure that the society's food supply is not subject to the whims of weather, international markets, or political blackmail. Food security is different from self-sufficiency, however, for in most countries domestic food production is even less stable than supplies available in international markets. Further, domestic food self-sufficiency within a generally interdependent world is an elusive concept. Does it mean self-sufficiency in a single staple grain, in all food, in all food-producing inputs (for example, feed grains for livestock or fertilizer for grain production), or even in all inputs to the input industries?

For a country bent on self-sufficiency, eliminating food grain imports is relatively easy. By raising grain prices high enough, consumption will be curtailed, production will be stimulated, and any import gap can be closed. Reaching self-sufficiency in this fashion, however, would surely be a hollow victory for food policy. Simply eliminating food imports does nothing to guarantee that poor people have enough to eat, and it may make matters much worse.

Most hunger is related to poverty, and so income generation through efficient employment creation is an important component of any strategy designed to improve household food security. Whether such employment creation leads to greater food self-sufficiency is obviously not a question of food supplies alone, but rather depends on the social profitability of increasing those supplies from domestic production. Policymakers may rightly value the higher rural incomes from increased domestic production somewhat more than the lower cost of similar food from imports and may feel that such production adds to the society's sense of food security. Beyond a 10 to 20 percent premium paid for that increased production, however, the wasted resources have very high opportunity costs for a poor country.

RURAL INCOMES AND COMPARATIVE ADVANTAGE. The argument that producing food should be a society's first priority until hunger is eliminated, after which diversification into cash crops can be permitted, has an emotional appeal when strawberries are being exported while landless peasants starve. The appropriate balance of crops—between cash crops and food crops and between cereals and legumes—has several dimensions in addition to the apparently simple question of whether all farm households are producing their own food first.

Several important crops are needed as industrial inputs, and increased cotton or jute output, for example, might permit more and higher-paying jobs in the industrial sector. The productivity of these jobs is a major factor in the social profitability of growing such crops. Farmers whose incomes are increased by growing cotton might be much worse off if forced to grow corn, and the greater home production of food might not offset the worsened poverty. At the same time, pushing tenants off the land on which they raised food for their families in order to grow export crops with mechanized farming techniques may contribute to significant rural hunger. The important issue, however, is not the nature of the crop being grown but the size of the income stream from growing the crop and the recipients of that income.

Efficient and widespread income generation is the most important role for any economy. From income stems the consumer's freedom to purchase a variety of desired goods; from lack of income stem restricted food purchases, hunger, and malnutrition. If a food system is creating many new jobs accessible to the ranks of rural workers dependent on wages for their livelihood, it is a success almost without attention to the composition of output. Well-paying jobs cutting sugarcane or carnations for export are superior to the hunger of marginal subsistence farming. It may be more desirable to have a well-fed, self-sufficient peasantry with adequate land to feed, clothe, and educate a family, but in many parts of the world, especially in much of Asia, this is not feasible. More productive jobs in the agricultural sector are then the only realistic escape route from rural poverty.

Rural jobs can be created in a wide variety of ways. They can come directly from a project that invests in a new agricultural endeavor, such as a sugar factory, an oil palm plantation, or an intensive livestock feeding operation. Many rural jobs are created, however, in a more roundabout fashion. Derived demand for labor is generated by the expenditure of income from basic agricultural production. Farmers consume some of their own produce directly with little downstream ripple effect on employment, but they also buy many goods and services from rural markets. Depending on the relative prices of those goods and services available for purchase in rural areas, and hence on the composition of demand, the secondary employment impact can be substantial. A strategy that pumps significant purchasing power into rural areas through incentive prices for agricultural produce can have a large, secondary impact on employment generation if other policies on industrial prices and wages are favorable to labor-intensive production of goods and services.

Incentive price policies also influence the second major source of employment in rural areas, wage labor on farms. An incentives-led agricultural development strategy encourages rapid growth in wage labor, and hence in jobs available to the rural landless, if macro policies and agricultural development programs do not offset this impact. Low interest rates, overvalued exchange rates, and direct subsidies to tractors and other labor-saving machinery, for example, can counteract the growth in demand for agricultural labor from higher agricultural prices.

Determining the appropriate degree of mechanization is very complicated. Tractors, for example, can be important to agricultural development in some circumstances. They might increase yields and absorb labor because more timely farm operations might make multiple cropping feasible. Such effects will make them privately profitable without the need for government subsidies. Just as subsidies for fertilizer induced the representative farm household in the tableau to use more fertilizer than was socially optimal, so subsidies to tractors cause farmers to use more tractors than is socially profitable. This is likely to increase their labor-displacing effects and reduce rural employment.

As the social profitability analysis showed, subsidies that distort prices have both production and income effects at the farm level. When important choices of production technique are also affected, subsidies and price distortions can have powerful consequences for employment and income distribution. Government policies in many developing countries have tended to price domestic food below international levels, to favor industry over agriculture, to favor export crops over food grain production, and to favor capital-intensive techniques relative to the employment of labor. The price distortions resulting from such policies have important consequences for the level and composition of agricultural output, rural employment and incomes, and the degree and distribution of hunger.

Social profitability analysis can illuminate and quantify some of these consequences. Not all the information or insight needed to do this analysis is yet in hand. Which prices to use and how to incorporate other food policy objectives into the analysis are topics for the next three chapters. But the social profitability analysis of actual decisions farmers must make year in and year out provides the essential foundation for an agricultural sector strategy that will be consistent with broader food policy objectives.

Elements of a Production Strategy

Four major lessons emerge from the farm decisionmaking analysis and are likely to influence most production strategies, especially when they are incorporated into a broader and consistent food strategy. These lessons include the desirability of broadly based programs for small farm households, the need for government policy to foster appropriate price incentives that increase agricultural output and to generate rapid increases in rural incomes, the importance of technical change for raising productivity and keeping food prices to consumers within reasonable limits, and the efficiency to be achieved by using international markets both as a source of gains from trade and as a measure of opportunity costs in policy deliberations when short-run trade is ruled out for other reasons.

Countries that have emphasized broadly based programs for small farmers have been more successful in achieving both their production and their consumption goals. Bimodal rural systems with a few large, modern farms and many small farms have sometimes achieved agricultural growth, but most have perpetuated or even exacerbated widespread poverty in the countryside. This poverty is the major constraint on solving the problems of hunger and on using new technology to increase agricultural productivity in the long run.

The need to make rapid and multiple decisions in field after field and day after day has also made centralized state farms difficult to manage. Socialist economies have found collective or communal farms less productive than private plots except where farm managers and workers have received clear incentives to improve efficiency of input use. In such circumstances, however, the incentives tend to skew the distribution of income and expose households to greater risk than if output were shared more equally. This tradeoff between incentives to produce efficiently and the distribution of returns, especially to poorer and highly risk-averse households, is not merely a problem for socialist economies, however. It contributes to the basic food price dilemma in market-oriented economies as well.

In these economies, farming systems with a large number of relatively small-scale farms have more effectively generated rural income and achieved a more equal income distribution than have systems of large farms. Given the decentralized nature of agriculture, government policies with respect to prices, both received and paid by farmers, are a crucial element in attempts to create a dynamic rural society. Even in the short run, price responsiveness can be important quantitatively. For the longer run, a continuation of "cheap food" policies, as pursued by many developing countries, is likely to have severely negative production effects. With an appropriate set of price incentives, a country can benefit from a decentralized system of management, where many individual farm households respond to changed economic conditions. Since farmers reap the rewards of good management, income incentives are important in all agricultural systems, both market-oriented and centrally planned.

The profitability of food production is related to technology as well as to prices. Outward shifts in the supply curve arising from technical change are more important to increasing agricultural productivity than are movements along it. Increasing productivity is a primary mechanism for sustaining longer-run profitability in agriculture without having to resort to higher food prices for consumers. For farmers to adopt new technology in response to price incentives, the improved technology must actually be available and appropriate to the ecological setting. Governments play an important role in developing new irrigation systems, fostering research to develop improved, locally adapted seed varieties, and investing in rural infrastructure and marketing to facilitate the flow of productive inputs and output. In the absence of such technical improvements in farming systems constrained by traditional technology, government policies can have only a limited effect in raising agricultural productivity.

Interaction with international markets provides a standard of efficiency for both domestic industry and agriculture. For poor societies, such efficiency is critical to the mobilization of domestic resources to cope with poverty and hunger. Attempts by countries to become completely autarkic and to insulate themselves from international prices have often led to severe price distortions and disincentives within agriculture, with a stagnant rural economy as a result. For every country that followed international price signals too closely and experienced roller coaster instability, there must be ten countries that have not read the signals closely enough and are saddled with inefficient and stagnant rural sectors. Both types of countries are likely to face significant problems of hunger in rural and urban areas, and both need to seek the middle ground defined by a broader food policy perspective.

This broader food policy approach includes reading long-run international market trends and using the signals to measure the efficiency of domestic price policy initiatives. It also includes careful attention to the domestic food marketing sector, which is the primary carrier of both price signals and food commodities from producers to consumers. For many commodities, price formation itself takes place in domestic markets, and these prices influence farmers and consumers and the options available to policymakers as they try to alter decisions made by both. Because of the marketing sector's role in generating and signaling prices, the food policy discussion is inevitably broadened to include other prices important in rural decisionmaking, especially wage rates, interest rates, and foreign exchange rates. Policy for farmers must fit within this broader marketing and macro context. At the same time, however, farm productivity fundamentally conditions the options available to policymakers to achieve a wide range of food policy objectives, including the reduction of hunger.

Bibliographical Note

Much of the vast literature in agricultural economics deals with the analysis of agricultural production systems. The analytical base connecting neoclassical economics with rural resource allocation appears in the classic book by Earl O. Heady, *Economics of Agricultural Production and Resource Use* (Englewood Cliffs, N.J.: Prentice-Hall, 1952). More recent and accessible treatments of how farmers allocate resources are provided by John Doll, V. James Rhodes, and Jerry West, *Economics of Agricultural Production, Markets, and Policy* (Homewood, Ill.: Richard D. Irwin, 1968), and by a set of essays collected by Bock Thiam Tan, Kamphol Adulavidhaya, Indirjit J. Singh, John C. Flinn, and Shao-er Ong, eds., *Improving Farm Management Teaching in Asia* (Bangkok: Agricultural Development Council, 1980). A thorough discussion of social profitability analysis as applied to agriculture is contained in Scott R. Pearson, J. Dirck Stryker, Charles P. Humphreys, and others, *Rice in West Africa: Policy and Economics* (Stanford, Calif.: Stanford University Press, 1981).

Issues involving risk in the agricultural production process are covered extensively in volumes by Jock Anderson, John Dillon, and Brian Hardaker, *Agricultural Decision Analysis* (Ames: Iowa State University Press, 1977), and by James A. Roumasset, Jean-Marc Boussard, and Indirjit J. Singh, *Risk, Uncertainty and Agricultural Development* (Laguna: Southeast Asian Regional Center for Graduate Study and Research in Agriculture, 1979). Both of these books require mathematical competence.

Several excellent books deal specifically with the application of linear programming to decision problems within agriculture. A useful introductory discussion is provided in chapters 2 and 3 of R. C. Agrawal and Earl O. Heady, *Operations Research Methods for Agricultural Decisions* (Ames: Iowa State University Press, 1972). Researchers interested in solution techniques will find the analysis by Raymond R. Beneke and Ronald Winterboer, *Linear Programming Applications to Agriculture* (Ames: Iowa State University Press, 1973), an essential reference. Several examples of policy application of programming methodology are contained in the collection of essays on Pakistan edited by Carl H. Gotsch, "Linear Programming and Agricultural Policy: Micro Studies of the Pakistan Punjab," *Food Research Institute Studies*, vol. 14, no. 1 (1975). Finally, a state-of-the-art volume edited by Louis M. Goreux and Alan Manne, *Multi-Level Planning: Case Studies in Mexico* (Amsterdam: North-Holland, 1973), provides an illustration of how a series of programming tableaux can be connected across farms and regions.

There is an extensive bibliography on supply functions and the price responsiveness of farmers. The initial formulation and empirical application of the Nerlovian distributed lag adjustment model is in Marc Nerlove, *The Dynamics of Supply: Estimation of Farmer's Response to Price* (Baltimore, Md.: Johns Hopkins University Press, 1958). An excellent review of the earlier literature is provided in an essay by Raj Krishna, "Agricultural Price Policy and Economic Development," in Herman M. Southworth and Bruce F. Johnston, eds., *Agricultural Development and Economic Growth* (Ithaca, N.Y.: Cornell University Press, 1967). Recent case studies by the World Bank also illustrate various pricing principles, as in Lucio G. Reca, *Argentina: Country Case Study of Agricultural Prices, Taxes, and Subsidies*, World Bank Staff Working Paper no. 386 (Washington, D.C., 1980), and Carl H. Gotsch and Gilbert Brown, *Prices, Taxes, and Subsidies in Pakistan Agriculture, 1960–1976*, World Bank Staff Working Paper no. 387 (Washington, D.C., 1980). The best summary of empirical estimates of supply elasticities can be found in Hossein Askari and John T. Cummings, *Agricultural Supply Response: A Survey of the Econometric Evidence* (New York: Praeger, 1976). A more theoretical treatment of response is contained in the book by John Dillon, *The Analysis of Response in Crop and Livestock Production*, 2d ed. (Sydney: Pergamon, 1977). A provocative essay by Willis Peterson, "International Farm Prices and the Social Cost of Cheap Food," *American Journal of Agricultural Economics*, vol. 61, no. 1 (1979), and a collection of essays edited by Theodore W. Schultz, *Distortions of Agricultural Incentives* (Bloomington: Indiana University Press, 1978), offer new evidence on the aggregate price elasticity of supply for agriculture.

Although this book on food policy does not deal extensively with benefit-cost techniques for investment projects, agricultural policy analysts will find helpful the manual on project analysis prepared by J. Price Gittinger, *Economic Analysis of Agricultural Projects*, 2d ed. (Baltimore, Md.: Johns Hopkins

University Press, 1982). The Gittinger book, especially if supplemented with additional case materials from the Economics Development Institute of the World Bank, illustrates important production policy issues including shadow prices, discounting, and with/without calculations. Several methodological approaches to dealing with choices of production technique, in the context of case studies, appear in C. Peter Timmer and others, *Choice of Technique in Developing Countries: Some Cautionary Tales*, Occasional Paper no. 32 (Cambridge, Mass.: Harvard Center for International Affairs, 1975).

A huge literature exists on agricultural development strategies. Some of the basic contributions in this field are Theodore W. Schultz, *Transforming Traditional Agriculture* (New Haven, Conn.: Yale University Press, 1964); Arthur T. Mosher, *Getting Agriculture Moving* (New York: Praeger, 1966); John W. Mellor, *The Economics of Agricultural Development* (Ithaca, N.Y.: Cornell University Press, 1966); Clifton W. Wharton, Jr., *Subsistence Agriculture and Economic Development* (Chicago: Aldine, 1969); and Yujiro Hayami and Vernon Ruttan, *Agricultural Development: An International Perspective* (Baltimore, Md.: Johns Hopkins University Press, 1972). The book by Uma J. Lele, *The Design of Rural Development: Lessons from Africa* (Baltimore, Md.: Johns Hopkins University Press, 1975), summarizes much of the World Bank's experience in Africa trying to broaden production strategies to include rural welfare issues. Bruce F. Johnston and Peter Kilby, *Agriculture and Structural Transformation: Economic Strategies in Late-Developing Countries* (New York: Oxford University Press, 1975), discuss bimodal and unimodal agricultural development strategies and emphasize the importance of technical change within a broader strategic vision. This strategic perspective is developed further and broadened in its scope in Bruce F. Johnston and William C. Clark, *Redesigning Rural Development: A Strategic Perspective* (Baltimore, Md.: Johns Hopkins University Press, 1982). An aggressive small-farmer development strategy is articulated in Sterling Wortman and Ralph W. Cummings, Jr., *To Feed This World: The Challenge and the Strategy* (Baltimore, Md.: Johns Hopkins University Press, 1978). The role of agriculture as a resource reservoir is summarized in the introduction to Lloyd G. Reynolds, ed., *Agriculture in Development Theory* (New Haven, Conn.: Yale University Press, 1975).

A small book by Arthur T. Mosher, *An Introduction to Agricultural Extension* (Singapore: Agricultural Development Council, Singapore University Press, 1978), is extremely useful. Data collection procedures relevant for the Mosher framework are covered in a new manual published by the International Maize and Wheat Improvement Center (CIMMYT), *Planning Techniques Appropriate to Farmers: Concepts and Procedures* (Mexico City, 1980). The international data needed to supplement the analysis of this chapter can be found in many sources, but the monthly *Food Outlook* series of the Food and Agriculture Organization of the United Nations is among the most helpful.

4

Marketing Functions, Markets, and Food Price Formation

The food marketing sector transforms the raw agricultural commodities produced by farmers into the foods purchased and eaten by consumers. The costs of storage, transportation, and processing—the marketing transformations—are an integral component of food price formation. Because the producer and consumer are typically different individuals even in developing countries, commodities must pass from one owner to another, frequently many times, before reaching the family table. This process of exchange takes place in markets and can be conducted only when a price has been agreed on between buyer and seller. In any but a purely subsistence economy, these three topics are inextricably linked—the productive functions of marketing, the role of the market as an arena of exchange, and the formation of food prices at which exchange takes place. For both socialist and capitalist economies, it is impossible to discuss any one of these without at least implicitly discussing the others as well.

This chapter is designed to provide food policy analysts with an understanding of all three topics. It employs the same general structure that was used to present the analysis of food consumption and production: an introduction to the issues that make marketing, markets, and price formation important to food policy analysts; a guide to the data needed to describe and understand the marketing sector and price formation; an outline of the theoretical perspectives and empirical techniques of analysis that permit analysts to reach rough judgments on the extent and social costs of inefficiencies in marketing and distortions in price formation; and a summary of the instruments available for government intervention in both marketing and price formation and a policy discussion of the likely costs and benefits of such interventions.

For the sake of convenience, the term "marketing" will be used inclusively to refer to all three topics treated in this chapter, and much of the discussion will be oriented toward those economies that use markets to determine prices and allocate resources. The term "marketing functions" is used to refer specifically to the commodity transformations in time, space, and form that are associated with storage, transportation, and processing. These functions must be performed in socialist and capitalist economies alike. Even in socialist economies, prices provide producers and consumers with signals about how to allocate their inputs and household budgets. Consequently, how socialist economies set their prices and what impact they have are important analytical questions. Because marketing encompasses so many activities that are at the core of all food systems, understanding the full range of marketing issues is a central task for food policy analysis.

Marketing Issues

Just as with food production, marketing is a means to an end. The objectives a society can reasonably hold for its marketing sector are analogous to the four basic objectives for the food system as a whole: efficient economic growth, a more equal distribution of incomes, nutritional well-being, and food security. Because it links the production and consumption sectors, marketing can contribute to all four objectives through the efficiency with which it communicates signals of scarcity and abundance to decisionmakers. Because it is the source of productive activities involving many jobs, marketing can contribute directly to economic growth, income distribution, and nutritional objectives. Because of its capacity to link domestic markets to international markets and to provide signals to policymakers concerning food shortages, the marketing sector is integral to the design of mechanisms to improve food security.

Why is it, then, that marketing activities are frequently thought to be unnecessary and against the interests of society, especially the interests of poor people in developing countries? The labels "middleman" and "speculator" almost universally carry negative connotations or actual opprobrium. The tendency is too widespread to be attributed wholly to a bad press. In fact, markets do not always function in the best interests of a broad cross section of society, especially in poor countries where communications and transportation facilities are poor, markets are highly segmented, and access for marketing participants is greatly restricted, sometimes to particular ethnic groups. Highly unequal financial bargaining power is often brought to the exchange relationship between seller and buyer. In short, the efficiency and economic gains potentially available from successful market coordination of a society's food system are an empirical issue, not a matter of faith and logic.

Because the public image of marketing is so negative, especially in most developing countries, it is important for the food policy analyst to determine how effectively marketing institutions and marketing agents are performing their dual roles of transforming commodities in time, space, and form while reflecting relative abundance and scarcity through the price signals communicated to producers and consumers. These price signals can be generated in the process of exchange in markets, in which case the competitiveness and efficiency of the markets must be examined. Alternatively, if governments set these prices to reflect other criteria and objectives, their effectiveness and costs in other dimensions must be examined.

Elements of Market Efficiency and Market Failure

Markets are the arena for two important tasks required in all societies: the physical marketing functions, and the communication of signals to producers and consumers about the costs of buying something or the benefits of selling it. Governments concerned about equal distribution of economic welfare to all citizens are understandably loathe to allow those price signals to be generated by anonymous market forces when the values of such important commodities as food and fuel, for example, or services, especially labor, are at stake.

A shortage of food means high prices in a market economy, with only the well-to-do able to purchase it. A food shortage in a socialist economy means rationing, with perhaps long lines and little choice about what goes into the food basket. In the short run, the socialist approach may deal more effectively with hunger, but hunger is also a long-run problem of development and efficient use of resources. Here the allocative role of prices becomes important, in addition to their role in income distribution. Much of the chapter is devoted to understanding the tension between these two roles. The last section seeks ways to improve the efficiency of allocation by using appropriate price signals without relinquishing all food distribution authority to the free workings of the market.

COMPETITION AND THE NUMBER OF MARKET PARTICIPANTS. Virtually all of the positive welfare implications of market coordination are derived from economists' models that use "perfect competition" assumptions to drive the logic of decisionmaking behavior on the part of market participants. Competition is a powerful force in economies. It is the "invisible hand" that guides private self-interest into maximizing social welfare. For competition to play this powerful role, however, there must be an adequate number of participants on both sides of the exchange relationship so that no single agent can significantly influence the outcome of the exchange. The only time the condition is clearly violated is when only a single participant sits on one side or the other. Even two sellers can provide strong competition for each other if they compete. Alternatively, twenty sellers may not be competitive if a mutual understanding exists about their appropriate market behavior. Very large numbers of participants—millions of farmers and millions of consumers—guarantee competitiveness at each end of the food system. The issue is the number of participants in the chain in between and the potential access of additional participants if the returns to providing marketing services rise above the level dictated by competitive equilibrium.

The farmer is concerned to get the highest possible price for the output to be sold (or the lowest possible price for the inputs to be purchased) for a given level of ancillary conditions, such as credit, speed of payment, and discounts for moisture. The farmer must determine which marketing agent to sell to. The more agents there are competing to buy the farmer's grain, the better the information available to the farmer about the prevailing price and the easier it is to switch from one buyer to another whose terms are relatively better. Where there are many potential secondary buyers, such as rice mills or export firms, many farm-level buying agents will offer the farmer great freedom of choice. If only a single end buyer exists, as in the case of pineapples for canning, the farmer may have little choice but to sell to the buyer from the cannery or to take a very large discount in a small local fruit market. Identifying the farmer's range of choice at the initial point of sale is the first step in understanding how competitive price formation is likely to be.

A similar approach holds at the opposite end of the marketing chain, where consumers buy foods for home consumption. Individual consumers have no influence over the prices they pay, but if many alternative retail stalls offer similar commodities and services, the freedom of consumers to choose one retailer over another prevents excess profits from high margins accruing to the retail marketing agents. If only a single retailer is available for miles around, the potential for high profits is great. In such circumstances the analyst must wonder why other retailers do not join the action. If significant barriers to entry impede the addition of more retailers, government steps to improve access to retail trade may pay considerable dividends to food consumers. If the monopoly position is caused by government regulations or is held by the government itself, the impact on consumers through reduced freedom of choice and higher prices must be balanced against any potential benefits that result from the government's role.

TRANSFER OF OWNERSHIP AND THE BALANCE OF MARKET POWER. When both seller and buyer agree on the terms of a sale, a price is established for the exchange. Both parties must be satisfied, but who actually decides what the price will be? Economists have been puzzled by this question for centuries. Some have invented quite fanciful arrangements, such as Leon Walras's auctioneer who permitted recontracting among parties until overall equilibrium was reached. Kenneth Arrow's suggestion is more relevant to the issues here. He sees all exchange relationships as having at least small elements of monopoly, or market, power on one side of the exchange or the other. Each exchange is to some extent unique because each party has barriers of time and distance between an alternative exchange party. Each party comes to the exchange with different knowledge about the characteristics of the underlying market forces for the item of exchange. Arrow argues that the party with the relatively greater knowledge actually sets the initial price. The other party then decides whether to accept or reject the offered or posted price. If little competition exists, there will be little pressure to set the posted price close to the actual costs of offering the product in that time, place, and form. Heavy competition, however, improves the other party's knowledge of market conditions, and it forces an adjustment in posted price by either direct negotiation or the patronizing of alternative dealers.

In such a framework of price formation, market knowledge is market power. One of the most important steps governments can take to improve the fairness of market price formation so that it discriminates less against the small farmer at one end and the consumer at the other is to provide these individuals with timely and accurate information about actual market conditions. Such information enables them to bargain more equally with purchasing agents or retailers who are naturally intent on widening their margins whenever possible. More equal balance of knowledge provides a more equal distribution of the gains from efficient market price formation.

EFFICIENCY OF PRICE FORMATION. Prices are formed efficiently when large numbers of buyers and sellers, all with similar access to relevant market information, interact to agree on a basis of exchange, a price. This price sends signals to consumers about the resource costs of supplying the commodity to them. It simultaneously sends signals to producers about the willingness of consumers to pay the resource costs of production. Efficient price formation is essential to the efficient allocation of resources in a market-directed economy.

This picture of price formation is essentially static, or at most it captures a sequence of static equilibria. However, expectations about future conditions are also likely to be important in the actual formation of prices. If expectations are precisely fulfilled in each period, a perfectly predictable dynamic pattern of prices results. Of course, the real world is never so accommodating. The essence of the interaction between expectations and price formation is that some market participants' expectations about the future are constantly being contradicted as new market information becomes available. In what amounts to a continuing wager against alternative expectations, large sums of money are made and lost when drought hits or bumper crops roll in.

Is this somehow inefficient? It is tempting to think that governments should simply set prices for basic grains (and other important commodities) at some "fair" level and prohibit the kind of trading that leads to speculative gains and losses. The capital tied up in such trading could be put to more productive social use through investments in factories or dams. Alas, this approach fails to recognize the dual role of dynamic price formation. It integrates information about future crops and alternative supplies, demand pressures, and storage costs to allocate the supplies in hand to future time periods. At the same time, the temporal pattern of prices established, or the price expectations formed, signal producers, consumers, and the suppliers of storage as to the opportunity costs of their production, consumption, and storage decisions.

Failure to receive accurate signals about these opportunity costs can cause enormous misallocation of resources in food production and consumption and very serious disruptions to the smooth temporal flow of food supplies to consumers. Many socialist economies, for example, try to use markets as a vehicle for achieving short-run efficiency in the distribution of goods in the economy while the government determines price signals that the markets will reflect to producers and consumers. Such government-set price signals in command economies tend to communicate in only one direction, from the top down. When the price signals fail to reflect the opportunity costs to the society of actual production and consumption decisions, no mechanism communicates this information back up to the price control commission. As the signals become more and more unbalanced, they frequently lead to severe shortages in the food system, as in Poland, or to massive budget subsidies for food producers or consumers, as in Egypt and China. Truncating the dynamic aspects of price formation caused by expectations also hobbles the mechanisms that produce static efficiency in the allocation of resources. It is not possible to have one without the other.

MARKET FAILURE. For all of its efficiency in allocating economic resources, a competitive market economy cannot accomplish some important social goals without careful government intervention. Some of these broader goals also relate to economic efficiency; others concern the distribution of income, nutritional well-being, and security of the society and its food supplies.

Even competitive markets with efficient price formation fail to provide a socially efficient allocation of resources if externalities exist within the economic system. Unfortunately, the food system is full of externalities. Irrigation decisions upstream affect water supplies downstream. Privately profitable applications of pesticides have consequences for public health and for the environment. When farmers cultivate hillsides and marginal lands in pursuit of food for their families (for example, on Java) or profits (for example, in Nebraska), soils erode. Major changes in food policy by large countries in the world food system, such as the U.S.S.R., the United States, and China, have an impact on producers and consumers in other countries.

The existence of such externalities and the failure of market-determined outcomes to provide efficient solutions are reasons for the analysis and design of food policies where government is an important participant in the food system. At the same time, an understanding of these factors should provide insight into the areas of economic resource allocation in which markets do an efficient job and government intervention is likely to make matters worse, not better. Rather than telling farmers how much pesticide to use and trying to enforce the rule, pesticide prices might be set to reflect full social costs. Incentives to plant crops that cause less soil erosion or replanting schemes to stabilize barren lands may be more effective than police action to prevent farmers from cultivating hillsides or villagers from poaching firewood from public lands.

The tension between intervening in markets and letting markets work is very strong in most countries. Intervention is frequently predicated on the existence of market externalities. In the context of a careful empirical understanding of the quantitative impact of such externalities, their existence does indeed call for specific government intervention. Typically, however, such interventions call for a scalpel rather than a sword.

Private market economies also fail to provide adequate quantities of public goods, such as national defense, police protection, scientific research, even roads and education. These "goods" all yield benefits to the population at large that cannot be priced and directly charged to the users by the (private) suppliers. An important role for government is to use general tax revenues to provide such public goods in socially optimal amounts.

Certain components of the food system are like public goods. Agricultural research is no doubt the most important, and governments of virtually all countries accept responsibility for financing agricultural research and adapting it to local environments. Rural education, roads, and communications networks all have at least an element of public good in their supply and demand and hence call for a government program to supplement private supplies.

Many observers regard the entire food marketing system as a public good because of the synergies and interdependence among its various components. A smoothly functioning marketing system depends on the simultaneous availability and interaction of these components: efficient communications, transportation, and storage facilities; common grades and standards to facilitate trading at a distance; legal codes to enforce contracts; credit availability to finance short-run inventories and processing operations; and a market information system to keep all market participants, from farmers to consumers, fairly and accurately informed about market trends. No private investor could hope to capture the total gains from the interactive synergy of this system, and individual investments in pieces of the system do not produce the overall synergy. Consequently, a vision of the ultimate productivity of an efficient marketing system provides a powerful impetus for extensive government involvement in the design, construction, and possibly the operation of the food marketing system.

Such a vision has much to recommend it. But it is not a vision that is easily put in focus by looking at the food marketing systems of the United States or Western Europe. The efficient functioning of marketing systems is particularly sensitive to local, cultural, and social conditions and especially to the local availability of resources. These resources include labor and capital, of course, but for marketing systems they also include managerial, administrative, and entrepreneurial resources, which are in very short supply for most governments. Consequently, massive government efforts to "modernize" food marketing sectors, especially if private investment and participation are not included, are likely to run afoul of the very complexity of the system itself.

It is well understood by both economists and politicians that the efficient outcome of market forces does not necessarily imply a satisfactory distribution of income or of food consumption. Most economists would like to "fix" the income distribution with some sort of neutral income transfer via the government budget, rather than alter prices for important commodities that influence the distribution of economic welfare. This approach preserves the efficiency of the market solution by not distorting producer or consumer choices, but most government policymakers find it impossible in practice. A typical response has been to use government interventions not to transfer income directly to poor people, but to alter important prices that significantly affect real incomes, because governments have more short-run control over prices than over individual incomes.

In the name of improving income distribution and the adequacy of food intake, therefore, many governments try to keep food prices low, wage rates high, interest rates low, and imports cheap through an overvalued foreign exchange rate. All these prices do have important implications for the real income of virtually everyone in a society, but they also are absolutely critical as signals for the efficient allocation of resources. Here again is the dilemma over the short-run welfare of the population, especially the poor whose food consumption can least stand to be reduced, and the longer-run efficiency of resource allocation that comes from allowing the scarcity of commodities and factors of production to be reflected in the prices paid for their consumption or use. This dilemma appears repeatedly in this book. The elements of a resolution are assembled in the consumption and production chapters, while the vehicles for their implementation are analyzed later in this chapter. First, the task of analyzing marketing functions, markets, and price formation lies ahead.

Marketing Functions and Price Formation

Suppose the farmer represented in the tableau of chapter 3 chose the optimal technique and has just harvested 6 tons of rice in Season I. Three questions are now pressing: how much rice should be sold (and how much kept for home consumption), what price will it bring, and who will buy it? These questions lead straight to the heart of the marketing issues, for answering them begins the process of understanding how rice harvested in the farmer's field is transformed into a meal of rice to be consumed in another time and place.

The farm family is both a producer and a consumer. How much rice will this farm household wish to consume? In terms of consumption, the most important determinants of the answer will be habits, income, and rice prices relative to other staple food prices. But when marketing considerations are added, the issue becomes complicated because the farm household income *depends* on the price of rice. In some circumstances a higher price for rice could lead the farmer to consume greater amounts because of a strong income effect. Most empirical evidence suggests, however, that farm families have negatively sloped demand curves for the foodstuffs they grow. Although perhaps less elastic in response to price changes than those of nonfarmers living in rural areas where a wide choice of foodstuffs is available, the demand curves of most farmers slope downward like the one shown in figure 4-1. Both the vertical postharvest supply function and the demand function are depicted for a representative farmer. Naturally, the supply function for future periods would be expected to have a positive slope, reflecting the farmer's ability and willingness to expand output in the face of greater price incentives.

With the farmer's rice supply fixed in the short run by the size of the harvest and with the quantity to be consumed at home determined by the market price for rice, the amount the farmer is willing to sell to the market will also be a function of that market price. At high rice prices the farmer prefers to consume somewhat less rice (and more corn, wheat, cassava, or other staples that are relatively cheaper when rice prices are high) and consequently is able to sell more rice. The amount offered to the market, the difference between the fixed supply Q_h and household consumption, is a rising function of price (at least up to the total available supply Q_h) and is shown in figure 4-1 by the dashed excess supply curve. This line reflects the amount of rice the farmer will offer to the market at each market price and is constructed by subtracting household rice consumption, itself a negative function of the market rice price, from the farmer's rice production. The excess supply curve relates the farmer's market sales of rice to the price received. If the market price is P_m, the farmer sells Q_s and consumes Q_c. The geometry of the excess supply curve guarantees that Q_s plus Q_c equals Q_h.

From whom does the farmer receive this "market price"? Although economists are prone to think of exchange and price formation as neutral concepts which happen automatically, market participants know better. Marketing agents are real people making decisions designed to improve their economic well-being (and contributing to economic output in the process). The farmer must find someone to buy the rice, or some marketing agent must find the farmer.

What motivates such a marketing agent? By purchasing an amount Q_s of the farmer's rough rice in the farmer's field at an agreed market price P_m, the agent hopes to do one or more of three things. First, the agent might transport the rough rice to a bulking point or a rice mill and resell it im-

Figure 4-1. Short-run Supply and Demand Curves
for a Representative Rice Farmer

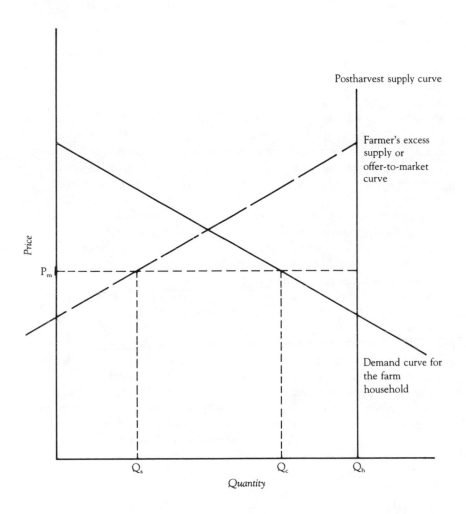

mediately, hoping to recover in the resale price a margin for the effort and
the risk involved in the transaction, for the rice mill may not be willing to
pay more than the agent paid the farmer.

Second, the agent might have a rice mill nearby. When the rice is milled,
it becomes more valuable to consumers, who prefer to eat milled rice instead
of paddy or brown rice. If the willingness of consumers to pay more for milled
rice is sufficiently great, the marketing agent might be able to recover the
costs incurred for the rough rice when it was purchased from the farmer, plus
an adequate margin to pay the full costs of processing, including a return for
investment costs and risks.

Third, the agent might store the rice in a warehouse and hope to sell it for a higher price later in the year, after the abundant harvest supplies have been absorbed. This process involves even more risk, for the agent must pay additional costs to store the rice—interest on the money invested in the rice, handling the rice as it is moved in and out of the warehouse, rental costs (or maintenance and depreciation charges) for the warehouse, losses while the rice is in storage, and insurance against fire and other hazards. When the rice is removed from storage, there is no guarantee that the agent will be able to sell it for a price sufficiently higher than the price paid to cover these costs plus a return for the time, effort, and risk involved. If the price is too low to cover these costs fully, the agent is likely to stop buying rice for storage or to offer the farmer a lower price at the next harvest. Although each of these functions—transportation, processing, and storage—was treated independently, the same agent could be involved in any or all of them.

COSTS AND PRICES. It is apparent that an array of prices for rice is being formed during the performance of the marketing functions. Consumers express a willingness to buy milled rice via their demand curves, farmers express a willingness to sell rough rice through their excess supply curves, and marketing agents connect the two parties by being willing, for an economic return to their time, capital, and risk-taking, to pay the farm price and to transport, store, and process the rice in order to sell it to the consumer in the time, place, and form desired. Prices are determined at each stage of this complicated marketing process. Although it is possible to get lost in the complexity, it is important to understand the basic forces that explain this process of price determination in markets. The example presented here focuses on temporal price formation, that is, the relationship between prices during the harvest and prices during the "short" season before new supplies from the next harvest become available. The transportation and processing functions can also be understood within this framework. They are held in abeyance for the moment in order to concentrate on the essence of price formation and its effects on quantities supplied and demanded in each period.

Figure 4-2 carries forward by two steps the analysis of the supply, demand, and market offers of the representative farmer shown in figure 4-1. First, figure 4-2 deals with market aggregates rather than an individual farmer. Consequently, the farm market supply function (offer curve) during the harvest period shown on the right side of figure 4-2 is the sum of all farmers' offer curves at each possible harvest period price P_h. It is positively sloped in the short run because farmers consume less rice at higher prices. In the longer run it will be even more elastically sloped because farmers will also react to higher prices by increasing output. The market demand curve for rice during the harvest period, also shown on the right side of figure 4-2, reflects the willingness of consumers to buy rice from the market at various prices (it is net of farm consumption from retained supplies). If this were all

Figure 4-2. A Back-to-back Supply and Demand Framework
for Understanding Seasonal Price Formation

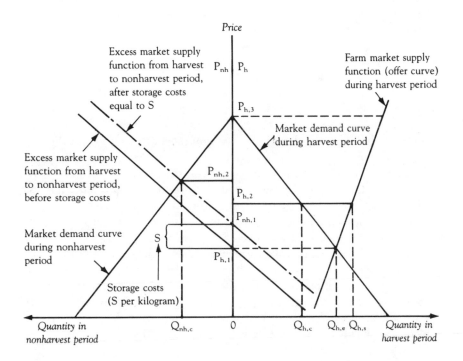

there was to the story, competitive forces in the market would be expected
to bring about an equilibrium where both consumers and farmers were satisfied
with the available price-quantity relationship. In this example, the supply
and demand curves intersect at $P_{h,1}$ and $Q_{h,e}$.

But there is more to the story. The left side of figure 4-2 introduces the
second step into the analysis by showing that consumers wish to eat rice even
during the time it is not being harvested. By arbitrarily dividing the rice
calendar into two periods, a harvest and a nonharvest period, figure 4-2 is
able to show the supply, demand, and price consequences of linking the two
periods through the storage function. The vertical axis measures the price of
rice for both periods, for the harvest period extending to the right and for
the nonharvest period extending to the left. The right side of the horizontal
axis measures quantities in the usual way of a supply and demand diagram;
the quantity increases from the origin to the right. To the left, however,
quantities are measured by reflection, as in a mirror image. Increasing quantities are shown by moving to the left of the origin, and so the nonharvest
period demand curve must slope down to the left, as a mirror image of the
demand curve during the harvest period. Because the two supply and demand

diagrams in price-quantity dimensions are placed next to each other with a common price axis, such figures are called back-to-back diagrams. Their usefulness will become apparent when the opportunity to save rice from the harvest period for consumption in the nonharvest period is considered.

No rice is produced in the nonharvest period—on the left side of figure 4-2. At all prices (within a normal range) during the nonharvest period, zero supplies from production are forthcoming. But with zero supplies and substantial demand for rice, prices in the nonharvest period would skyrocket. If prices in the nonharvest period are sufficiently higher than in the harvest period, someone, a marketing agent, is likely to take the risk of purchasing rice during the harvest and storing it for later sale at the higher price in the nonharvest period.

Figure 4-2 shows how this process works. In the figure, S equals the costs per kilogram that a marketing agent will incur to store rice from the harvest to the nonharvest period. These storage costs include a suitable reward for time, effort, opportunity costs of capital invested, and return for risk-taking. If costs equal to S are actually covered by the difference in price between the two periods, the marketing agent will be willing to continue these activities year after year. If the price difference is less than S, some marketing agents will find it unprofitable to continue in business as transfer agents between the harvest and nonharvest periods. If the price difference is greater than S, the agents will expand their storage operations, and others may join the activity. Figure 4-2 is constructed on the assumption that the price rise will just equal the storage costs S.

It is now possible to see where supplies will come from in the nonharvest period despite the total lack of production. Speculators—the name for marketing agents who buy when the price is low in the hope that it will rise after the harvest—will be willing to supply from storage an amount of rice that depends on the relative market prices prevailing in the two periods. The two prices must be different by the cost of storing rice from one period to the next. In figure 4-2 the nonharvest price $P_{nh,1}$ is higher than the equivalent harvest price $P_{h,1}$ by the storage costs S.

$P_{h,1}$ is a particularly important price. If it were to prevail during the harvest period, as indicated above, harvest period market supplies would equal harvest period market demand, and no rice would be available for purchase by speculators for storage. In the absence of storage costs, the excess market supply curve for the nonharvest period would start at zero quantities for price $P_{h,1}$ in the harvest period. Consequently, no rice would be available for consumption in the nonharvest period, and consumers then would have to find other sources of food or go hungry. If speculators bid up the harvest period price to a level higher than $P_{h,1}$, however, consumer demand in that period would be less, market supplies forthcoming from farmers would be greater, and speculators would move the excess supplies into storage for later sale and consumption in the nonharvest period. The amount of these excess supplies available for the second period is a function of the price prevailing in the harvest period.

The excess market supply function from harvest period to nonharvest period shown in figure 4-2 reflects this price-quantity relationship. The solid line shows the excess supplies available in the nonharvest period before storage costs are incurred. The dashed line shows the supplies available in the nonharvest period after the costs of storage S have been paid. For each price-quantity relationship showing excess supply at a price during the harvest period, the dashed line shows the equivalent price that must prevail in the nonharvest period to cover the costs of storage.

What happens? This equilibrium price-quantity relationship, shown in figure 4-2 at $P_{nh,2}$ and $Q_{nh,c}$, can be located by determining the price at which the excess supply available in the nonharvest period is equal to the demand during the period. Then, because the harvest price must be lower than the nonharvest price by the costs of storage, the harvest price is located at $P_{h,2}$. From this price the decisions of consumers and farmers in the harvest period can be determined. In the example shown, market demand will be $Q_{h,c}$ and market supplies will be $Q_{h,s}$. The difference between the amounts supplied and demanded is $Q_{h,s}$ minus $Q_{h,c}$, which must equal the amounts stored and consumed in the nonharvest period, $Q_{nh,c}$. The excess supply curve is constructed so that this is precisely what happens. The construction is easy with the linear supply and demand curves in the example. It can be quite complicated with more complex shapes.

THE MARKET PERSPECTIVE. Figure 4-2 shows that marketing functions and price formation are simultaneously connected. One affects the other. If storage costs rise because, for example, interest rates rise, the price of rice will be higher in the nonharvest period than before and lower in the harvest period. These price changes will affect total supplies available and the allocation of those supplies between consumers in the two periods. To continue the example, the higher storage costs would cause marketed supplies in the harvest period to fall, as farmers faced lower prices. Harvest period consumers would buy more because they also face lower prices. The entire burden of reduced supplies would fall on nonharvest consumers through the higher prices in the second period. Chapter 2 noted the potential nutritional significance of reduced consumption during nonharvest periods of high seasonal prices. Figure 4-2 shows why high seasonal prices are an essential element in supplying food to the short season in the first place. In the absence of subsidies to reduce the real economic costs of storage, the seasonal price rise and reduced seasonal consumption are necessary to have any food at all in the nonharvest period.

Marketing functions can thus be seen as the essential link between producers and consumers in two very different and yet simultaneous and connected ways. First, the marketing agents link producers and consumers physically, by actually buying, storing, transporting, processing, and selling commodities. Those societies that lack adequate numbers of such marketing agents know best their value. Empty stores and markets, long queues, furtive dealings on side streets or in back rooms testify to the valuable equilibrating role provided by marketing agents as they balance their purchase, transformation, and sales decisions against the likely economic reward. Simultaneously, however, because exchange of commodities is taking place, open or implicit price signals are being generated and transmitted to the active economic agents in the food system, influencing their production and consumption decisions. And by the cumulative reverberations of those decisions back on the marketing agents, and back on price formation, and back on decisionmaking, and so on in the endless repetitive flows characteristic of economies with markets, a dynamic equilibrium process is established by which resources are allocated both to goods the consumers most want and to areas where the resources are most productive in the farm system that supplies the goods.

Because socialist economies tend to use marketing systems in one direction only, the information generated by imbalances in the exchange markets is largely lost as signals to producers and consumers below and to policymakers above. To be sure, parallel markets in rural areas, or even gray-to-black markets in urban areas, transmit some of this information on relative scarcity. Such informal markets provide much of the food and rural income in a few economies where official prices and rigid market regulations have driven supplies underground. The point is not the failure of state interventions in marketing and price formation, although it happens often enough, but rather the importance of the information generated in markets for the efficient use of a society's economic and human resources.

Understanding the Marketing System

When markets work, the automatic adjustment processes perform an awesome task of coordination with a minimum of fuss, and economic resources are allocated efficiently. When markets fail, participants with inside information and economic power are able to exploit both producers and consumers, to the special detriment of the poor at each end. The task of this chapter is to help analysts know when markets are working, identify markets that are failing and understand why, and determine which government interventions would improve both the efficiency of market operations and the distribution of gains generated when markets work efficiently.

The questions of most importance in the marketing sector—the costs and efficiency of providing marketing services and the dynamic capacity of the system to create and transmit signals about incentives to producers and consumers that are consistent with resource availabilities and long-run structural transformation—are not easy to answer. Because direct approaches are frequently constrained by unavailable or unreliable data, indirect approaches that rely on normative competitive models are often used to provide additional insight. In such circumstances, no direct listing of the data needed can lead straight to the analytical techniques. A constant interplay is necessary between the availability and reliability of data on the one hand and the analytical approach used to address important marketing questions on the other.

A number of empirical questions are addressed in analyzing marketing systems. What are the marketing channels for important commodities and who are the participants? What are the costs, margins, and profits that result from this process? What do price data at various levels of the marketing system reveal about the process of price formation and the degree of connection among markets? How are international market prices determined and how do they influence domestic price formation?

As with both consumption and production data, published sources provide the analyst with an efficient first cut at the task of understanding how the marketing system works. But data from field observations, even informal weekend surveys, add critical flavor and insight into the mechanisms that generate published statistics. For example, riding with a bag of rice as it changes hands repeatedly between the farm gate and retail stall and understanding all the decisions made along the way will guarantee the analyst a better perspective on market decisionmaking and price formation than a host of statistical analyses done in the office.

Elements of a Competitive Market

One indirect way to measure market efficiency is to ask whether the elements of a competitive market are present in the marketing system under study. These elements include the following set of conditions: items of the traded commodity are fungible (interchangeable) and divisible; buyers and sellers act in an economically rational fashion (they want more, not less, incomes and goods); firms are small and numerous enough that their decisions have no impact on prices; all participants have equal access to activities of the market on the same terms; and everyone has complete knowledge of forces likely to influence supply and demand.

If these five conditions—divisibility, rationality, small firms, equal access, and complete knowledge—characterize a marketing system, the market will perform efficiently with no scope for excess profits. Fulfillment of these conditions is sufficient, but not necessary, for a market to be competitive. For example, price formation can occur efficiently in a market where only three or four large firms are selling or buying if these firms compete rather than collude with one another. The main difficulty with this indirect approach, therefore, is how to determine from a survey of market participants whether the system is operating under circumstances that approximate the competitive ideal closely enough to rule out collusion and excess profits.

Of the five conditions needed for a competitive market, two are usually not at issue in food crop marketing. Divisibility is a characteristic of nearly all food commodities, and virtually all market participants react appropriately to economic signals. The third condition, numerous small firms, is also a feature of most marketing systems in developing countries unless the government has created an effective parastatal monopoly or has policies restricting the access of new entrants to the marketing system. Large-scale export marketing firms are sometimes an important exception.

The principal focus is on the conditions of market access and knowledge. Because no system can have perfectly equal access and complete information, the matter is one of degree, that is, whether entry is free enough and information is good enough for the market to work with a reasonable degree of competitiveness—enough to bring about an efficient result. Much can be learned from surveys that inquire about modes of entry into trade (periods of apprenticeship, capital requirements, and age distributions of merchants) and about market information (credit arrangements and risk sharing, bargaining positions of farmers at the first point of sale, and sources of price information for nearby and distant wholesale markets).

Ease of entry into the marketing system (as a petty trader or operator of a small-scale rice mill, for example), in combination with reasonably accessible market information, carries a strong presumption of a competitively efficient marketing system. If the marketing system is characterized by limited access and information, government efforts to provide wider access to working capital, better gathering and dissemination of price statistics and information about crop conditions, or the dissolution of state-sanctioned market-area monopolies may well improve market efficiency.

To find out how many traders are operating in a marketing system, and at what points a commodity changes hands, it is helpful to sketch its flow through the marketing chain. The competitiveness of a market and the structure of the marketing chain are obviously related. If at some point in the chain only a single buyer or seller exists, then noncompetitive behavior is likely. Alternatively, the presence of many active buyers and sellers all along the chain carries a strong presumption of competitive behavior and efficient market performance.

Market Flows and Participants: Marketing Chains

Construction of food crop marketing chains helps organize the links between production and consumption. Some typical marketing chains for a commodity are shown in the following tabulation:

1. Farmer $\underbrace{S,P,T}$ rural consumer

2. Farmer ___S,P,T___, rural retailer ___T___, rural consumer

3. Farmer ___S,T___, resident processor or assembler ___P,S,T___,
   rural retailer ___T___, rural consumer

4. Farmer ___S,T___, resident processor or retailer ___P,S,T___,
   nonresident wholesaler ___S,T___, urban consumer

5. Farmer ___S,T___, nonresident wholesaler ___P,S,T___,
   urban wholesaler or consumer

where T = transfer operation, such as transportation or exchange of own-ership; P = processing activity; and S = storage function.

Estimating volumes and percentages of commodity transformations at each link in the chain provides an overview of the marketing system's structure. How much of total production do farmers sell, and how much is sold directly to rural consumers (marketing chain 1)? How much is sold to rural retailers in a nearby marketplace (chain 2)? How much is sold to resident processors or assemblers, who then sell either to rural retailers in the region (chain 3) or to nonresident wholesalers for shipment to urban markets (chain 4)? How much is sold to nonresident wholesalers who travel to producing areas to buy supplies for urban markets (chain 5)?

Using formal or informal market surveys, the analyst attempts to replace the arrows in the marketing chains with quantities or percentages, as for the rice marketing chain shown in figure 4-3. In this example, farmers sold 50 percent of their marketings to local assemblers, 40 percent to local processors, and 5 percent each to district assemblers and processors. These quantities then moved on through the system until 85 percent was exported from the district and 15 percent was consumed locally.

Marketing chain diagrams thus specify market linkages that connect one price series to another to determine, for instance, whether rural food prices are influenced by urban demand or whether expectations of high preharvest prices work back to influence the harvest price. Knowing when and where the crops are sold, their transportation and storage destinations, and who the ultimate consumer is permits the analyst to specify the likely causal direction of market connections.

Marketing Costs and Margins

Large marketing margins—the spread between farm prices and consumer prices—can occur for two reasons: either high real marketing costs cause consumer prices to be much higher than farm prices or monopolistic elements in the marketing system are earning excess profits. Both a direct and an indirect approach can be used to determine whether there are excess profits and serious inefficiency in food crop marketing or whether wide margins are

Figure 4-3. Marketing Chain for Rice, Atebubu District, Ghana

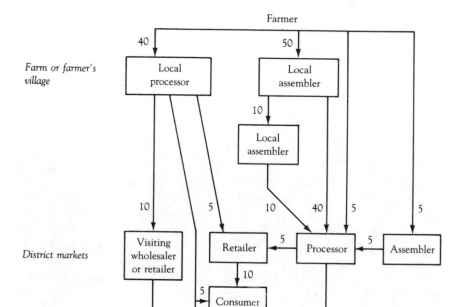

Note: Amounts represent percentage of total marketings.
Source: V. Roy Southworth, "Food Crop Marketing in Atebubu District, Ghana," Ph.D. dissertation, Stanford University, 1981.

due to high real costs which might be reduced through appropriate government investment in marketing infrastructure. Because of serious data restrictions in most circumstances, both approaches—one that looks at costs, the other at prices and price margins—are usually needed to allow cross-checking with each other.

MEASURING MARKETING COSTS. The direct approach looks at the three marketing functions whose combined costs constitute the marketing margin. This kind of efficiency analysis of marketing has clear analogues with that of any productive activity, including agricultural production. Such empirical applications, however, are usually difficult and sometimes out of reach because data requirements are very demanding.

Records are needed of representative costs and returns from the main participants in transportation (merchants, transporters, and brokers), processing, and storage. Analysts estimate the costs of all inputs, including management costs. Subtracting costs from returns then gives profits at each level of the system. An example of a marketing margin for rice in Ghana is presented in table 4-1. In the example, farmers received 70 percent of the urban retail price, and net returns to assemblers, processors, and retailers each ranged between 4.6 and 6.5 percent of the urban retail price.

Table 4-1. Average Marketing Margins for Rice Produced in Atebubu District and Retailed in Kumasi, Ghana, January through July 1977

Item	Cedis per ton[a]	Percentage of retail price
Atebubu market wholesale price[b]	2,216.93	83.0
Producer price[c]	1,894.38	70.9
Assemblers' gross margin	322.55	12.1
Commissions	(20.06)	(0.8)
Transport	(90.28)	(3.4)
Handling and storage	(8.00)	(0.3)
District tax	(30.10)	(1.1)
Assemblers' net margin	174.11	6.5
Kumasi wholesale price[b]	2,525.00	94.5
Atebubu market wholesale price	2,216.93	83.0
Processors' gross margin	308.07	11.5
Transport	(50.06)	(1.9)
Parboiling	(40.13)	(1.5)
Milling	(60.19)	(2.2)
Handling	(16.03)	(0.6)
Commissions	(20.00)	(0.7)
Processors' net margin	121.66	4.6
Kumasi retail price[b]	2,671.80	100.0
Kumasi wholesale price	2,525.00	94.5
Retailers' gross margin	146.80	5.5
Handling	(6.50)	(0.2)
Stall rental	(7.00)	(0.3)
Retailers' net margin	133.30	5.0

a. Paddy prices at the producer and Atebubu market wholesale level were converted to their milled equivalent at a 0.62 milling ratio. One cedi = 0.87 U.S. dollars.

b. Market prices are the average of monthly price figures collected by the Ministry of Agriculture from January through July 1977.

c. The producer prices are the average of prices recorded in the farm survey for producers in the Kwame Danso area.

Source: V. Roy Southworth, "Food Crop Marketing in Atebubu District, Ghana," Ph.D. dissertation, Stanford University, 1981.

Because normal profit is the return to capital (including working capital as well as equipment and buildings), data are needed on capital used in the marketing enterprises. Rates of profit are calculated by comparing estimated profit levels with the amount of capital in use. To determine if the return to capital represents normal profits, the analyst must compare it with the prevailing interest rates in the credit markets to which the food crop merchants have access. If the prevailing interest rate (which contains a premium for the riskiness of the marketing investment) is less than the earned rate of return, the earned level of profit is above normal.

Although this type of analysis is time-consuming and the data requirements are extensive, it is worth attempting for policy purposes if there is some prior evidence of excess profits or if policymakers believe that marketing inefficiencies are so pervasive that only solid empirical evidence will prevent implementation of marketing policies based on that belief.

PRICE DATA. Price analysis is an indirect approach for determining market efficiency. Efficient marketing systems are characterized by a high degree of price integration—closely correlated movements of connected series of prices—over space, form, and time. In an efficient market economy, price integration is caused by arbitrage. In these economies market participants respond when they notice that prices in two markets are sufficiently different that profits can be made by buying in the low-price market and selling in the high-price market. If competitive conditions prevail and enough merchants respond in this way, the abnormal price difference disappears because supplies in the low-price market decline, placing upward pressure on prices, and supplies in the high-price market increase, causing prices to fall. Hence, prices in all efficient markets are linked by the arbitraging decisions of merchants, and price differences should reflect only normal costs. However, expectations about future price levels are an important ingredient in price formation. Because future price levels are uncertain, merchants bear risks when holding commodities, and the costs of risk-bearing are also included in marketing margins.

Price analysis of marketing margins involves statistical comparisons of pairs of price series that should be connected by the marketing system, and it applies to interrelated markets (over space), degrees of product processing (in form), and periods of storage (over time). In using price data to determine the degree of correlation in price movements, it is essential to be clear about the level in the marketing chain to which the prices apply. So-called farm-level prices, for example, might have been calculated from other prices in the system. The prices must pertain to a comparable quality and form of product, for example, milled rice of a particular variety with a specified percentage of brokens. Prices do need to be reliably collected, and actual prices prevailing in markets are to be distinguished from officially announced prices.

Low correlation coefficients mean the markets are unconnected by actual movements of commodities from one town to another. High correlation of price series between markets, indicating strong price integration, can result from several factors. First, stable prices in all cities can cause high correlation simply because little price movement was observed. Second, high correlation among price movements might indicate perfect competition and efficient price arbitrage. Alternatively, the strong correlations might result from monopoly or effective government policy with little actual market connection occurring among towns. Corroborative evidence is needed to understand the actual formation of prices between markets and hence to explain the reasons for high correlation.

MAPPING ZONES OF COMPETITIVENESS. Maps of zones of competitiveness associated with the main marketing chains serve to summarize the description of a marketing system. These maps, or the tabular information that go into their construction, reveal the extent to which marketing costs for a commodity, together with the farm costs of producing it, permit merchants in food producing areas to collect, process, store, and deliver foodstuffs competitively—that is, without government subsidy or protection—to principal consuming centers. This mapping can also be used to show how the national food system is linked to international commodity markets. The connection and relationship between international and domestic grain prices are key elements of domestic food policy and are discussed further in this chapter and in chapter 6. The domestic marketing sector provides the facilities and connecting mechanisms that permit a food price policy to function effectively in an international market context.

Comparing the cost of a domestically produced foodstuff delivered to a port city (the farming cost plus marketing cost) with the locally quoted price for export of the same commodity indicates whether that commodity can be exported without government export subsidy. A similar comparison made with the full import price shows whether the locally produced foodstuff can survive international competition in the port city's wholesale markets and subsequently in interior markets where locally produced foodstuffs have more of a competitive cost advantage. If the commodity is not competitive with imports, a government may choose to limit imports with tariffs or quantitative restrictions. Isocost lines (connecting points of equal costs) can be drawn on the map to indicate, at a given world price for a foodstuff, the limits of production areas able to export competitively and of farming regions able to meet import competition without protection. The likely effects of reductions in production or marketing costs can also be examined by identifying how much additional output would be marketed competitively and where those marketings would originate.

The type of information needed to identify zones of competitiveness is shown in table 4-2. Rice production and marketing in one coastal country,

Table 4-2. Net Social Profitability of Rice Production at Alternative
Locations in West Africa
(francs per kilogram of rice)

Location of domestic rice production and consumption	Social returns[a]	Social costs[b]	Net social profitability
Consumption at the production center in the interior countries (Mali, Niger, and Upper Volta)	99.2	84.0	15.2
Production at the average distance with consumption at the main center in interior countries	97.0	86.2	10.8
Production at the greatest distance with consumption at the main center in interior countries	97.0	89.9	7.1
Production and consumption in Senegal, distant from the port	84.9	84.0	0.9
Consumption at the production center in Senegal	81.2	84.0	−2.8
Production at the average distance with consumption at the main center in Senegal	79.0	86.2	−7.2
Production at the greatest distance with consumption at the main center in Senegal	79.0	89.9	−10.9

a. Social returns are the opportunity cost of imported rice delivered to the consumption location, according to the following assumptions (in francs per kilogram of rice):

	Senegal	Interior countries
Price of rice, c.i.f. West African port	74	74
Handling and port charges	5	5
Inland transportation and distribution costs to main consumption center	0	18
Delivered cost of imported rice at main consumption center	79	97

Various additional transportation charges are incurred in delivering imported rice to alternative consumption locations.

b. Social costs include farm production costs of 67.7 francs per kilogram, costs of collection and of milling with a small-scale huller of 12.0 francs, and costs of transportation to a main consumption center of 6.5 francs.

Source: Data taken from Charles P. Humphreys and Scott R. Pearson, "Choice of Technique in Sahelian Rice Production," Food Research Institute Studies, vol. 18, no. 3 (1979–80).

Senegal, is compared with that in three interior countries in West Africa—
Mali, Niger, and Upper Volta. Results are reported in social costs, returns,
and profits so that the effects of government policies on actual market prices
are removed.

Table 4-2 is constructed to illustrate the decreased social profitability of
growing rice the closer the production area is to the port that imports rice.
With both production and consumption taking place at the production centers of the interior countries, Mali, Niger, and Upper Volta, social returns

are 99.2 francs per kilogram (because of the high cost of bringing imported rice to these areas), while the social cost of production is only 84.0 francs (production plus milling costs and a small transportation charge). The resulting net social profitability is 15.2 francs per kilogram. This profitability declines as domestically produced rice must be transported further while imported rice incurs smaller transportation costs. In the interior countries net social profitability of rice production falls to 7.1 francs per kilogram under the least favorable combination of assumptions for producing area and consuming location.

In the coastal country of Senegal, domestic rice production is barely socially profitable under the most favorable set of locational assumptions. All other combinations show negative social returns, which indicate that Senegalese rice production is not competitive against imported rice without government protection or subsidies for the rice sector. The design of alternative protection and subsidy policies, as well as the analysis for determining their impact or desirability, are treated later in the chapter. The possible mechanisms, however, for increasing the private profitability of growing rice in Senegal are apparent from table 4-2. First, and perhaps easiest, imported rice could have a tariff put on it. A duty of 10 francs per kilogram would ensure the private profitability of rice production except in the most remote rice-growing areas in Senegal. Alternatively, subsidies to farmers, perhaps through subsidized fertilizer or credit, subsidies to rice millers, or subsidies to the transportation system, could accomplish the same goal.

Analytical Techniques for Measuring Marketing Efficiency

The scope for government intervention in marketing is determined by the efficiency and costs of performing the basic marketing functions. If high costs exist, government investments can lower them. If serious inefficiency exists, government policies might improve competitiveness or provide direct competitive standards. Either way, the first task for analysts is to identify empirically the high costs or inefficiencies. If analysts were able to examine the detailed records of marketing agents' costs and returns for transportation, storage, and processing, monopoly profits and inefficiencies might show up directly. Such records are extremely difficult to obtain, however, and those that are available may be of dubious accuracy. The indirect approach of examining price formation at various levels in the marketing chain is frequently more feasible and the data more reliable. Where evidence of inefficiency shows up from such price analysis, more detailed checks of books and records might then be very effective in uncovering the source of high marketing costs.

Marketing efficiency can be analyzed by comparing seasonal price rises with the costs of storage and by correlating market prices in different locations. More extensive analysis focuses on the full marketing margin between farmers and consumers. Models of actual margins between product form and location test the efficiency of processing, the direction of market connection, and the size of margin needed to establish a connection. These techniques usually cannot "prove" that price formation is efficient or inefficient, but each can point to more detailed field surveys which will have a high payoff to further data gathering, analysis, and policy insight.

SEASONAL PRICE ANALYSIS AND THE COST OF STORAGE. Seasonal price analysis tests the effectiveness of arbitrage over time. Prices of food crops typically follow a seasonal pattern, falling immediately after the harvest and rising thereafter until the next harvest, as farmers and merchants store some supplies to meet consumer demand throughout the year. In a competitive market, the seasonal price rise should just cover the costs of storage, which consist of interest charges on working capital tied up in the form of stored commodities, provision for commodity losses, the cost of labor and facilities used in storage, and normal profits (including risk-bearing).

By comparing monthly price rises with the monthly costs of storage, analysts can test whether there are excess profits in the storage function. The monthly price rises are derived from an index of wholesale prices, which are usually calculated as the average monthly percentage of a twelve-month moving average. This version of price analysis seeks to identify excess profits in the storage cost portion of the marketing margin. Even if data on storage costs are not available, much insight into the time dimension of the marketing system can be gained by contrasting seasonal price indexes for the main food crops.

An example of seasonal price indexes for four commodities in Ghana is shown in table 4-3. The prices of yams and corn nearly doubled from harvest to preharvest, while those for paddy rose 35 percent and for dried cassava 50 percent. The additional information needed to estimate costs of storage is detailed in table 4-4, which contains storage costs for eight months under different assumed pairs of monthly interest rates and commodity losses in storage. It is known from table 4-3 that corn prices on average rose 95 percent during an eight-month season. This seasonal price rise is consistent with storage losses of 20 percent and a monthly interest rate of 5.7 percent— magnitudes that correspond to a cost of storage for eight months of 99 percent of the purchase value. Alternatively, storage losses of 20 percent, an interest rate of 4.7 percent per month, and other storage costs (such as rent on facilities, labor, and profit) of 1 percent per month also correspond to the cost of storage for this period. Seasonal price rises for corn thus may reflect actual costs of storage although these costs are quite high. Research in South Asia has tended to show significantly smaller on-farm storage losses and seasonal price rises commensurate with these lower costs of storage.

INTERMARKET PRICE CORRELATIONS. Correlations of wholesale prices can

Table 4-3. Index of Monthly Wholesale Prices of Yams, Paddy, Corn, and Dried Cassava in Atebubu Market, 1965–74

Crop	Jan.	Feb.	Mar.	Apr.	May	Jun.	Jul.	Aug.	Sep.	Oct.	Nov.	Dec.	Range
Yams													
Mean	104	111	109	126	135	139	90	67	66	67	91	95	73
Standard deviation	11	20	10	19	17	20	28	15	16	15	16	22	
Paddy													
Mean[a]	91	93	96	105	111	110	109	109	110	99	85	82	29
Standard deviation	10	15	5	12	8	11	16	30	13	6	9	11	
Corn													
Mean[b]	97	99	104	125	141	136	102	74	66	78	92	90	75
Standard deviation	9	8	7	18	14	26	15	10	6	10	11	6	
Dried cassava													
Mean	101	103	83	83	97	102	103	120	126	103	95	83	43
Standard deviation	42	40	13	13	14	18	15	54	51	26	23	12	

Note: Index is average monthly percentage of twelve-month moving average.
a. January 1969 to July 1974.
b. January 1968 to March 1974.
Source: V. Roy Southworth, William O. Jones, and Scott R. Pearson, "Food Crop Marketing in Atebubu District, Ghana," Food Research Institute Studies, vol. 17, no. 2 (1979), p. 180.

Table 4-4. Estimated Cost of Storage for Eight Months at Various Rates
of Interest and Storage Loss

Interest rate per month[a]	Storage loss (percent)				
	30	20	15	5	None
0	30	20	15	5	0
1	54	35	27	14	8
2	67	46	38	23	17
3	81	58	49	33	27
4	96	71	61	44	37
5	111	85	74	56	48
6	128	99	88	68	59

Note: The cost-of-storage figures in the body of the table are percentages of the purchase value of the amounts left for sale at the end of eight months.

a. Calculations assume interest is compounded annually.

Source: V. Roy Southworth, "Food Crop Marketing in Atebubu District, Ghana," Ph.D. Dissertation, Stanford University, 1981.

be calculated between pairs of markets to test market integration. Results from one such analysis are reported in table 4-5 and mapped in figure 4-4. Wholesale prices of corn were strongly correlated between pairs of markets in Ghana. Where a coefficient of 1.00 would indicate identical price movements in the two markets, more than half the correlation coefficients were 0.85 or above, and nearly one-fourth were at or above 0.90. A simple correlation coefficient of 0.90 means that 81 percent of the variation in one price series is correlated with variations in the other price series.

Because correlation coefficients are influenced by inflation and by very large seasonal price movements, it is best to choose periods for analysis in which inflation was moderate or to correct for the effects of inflation by correlating price changes rather than actual prices. The price changes are found by subtracting each monthly observation from the one preceding it to obtain first differences.

The map in figure 4-4 shows lines drawn between pairs of cities that have corn price correlation coefficients greater than or equal to 0.90. This mapping includes all but four markets, a result which suggests an integrated marketing system for corn during the period tested. These high correlations indicate a significant degree of spatial arbitrage so long as there are no extreme monopoly conditions or effective government controls. If the analysis shows low correlation coefficients, communication and transportation networks may be inadequate for effective integration of markets.

More significant judgments about the efficiency of spatial arbitrage cannot be made with this technique, for relatively small differences in correlation coefficients can reflect highly profitable market manipulations. The real purpose of intermarket price correlation analysis is to demonstrate that a domestic marketing system really does exist and that it serves to connect the food

Table 4-5. Correlation of Wholesale Prices among Pairs of Markets, Ghana, 1965–72

Correlation coefficient	Proportion of total coefficients by commodity			
	Yams	Rice	Corn	Dried cassava
0.95+	0.02	0.04	0.02	0
0.90–0.94	0	0.03	0.20	0.01
0.85–0.89	0.02	0.03	0.43	0.03
0.80–0.84	0.06	0.08	0.17	0.03
0.75–0.79	0.11	0.13	0.06	0.08
0.70–0.74	0.07	0.17	0.01	0.08
0.65–0.69	0.11	0.13	0	0.17
0.60–0.64	0.13	0.09	0.03	0.09
0.55–0.59	0.07	0.07	0.03	0.13
0.50–0.54	0.11	0.03	0.04	0.10
0–0.49	0.30	0.18	0.02	0.23
<0	0	0.03	0	0.06
Total	1.00	1.00	1.00	1.00
Number of markets	16	16	16	16
Number of pairs	120	120	120	120
First quartile	0.70–0.74	0.75–0.79	0.85–0.89	0.65–0.69
Second quartile	0.60–0.64	0.65–0.69	0.85–0.89	0.55–0.59

Source: V. Roy Southworth, William O. Jones, and Scott R. Pearson, "Food Crop Marketing in Atebubu District, Ghana," *Food Research Institute Studies*, vol. 17, no. 2 (1979), p. 189.

markets of various cities and towns in the country. This simple demonstration can have a powerful effect on policymakers who believe that each market is controlled by a protected monopoly reacting only to local conditions.

MARKETING MARGIN ANALYSIS. If farmers, consumers, and policymakers alike think the marketing margin is too large, an obvious question is "how large is it?" The question is deceptively simple, for the measured size of the margin between the farm-gate price and the retail price can change over time as conditions change in the marketing system. In addition, the margin is calculated as the difference between the retail price and the farm-gate price, but this calculation assumes implicitly that the commodity is actually being marketed through the entire chain from farmer to retail consumer. This may be the right assumption during part of the year—for several months after the harvest, for instance. During other parts of the year, however, no commodities may be flowing from farmers to urban centers. During these periods when no market connection exists between rural and urban markets (or at least the connection is not in the regular direction), comparisons of farm prices and retail prices reveal nothing whatsoever of the size of the marketing margin.

Simple attempts to measure the size of the overall marketing margin by

Figure 4-4. Intermarket Correlation of Wholesale Corn Prices

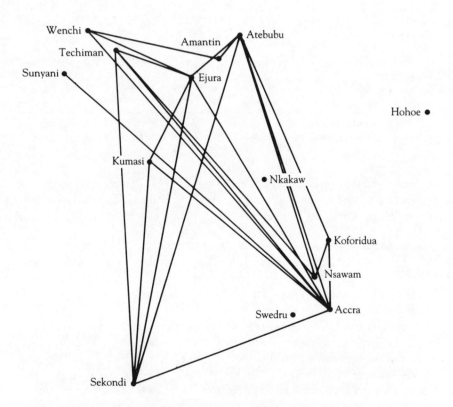

Note: Corn correlations ≥ 0.90.
Source: V. Roy Southworth, William O. Jones, and Scott R. Pearson, "Food Crop Marketing in Atebubu District, Ghana," *Food Research Institute Studies*, vol. 17, no. 2 (1979), p. 184.

calculating the difference between average annual retail and farm-gate prices may significantly underestimate the true costs of connecting these two markets with actual flows of commodities. The alternative is to specify carefully a simple model of market connection and to use monthly or seasonal data to measure the size of the marketing margin.

One such model is illustrated in figure 4-5, where rice prices are measured on the vertical axis and time during a year along the horizontal axis. Both urban and rural rice prices (in milled rice equivalents) are shown, separated by the full costs of transforming paddy at the farm gate to milled rice at the retail stall. These price observations are all within the same month of observation so that no significant storage costs are incurred. Figure 4-5 is designed to show what happens to the short-run flow of rice from rural to urban

Figure 4-5. Marketing Margins and Connections between Urban and Rural Markets

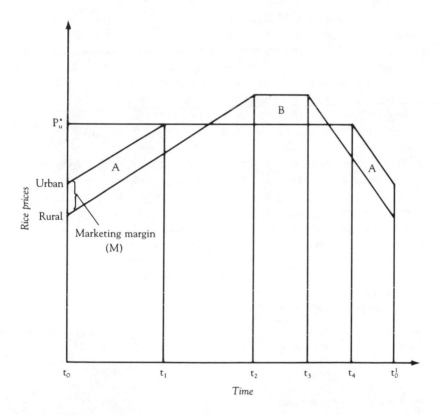

Source: C. Peter Timmer, "A Model of Rice Marketing in Indonesia," *Food Research Institute Studies,* vol. 13, no. 2 (1974), p. 151.

areas and the consequent impact on the observed price margin of any inter-
ruption of that flow.

At time t_0 the rice harvest has ended, and both rural and urban rice prices
begin their seasonal rise. Urban prices are higher than rural prices by the
size of the actual marketing margin M. This margin reflects full competitive
costs of connecting the two markets with a physical flow of rice. At time t_1,
the urban rice price reaches a ceiling dictated either by government policy
and supplies from a buffer stock or by the availability of imports at price
P_u^*. Consequently, urban prices cease to rise. Costs of storage in rural areas
continue to mount, however, and so rural prices continue to rise from time
t_1 to time t_2, when rural prices actually exceed urban prices by the marketing
margin M, and supplies begin to flow back to the rural areas until time t_3,
when the rural harvest begins in the new season. Rural rice prices fall until
they reach their seasonal low at time t_0^1, and the cycle begins again. The
urban rice price does not begin to fall until time t_4, when the rural rice price
has fallen below P_u^* by the size of the marketing margin M, and hence the
two markets are again connected by physical flows of rice.

How can M be measured? Figure 4-5 shows that only during the periods
marked A, from t_0 to t_1 and from t_4 to t_0^1, is the actual marketing margin M
reflected in the difference between the urban and rural rice prices. During
those times the analyst can observe the costs the marketing system is incurring
to connect the rural and urban markets. Naturally, there is no guarantee
that these costs reflect efficient marketing or lack of monopoly influence,
but they are the actual costs that must then be compared with estimates of
efficient costs. However, the fact that the "measured" margin between t_1
and t_2, or between t_3 and t_4, is less than M (and may even be negative) is
not evidence that the margins from t_0 to t_1 and from t_4 to t_0^1 are excessive.
Only the latter measurements have any meaning at all.

Measuring marketing margins in this manner can quickly provide insight
into the dynamics and costs of basic food grain marketing. Published or readily
available price data can often be used for the analysis. What the analyst must
provide is careful thought about how the marketing system actually works
and its seasonal variations. This information comes from many sources and
especially from field trips to look at markets. Knowing where the prices are
collected and how the markets function are important precursors to estimation
of even simple marketing models.

International Commodity Markets

Marketing analysts cannot be content when they understand how their
domestic food markets work. Nearly all countries are connected either directly
or indirectly to international food markets as well. These connections influence domestic price formation, and so they are important to the immediate
issues being treated here. International prices are also integral components

of the social profitability analysis outlined in chapter 3 and to the issues of
food security that permeate the discussion throughout the book. Food policymakers face a basic issue in deciding whether future food supplies should be
produced domestically by the country's own farmers or imported in exchange
for other goods and services the country can produce more cheaply and
efficiently. The answer can be given only in the context of what level of
international prices will prevail when the time comes. These prices are highly
unstable, and predicting them is no easy task.

INTERNATIONAL PRICE FORMATION. At one level, a food policy analyst can
find out about grain prices on international markets with a simple telephone
call to one of the major grain export firms, which will be only too happy to
quote prices, delivery dates, and conditions of payment. In a very real sense,
such a conversation reveals *the* international price for grain. For the food
agency that needs 50,000 tons of wheat for sixty-day delivery, the quoted
price is the beginning and end of the story.

Other participants in the country's food system, both public and private,
have additional concerns, however. Two in particular are important: how
long will the quoted price be relevant, and is the trend of real prices (that
is, corrected for inflation) up or down? At any given time experts are more
or less evenly divided on these questions. For commodities that are actively
traded on futures markets (such as wheat, corn, and soybeans), the best
information available to market participants is reflected in quotations for
contracts with specific delivery dates, up to a year or somewhat more into
the future. Even for commodities without active futures markets (such as
rice), forward contracts are usually available from major suppliers and give
some sense of how market participants view price trends for the near future.

For planning horizons of a year or so, these futures and forward markets
provide the best information available on likely price trends. Of course, they
may not be right. But the evidence of the postwar era shows that no country
has been able to outguess these markets in a consistent fashion, and most
grain importers have paid higher prices than were available simply by using
forward contracts and futures markets to hedge against price risks. Considerable savings seem to be available to countries that develop the skills and
bureaucratic rules permitting active use of futures markets to provide the
lowest and most stable costs of grain for any given overall market environment.

For the longer run, even futures markets are of little help to planners trying
to determine the opportunity costs of investments to raise food production
or to lower losses in storage or processing. When investments have payoffs
several years in the future, some sense of longer-run price trends in international markets is needed. One way to achieve this is simply to plot over
time the real prices of wheat, for example, averaged over a five- or ten-year
period to eliminate year-to-year variations and see whether the trend is up

or down. To most people's surprise, the trend for the past century has been significantly downward for wheat and corn, except for occasional and short-lived spurts upward, as in 1951 or 1973.

An alternative to such a simple approach, but one that must ultimately be consistent with the trends generated in the markets, is to look at the basic supply and demand factors which generate equilibrium prices in world markets. It must be recognized when taking a supply-demand perspective that world markets for grain do not reflect world supply and demand conditions in total, but rather the economic forces that clear a *residual* market after internal supply has been balanced against demand inside most countries' borders. Only a few countries permit world grain prices to set directly the signals communicated to domestic consumers and producers; of these few, the United States is by far the most important. When the United States permits free trade of grain across its borders in response to prices foreign consumers are willing to pay, which is most of the time, then its major grain markets, especially the Chicago grain markets, *are* the world markets. That is where international grain price formation actually takes place.

The longer-run price trends generated in these markets depend on whether supply curves reflecting available export supplies are shifting outward faster or slower than demand curves. The relevant demand curves reflect desired (and affordable) purchases by countries whose domestic production is insufficient to meet domestic needs within their actual price environment set by trade and subsidy policies. Consequently, the most useful analytical framework for understanding grain price formation on international markets is the same type of excess supply and excess demand curve framework presented in figure 4-2.

In such a framework the protectionist policies of the European Economic Community or the fluctuating grain needs of the U.S.S.R. to meet livestock feed requirements can be incorporated directly into the location and shape of the world market supply and demand curves. Consequently, the analysis can reflect policy environments as well as the longer-run trends in population and income growth on the demand side and technological change, area expansion, and weather and climate on the supply side.

Figure 4-6 illustrates one of two alternative international grain market environments. In this example demand forces are rising more rapidly than factors shifting out supply curves, and the trend of real prices is upward. Such a scenario was widely accepted in the late 1970s in the aftermath of the world food crisis of 1973–74. It would represent a shift in long-run historical trends, however, especially a dramatic slowing in the rate of technical change in agriculture and in area expansion. Both changes are entirely possible, of course, and a slower growth in new areas brought under cultivation is likely. However, if both technical change and area of cultivation (particularly irrigated area) are to some extent a function of earlier incentives to grow more food, then the high prices of the mid-1970s may have been partly self-correcting in the long run through both shifts in the supply curve and in the elasticity of supply itself. As the more elastic, dashed supply curves in figure 4-6 show, even when the shifts are identical to shifts in the inelastic supply curves, the greater elasticity of supply response prevents prices from rising as rapidly.

The second possibility is illustrated in figure 4-7, which shows supply curves shifting out more rapidly than demand curves. As was noted, this is consistent with historic patterns but may not reflect future trends if demand pressures increase more quickly because of population and income growth or if supply curves do not shift out as rapidly as has been the case historically. The important role of demand elasticities is illustrated in this figure. If food grain demand is highly inelastic when supply shifts out rapidly, then the trend of real prices is sharply lower. However, if grain demand is more elastic, even

Figure 4-6. International Grain Market Price Formation: Demand Curves Shift Faster than Supply Curves; Prices Rise over Time

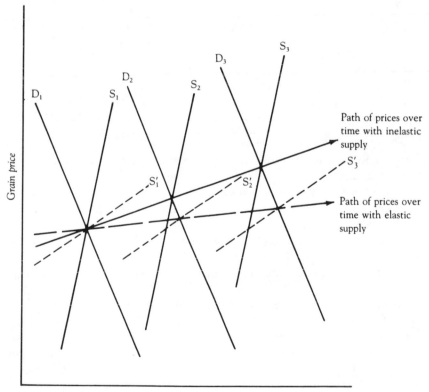

Figure 4-7. International Grain Market Price Formation: Supply Curves
Shift Faster than Demand Curves; Prices Fall over Time

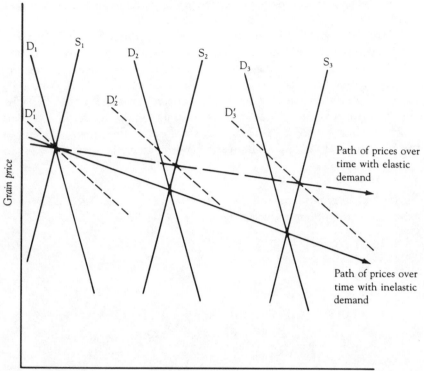

with exactly the same *shifts* in demand, then grain prices do not fall so sharply
as more demand is induced by the lower prices.

The elasticity of demand for grain is connected to its price level because
more end uses become economical as prices drop. Although the distinction
between food grains, feed grains, and industrial raw materials is commonly
understood, the distinction is basically one of price. The elasticity of demand
for wheat, for example, varies with price levels. Grain will be used primarily
for direct human consumption at high prices and exhibit a very low demand
elasticity. As figure 4-8 shows, at lower prices grain will be fed to animals
and eventually even be used industrially. Generally speaking, the lower the
price of a commodity or the higher the price of its substitutes, the more likely
there can be end-use substitutions. New technical processes, specific government policy, and relative prices of other commodities all influence the
degree of substitution. High prices for corn, for example, would shift the
feed use portion of the demand curve for wheat, while sharply higher petroleum prices might add to the demand for wheat for energy use.

Figure 4-8. Effects of Changing End Uses on Demand Elasticities

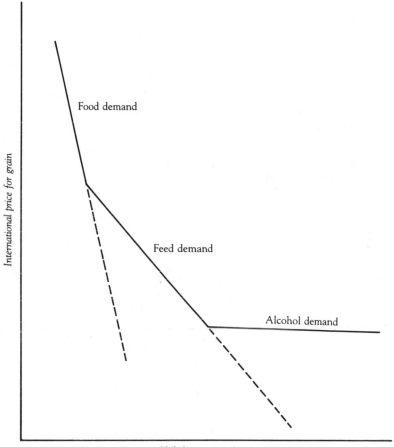

Global *quantity of grain*

From decade to decade, international price movements are driven fundamentally by world supply and demand forces. This "longer run," however, is composed of a series of annual "short runs," which are in turn affected by other causal variables. These short-run forces tend to be less stable and predictable than population growth or technical change. Moreover, this annual price variability is frequently large enough to obscure the longer-run trends in prices.

Poor weather is one factor that often accounts for substantial leftward shifts in export-supply curves or rightward shifts in import-demand curves. This is especially true when abnormal weather affects a country that is a major actor on either the supply or demand side of an international market. The other significant destabilizing force in world markets is government policy change

in one or more key countries. Unexpected changes in domestic policy—
embargoes, export bans, special barter arrangements, and so forth—often
accentuate price effects induced by weather or other short-term variables.

International trade in rice presents a good illustration of all these points.
Rice is traded primarily among Asian countries. Bad weather in Asia often
affects the rice production of both exporters and importers at the same time.
In figure 4-9 poor weather, such as a bad monsoon that affects several countries in South or Southeast Asia, simultaneously causes a leftward shift in
the export-supply curve and a rightward shift in the import-demand curve.
The consequence is very high prices in years of poor weather and low annual
prices in years of good weather in Asia.

Figure 4-9. Effects of Weather on Price Fluctuations
in the International Rice Market

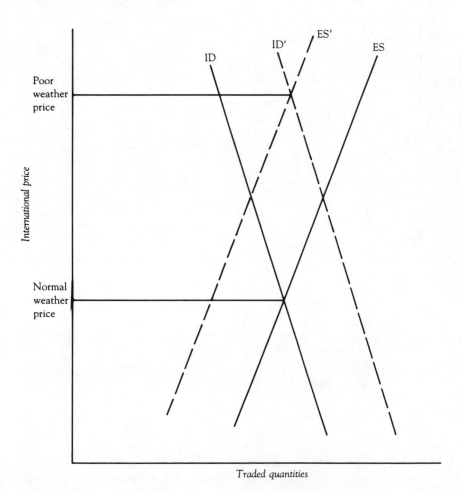

Weather-induced variability in rice prices is compounded by two other sets of factors. First, rice is traded in a "thin" market—a market where only a small percentage of production enters international trade. With world production at approximately 350 million tons (milled rice equivalent) and trade at only 12 million tons, the international market can be extremely sensitive to small changes. A variation of 5 million tons in rice production in Thailand, a major export supplier, would not affect world rice output very much, but it could eliminate 2 million tons of Thai rice exports and reduce world export supplies by one-sixth.

Second, most governments in Asia try to protect producers and consumers from short-run price instability in the rice market by undertaking actions—such as setting up import and export monopolies, long-term purchase arrangements, barter deals, import subsidies, and export taxes—that have the effect of isolating their domestic rice price from changes in the international price. In most countries, movements in international food prices, especially for basic food grains, are *not* passed on to consumers or producers. As more domestic markets are isolated from international markets by trade and subsidy policies, the international markets themselves become more subject to wide price fluctuations because of the thinness of export supplies and import demands that are price responsive. These fluctuations thus add to pressures on domestic policymakers to isolate themselves from world markets.

THE BORDER PRICE. The tendency to protect a country's food producers and consumers from unstable world markets is quite understandable, especially in countries that do not use market systems to generate price signals or to reflect relative scarcity to producers and consumers. Such autarky has its costs, however, including lower overall levels of consumer welfare (although some countries may achieve a more equal distribution of important commodities through such policies). Slow growth in agricultural production is also a common result because signals are missing as to what should and should not be grown. Even in a context of nontrade, the opportunity costs involved are of considerable interest and importance, and these depend on international prices. The important question that remains is what international price should be used as the standard of reference for social profitability analysis or for analysis of various price and trade policies? There will be different answers depending primarily on the time frame of analysis, and an important issue is how to distinguish short-run price fluctuations from long-run trends.

For countries actively trading in international commodity markets, the question has a day-to-day immediacy. Short-run international price fluctuations can be buffered to provide a more stable decisionmaking environment for domestic producers and consumers. But such buffering, whether done through physical storage of grain or trade policy and subsidies, is extremely expensive if domestic prices remain out of line with international prices for very long. At some point—and the point depends on financial and logistical flexibility—domestic price policy faces strong pressures to conform to the opportunity costs of the outside world. Otherwise budget subsidies play havoc with fiscal policy, and the dynamic distortions become entrenched in the domestic economy.

To follow international market trends as an element of domestic food price policy, three components must be distinguished: the short-run trends over several months that influence import purchases; the medium-run trends that affect consumer and producer prices; and the long-run trends that affect government investment decisions with regard to agricultural infrastructure and research. Analysts can identify these trends by plotting moving averages of real (deflated) prices for the relevant period for decisions. Three-month, two-year, and five- or ten-year moving averages can provide simple and mechanical, yet persistent, reminders that the long run is made up of a sequence of short runs.

These three trends reflect the different time horizons of government decisions that are closely tied to the world price. Whether to use grain from a buffer stock rather than to import grain is a relevant decision over a two- or three-month period, but probably not for a six-month period and almost certainly not for twelve or eighteen months. Similarly, consumer and producer prices can be stabilized for a year or perhaps two by using budget subsidies or import duties to counteract movements in world prices, but the budget costs mount and the distortions begin to get locked into production and consumption patterns before very long. Long-run government investment decisions need a long-run perspective.

A food price policy that actively uses world markets thus requires a sequence of increasingly tighter links as the time horizon of decisions gets shorter. This calls for a complex and somewhat muddy arrangement. Managers of food logistics agencies should often be using an entirely different set of price signals from that used by their own investment departments planning new marketing facilities. Market operatives who are busy buying and selling grain to maintain a buffer stock can be enforcing floor and ceiling prices that are different from either the short-run import price or the long-run investment price. Flexible financing arrangements and a carefully managed buffer stock permit these multiple links between domestic and international prices to serve national food policy objectives.

To further these objectives, two types of analysis are needed. The first looks at the costs and benefits of price policies that use trade barriers or budget subsidies, or both, to place a wedge (or even an iron door) between domestic and international prices. The second is an analysis of policies aimed at narrowing marketing margins, especially dampening seasonal movements in prices and reducing geographical differences. These policies are often implemented with government-operated buffer stocks supplied by imports. Consequently, an understanding of efforts made to narrow marketing margins also provides insights into the potential usefulness of links between domestic and international prices.

Domestic Markets and Price Policy

"Food prices are too high." "Crop prices are too low." Both complaints are heard in virtually all countries. All consumers would like food prices to be lower, to take a smaller portion of their family budgets. All farmers would like their crop prices to be higher, to provide them greater return for their effort and investment. The tension between the two, the food price dilemma, inevitably focuses the attention of consumers, producers, and policymakers alike on the margin between farm prices and consumer prices. All these groups point to the middleman and say "marketing costs are too high."

Several factors common to all food marketing systems lead to this impression, whether it is true or not. First, the marketing system is the narrow point in an hourglass-shaped distribution pattern which first concentrates the crop sales from millions of farmers and then disperses the food to millions of consumers in the time, place, and form in which they want it. Politically, millions of farmers or millions of consumers are forces to be reckoned with; the hundreds or thousands of middlemen usually are not.

Second, operating as a middleman is a very risky business even in developed countries where information is excellent. In developing countries the risks are even larger. Only the highly skilled can survive for very long in such circumstances, and the economic return to these skills is large. In short, many middlemen are quite rich, in sharp contrast to the poverty of both their supplying farmers and consuming households. It is a very short step between the observation of rich middlemen and the conclusion of high-cost, inefficient, and monopolistic marketing. The conclusion, however, is wrong as a logical necessity, and, in a broad array of developing countries, wrong as a matter of fact.

A third reason for the strong perception that marketing margins in developing countries are too high is that they *are* high. Marketing costs are high when roads and communications are poor, when interest rates and storage losses are high, and when processing facilities are poorly maintained and operated because of difficulties in obtaining working capital or spare parts. In other words, marketing margins are high because the real costs of marketing are high. It is not a matter of short-run private inefficiency and monopoly profits accruing to a few greedy middlemen. Significant opportunities exist for socially profitable investment in the marketing system that will reduce these high costs. The purpose of marketing analysis is to locate these areas of high costs, to identify any inefficiencies and monopoly profits if they exist, and to propose policy initiatives and investments that will lower the real costs of marketing.

Marketing analysis is concerned with both price levels and price margins since the marketing system connects farm prices to consumer prices; in market economies it serves as the arena for price formation at each level. Governments can attempt to set all the important prices to reflect social priorities, or, through a variety of trade and subsidy policies, governments can affect the level of the overall price structure. This analysis is relevant to socialist economies as well as to market economies because allocating resources efficiently and generating and utilizing information are important to both kinds of societies.

The market and welfare aspects of price level interventions are outlined to provide the analyst with a set of tools for assessing the impact of trade and subsidy policies on the welfare of producers and consumers and on the national budget. Determining the welfare impact requires the use of world prices as a standard of reference to judge the opportunity costs of particular policies. Government policies can significantly affect both price levels and margins, and this chapter also presents a wide range of potential interventions that subsidize marketing margins and thereby deal with the food price dilemma.

Price Policy Analysis

In market economies nearly all government economic policies influence the rural-urban terms of trade, defined roughly as the price of food crops relative to the prices of goods and services, including consumer products and farm inputs, purchased by farmers growing food crops. The rural-urban terms of trade is a major factor determining incentives to increase agricultural output while simultaneously signaling consumers about the relative costs of food. For convenience and clarity, the terms of trade will be called the "food parity price." This term is a reminder that farm incentives can be raised in two ways: higher output prices or lower input prices (or lower prices for consumer goods that farmers purchase with their incomes).

The food parity price is principally influenced by two sets of policies: foreign exchange rate, interest rate, and wage rate policies (the macro price policies discussed in chapter 5); and the subsidy and trade policies that drive a wedge between the world price of a product (output or input) and its domestic price. These price policies are illustrated here with food crops in mind, although the reasoning applies equally well to manufactured goods or agricultural inputs, such as fertilizer.

Price policies are judged by their effects on the four food policy objectives—promoting economic efficiency and hence faster growth of income, distributing incomes more equally, guaranteeing adequate nutritional status for all people, and providing security of food supplies. Empirical analysis of a policy requires measurement of the size as well as the likely direction of its impact. In addition, the weights given by governments to the several objectives and the constraints on choice of policy, including international repercussions, determine the actual feasibility and efficacy of a price policy.

Each price policy uses a subsidy or a trade restriction to cause the domestic producer or consumer price, or both, to differ from the world price. A simple consumer subsidy causes both producers and consumers to face lower prices than those in the world market. A specific producer price subsidy can raise the farmers' decision price above world levels while leaving the consumer price at the world price. In the absence of specific policy intervention, the domestic price and world price for a commodity will be the same for both producers and consumers.

A price policy intervention has an impact on the four food policy objectives in the following ways: it affects economic growth by the extent of efficiency losses; income distribution by the direction of income transfers; food security by increases or decreases in quantities traded internationally; and nutritional status by the income transfers price policies effect to or from consumers. (The differential impact on poor consumers of food price changes is not captured within this analytical framework.) The effect of the policy on the food parity price itself depends on whether the policy is applied to a food crop or to a manufactured product purchased by farmers and on whether the policy raises or lowers the domestic price of the commodity. A subsidy on rice imports lowers the food parity price by reducing the food price. A subsidy on fertilizer raises the food parity price by lowering the cost of an important input for food crop production.

SUBSIDY POLICY. A consumer subsidy on importables—goods for which domestic supplies are less than domestic demand in the absence of price policy—is a common price policy intervention in developing countries. Subsidizing rice imports, for example, causes the domestic price of rice for both consumers and producers to be less than the world price. As a result, the quantity of rice produced domestically declines, the amount consumed locally increases, and rice imports are greater than before the subsidy was introduced. The government must use budget resources to lower the price of rice, and this makes consumers better off. In this short-run, static model, when consumers gain, however, the producers of rice lose because their production, sales, and profits are reduced because of the lower price of rice. In effect, producers are forced to transfer income to consumers. A subsidy on rice imports also causes the food parity price to fall because the domestic rice price is reduced.

All four effects of subsidy policy—on quantities, transfers, efficiency losses, and the food parity price—are shown in figure 4-10. The initial situation, before the subsidy policy, has the domestic price equal to the world price, and so domestic supply is Q_1 and domestic demand is Q_3, with imports making up the difference ($Q_3 - Q_1$). When the government introduces a subsidy on rice prices, thus lowering the domestic price below the world price by $P_w - P_d$, demand increases to Q_4 and domestic supply drops to Q_2, both because of lower prices. The import gap widens to $Q_4 - Q_2$.

Figure 4-10. Effects of a Subsidy Policy on a Consumer Import, Rice

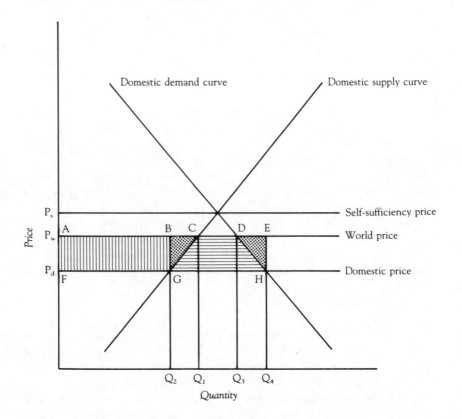

The government must pay a budget subsidy on all imported rice since the world price is higher than the domestic price. The total subsidy is $(P_w - P_d) \cdot (Q_4 - Q_2)$, or the per unit subsidy times total imports. This amount shows up in figure 4-10 as the rectangle BEHG. The rest of the subsidy is paid implicitly by farmers because of the lower price they receive. Their income transfer to consumers is equal to the unit subsidy times total production, or rectangle ABGF, plus the profits lost by reducing output, the triangle BCG. It is clear that the total economic costs of the subsidy policy are much larger than just the cost of the budget subsidy itself.

Although consumers clearly benefit by this price subsidy on rice, their total gain is less than the sum of the budget subsidy and implicit transfer from farmers. The difference is due to the efficiency losses caused by the price distortions introduced by the wedge between domestic and international rice prices. In this example, there are efficiency losses in both the producing and consuming sectors.

The production efficiency losses are measured by the dotted triangle BCG.

Because domestic resources can be used to produce rice more cheaply than the opportunity cost of imports as long as the domestic supply curve is below the world price, the triangle between the world price, the domestic price, and the domestic supply curve is an area of wasted resources. The cost of this waste is paid by the budget, but no commensurate gains accrue to consumers.

On the consumer side, the demand curve represents the price consumers are willing to pay for each quantity; so a lower price produces benefits for consumers who were willing to pay a higher price but no longer have to. This consumer surplus is reflected by the area under the demand curve but above the consumer price. In figure 4-10 the increase in consumer surplus is measured by the quadrilateral figure ADHF. The government budget subsidies needed to move the domestic price from P_w to P_d are greater than the gain in consumer surplus that comes from the lower prices. The consumption efficiency loss is shown by the triangle DEH.

One last lesson is apparent from the figure. The country using subsidies to provide consumers with imported rice at prices lower than those in the international market has reduced the degree of food self-sufficiency achieved relative to what would have occurred with free trade. An entirely different result would come from restricting imports and causing domestic rice prices to rise above world levels. If pursued far enough, a policy of pushing up rice prices could result in self-sufficiency for the country illustrated in figure 4-10. In fact, if domestic rice prices were maintained at P_s, the country would exactly reach self-sufficiency, with domestic rice consumption just equaling domestic production. The point is not that pursuing such self-sufficiency is a good or a bad policy, but rather that any policy debate about food self-sufficiency can be conducted only in the context of the domestic price environment relative to world prices. Self-sufficiency at price P_s could be a bitter policy victory if it reduces food consumption and displaces the production of other important agricultural commodities.

TRADE RESTRICTIONS. Trade policies that place restrictions on the flow of imports or exports of a commodity can be analyzed by using diagrams similar to figure 4-10. A trade restriction can be applied to either the price or the quantity of the commodity to reduce the amount traded internationally and to drive a wedge between the world price and the domestic price. For imports, the trade policy imposes either a per unit tariff (import tax) or a quantitative restriction (import quota) to limit the quantity imported and raise the domestic price above the world price. Likewise, trade policy for exports limits the quantity exported through imposition of either a per unit export tax or an export quota, and the result is to cause the domestic price to be lower than the world price.

If, for example, a trade policy restricts imports of textiles through imposition of a tariff, producers of textiles gain because the domestic price rises

above the world price. In response to higher local textile prices, production
expands, consumption declines, and the quantity of imports is reduced. Since
the domestic price is raised, consumers transfer income to producers and to
the government budget because of the duties paid on imports. As with the
consumer subsidy on rice, efficiency losses occur in both production and
consumption because the policy-adjusted price is higher than the world price,
which represents the actual opportunity costs of imports. A tariff on textiles
reduces the food parity price because textile prices rise for farmers, thus
increasing the price index of manufactured items purchased by farmers. Hence
the relative food parity price falls.

EFFECTS OF PRICE POLICIES. Price policies can be classified into six categories:

	Policies benefiting producers	Policies benefiting consumers
Subsidy policies	Producer subsidies on importables	Consumer subsidies on importables
	Producer subsidies on exportables	Consumer subsidies on exportables
Trade policies	Restrictions on imports	Restrictions on exports

Each price policy can be analyzed graphically (as in figure 4-10) to determine
the impact on quantities produced, consumed, and traded; on income transfers among producers, consumers, and the budget; and on efficiency losses
in production and consumption. The results of these analyses are shown in
table 4-6, which summarizes the impact of each price policy and reveals
several important effects of price policy interventions.

In the short-run, static world of this analysis all price policy interventions
incur efficiency losses in either production or consumption relative to an
international price standard. The only exception is when a price policy
intervention specifically offsets an existing source of static inefficiency, such
as a divergence between public and private profitability that occurs because
of externalities or economies of scale. Most policies have efficiency losses in
both production and consumption. Long-run efficiency gains are possible if
the subsidies call forth dynamic forces leading to technical change or the
maturation of infant industries, but these forces are not automatic. In many
circumstances the short-run efficiency losses have tended to accumulate and
widen the distortions in the economy.

A government uses food price policy to bring about basic changes in the
food system. Incentive prices can encourage production, discourage consumption, and reduce imports. Alternatively, food subsidies can reduce production, increase consumption, and increase imports. All price policies have
opposite (or at least neutral) effects on production and consumption. To
increase both the production and consumption of food would require maintaining a dual price policy involving subsidies to both producers and con-

Table 4-6. Summary of Effects of Price Policies

Type of policy	Quantity (increase, no change, or decrease)			Transfer (gains, no change, or losses)			Efficiency loss (incurred or no change)	
	Production	Consumption	Trade	Producers	Consumers	Budget	Production	Consumption
Producer subsidy on importables	+	0	−	+	0	−	X	0
Producer subsidy on exportables	+	−	+	+	−	−	X	X
Consumer subsidy on importables	−	+	+	−	+	−	X	X
Consumer subsidy on exportables	0	+	−	0	+	−	0	X
Restrictions on imports	+	−	−	+	−	+	X	X
Restrictions on exports	−	+	−	−	+	+	X	X

Note: X indicates an efficiency loss is incurred.

sumers. Such combined policies can also be analyzed within the framework used here, but the analysis is somewhat more complicated than the "pure" examples illustrated in figure 4-10 and summarized in table 4-6.

All price policies have an impact on quantities traded internationally since, by definition, the policies apply only to tradable commodities. The welfare effects of price policies for nontradables are difficult to measure because of the absence of an international price standard of comparison. Table 4-6 shows that most price policies reduce trade. This tendency is related to the pervasive efficiency losses incurred by price policies. Because trade leads to gains in economic efficiency through better allocation of productive resources, policies that reduce trade will likely incur efficiency losses.

The allocative effects of price policies on quantities produced, consumed, and traded have corresponding income distribution effects that occur as transfers are made among producers, consumers, and the budget. The full incidence of such transfers can be understood only in the context of the burden of raising tax revenues for the budget, but the direct gains to producers and consumers, before taxes are netted out, are shown in table 4-6. Transfers to producers and consumers tend to mirror the effects on quantities produced and consumed. More important, all subsidy policies incur negative budget transfers while trade restrictions earn the government a budget surplus. Such budget losses or gains are only a part of the total economic transfers occasioned by price policy, and frequently only a tiny part if traded quantities are small relative to total domestic production and consumption. The implicit transfers between producers and consumers are often the most important aspects of food price policy and yet are the least visible.

For some purposes of food policy, knowing the direction of policy effects is enough. In most situations actual measurement is required. Demand and supply elasticities permit the empirical analysis of trade, transfer, and efficiency effects. Because of the static nature of this analysis, these measured effects reflect short-run adjustments only. The dynamic adjustments of the food system to long-run price distortions are at least as important, as is the disaggregated welfare impact relative to the average impact reflected in this analysis. Income and price elasticities for each income class (assembled with the techniques outlined in chapter 2) are necessary to disaggregate the impact on the poor of the various subsidy and trade policies. Typically the nonfarm poor will be disproportionately benefited by price policies that lower food prices and transfer income to consumers at large and will be disproportionately hurt by higher food prices and income transfers to farmers, at least in the short run. Price policies designed for efficiency and more rapid growth of farm output will have a dynamic side effect of creating more jobs in rural areas and probably in urban areas as well.

The policy problem is one of finding mechanisms to protect the food intake of poor urban and rural landless consumers while the dynamic growth process has time to build momentum. The dynamic relationship between an efficient food price policy and performance in the rest of the economy is treated in detail in chapter 5, and the reconciliation of short-run consumer interests with long-run rural productivity is a major element of chapter 6.

While food subsidies that favor consumers can operate within the general price policy environment created by trade and subsidy policies with respect to international border prices, specific subsidies targeted to reach poor urban and rural landless consumers are likely to be implemented through the marketing system. The mutual interaction of food subsidies and the marketing system can be analyzed with the same tools that were used for supply and demand analysis and for determining the effects of trade and subsidy policies.

Subsidies and the Food Price Dilemma

Both socialist and capitalist economies use a variety of subsidies to protect their producers and consumers from the full brunt of the food price dilemma. Developed countries with highly productive farmers often end up paying huge price subsidies to prevent their productivity from driving many farmers into bankruptcy. Developing countries use subsidies to their consumers to allow small household budgets to be stretched just a bit further, thus saving some of the very poor from the brink of starvation itself. Socialist economies often face the food price dilemma directly by attempting to maintain entirely separate and unconnected prices for producers and consumers. This requires that the state carry out all of the functions of the marketing system.

Some countries have managed these respective tasks quite efficiently and have equitable food distribution and vigorous food producing sectors to show for it. Hungary and Costa Rica are examples. Others have been trapped by the size of budget deficits or by the lack of information and the inability to make appropriate allocative decisions. The failure is characteristic of bureaucratic behavior in the absence of markets where price formation takes place. For countries with such problems, the following analysis of marketing subsidies provides insights into the nature of these difficulties. Even for countries that rely extensively on markets to allocate resources and generate price signals, analysis of marketing subsidies can identify cost-effective mechanisms to reach poor consumers.

Subsidizing Marketing Costs

One obvious way to keep farm prices high and consumer prices low is to minimize the marketing margin. Since real economic resources are required to transform food crops in space, time, and form to food that consumers buy and eat, keeping margins below their private costs requires a government subsidy. Most socialist governments and many even in market economies believe that marketing is somehow an unnecessary function. One response is to carry out all marketing tasks directly; another is to legislate narrow (or even zero) margins. Other countries recognize the real value and costs of marketing services and find mechanisms to subsidize the margins as a way of narrowing the price spread between producer and consumer.

The impact of a marketing subsidy depends on whether consumers, producers, or both realize the price benefits made possible by the subsidy. Figure 4-11 illustrates the alternative effects in a simple supply and demand framework. The figure shows a retail supply function for food grain uniformly shifted above the farm supply function by a constant marketing cost equal to $P_m - P_f$. These are real economic costs incurred in providing essential marketing services between producers and consumers. The retail demand curve for food grain shows the amounts consumers purchase at each price level. The intersection at price level P_m and quantity Q_m indicates the market equilibrium in the absence of government intervention or subsidy.

Figure 4-11. Effect of a Marketing Subsidy on Supply and Demand for Food Grains

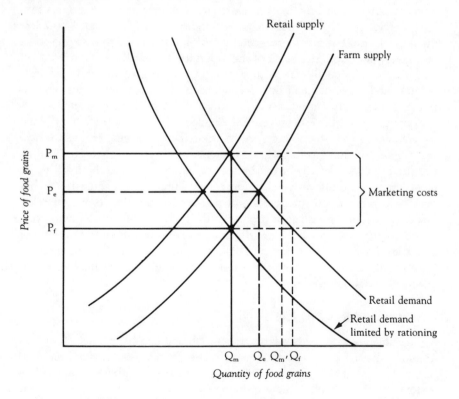

Source: C. Peter Timmer, "China and the World Food System," in Ray A. Goldberg, ed., Research in Domestic and International Agribusiness Management, vol. 2 (Greenwich, Conn.: JAI Press, 1981), p. 111.

A government subsidy on marketing costs equal to $P_m - P_f$ can have a range of results, depending on whether farmers or consumers receive most of the subsidy. Three possibilities are shown in figure 4-11. In the first possibility, farmers receive the entire subsidy so that consumer prices remain at P_m, but farm prices rise to P_m also. Farm output then rises along the farm supply function from Q_m to Q_m', and the additional output must be disposed of by the government, usually by subsidizing exports.

Alternatively, consumers receive the entire subsidy so that farm prices remain at P_f, but consumer prices drop to P_f as well. Consumer demand then increases along the retail demand curve to Q_f, and the government must either ration supplies at price P_f to the quantity Q_m that farmers are willing to produce or import additional quantities of food grain equal to $Q_f - Q_m$. Whether such imports will require subsidies depends on the relationship between domestic and international prices.

In the third alternative, producers and consumers split the marketing subsidy in such a way that a new equilibrium price and quantity is reached. In figure 4-11 this new position is shown at price P_e and quantity Q_e where farmers are just willing to produce along the supply function at price P_e a quantity that consumers are willing to consume at P_e. The government must continue to provide the full marketing subsidy of $P_m - P_f$, but no rationing or subsidized imports or exports are required.

The three examples examined here are taken from a continuum of potential effects of a marketing subsidy. The actual impact will depend on the structure of the marketing sector, how the subsidies are actually implemented, the elasticities of the supply and demand curves, and how carefully the government attempts to regulate the outcome to favor consumers or producers.

The mechanisms by which the government might implement such marketing subsidies are quite diverse. Storage costs can be subsidized with low rental rates in government-owned warehouses or with cheap credit for financing inventories. Gasoline for trucks can be subsidized, and special rates for shipping food crops on a state-owned or regulated rail system can be implemented. Imports of food processing machinery can be subsidized by special tariff and tax concessions and by an overvalued exchange rate or preferential access to foreign exchange. Working capital can be supplied cheaply from the state banking system. All of these explicit or implicit subsidies can be used to reduce the actual costs incurred by the private marketing system.

A more direct subsidy can also be used to lower the marketing margin. Wholesalers, for example, could be paid a per unit subsidy to enable them to sell a particular foodstuff for less than their costs of purchase plus costs of marketing. Rice that cost a merchant Rp 100 per kilogram to buy, store, mill, and transport to the city could be sold for Rp 60 per kilogram if the government provided a subsidy of Rp 40 per kilogram.

Alternatively, the state might simply take over the marketing tasks itself by setting up a parastatal marketing agency with monopoly control over farm sales and consumer purchases. Farm prices and consumer prices thus become a "simple" government policy decision, and a budget subsidy covers any losses on actual operational expenses. When given total monopoly power to handle food commodities, such parastatal marketing agencies have done a rather poor job of defending incentive farm prices and protecting consumer prices without massive subsidies and inefficiencies. When parastatals are used to provide a standard of competitive behavior relative to a private sector, the result is more favorable, although the private sector does tend to have lower real costs of marketing than does the typical parastatal. Consequently, some subsidy is required even in these more limited endeavors.

Both approaches to simple subsidization of marketing margins, either through the private sector or parastatals, run into a very awkward problem. Unless a simple way can be found to separate the "purchase" market from the "selling" market, there is an inevitable tendency for the cheap retail commodity to find its way back to be bought again at the higher farm price. Clearly, this transaction can happen only when the farm price is higher than the retail price for the same commodity, but it is surprising how many governments have tried to implement just such a pricing arrangement. The subsidy burden is quite large when each ton of rice, for example, is subsidized only once. When it appears two or three times on the subsidy rolls, the costs quickly mushroom out of control.

Even success in subsidizing marketing margins does not eliminate marketing costs, for another segment of society is paying them through general tax revenues for the benefit of food producers and consumers. The actual incidence of such a revenue transfer could be socially desirable, but the transfer is still occurring.

The long-run efficacy of subsidized marketing costs is difficult to judge. Future productivity gains are likely to come primarily through more efficient resource allocation led by price mechanisms based on real opportunity costs. If so, state food logistics agencies have a poor record of receiving and transmitting signals of relative scarcity, and better communication of such information will be needed. At the same time, an active government role in dampening the transmittal of sharply fluctuating international prices is likely to be desirable, as is some capacity to smooth out year-to-year fluctuations in domestic price formation.

Subsidizing Poor Consumers

The efficient way to deal with poverty is to transfer general government revenues to poor people and let them make their own allocative decisions about how best to improve their consumption bundle. Few societies wish or are able to accomplish such neutral income transfers, and yet most societies want very much to alleviate the worst manifestations of extreme poverty. Providing direct subsidies to poor consumers in the form of preferential access to or prices for special merit goods—goods whose social value is higher than their market value—is the most common approach in societies as diverse as Sri Lanka, Mexico, and the United States. Because food is considered a merit good in all societies, a number of special food subsidy schemes for poor consumers have been designed and implemented. Chapter 2 categorized these into targeted and nontargeted interventions. Three of the most important targeted food subsidy mechanisms are discussed here: dual price systems, food stamps, and subsidies for foods consumed primarily by the poor.

DUAL PRICE SYSTEMS. Several countries with market economies, especially in South Asia, have experimented with dual price systems for basic food grains. Although program details vary considerably, the logic of the approach for a closed economy, that is, one with no food imports, calls for farmers to pay a grain tax based on land cultivated or on historic yields but not on current output. Farmers thus treat the grain tax as a fixed cost of production which does not alter their resource allocation decisions or short-run incentives to produce. The grain obtained from this tax is made available in government-operated or licensed fair-price shops where low-income consumers are permitted to buy a ration quantity at very low prices. Farmers are free to sell their surplus production in an open market where consumers, including the poor, are free to buy whatever quantity they wish at the market-clearing price. Hence, there are two food prices in the system, the cheap ration price set by the government in the fair-price shops and the free-market price set by the equilibrium of supply from farmers and demand from consumers. In some systems the farmers are also paid a low "procurement price" for their grain taken by the state, thus reducing but not eliminating the tax element in the transfer.

The logic and mechanics of this dual price system also apply to a number of socialist economies that maintain parallel rural markets for state purchases and private transactions. Important information is thus generated about relative commodity scarcities, even though state purchases take place at fixed prices. In China these markets are used to provide added sources of income for rural commune members; the price signals indicate to planners how realistic their own purchase prices are for state procurement. Ration shops in cities distribute the procured grain (as well as imported supplies) at low prices to protect the purchasing power of Chinese industrial workers.

The analytics of a dual price system are quite complicated. Food production, consumption by low-income and high-income consumers separately, and an equilibrium supply and demand framework must be integrated into a consistent picture of the food system. The dynamics are illustrated sequentially in figures 4-12 to 4-14.

In figure 4-12, the original supply curve S_0 and demand curve D_0 intersect

Figure 4-12. Market Supply and Demand Framework Illustrating the Effect of a Dual Price System

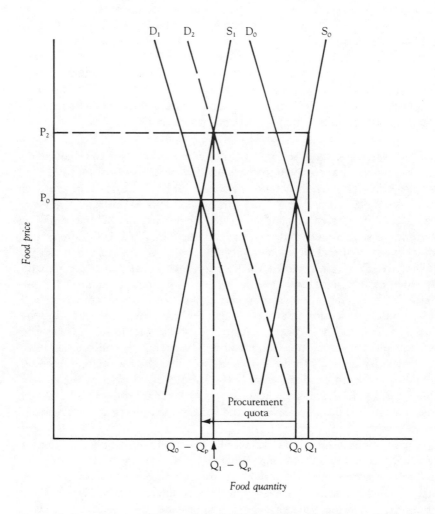

Source: C. Peter Timmer, "China and the World Food System," in Ray A. Goldberg, ed., *Research in Domestic and International Agribusiness Management*, vol. 2 (Greenwich, Conn.: JAI Press, 1981), p. 113.

to produce a market price P_0 and a quantity produced and consumed Q_0. The dual price scheme is implemented by government procurement of quantity Q_p (in figure 4-13). In the absence of any price response, this procurement of grain supplies shifts the supply and demand curves to S_1 and D_1, respectively, with the same price and the new market quantity equal to the original quantity less the procurement quantity.

Figure 4-13. Food Production Framework Illustrating the Effect of a Dual Price System

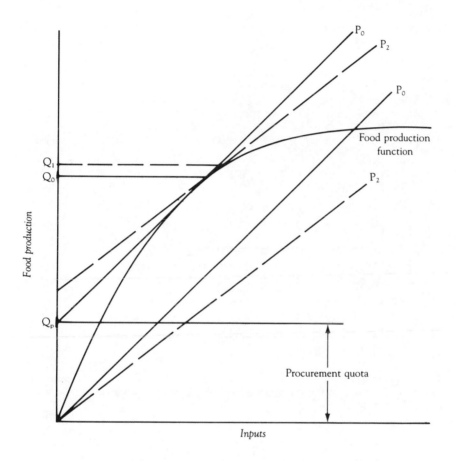

Source: C. Peter Timmer, "China and the World Food System," in Ray A. Goldberg, ed., *Research in Domestic and International Agribusiness Management*, vol. 2 (Greenwich, Conn.: JAI Press, 1981), p. 114.

The procurement quantity Q_p is sold in fair-price shops to poor consumers at, for example, half the original market price of P_0. The effect on poor consumers is shown in figure 4-14, where I_p^0 is the original indifference curve for poor consumers before the implementation of a dual price system. After the system is put into effect, poor consumers are able to reach indifference curve I_p^1 by purchasing their entire ration quantities at the ration price, plus small additional quantities of food from the open market at price P_2. The low ration price raises the quantities consumed by poor consumers because of an income effect. The added demand shifts overall market demand from

Figure 4-14. High-income and Low-income Consumer Decisionmaking
Framework Illustrating the Effect of a Fair-price Shop

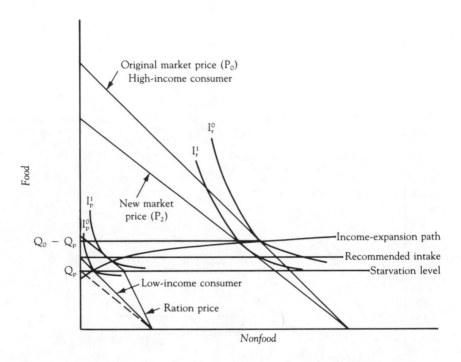

Source: C. Peter Timmer, "China and the World Food System," in Ray A. Goldberg, ed.,
Research in Domestic and International Agribusiness Management, vol. 2 (Greenwich, Conn.: JAI
Press, 1981), p. 115.

curve D_1 to demand curve D_2 (in figure 4-12). The added demand causes
supplies to increase along supply curve S_1, resulting in a new price equilibrium
at P_2. A small additional quantity is thus supplied to match the added demand
from low-income consumers (and a small decrease in demand from well-off
consumers because of the higher price in the market). By assumption, high-
income consumers may not buy food at the lower prices of the fair-price
shops.

The effects on farmers are illustrated in figure 4-13. The added production
is generated by higher food prices, relative to input prices, which cause more
intensive use of inputs along the food production function. Total output thus
rises from Q_0 to Q_1 when food prices rise from P_0 to P_2. (For simplicity,
marketing costs are ignored in this discussion.) The government procures a
fixed amount of food Q_p from farmers, who are free to produce and sell as
much as they like in the market. At the original price P_0, total production
is Q_0. At the new market equilibrium price of P_2, farmers increase the

intensity of cultivation and produce Q_1. This increase in output at price P_2 must be equal to the increase in demand from consumers through the combined effect of low prices in fair-price shops and higher market price P_2 to other consumers.

The effects on low-income and high-income consumers are shown in figure 4-14. The initial quantities of food consumed, $Q_0 - Q_p$ and Q_p, respectively, add up to total initial food production Q_0. The poor consumer is shown at "starvation" level, while the high-income consumer is well above the "recommended" level of food intake. Both consumers are located on a general income expansion path for food.

After the government procures quantity Q_p from farmers, it makes the food available to poor consumers in fair-price shops at a price just half the original price of P_0. The income effect of this cheap price raises food consumption of poor consumers, with the supplemental quantities being purchased at the new higher market price P_2. The new higher market price P_2 forces well-off consumers from indifference curve I_r^0 to I_r^1, and their food intake is lowered slightly. The increase in food consumption among the poor minus the small decrease among rich consumers must equal the increased quantity of food produced by farmers as a result of the new higher price P_2. The supply and demand framework of figure 4-12 must be consistent with the production function results of figure 4-13 and the consumer decision-making results in figure 4-14. Although these shifts are difficult to demonstrate graphically, markets automatically make the necessary adjustments to reach consistency.

The three figures can also be used to show the impact on poor consumers who might be excluded from the fair-price shops. The new higher market prices may force them below the starvation level. In addition, if fair-price shops do not limit the quantity for sale or restrict their sales to low-income consumers, procurement quantities will be inadequate to stock the shops. Food imports will be needed to fill the gap. Otherwise the fair-price shops may be sold out and not provide low-cost food grain on a regular basis.

The successful dual price system has several key ingredients that are identified by this analytical approach. First, it requires access to significant quantities of low-cost grain from farms large enough to produce sizable marketings. Second, it requires careful control over access to the cheap grain available in the fair-price shops. For the system to work, the ration quantities must be limited to the amounts available, and the rations must be restricted to those at the bottom end of the income distribution, possibly by choosing commodities only the poor will consume. If some of the poor are excluded from the system, they are doubly disadvantaged, for not only are they denied cheap grain from the fair-price shop, but the free-market price is now substantially higher than it would have been in the absence of the dual price system.

Although it might appear that a carefully designed system can operate without a subsidy, especially if the procurement price is sufficiently low (even zero) so that revenue from ration sales pays for procurement and distribution costs, the system clearly requires resource transfers from farmers to consumers. If the burden of the transfers is on large wealthy farmers to benefit low-income consumers, income distribution may become more equal. However, much experience points to the burden falling primarily on low- or middle-income farmers to the benefit of middle-income urban consumers—typically a regressive income transfer. The very poor are frequently excluded from the benefits.

A very carefully designed procurement program can minimize the disincentive effects on agricultural production and hence prevent large efficiency losses, but most existing programs have been neither designed nor implemented so carefully. A common outcome is that prices for all farm output are depressed through the procurement program and incentives are sharply diminished. Even for the most carefully designed program, the tax equivalent of the grain procurement reduces savings available for private, farm-level investment in raising agricultural productivity. Such farm-level investment, when permitted, typically has a high payoff.

Food stamps. Food stamps have been widely used in the United States as the main government program for reducing hunger among poor people. Nearly 20 million people received a net value of over $6,000 million in food stamps in 1981. This large government program remains very controversial, and widely publicized reports of fraud and cheating as well as evidence of significant disincentives for food stamp recipients to take low-paying jobs have eroded public and congressional support. Strongest support for the program comes from labor and social welfare groups and farm lobbies. Farmers have found that the food stamp program adds to demand through the regular food marketing system and thus contributes significantly to farm incomes.

Only a few developing countries have attempted to subsidize their poor consumers by using food stamps—Sri Lanka, Trinidad and Tobago, and Colombia. Despite the theoretical efficiency of food stamps in providing food subsidies targeted precisely to those most in need, the actual implementation record so far is quite mixed. If no serious attempt is made to implement a means test, then food stamps transfer commodity-specific income to a broad range of consumers. If poor consumers are already allocating much of their budgets to these commodities, the transfer serves as a general income transfer rather than as a food-specific transfer. Of course, without a discriminating means test, a large proportion of the population may try to use the program.

Where serious attempts are made to limit food stamps to the most impoverished households, all the problems of implementing an honest and efficient means test arise. Many relatively well-off households slip into the system, many of the most destitute fall outside, and the bureaucratic costs become very large. Food stamp programs as an efficient targeting mechanism for food subsidies can probably be used effectively only in middle-income countries with a skilled civil service and accurate statistical records on at least the urban population. For poorer countries and in the rural areas of even the middle-income countries food stamps are not likely to be effective.

POOR PEOPLE'S FOODS. The poor in most societies eat different foods from those consumed by middle- and upper-income groups. As chapter 2 showed, even in those countries where 70 to 90 percent of calories come from starchy staples, the diets of the poor are remarkably different from the average availability shown in a food balance sheet. Poor people's foods tend to be root crops (cassava, sweet potatoes, Irish potatoes) or coarse grains (corn, sorghum, millet, and others). The preferred staple in most societies is either rice or wheat although corn is preferred in some African and Latin American countries. In rice cultures wheat is sometimes regarded as an inferior good.

Such sharp contrasts in food consumption patterns by income class within a country are not caused by differences in taste but by economic necessity. The poor in Indonesia eating cassava and corn would prefer to eat rice, as would the barley eaters in the Republic of Korea in the early 1970s. If a society does not have the bureaucratic and financial resources to provide subsidies for the more expensive preferred foods, subsidies to poor people's foods can be effectively self-targeting. If only the poor choose to eat the subsidized inferior staples, only the poor capture the subsidy.

At the same time, many of the inferior foods are produced by very poor farmers on marginal lands at considerable distance from major urban centers. Marketing subsidies that raise the returns to these farmers while lowering the costs to the consumers may work simultaneously on both dimensions of poverty. Simply forcing down prices, however, would have a devastating impact on the incomes and welfare of some of the poorest of the rural poor.

Such subsidies have both short-run and long-run costs. In the short run, implementing subsidies for commodities that do not travel or store well (root crops) or for which well-developed marketing systems do not exist is usually not feasible without significant investment in food technology and improved marketing infrastructure. Because farmers tend to switch to growing more profitable crops, obtaining supplies of these commodities when market prices are being forced down is an obvious problem. Providing subsidies to poor consumers via commodity-specific food stamps (available with minimal bureaucratic processing) while allowing incentive prices for farmers in commercial markets might be more feasible. Alternatively, an imported commodity can be an efficient carrier of subsidies to poor consumers and have less impact on domestic farmers. A subsidized low-quality wheat flour might have this effect in Sri Lanka, for example.

The longer-run effects are more troubling and suggest that disaggregated commodity price policies probably can serve only as short-run bridges across the food price dilemma. The distortions introduced by significant subsidies on a single commodity can eventually be very powerful. Low prices for high-quality wheat at one time led to almost one-third of Sri Lanka's calories being provided by a foodstuff it could not grow. Livestock industries find heavily subsidized corn or wheat a cheap, high-quality animal feed. Such grain-fed livestock industries redirect the subsidy from poor people to rich people. The lower prices for these inferior foods almost inevitably dampen incentives for research and development of new technology for the crops and reduce the profitability of growing them.

The implementation of food subsidies for poor consumers through the regular channels of the marketing system is the most efficient way to protect food intake of the poor when price incentives to farmers are improved. But both the analytics of the design and the historical implementation record suggest great difficulties in isolating the targeted food subsidy programs for poor people from more general food subsidies for all consumers, or all urban consumers. Such general subsidies have enormous fiscal effects and serious disincentive consequences for agriculture. Both the problems and the potential rewards of successfully implementing targeted food subsidy programs explain the extensive attention in this book to these topics.

Government Intervention and Policy Perspective

Developing a marketing strategy for government intervention requires a clear vision of what the marketing system should accomplish in the future plus a suitably detailed empirical understanding of what it actually does accomplish now. This chapter has attempted to provide both the vision and the analytical tools to address the empirical questions of market performance. The elements of a marketing strategy can be identified by combining these two approaches.

MARKETING EFFICIENCY. Marketing analysis shows that the formation of price margins is largely a function of two elements: the costs of transportation, storage, and processing; and the efficiency with which these marketing services are provided. The government's role is to invest in the components of a marketing system to the extent that social benefits from lowered marketing costs match the social opportunity costs of the public resources needed for the investment. Lowering marketing costs is clearly a good thing as long as more resources are saved than are needed to save them.

In addition to a concern for lowering the real costs of marketing, governments need to focus on the efficiency with which marketing services are provided. In market economies, inefficiency means excess profits, and excess profits mean monopolistic middlemen or collusion in price formation. Both sources of excess profits are extremely difficult to regulate directly because of enforcement problems. In the face of solid evidence of market inefficiency (as opposed to high costs), governments are faced with two quite divergent alternatives. The first is to improve the competitiveness of the marketing system by creating better market access for potential participants who might provide marketing services and by distributing better information for consumers, producers, and marketing agents about factors likely to affect price formation.

The second alternative is for the government to provide the marketing services directly, setting a competitive standard that all other marketing participants must meet. In most countries that have followed this course, it was the government which could not meet the competitive standard of the existing marketing participants. Continuing the government's marketing role thus would require either significant budget subsidies to cover the high costs or the banning of private market activities to eliminate the competition, thereby forcing consumers to pay the costs of government inefficiency.

Banning private marketing activities never improves the welfare of broad groups of either farmers or consumers. No government has ever been completely successful with such a ban, although many have tried. Subsidized government marketing agencies, however, can play an important and socially profitable role. If the subsidy is not too large, the agency can reflect a competitive standard for private marketing agents without driving them out of business. At the same time, a public marketing agency can implement a price stabilization policy that requires active government intervention to defend a floor price for farmers and a ceiling price for consumers—a particularly useful role for a government agency in reducing extreme and unexpected seasonal price swings. Again, the margin between the two will determine the amount of budget subsidy required by the public agency to cover its own real costs as well as the ability of the private trade to continue to provide a significant share of marketing services. Forcing the entire food marketing burden into government hands either by active policy or by default presents an awesome task of coordination, physical handling, and price formation. No government has handled the task on its own even when it wanted to, and those that have tried to handle more rather than less have achieved less rather than more.

The purpose of having efficient and low-cost marketing services provided to the food system in particular, and to the whole economy in general, is twofold. First, and most important in the short run, low marketing costs are the most efficient and sustainable solution to the food price dilemma. The narrower the margin because of genuinely low marketing costs and highly efficient price formation, the more consumers and producers both can share in the productivity potential of a healthy agricultural economy.

The second purpose is to enable markets to function in their dynamic role of coordinating resource allocation and providing accurate signals to producers and consumers that reflect the opportunity costs of their decisions. Implicit in this role is the ability of producers and consumers, and indeed of the marketing agents as well, to react quickly and efficiently to new price signals from the market. Although most economic models show decisionmakers moving from one equilibrium to another equilibrium after, for example, a price change, the actual process of adjusting to a new disequilibrium environment is much more complicated.

Economic development is inherently a process of continuing disequilibrium. The economic value of being able to cope successfully and efficiently with disequilibrium rises sharply as new technology, new markets, and new opportunities are thrust into traditional economies. T. W. Schultz has emphasized how important education is in building the capacity to process new information and decide quickly on appropriate responses. Education, at least at the level of functional literacy, is considered by most governments to be a basic human need. Beyond this, however, education is essential to the dynamic efficiency of market systems and their distributional outcome. Poor people tend to be the least educated and thus have the least capacity to respond appropriately to the opportunities offered by disequilibrium situations.

THE LEVEL OF PRICES. In a competitive food marketing system the level of prices is determined simultaneously with the various margins among prices. Because real economic resources must be used to provide marketing services, the formation of price margins is the major determinant of the efficiency of resource allocation in the marketing sector. Similarly, the formation of price levels determines the efficiency of resource allocation in food production and consumption. These price levels are also crucial determinants of income distribution, especially between urban and rural sectors, and of the distribution of food intake.

Many governments in both socialist and market systems have intervened in the formation of price levels to influence the distribution of income and food and have willingly sacrificed efficiency goals to do so. Through trade and subsidy instruments that most governments can implement quite effectively, food prices can be set (at least for short periods) with wide discretion.

The tension between the desire to set food prices for short-run distributional reasons and the need to avoid long-run productivity losses that mount from such seriously distorted prices is not easily resolved, even with collective ownership and decisionmaking. The dilemma is not so sharp for wealthy societies which have the budgetary and management resources to use food stamps or other welfare programs to protect the consumption levels of very poor people. For less fortunate societies more structural compromises have seemed inevitable, with at least part of the price and market system being used to deliver food to the poor.

To reconcile the conflict between food prices set for efficiency purposes and food prices set for distributional purposes, ways must be found to target the effects of price policy interventions. Food stamps target benefits to poor people very effectively if the bureaucratic capacity exists to identify and reach them with appropriate amounts of stamps. This is a big "if." Fair-price shops in the context of a dual food price system have been tried extensively in South Asia. Research by the International Food Policy Research Institute points to positive consumption consequences of the systems in both Bangladesh and India. The programs, however, have had very large leakages to nonpoor consumers and significant disincentive effects for farmers. Most rural consumers have been out of reach of the system. Price targeting by commodity, with subsidies paid only for food consumed primarily by the poor, has not been tried extensively anywhere, but the strategy must face problems of supply and the potential use of subsidized inferior foods as livestock feed. All three approaches used simultaneously in an intersecting targeted program—food stamps to gain access to fair-price shops that sell foods consumed primarily by the poor—might offer a financially feasible and effective alternative.

The temptation for governments to intervene in food marketing and price formation is very great. A variety of interventions can contribute to important social goals. Investments can lower marketing costs. Well-managed public buffer stocks can improve price stability and set competitive standards for private markets. Appropriate price levels can improve production incentives or increase food consumption. But an even greater variety of interventions can disrupt the food system or bring it to a standstill. Narrow margins set by legislation can drive most food marketing activities into hiding. Heavy consumer subsidies for the major foodstuff can distort producer incentives and place enormous burdens on the budget. Parastatal marketing agencies with monopoly power can immobilize the efficient allocation of resources and simultaneously damage the welfare of both poor farmers and poor consumers.

Marketing systems are at once fragile and robust. They are fragile because government actions can, with ease, drastically raise the risks of storing, transporting, and processing food. With higher risks come higher marketing costs and a distortion of price signals to producers, consumers, and marketing agents alike. Poor societies can ill afford the waste from such distortion and inefficiency, especially when caused by the actions of their own governments.

The robustness of marketing systems comes from the flexibility, adaptability, and sheer drive to survive and do better that is characteristic of most decisionmakers in most marketing systems. Markets never entirely disappear. They are too important for both people and society. A strategy that nurtures their development by encouraging equal access, rather than forces them into hiding, is likely to pay handsome social rewards.

Bibliographical Note

Discussions of markets and prices and of price policies can be found in a number of books on microeconomic theory, but no textbook deals with these topics explicitly in the context of food crop marketing in developing countries. The two texts that best complement this chapter are Raymond G. Bressler, Jr., and Richard A. King, *Markets, Prices, and Interregional Trade* (New York: John Wiley, 1970), and William G. Tomek and Kenneth L. Robinson, *Agricultural Product Prices* (Ithaca, N.Y.: Cornell University Press, 1981). Analysis of price formation in the presence of divergences between private and social valuations in supply or demand is presented in W. M. Corden, *Trade Policy and Economic Welfare* (Oxford: Clarendon Press, 1974). A modern statement of trade theory and a complete discussion of international price formation are contained in Richard E. Caves and Ronald W. Jones, *World Trade and Payments: An Introduction* (Boston, Mass.: Little, Brown, 1981). An important but quite sophisticated analysis of international buffer stock schemes to stabilize commodity prices is presented in David M. G. Newbery and Joseph E. Stiglitz, *The Theory of Commodity Price Stabilization: A Study in the Economics of Risk* (Oxford: Clarendon Press, 1981). Their conclusions cast serious doubts on the workability of and benefits from such schemes. This reinforces this chapter's emphasis on domestic price policy and the use of international markets to further domestic objectives.

A discussion of market power and price formation is in Kenneth Arrow, "Toward a Theory of Price Adjustment," *The Allocation of Economic Resources* (Stanford, Calif.: Stanford University Press, 1959). This volume also contains a classic article by Hendrik Houthakker on seasonal price formation, "The Scope and Limits of Futures Trading." Further discussion of market failure is in Francis Bator, "The Anatomy of Market Failure," *Quarterly Journal of Economics* (August 1958). The role of education in coping with disequilibrium is discussed in Theodore W. Schultz, *Investment in Human Capital: The Role of Education and of Research* (New York: Free Press, 1971).

Examples of the analytical methods introduced in the chapter are presented in a variety of books and articles. Techniques of price analysis are explained in Frederick V. Waugh, *Demand and Price Analysis*, Technical Bulletin no. 1316 (Washington, D.C.: U.S. Department of Agriculture, Economic and Statistical Analysis Division, 1964). An empirical analysis of seasonal price formation is presented in Richard H. Goldman, "Seasonal Rice Prices in Indonesia, 1953–69: An Anticipatory Price Analysis," *Food Research Institute Studies*, vol. 13, no. 2 (1974), pp. 99–143. A study of marketing margins is contained in C. Peter Timmer, "A Model of Rice Marketing Margins in Indonesia," *Food Research Institute Studies*, vol. 13, no. 2 (1974), pp. 145–67. A discussion of range of farmer choice in crop sales is in Ammar Siamwalla, "Farmers and Middlemen: Aspects of Agricultural Marketing in Thailand" (Bangkok: United Nations Asian Development Institute, 1975).

Techniques that can be used to analyze proposed projects for expanding marketing capacity are discussed in J. Price Gittinger, *Economic Analysis of Agricultural Projects*, 2d ed. (Baltimore, Md.: Johns Hopkins University Press, 1982). The analysis needed to generate data for mapping marketing margins is illustrated in Scott R. Pearson, J. Dirck Stryker, Charles P. Humphreys, and others, *Rice in West Africa: Policy and Economics* (Stanford, Calif.: Stanford University Press, 1981). An analysis of the benefits of price stabilization is presented in Saleh Afiff and C. Peter Timmer, "Rice Policy in Indonesia," *Food Research Institute Studies*, vol. 10, no. 2 (1971), pp. 131–59. The use of rice prices as a major policy instrument by Asian governments is analyzed in two special issues of *Food Research Institute Studies* edited by C. Peter Timmer, "The Political Economy of Rice in Asia," vol. 14, nos. 3 and 4 (1975).

Various approaches have been used to describe and analyze marketing systems and policies for food crops. Elements of the perspective used here draw on the work of William O. Jones, especially *Marketing Staple Food Crops in Tropical Africa* (Ithaca, N.Y.: Cornell University Press, 1972). A case study using the Jones approach is reported in V. Roy Southworth, William O. Jones, and Scott R. Pearson, "Food Crop Marketing in Atebubu District, Ghana," *Food Research Institute Studies*, vol. 17, no. 2 (1979), pp. 157–95.

The issues of postharvest losses during storage, transporting, and processing are treated in a major section of Nevin S. Scrimshaw and Mitchell B. Wallerstein, eds., *Nutrition Policy Implementation: Issues and Experience* (New York: Plenum Press, 1972), which includes a comment by Michael Lipton that cites important work done at the Institute of Development Studies at Sussex. See, for example, Martin Greeley, "Appropriate Technology: Recent Indian Experience with Farm-level Food-grain Research," *Food Policy*, vol. 3, no. 1 (February 1978), pp. 39–49.

Three review papers place many of the food crop marketing issues discussed in this chapter in development perspective: John C. Abbott, "The Development of Marketing Institutions," in Herman M. Southworth and Bruce F. Johnston, eds., *Agricultural Development and Economic Growth* (Ithaca, N.Y.: Cornell University Press, 1969), pp. 364–93; Vernon Ruttan, "Agricultural Product and Factor Markets in Southeast Asia," *Economic Development and Cultural Change*, vol. 17, no. 4 (July 1969), pp. 501–19; and Barbara Harriss, "There Is a Method in My Madness: Or Is It Vice Versa? Measuring Agricultural Market Performance," *Food Research Institute Studies*, vol. 17, no. 2 (1979), pp. 197–218.

Book-length case studies include: Paul J. Bohannon and George Dalton, eds., *Markets in Africa* (Evanston, Ill.: Northwestern University Press, 1962); Uma J. Lele, *Food Grain Marketing in India: Private Performance and Public Policy* (Ithaca, N.Y.: Cornell University Press, 1971); and Leon A. Mears, *Rice Marketing in the Republik of Indonesia* (Jakarta: P. T. Pembangunan, 1961). Results from a number of West African studies are contained in Elliot Berg, "Marketing, Food Policy and Storage of Food Grains in the Sahel" (Ann Arbor: University of Michigan/USAID, Center for Research on Economic Development, 1977). A series of Latin American studies is summarized in Kelly Harrison and others, "Improving Food Marketing Systems in Developing Countries: Experience from Latin America," Research Report no. 6

(East Lansing: Michigan State University, Latin American Studies Center, November 1976).

Trade protection has been an important topic of recent research. D. Gale Johnson's book, *World Agriculture in Disarray* (New York: Macmillan, 1973), documented many of the inefficiencies in agricultural trade patterns and their high cost to consumers in rich and poor countries. Alex McCalla and Timothy Josling, eds., *Imperfect Markets in Agricultural Trade* (Montclair, N.J.: Allenheld-Osman, 1981), has an extensive bibliography and assessment of research needs. Studies by International Food Policy Research Institute, *Agricultural Protection in OECD Countries: Its Cost to Less Developed Countries* (Washington, D.C.: IFPRI, December 1980), and Jimmye Hillman, *Nontariff Agricultural Trade Barriers* (Lincoln: University of Nebraska Press, 1978), look specifically at the problems of developing countries caused by the agricultural trade barriers of developed countries.

5

Macroeconomic Policies and the Food System

Food policy analysts would seem to have enough to worry about with food consumption and nutrition, food production and rural employment generation, domestic food price formation and the efficiency of storage, transportation, and processing, and the effects of international prices on both domestic prices and the opportunity costs of domestic policies. Indeed, "getting the issues right" in all these areas is a large task, and designing effective policies to deal with the issues an even larger one. Few countries are this far along in understanding and implementing consistent policies designed to reach the four basic objectives for the food sector. Certainly much can be done to improve sectoral policies and performance without looking beyond the micro sectors.

Still, that is not enough. In the long run, macroeconomic forces are too pervasive and too powerful for micro sectoral strategies to overcome. When they work at cross-purposes, as they do in many developing countries, an unfavorable macroeconomic environment will ultimately erode even the best plans for consumption, production, or marketing. A simple example that integrates issues from all three sectors into a macro context illustrates why this is so.

Before rice can be eaten, it must first be grown and then processed into the milled rice preferred by consumers. Exactly how the milling is done turns out to be very important because it affects employment, income distribution, the amount of rice available to consumers (or the amount of rice imported or exported), and incentives to producers to grow rice. The range of technology available for milling rice varies enormously—from hand-pounding with a pole in a hollowed log to very sophisticated and expensive multiple-pass milling machines integrated with large-scale drying and storage facilities that provide optimal control over the rice grain from delivery after harvest to packaging for consumers.

Rice milling facilities in between these two extremes range from very small, self-contained mills, which offer labor savings over hand-pounding at modest capital expense, to larger mills, which become progressively more expensive, more labor-saving, and more technically efficient in converting paddy into milled rice. The choice is not restricted to the extremes although either can be appropriate in particular circumstances. The choice is wide. The opportunity exists to find just the right combination of investment cost, use of labor, and technical efficiency to fit a particular local environment.

What is the appropriate choice of technique in rice milling? The more costly techniques in terms of investment per ton of milling capacity are also more technically efficient. For each ton of rough rice input, the more sophisticated facilities produce higher quality rice with less waste. The smaller and cheaper mills, however, need more labor per ton of capacity and will create more jobs than larger-scale mills. If a private entrepreneur is trying to make a decision about investing in a rice mill, asking which technique is appropriate is similar analytically to asking how farmers should produce their output—the factor-factor decision analyzed in chapter 3 with the isoquant in figure 3-2. When the private sector is making the investment decision in the context of market prices, the technique which is least costly per ton of output will be installed.

Like the fertilizer and rice prices facing the farmer in chapter 3, the relevant prices in the rice miller's decision are not set solely by market forces, but are susceptible to policy influence. The miller's calculations depend on nearly every important macroeconomic variable in a country: foreign exchange rates, interest rates, wage rates, and rice prices. Foreign exchange rates dictate the cost of imported machinery for the rice mill, interest rates determine the cost of the loan to pay for the machinery and the building, wage rates determine the labor costs of running the establishment after it is operational, and rice prices determine the value of the additional milled rice produced from each ton of paddy input by more technically efficient facilities.

When macro policy alters these important prices from their equilibrium values based on existing domestic abundance and scarcity of the factors, the impact on choice of technique can be dramatic. When grain prices are kept low, storage and processing facilities that save grain are not so profitable; few investments are made to save grain, and little management effort is exerted to run the available facilities efficiently. When interest rates are heavily subsidized and wage rates for unskilled labor are raised by legislation, large-scale, capital-intensive mills are installed in the midst of widespread unemployment. If foreign exchange is allocated to preferred investors at a cheap price, they will invest heavily in imported machinery, which tends to be labor-displacing, while other investors outside the allocation process may not even be able to purchase spare parts for their trucks or small-scale mills. Although the example here uses rice mills, the impact of distorted macro prices on domestic investors obviously extends to nearly every sector.

For analysts to determine both the impact of existing macro policies on

private investors in rice mills and the appropriate milling technique to maximize social profitability, two separate issues must be addressed. First, social
profitability analysis of the alternative techniques will indicate which one
adds most to the social value of milled rice relative to rough rice. Second,
this analysis will include a calculation of the budget allocations needed to
translate the desired level of macro prices that reflect social profitability into
actual market prices that private investors will use to make decisions. Determining the desired levels for these prices places the issue of appropriate
rice milling investments in a larger social context.

The answer to which technique is appropriate in social as opposed to private
terms depends on how society values job creation, the alternative uses of
investment funds, and the foreign exchange needed to pay for milling machinery and the rice imported to replace that lost in processing when a less
technically efficient mill is chosen. In other words, what is the scarcity value
of labor? What is the opportunity cost of capital? What is society's capacity
to produce goods for export in order to import?

Empirical analysis of these questions often shows that existing market prices
diverge from social opportunity costs. In the terminology of the programming
tableau of chapter 3, the shadow prices for labor, capital, and foreign exchange may be different from market values used by private decisionmakers
in the economy. Sometimes this happens because of government intervention.

For example, if interest rates are subsidized in the hope of inducing investment in modern plants and equipment, rice millers may buy facilities
that are technically sophisticated but difficult to manage in a traditional rural
economy where the marketing infrastructure is inadequate to supply the daily
input needs of a large modern unit. Then the private interest costs are being
distorted by government policy.

Alternatively, if widespread rural unemployment exists, the social cost of
employing labor may be much less than the actual market wage for the reasons
discussed in chapter 3. Here the failure is in the market mechanism itself,
and policymakers may then seek interventions to reduce the profitability of
more capital-intensive, labor-saving mills in order to generate more jobs.

Several important tradeoffs are involved in these policy decisions. Keeping
wages high will help those with jobs, but may induce firms to choose technologies that use little labor. Forcing interest rates down may prevent owners
of capital from receiving large earnings on their savings, but it may force
capital into unproductive uses. In addition, closing any gap between social
and private prices for important factors of production and commodities usually
requires government subsidies. Consequently, finding the socially appropriate
policy environment depends on the difficulty of raising funds to pay for these
budget subsidies.

These subsidies can be used to narrow the marketing margin and soften
the food price dilemma, but at the same time they will also favor investment

in more technically efficient mills that displace labor. Only technically efficient mills can survive the pressure caused by very narrow margins between paddy and milled rice prices. Price policies that lower domestic rice prices will favor consumers at the expense of producers, but lower rice prices also favor labor-intensive rice mills. These smaller mills waste more rice and generally produce a lower quality of output. Some clear and obvious tradeoffs are apparent in making this choice.

Government policies strongly condition the macro environment in which micro decisions are made by consumers, producers, and marketing agents in the food system. When it is recognized that fiscal and monetary policies are intimately connected to the real values of policy-determined factor prices, it is apparent that macroeconomic policy has a pervasive influence on the structure of incentives and performance in the entire food system. Especially in the long run, macroeconomic policy determines the rate of growth of both urban and rural sectors and also conditions the structure of that growth. In particular, the degree of job creation and the distribution of income (and food consumption) are more a function of macroeconomic policy than of sectoral investments and project design.

A major dilemma exists over this powerful role of the macro economy because short-run income distribution consequences of a policy are frequently the opposite of its long-run effects. Consequently, the food price dilemma which is the focus of much of this book has its parallel in macro policy. Because of the important two-way connections between food policy and macro policy, it is necessary to integrate the food price dilemma into this basic equity-efficiency tradeoff for macro policy, a task for later in the chapter. First, a review of the simple elements of macroeconomics in a food policy context is necessary. Analysts should hope to draw from this review not the skills needed to design better macro policies, but rather the insight and language needed to participate in the debate over macro policy reforms. These reforms have enormous implications for the food sector.

The Macro Economy and Macro Policies

Comprehending the relationship between the food system and the macro economy helps identify the policy issues and range of choices available to policymakers. A distorted set of macro policies—which typically includes rapid inflation, an overvalued exchange rate, subsidized interest rates for preferred creditors, minimum wages for an urban working class elite, and depressed rural incentives—makes rapid growth in agricultural output extremely difficult, while it simultaneously skews the distribution of earned income. Short-run interests of poor people are often protected to some extent by such policies because they tend to make cheap food available through subsidized imports.

When macro policies are badly distorted, their cumulative impact puts pressure on the economy for major policy reforms. As these pressures build, the options available to food policymakers are extremely limited: more investment in irrigation, a better agricultural research and extension program, perhaps a subsidy on fertilizer and modern seeds. These will contribute to agricultural growth, but in the constraining environment of distorted macro policies, such programs will not provide the basis for long-run dynamic growth of rural output and incomes, which is the essential base for a food policy that simultaneously increases food production while reducing hunger.

Consequently, policy analysts need to understand the elements of an effective macro reform and determine its impact on food policy objectives. It is not the mandate or the prerogative of food policy analysts to design and implement such reforms. But the reforms do come eventually because serious macro distortions generate powerful forces for macro policies more consistent with real scarcity values in the economy. Either external creditors—the International Monetary Fund, World Bank, bilateral donor agencies, or the multinational commercial banks—force these painful adjustments when a crisis is reached, or else a country's macro policymakers stay ahead of the situation and design new policies that avert a crisis.

At one level these macro reforms are simple and obvious—remove the distortions in macro prices and change fiscal and monetary policies to slow the rate of inflation. Even without specific concern for the food sector, such a macro reform is likely to raise farm incomes by improving the rural-urban terms of trade. The food price will rise to its international opportunity cost. More broadly, the devaluation that brings foreign exchange rates into equilibrium usually will pump new purchasing power into rural areas, with positive effects on rural employment and improved income distribution. Eventually, scarcity values for labor and capital will induce a new efficiency in resource use which leads to greater employment creation and faster economic growth.

Governments, however, are usually very reluctant to take these steps, for there are major short-run political and welfare consequences. For the reforms to be effective, many price increases will be needed, and overall budget subsidies must be cut. The real incomes of many workers and civil servants will be sharply reduced, and the urban political base of a government can be seriously threatened in the wake of the painful adjustments needed. With regard to food policy, those adjustments hinge critically on the likely reductions in food consumption by poor households caused by the higher food prices that almost inevitably accompany a macro reform. Here lies a major concern of the food policy analyst, for if a macro reform is in the works, those responsible for food policy had best be prepared with a set of food consumption interventions that will prevent the worst manifestations of such a squeeze on the poor.

A more active role is also possible. By carefully laying out the conflict between food consumption and productive efficiency to macro policymakers and by designing short-run targeted food consumption subsidies—of the types described in chapters 2 and 4—to help poor people across the bridge to long-run economic growth, food policy analysts can make it easier for macro policymakers to proceed with the needed reforms. The political inertia so often observed in the face of macro economies run amok is entirely understandable. It is an almost inevitable result of the basic food price dilemma itself, as extended to the macro context. An analytically sound food policy offers macro policymakers a new potential for action. Capturing this opportunity requires a dialogue between food policy and macro policy analysts; for this exchange the food policy analyst needs to understand the world from the macro analyst's point of view.

Describing Macro Economies

Macro economies can be described in four quite different, and yet ultimately identical, ways: in terms of demand, supply, and income, and in monetary terms. In the demand approach the total of a nation's economic activity is disaggregated into the major components of final demand—usually consumption, private investment, government expenditures, and any excess of exports over imports. When totaled, these components make up a country's gross domestic product, or GDP. When net income transfers to or from abroad are added, the total is gross national product, or GNP. The composition and overall aggregate of demand has provided the main focus of macroeconomic theory and policy in market economies since the Keynesian revolution began in the 1930s.

Just as food cannot be consumed unless it is first produced, aggregate demand cannot be met without a supply of goods and services. The supply approach focuses on the structure by sector of production in an economy. When output from agriculture, industry, services, and government is totaled, the result is also GDP, and hence aggregate supply equals aggregate demand. Political and theoretical attention in developed countries has recently been directed to this "supply side," as declining productivity and "stagflation"—the combination of economic stagnation and rapid inflation—have discredited much of modern macroeconomics as practiced in the industrialized countries. The supply approach to macroeconomics has a long tradition, however, as classical macroeconomic theory focuses attention on the dynamics of long-run aggregate supply. This concern for expansion of output has obvious relevance to developing countries—a relevance that concern for the adequacy of aggregate demand often does not have.

The production of goods and services requires the employment of factors of production—labor, capital, land, entrepreneurship and management—which earn income in return for their services. These incomes provide the wherewithal to purchase the goods and services that have been produced. Incomes thus provide a third way of tallying up national economic activity.

In market economies the total of wages, interest, rent, and profits is spent on the components of aggregate final demand, and so total incomes also equal GDP. Aggregate income and its distribution among the basic claimants in the economy are major concerns of macroeconomic analysis.

In socialist economies where rationing is used to distribute many goods and services and where the domestic currency is not convertible into foreign exchange (and hence into imports), the total national economic output is much more difficult to tally. Excess consumer purchasing power, arbitrary accounting prices, and the direct allocation of housing, health services, and even public transportation make Western macroeconomic accounting systems of little use. At the same time, the distribution of incomes is determined primarily by the availability of rationed goods and services, not by money incomes as such. For this reason, the extremes of poverty and wealth often seen in market economies are not so prevalent in those socialist economies that are well managed.

Each of these three ways of describing a macro economy—demand, supply, and income—will be equally valid even in a traditional, subsistence economy where exchange of goods and services takes place only by physical barter. Nearly all economies have found a more efficient mechanism of exchange— the use of money as a medium in which the prices of all goods and services are quoted. Indeed, it is through prices that all the components can be added in a meaningful way. The use of monetary units, however, should not hide the "real" nature of the economy being examined. Even when the real level of activity is constant, the monetary total of economic activity can change because of changes in the general level of prices.

A general increase in prices—inflation—is a monetary phenomenon caused by changes in the amount of money in circulation (or the rate at which it changes hands). The monetary policies that bring about inflation, however, also involve variables that affect the real economy. A complex and poorly understood relationship exists among the money supply, interest rates, inflation, price expectations, investment, and the distribution of income. Money is more than just a convenient medium of exchange. It is also a significant factor with direct influence on the level of macroeconomic activity. The description and analysis of a macro economy in monetary terms is as legitimate and important as its description and analysis in terms of demand, supply, and income.

These various macroeconomic approaches would seem to be of scant concern to food policy analysts. As seen in the rice milling example, however, most governments try to influence the level and distribution of macroeconomic activity with a variety of policy instruments, nearly all of which have powerful direct or indirect effects on the food system as well as on overall economic performance. Some of these effects on the food system are intended, but most are simply accidental fallout. Much of macro policy is designed with little thought given to its ultimate impact on such important food system variables as production, prices, distribution of consumption, and volume of food imports.

Three main areas of macroeconomic policy will receive attention here: the budget, fiscal and monetary policy, and macro prices (foreign exchange rates, interest rates, and wage rates). In addition, macro policy has an indirect but powerful impact on food prices specifically and on the overall terms of trade between rural and urban sectors more broadly. The terms of trade will also be considered as an element of macro policy.

The impact of macro policy on the formation of food policy, and on the food system itself, is summarized in figure 5-1. Although in the figure all the arrows connecting macro policy to food policy flow in one direction only, feedback effects can be important in particular circumstances. The diagram emphasizes the dual nature of macroeconomic policy: its fiscal and monetary component primarily expressed via budgetary policy and subsequent implications for monetary growth; and its policy component with respect to the three macro prices—foreign exchange rates, interest rates, and wage rates. Inflation plays a central role in conditioning the real levels faced by the micro decisionmakers in an economy of policy-determined, nominal macro prices. In addition, the border policies discussed in chapter 4 are a major determinant of food prices directly and of the rural-urban terms of trade more broadly. Figure 5-1 assembles all the components that comprise a country's food policy.

Budget Policy

No government budget anywhere in the world is allocated solely on the basis of economic criteria. The budgetary process involves hearing and judging competing claims for budget revenues, and the judgments cannot avoid such noneconomic intangibles as national security and political expediency. Most claims on budget revenues are challenged and compromised, and few participants end up entirely happy with the outcome.

Budget allocations to the food sector are no exception, whether for consumer subsidy programs or agricultural research and extension. Food policy analysts cannot take for granted a guaranteed share of the budget for food programs. Two questions are of chief concern to food policy analysts: how large should overall budget allocations for the food sector be; and how should resources be allocated to various programs within the food sector, between consumption and production and between recurrent expenditures and investment? Because the implementation of many food price policies, such as those discussed in chapters 2 and 4, requires budget subsidies, to join the budget debate is to join virtually the entire food policy debate. Out of this debate emerge the nuts and bolts of a country's actual food policy.

Figure 5-2 shows the elements of the budget allocation process important

Figure 5-1. Major Connections between Macroeconomic Policy
and Food Policy

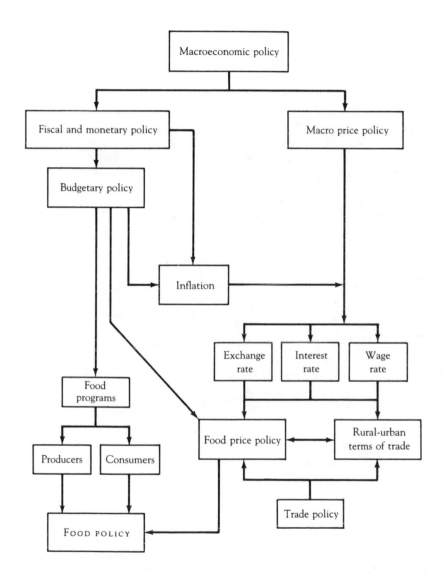

for food policy. The size of the government budget is determined by total
tax revenues and the size of the deficit (or surplus), which together make up
fiscal policy. The total budget is allocated between the food and nonfood
sectors (although the distinction is sometimes arbitrary, as with investments
in roads or port facilities). As noted above, the basis for making this allocation

Figure 5-2. Budget Allocations and the Food Sector

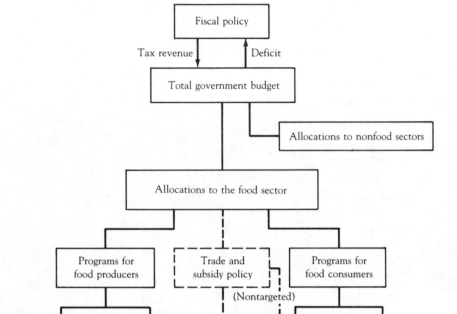

extends well beyond the results of social benefit-cost analysis to include important political and security issues. Allocations to programs for food producers and allocations to programs for food consumers are not necessarily at the expense of each other from a fixed food sector budget. There is some tendency for each major program to compete with all other programs in the budget, not just with other programs within its own sector.

For many countries the major budget allocation to the food sector is for subsidies to producers, consumers, or both. At one time more than half of Sri Lanka's budget was devoted to food subsidies for consumers; in 1981 nearly one-third of China's budget was devoted to subsidizing both food consumers and producers. These subsidies have the implicit goal of dealing with the welfare consequences of the food price dilemma—an inability to keep farm prices high and food prices low. Often, as in China, this goal is quite explicit.

The relationship between the use of subsidies in effecting income transfers to producers and consumers and the role of subsidies in implementing food price policy is shown by the dotted lines in figure 5-2. As shown in chapter 4, most price policies for basic food grains rely on trade or subsidy instruments to force a wedge between international prices for the commodity and its domestic price to producers, consumers, or both. Trade restrictions on imports or exports produce revenue for the budget. But budget allocations are required for the food subsidies needed to keep domestic prices of imported food below the international price. As noted in chapter 2, unless these consumer subsidies are carefully targeted to particular consumer groups, they inevitably spill over to become part of food price policy. Producer subsidies have similar characteristics. In some countries budget policy, subsidy policy, and food price policy are the same thing.

Budget allocations are also required for recurring expenses, such as salaries and office expenses for an extension service or market information system, or interest on the public debt. Recurring expenses represent government consumption. They may be essential to the day-to-day provision of important government services, but they do not build new productive capacity except in a very indirect way, as when extension agents increase the decisionmaking abilities of the farmers they reach. Then the budget is being invested in human capital.

Budget allocations for investment are intended to build long-run productive capacity directly. Investments in the food sector are usually designed to increase food production—irrigation facilities, rural infrastructure, including electrification and roads, agricultural research, and so on. But important investments can also be made on behalf of food consumers. Because of the relationship among nutritional status, health status, and food intake, government investment in public health infrastructure—sanitation, clean water, rural clinics, and immunization programs—can significantly improve the efficiency of food consumers' expenditures. Equally important in the long run, investments in agricultural research benefit consumers as well as farmers. Improved agricultural technology lowers costs of production, and because agriculture tends to be a competitive industry, lower costs are passed on to consumers quite directly.

Fiscal and Monetary Policy

The overall size of the government budget (relative to the size of the economy) is determined by two factors: the willingness and ability of the government to tax the domestic economy to produce revenue and the willingness to run and finance budget deficits. Both are the province of fiscal policy and, because deficits typically are financed by increasing the money supply, of monetary policy. The inflationary consequences of rapid increases in the money supply can be quite severe, and most countries attempt to use tax policy to generate as much government revenue as possible. Raising taxes distorts the economy in other ways, however, and these distortions, plus the bureaucratic difficulties of administering complicated tax codes in developing economies, place tight limits on the size of tax revenues.

A fundamental principle of taxation in societies attempting to alleviate poverty and reach a more equal distribution of income is that the burden of taxes should fall proportionately heavier on higher-income citizens. With progressive taxation in many industrialized countries, not only do tax collections rise in proportion to a person's income, but also the legislated tax *rate* rises with income. In fact, effective tax rates actually paid are quite uniform even in rich countries, and few developing countries are able to use progressive taxation because of the difficulty of defining and accurately measuring personal incomes. The tax structures of some poor countries are regressive because the commodities that are the most easily taxed in such countries are those produced or consumed by poor people. Export taxes on smallholder agricultural products, for example, usually have a regressive incidence.

The costs of tax collection include administrative expenses and the costs taxpayers incur in complying with, legally avoiding, or illegally evading the tax laws. Because of the high level of administrative capacity required to enforce taxes, especially on factor income (private and corporate income taxes and land taxes), most developing countries raise large proportions of their revenues from commodity taxes, such as import, export, sales, and excise taxes. These taxes are not necessarily regressive, especially if efforts are made to exempt the commodities most important in the lives of the poor. Failure to make these efforts, however, often means that the tax burden falls predominately on poor people.

A handful of countries have access to significant budget revenues without having to tax their own citizens. Exporters of natural resources with low exploitation costs, especially petroleum, are able to generate large rents paid by foreign consumers. With appropriate government policies designed to capture the profits implicit in the gap between the domestic resource costs of producing the oil or copper and its sale price in world markets, these fortunate countries are able to transfer substantial revenues to the government treasury without domestic efficiency losses, income distribution effects, or the collection costs associated with raising local tax revenues.

These countries are not without macroeconomic problems, however. The large influx of foreign exchange supports an exchange rate and level of imported goods that can seriously reduce output and employment in domestic productive sectors, both agricultural and industrial. These macro problems of wealth are perhaps easier to deal with than the problems of a poor resource base and low tax revenues, and little attention is paid to the problems of countries with foreign exchange surpluses in the rest of this chapter. Significant inflows of foreign aid can also ease the domestic tax burden. Very few countries, however, can look to this solution.

THE MONEY SUPPLY. Given the limitations on raising tax revenues and the equally intense pressures to increase spending, most countries incur significant budget deficits. In principle, the deficit could be covered by borrowing from the domestic private sector or from abroad, but in practice most developing countries with budget problems finance large portions of their deficits through expansionary monetary policy, that is, through central bank purchases of government debt. For this reason fiscal and monetary policies are closely linked in developing countries.

Monetary policy affects the size and rate of expansion of the country's supply of money. Where up to half a country's GDP is produced seasonally in the agricultural sector, an important task of monetary policy is to manage the money supply flexibly to allow enough operating capital to finance seasonal requirements. Money, including cash, savings accounts, and demand deposits (checking accounts), represents purchasing power in an economy. If a government's central bank expands the money supply at about the same rate as the economy-wide growth of physical output of goods and services (or somewhat faster if the economy is still in the process of becoming monetized), the purchasing power of money creates an aggregate demand for goods and services that is just met by the available aggregate supply of physical output, and overall prices do not change. When a government has its central bank print money to finance a large budget deficit, upward pressure on prices results because aggregate demand exceeds aggregate supply. In revenue-poor developing countries, large budget deficits cause rapid growth of the money supply, which usually results in inflation.

INFLATION. Inflation is a continuing increase in the overall level of prices for a country's goods and services, as measured by consumer or wholesale price indices. In every economy's national income accounts, aggregate supply of goods and services produced must equal aggregate demand from the total of expenditures, as shown in the following identity (which holds by definition):

$$\text{Aggregate output} = \text{aggregate expenditures}$$
$$(\text{Origin of income}) = (\text{uses of income})$$
$$Y = P \cdot Q \equiv C + I + G + X - M$$

where Y = monetary value of national output or income
P = price index covering all goods and services produced

Q = quantity index covering all goods and services produced
C = national consumption expenditures in private sector
I = national investment expenditures in private sector
G = government expenditures on consumption and investment
X = total value of exports
M = total value of imports.

When the government runs a budget deficit and finances it by expanding the money supply, government demand for goods and services (G in the identity above) will rise. This increased demand can call forth increased physical supplies of goods and services (Q) if there are unemployed resources, such as idle labor, unutilized plant capacity, or open land, that can be quickly brought into production. But in developing countries supply bottlenecks rather than inadequate demand tend to be the constraint on rapid increases in output, and so Q does not increase. For the value of aggregate output (Y) to equal the value of aggregate expenditures after G has risen, either imports must increase (with an impact on the foreign exchange rate to be discussed shortly) or the general price level P must rise, thus causing inflation. If the balance of trade is held constant, more money is chasing the same amount of goods and services.

This demand-pull inflation results directly from macro policy and is the main, but not the only, source of inflation. Cost-push inflation occurs if suppliers of inputs, particularly labor unions, are successful in organizing to raise the costs of their services. Large wage settlements are then passed along by firms to consumers in the form of higher product prices. Cost-push inflation may be a significant problem in industrialized countries with strong labor unions, but it is relatively insignificant in developing countries where industrial sectors are small, and unions, if they exist at all, have limited power.

Inflation can also be imported. The prices of goods and services that countries buy from abroad rise along with inflation in the exporting countries. In recent years the prices of imports in developing countries have risen 10 to 15 percent annually, apart from petroleum products whose prices have risen much faster than other imports since 1973. Governments with fixed exchange rates have little effective control over imported inflation.

Macro Prices and the Food Sector

In Western economies most attention to macroeconomic policy has been focused on the budget, fiscal, and monetary issues and on the resulting levels of aggregate output and rates of inflation. Until recently, relatively little attention was devoted to another arena of government macro policy, the formation of prices for factors of production—labor, capital, and land—and the formation of two important terms of trade—between domestic and international goods and between rural and urban goods. These five prices—wage rates, interest rates, land rental rates, foreign exchange rates, and the rural-urban terms of trade (the food parity price)—are significantly influenced by basic macroeconomic policy in an economy.

The rice milling example illustrated the importance of the dual role of these prices in allocating resources efficiently and in determining levels and distribution of incomes. For both reasons, governments in developing countries frequently use macro policy instruments in conscious attempts to influence the levels of these prices. The direct role of government policy in determining three of them—foreign exchange rates, interest rates, and wage rates—makes it appropriate to call them macro prices. Land rental rates and the rural-urban terms of trade are influenced by macro policy in equally powerful but much more complicated ways. They are treated as an indirect result of macro policy, the outcome of a complex interplay among trade and subsidy policies, fiscal and monetary policies, and the other macro price policies.

Macro prices signal the scarcity of the factor of production concerned and, consequently, the incomes flowing to each factor. Because most governments wish to affect income distribution in their societies, they are greatly tempted to use government policy in an effort to set macro prices, rather than allow them to be determined by market forces. If wage rates can be set high, labor is no longer cheap, and poverty is eliminated. If interest rates can be set low, capital is not scarce, and a country can quickly have a modern industrial sector. If food prices are kept low, food is abundant, and no one will be hungry. Macro prices reflect the most basic conditions of a country's economy. A government that attempts to set these prices to express its urgent desire for a modern, prosperous society is trying to short-circuit the economic development process. It is no wonder that many countries have tried this approach. When it fails—as it must until the productivity base has been built that will support higher standards of living in the long run—the economy is riddled with serious price distortions. Resource allocations skew income distribution while much of the labor power of the work force is left untapped, and the government faces stagnant growth in both agricultural and industrial output. It is not easy to put such an economy back on track.

Some macro prices are easer to influence than others. The foreign exchange rate is most susceptible to government control. Except for cases of significant imbalance between the official rate and what private markets are willing to pay, most central banks are able to make the official rate widely reflected in actual transactions throughout the economy. Interest rates and wage rates are subject to progressively less effective government control. As already noted, the land rental rate and the rural-urban terms of trade are determined by even more complicated mechanisms than the specific macro prices. Macro policy and the food parity price, however, are functionally related to each other and need to be analyzed together. The rural-urban terms of trade cannot be understood independently of macroeconomic policy. A separate section of this chapter attempts to show the connections.

Foreign Exchange Rates

An exchange rate for a nation's currency establishes its value relative to the currency of another country. For many industrialized countries the price of foreign exchange is determined in international currency markets by the supply of and demand for a country's currency. These are established by the country's balance between imports and exports and international capital flows. Similar fundamental economic forces exist in developing countries, but their exchange rates are typically set by governments rather than determined in markets. Whether a government sets the foreign exchange rate at a level that will more or less clear the market determines whether imports or exports are priced (in domestic currency) at levels that reflect their economic scarcities relative to domestic goods and services that are not traded internationally.

THE EXCHANGE RATE. The exchange rate reflects the rate at which a country must give up its own currency to obtain foreign currency to import goods and services, and it simultaneously determines the value in domestic currency of goods and services that are exported. If the exchange rate between the Indonesian rupiah (Rp) and the U.S. dollar is set at Rp 625/$1, Indonesian importers must pay 625 rupiahs to receive one dollar's worth of imports, and similarly each dollar of export earnings is worth 625 rupiahs when translated into domestic currency.

A developing country typically ties or pegs its currency to that of a major trading partner, usually the U.S. dollar, which exchanges freely with currencies of other trading partners. As long as the rate is pegged, the currency follows the fate of the U.S. dollar in the foreign exchange markets, declining in value in relation to currencies of third countries as the dollar depreciates relative to those currencies and rising in value as the dollar appreciates. The exchange rate between the rupiah and the Japanese yen, for example, is thus determined by dollar versus yen movements as long as the rupiah remains tied to the dollar at a fixed rate.

A government can change the price of its currency in terms of the dollar (and hence also of all other currencies) by setting a new official exchange rate. To lower the value of its currency, that is, to devalue, a government simply announces that henceforth more domestic currency will be needed to exchange for one dollar. A change in the rate from Rp 625/$1 to Rp 700/$1 would be a 12 percent devaluation of the rupiah relative to the dollar [(700 − 625)/625]. Changes in the opposite direction, for example, from Rp 625/$1 to Rp 550/$1 would amount to a 12 percent revaluation [(625 − 550)/625].

OVERVALUED EXCHANGE RATES. Many developing countries choose explicitly or implicitly to maintain overvalued exchange rates. Such rates keep the cost of foreign exchange low and hence imports cheap. They cannot be maintained with free markets for foreign exchange, however, or there would be excess demand for foreign currency to pay for a flood of imported goods. The low rates can be maintained only by currency controls, import tariffs and barriers, and allocations of foreign exchange to preferred importers or for high priority uses (often, unfortunately, military hardware). The presence of such controls and trade barriers shows that a country's currency is overvalued, although by how much is a difficult topic beyond the scope of this analysis.

If a country's exchange rate is overvalued, commodities such as food crops that normally are traded internationally either as imports or as exports are undervalued. Farmers receive less for their crops than they would if the price of foreign exchange were market-determined. Hence overvalued exchange rates act as an implicit tax on agriculture. All consumers of food and other traded goods are thus subsidized indirectly because of the low prices for these items. The government budget is also relieved of part of the direct burden of providing any food subsidies since these are shifted to food producers through lower prices. Consequently, the tendency toward overvalued exchange rates has a strong biasing effect on the food system, favoring urban food consumers and penalizing rural food producers.

Providers of nontraded domestic services, such as marketing agents and civil servants, and of goods that do not enter world trade, such as bulky commodities with high transportation costs, benefit from an overvalued exchange rate. The domestic prices of the nontraded goods and services are relatively high (and profitable) compared with the prices for food and imported goods, which are relatively unprofitable.

Overvalued exchange rates are a major reason the rural-urban terms of trade are so unfavorable for agricultural producers in developing coutries, and they are a major source of the "urban bias" that, according to Michael Lipton, leaves poor people poor. This urban bias has strong political roots in the student–industrial worker–civil servant power base of most governments in the developing world. But overvalued exchange rates are usually not the result of an overt and conscious choice of the government, even though the urban political support is welcome. In most cases, overvalued exchange rates are generated without specific policy decisions by differential inflation rates and are sustained to some extent by the prevalence of industrial protection.

If a country begins with a fixed exchange rate that correctly prices its currency relative to foreign currencies, then the demand for foreign exchange is matched by its supply. Domestic inflation, however, places pressure on the country's fixed exchange rate because import demand will increase in the face of lower relative prices for imported goods, export earnings will decline because of decreased demand for the goods the country sells, and the market for foreign exchange will not clear at the fixed exchange rate without capital inflows.

Because virtually all countries experience some inflation, the relevant comparison is between the domestic rate of inflation and the rate in countries that are major trading partners. If a country experiences an annual rate of inflation in its wholesale price index of 20 percent and if its main trading partners also experience 20 percent inflation during the year, domestic and foreign costs and prices would rise by the same amount, and there would be no pressure on the exchange rate (in the absence of other structural changes in the economy, such as differential productivity growth). If the inflation rate in the principal trading partners is only 8 percent, a figure more in line with recent experience of industrialized countries, the differential rate of inflation is 12 percent (20 percent in the developing country minus 8 percent in its trading partners). The exchange rate thus becomes overvalued by approximately 12 percent, even though no policymaker made any decisions at all about the exchange rate.

Many developing countries are able to maintain overvalued exchange rates because of protective trade policies, often supplemented by exchange controls and restrictions on foreign investment. Most governments impose tariffs or quantitative restrictions on imports in an attempt to promote more rapid industrialization or to raise government revenues. Taxes on exports also raise government revenues while keeping domestic commodity prices low.

Protection is an instrument of industrial policy and of agricultural policy in many industrialized countries as well as developing countries, but it has an important, and often fully intended, impact on exchange rates which is relatively more important for poor countries. Protection raises the domestic market prices of protected goods, which are or could be imported. In the absence of such protection the prices of these goods would drop, demand for them would rise, and more would be imported. Bidding for the foreign exchange to pay for these imports would cause the equilibrium value of foreign exchange to rise. When the government maintains protectionist policies, the domestic currency can be overvalued, although supply of and demand for foreign currency is in balance.

DEVALUATION. Overvalued exchange rates tend to divert the flow of purchasing power to urban areas, usually widening rural-urban income distribution disparities. The depressed rural incentives cause low growth in output and little gain in rural employment. Low food prices provide general subsidies to food consumers, which may protect the welfare of the poor and raise total food intake. But since domestic food production is depressed and foreign exchange is cheap, food imports tend to expand considerably. The strong tendency in developing countries toward overvalued exchange rates thus places heavy burdens on the design of a food policy.

The remedy for overvaluation of an exchange rate is devaluation, which is meant to permit the economy to regain its international competitiveness. Differential inflation distorts the price relationships between tradable goods and services whose prices are determined by international market prices and nontradable domestic goods and services. The latter are termed "nontradable" because transportation costs are so high for certain types of bulky, low-valued goods, such as sweet potatoes, that their prices are determined by local supply and demand conditions rather than by international market prices.

Because of differential inflation the prices of tradable goods in domestic currency are too low to clear the market for foreign exchange. At the fixed exchange rate, too many imports are desired and too few exports are supplied. A devaluation attempts to correct this situation by raising the prices of tradable goods relative to those of nontradable goods. Because the amount of domestic currency earned per unit of foreign currency is increased, producers of tradable goods receive higher prices relative to producers of non-tradable goods. It is as if there were only two goods produced in the economy, and the government raised the price of one (tradables) while leaving that of the other (nontradables) initially unaffected. In the example, a 12 percent devaluation results in a 12 percent increase in the price of tradable goods. Consumers switch some of their demand from the previously too cheap tradable goods to the now relatively less expensive nontradable goods. Because their prices have gone up, producers of tradable goods expand output, and because prices of nontradable goods have fallen, their suppliers contract production. Import demand falls, export supplies rise, and demand for nontradable goods increases. A devaluation thus brings about shifts in demand and supply by changing relative prices between tradable and nontradable goods. But the decreased supply of and increased demand for nontradable goods will push their prices up again unless fiscal and monetary policies reduce aggregate demand or changed expectations lead to greater investment and less consumption.

A devaluation by itself, especially if the extent of protection remains unchanged, cannot solve the problem. Differential inflation is the cause of the overvaluation. If domestic inflation is permitted to continue at levels exceeding inflation in the major trading partners, devaluation alone will be followed by a rise in the relative price of nontradable goods because of inflation. This rise will offset the initial price change and thwart the switching of demand from tradable to nontradable goods and of supply in the reverse direction. The exchange rate will again become overvalued (albeit at the new exchange rate). To be successful in the short run, a devaluation must be accompanied by fiscal and monetary policies that reduce inflation by cutting aggregate demand and lowering domestic expenditures. To be successful in the long run, the devaluation must change expectations and generate greater investment by both domestic and foreign firms.

Most governments, however, find it very difficult to adopt more stringent fiscal, monetary, and exchange rate policies. Devaluation is a politically sensitive topic largely because two groups are immediately worse off after a devaluation: owners or workers producing nontradable goods and services or using large amounts of tradable inputs—for example, civil servants and factory workers; and consumers, especially urban residents, who have a high propensity to consume tradable goods. Continued overvaluation subsidizes the real incomes of civil servants and urban residents in the short run and thus is politically popular. But it acts as an implicit tax on agriculture because part of the cost of food subsidies is transferred from the government budget to food producers. A devaluation usually raises food prices and thus shifts the food parity price (the rural-urban terms of trade) in favor of agriculture. Many rural dwellers produce tradable goods with the use of nontraded land and labor and few tradable inputs, and they often consume larger proportions of nontradable goods than do urban residents.

The failure to devalue in order to create better incentives for the rural sector lies not with urban-oriented government policy alone, although this is important. Many painful adjustments must be made by both producers and consumers in an economy when the exchange rate of the domestic currency is devalued. The food consumption adjustments of the very poor can be especially painful, and one important role for food policy analysts is to design programs that protect the short-run welfare of the very poor when a devaluation is needed. It bears repeating that the devaluation offers the long-run prospect of more jobs and faster growth. But the problem both for the government and for the poor is how to survive until then.

Interest Rates

Interest rates reflect two fundamental aspects of all economies. First, interest is the "wage" of capital and reflects its productivity in increasing output. Capital has an opportunity cost and can be rented just like labor and land. It must be compensated for its use at a competitive rate if owners of capital are not to withdraw its services. Second, interest rates reflect an essential time dimension, as owners of capital have the choice of consuming their capital in the present or saving it to reap potentially larger, but later, consumption returns. If capital markets were perfect and riskless, the productivity dimension of interest rates would just match the "liquidity," or time dimension, of interest rates because transactions between different opportunities for productive investments would produce an equilibrium rate of time discount.

In the real world, however, such perfection is seldom achieved. Investments are risky, access to capital markets is uneven, and, especially in developing countries, knowledge of actual investment opportunities and payoffs is highly imperfect. Consequently, the marginal productivity of capital, one determinant of the interest rate, frequently diverges from the rate at which society values future consumption as opposed to present consumption, the alternative determinant of the interest rate. An important goal of financial policy is to make this divergence as small as possible. The following discussion deals primarily with the interest rate as a reflection of the productivity of capital. In well-functioning international capital markets the productivity of capital will approximate its opportunity cost, with appropriate discounts for lenders' risks and borrowers' concerns for the burden of indebtedness. The social rate of time discount is incorporated in the policy perspective.

CAPITAL MARKETS. Many governments are reasonably effective at setting foreign exchange rates and making them widely applicable even if they diverge somewhat from equilibrium levels. As the divergence widens, gray and black markets for foreign currency spring up, and eventually the government loses control of the foreign exchange rate. In such cases most foreign currency is exchanged for domestic currency through unofficial channels at rates that more closely reflect its opportunity costs to importers and exporters. Furtive foreign exchange markets reflect a breakdown of government policy, but when government policy is generally effective, foreign exchange transactions are handled routinely through the banking system.

Capital markets are structured quite differently. Almost everyone in a monetary economy has the opportunity to be either a borrower or a lender, however small, while the great majority of a country's population seldom sees another country's currency. Each time a borrowing-lending agreement is transacted, a miniature capital market has been established. No matter what the central government may want the interest rate in the society to be, such individual capital transactions can and do go on. Consequently, understanding the functioning of a country's capital markets and the role of government policy in setting interest rates in those capital markets is much more complicated than understanding how foreign exchange rates are set.

Government policy with respect to capital markets is significantly affected by three related factors: interest rate formation, the development of financial institutions, and the impact of monetary policy as an outgrowth of budgetary and fiscal policy. Because there are two primary determinants of an interest rate, government policy is frequently caught between the scarcity value of capital in increasing production and a desire to make capital available at a rate that reflects the government's valuation of future consumption relative to current consumption. On the one hand, if a society can keep interest rates low, then future events have greater present value and the welfare of future generations becomes more important. Low interest rates make investment cheaper in a capital stock to bequeath to children and grandchildren, and it makes the conservation of natural resources and investment in social infrastructure with a long expected life easier to justify economically. However, the current generation may not save enough at low actual interest rates to finance those investments.

Keeping interest rates high, on the other hand, reflects the current scarcity and productivity of capital in production, induces greater savings, and comes closer to matching the rate of time discount of private decisionmakers in the economy. Consequently, the first issue for government policy with respect to capital markets is interest rate formation. Naturally, it is difficult to judge what interest rates would be in the absence of policy and how interventions actually alter those rates. Still, the direction in which policy is having an influence is usually readily apparent, and knowing this is an important starting point.

The second concern of government policy is the development of institutions that actually carry out the day-to-day functions of a capital market. In simple economies households with surplus cash can lend to their neighbors who need a temporary addition to their incomes. But the essence of a modernizing economy is its reliance on a network of financial intermediaries that provide convenient and safe places to save money as well as efficient vehicles for accumulating savings for further loans to farms and businesses for real investment to expand the productive capacity of the economy.

In most economies capital markets are better developed in urban centers and wealthier agricultural areas. There the services of financial institutions are widely available. Markets for local securities and bonds provide direct firm financing. Local financial intermediaries, such as insurance companies, banks, and savings and loan companies, provide indirect financing to firms and other investors.

This uneven development of financial institutions is one cause of segmentation of the capital market and a wide range of interest rates, even for similar risks and transaction costs. In addition, segmentation is caused by government regulation itself, especially of major (and visible) financial institutions in the capital or commercial center, as well as by a tendency of governments to subsidize their own banking institutions, thus providing significant cost advantages over private financial institutions. As a result, rural credit markets tend to be informal with very high interest rates, partly because of the high transaction costs and greater risk premiums attached to small loans. The underdeveloped financial institutions, fear of regulation, and resulting segmentation of the capital market inhibit the efficient flow of capital from savers to borrowers within rural areas and between urban and rural areas.

The third factor affecting government policy on interest rates is not unique to developing countries. The role of monetary policy in facilitating fiscal policy and financing government budget deficits is a topic of great concern in developed countries as well. To avoid inflation, the growth in money supply should not be significantly greater than the growth in real output (allowing for changes in willingness to hold money). But "tight money" means that a budget deficit must be financed from private savings (or from abroad), which tends to drive up interest rates as private borrowers compete with the government for the available capital. Recession and unemployment are the result. Alternatively, "monetizing" the budget deficit usually leads to inflation, which lowers the value of holding a monetary debt instrument, such as a bond or savings certificate. Lenders may understandably insist on higher interest rates to compensate for this decline in value. The resulting combination of high interest rates and inflation has come to be known as stagflation.

Capital moves relatively freely internationally as modern communications and a sophisticated global banking system permit billions of dollars to be moved anywhere in the world at a moment's notice. This mobility of capital further complicates the linkage between interest rates and monetary policy. High interest rates in a country attract an inflow of international capital; low interest rates tend to cause a capital outflow. These flows of international capital affect the supply of and demand for foreign currency and thus influence the foreign exchange rate.

Since the equilibrium exchange rate is significantly affected by differential inflation rates among trading partners, the connections among monetary policy and inflation, interest rates and exchange rates, and interest rates and monetary policy become obvious although they are extraordinarily complicated. In the past, when exchange rates were relatively fixed, macro imbalance tended to be reflected in changes in foreign exchange reserves. But with more flexible exchange rates and interest rates, imbalances tend to be reflected by changes in international prices and trade flows and ultimately in the real incomes of producers and consumers. This is especially true of those producers and consumers whose real incomes are very sensitive to prices of traded goods, such as farmers who produce food and consumers who buy it.

OFFICIAL INTEREST RATE. An official interest rate—the level legislated by the government as the maximum rate that can be charged by lenders—often exacerbates capital market segmentation. When the government sets the official rate of interest below the market-clearing rate, only privileged borrowers gain access to cheap, rationed credit. The residual market for credit, largely made up of traditional lenders and borrowers, continues to function, but it becomes a thinner market because of the exit of those able to use officially controlled institutions. Credit rationing and reduced savings result from an interest rate ceiling and cause the interest rate in the residual market to be higher than otherwise.

Official interest rates can be enforced mainly in large, visible financial institutions but only rarely in the traditional, informal lending markets. With an official interest rate ceiling, the segmentation of the capital market is increased because of the even wider differential between institutional and traditional lending rates. Farmers and merchants consequently pay more for credit in traditional markets, and industrialists pay less in financial institutions than they would in the absence of an official interest rate ceiling.

NOMINAL AND REAL INTEREST RATES. Inflation and the interest rate are related because inflation reduces the purchasing power of monetary assets. As prices rise, fewer goods and services can be purchased with a given amount of money. Interest payments are monetary assets that are transferred from borrowers to lenders within some specified time period. Because interest payments have a time dimension, lenders are concerned about inflation, which reduces the purchasing power of the interest payments at the time they receive them as well as the purchasing power of their capital when it is paid back.

Lenders thus consider not only the nominal rate of interest, that established in the borrowing agreement, but also the real rate of interest, the one remaining after adjustments for inflation. Since both the inflation and interest rates are denominated in annual percentages, the real rate of interest can be roughly approximated by subtracting the inflation rate from the nominal rate of interest. If the nominal rate of interest is 18 percent a year and the annual rate of inflation is 16 percent, the real rate of interest is about 2 percent (18 − 16). The precise formula is {[(1 + nominal annual rate of interest) ÷ (1 + the annual rate of inflation)] − 1}. For this example, the precise real rate of interest is 1.7 percent [(1.18/1.16) − 1].

If the annual inflation rate increases to 24 percent in this example and the government keeps the official interest rate at 18 percent a year, the real official rate of interest becomes negative: about −6 percent a year (18 − 24), or precisely −4.8 percent [(1.18/1.24) − 1]. A negative real rate of interest means that savers lose purchasing power by lending their money at the official rate and that borrowers are subsidized in real terms. While borrowers would prefer negative real interest rates, savers tend to put their money in land or commodities, for example, rather than in banks, to hedge against inflation. Inflation tends to cause financial disintermediation—the withering of financial intermediaries, such as banks, savings institutions, and insurance companies—when governments impose ceilings on interest rates.

A positive interest rate requires that the government, through the central bank, maintain the nominal official rate above the rate of inflation. This can be done by controlling inflation, adjusting the nominal official interest rate, or some combination of both. In practice, it is politically difficult to push up the official interest rate. Maintaining a positive real rate of interest is made easier with low rates of inflation.

Evidence accumulated from the development experience of poor countries over the past several decades shows that positive real rates of interest cause faster growth of financial institutions, and the faster growth leads to more rapid increases in national incomes. A positive real interest rate encourages domestic saving and investment, inflows of foreign investment, and thus domestic capital formation. The productivity of this new capital is enhanced because the credit is allocated to its most productive uses by the market rather than by rationing decisions of financial institutions and government agencies.

FINANCIAL POLICY. As the rice milling example suggested, subsidized interest rates make investment in modern, capital-intensive technology more profitable. It would seem to follow from this that raising interest rates would impede the development process, which depends on the accumulation of capital, and subsidized interest rates would lead to more capital investment and to more rapid economic growth. The flaw in this logic can be understood only by differentiating static and dynamic effects. Since economic development is an inherently dynamic process, the dynamic effects of interest rate policy will be crucial for judging its impact on development.

Figure 5-3 illustrates the alternative effects of two stylized interest rate policies. "Low" interest rates capture the full effects of official interest rate policy that causes negative real rates for privileged borrowers, financial repression, and increased segmentation of the capital market. "High" interest rates are meant to reflect a financial policy that allows market-clearing rates to encourage savings and to channel capital to its most productive uses, thus promoting financial deepening and reduced segmentation of capital markets.

Two related effects drive the conclusion from figure 5-3 that low interest rates lead to low investment, and vice versa. The first relates to the rate of savings and the second to the productivity of the resulting investment of the savings. Both are large topics that cannot be treated in depth here.

Private households in both urban and rural areas usually respond to a change from negative to positive real interest rates by increased savings. On average, more than half the total domestic savings in developing countries comes from the private, noncorporate sector. Hence, the positive supply response of these savings to the real interest rate can be of considerable quantitative significance. A country that wishes to increase its rate of growth must either increase the rate of investment, by generating the savings resources to make this possible, or increase the productivity of the new capital being invested.

Only a limited number of sources are available for increased savings: larger foreign capital inflows, higher public savings from increased taxes or profits from public enterprises, and positive real interest rates to call forth greater private domestic savings. Aid-financed foreign capital inflows are decreasing in per capita terms and as a share of world economic product. The profit-making record of public enterprises in both developed and developing countries is not promising, except for enterprises based on natural resources. Public enterprises frequently absorb more public savings than they generate. Hence, countries looking for increases in the supply of investable funds usually must look to positive real interest rates to encourage their own domestic savers.

At least as important, these positive real interest rates will also directly affect the productivity of the investments made possible by the savings. The

Figure 5-3. Effects of Alternative Financial Policies

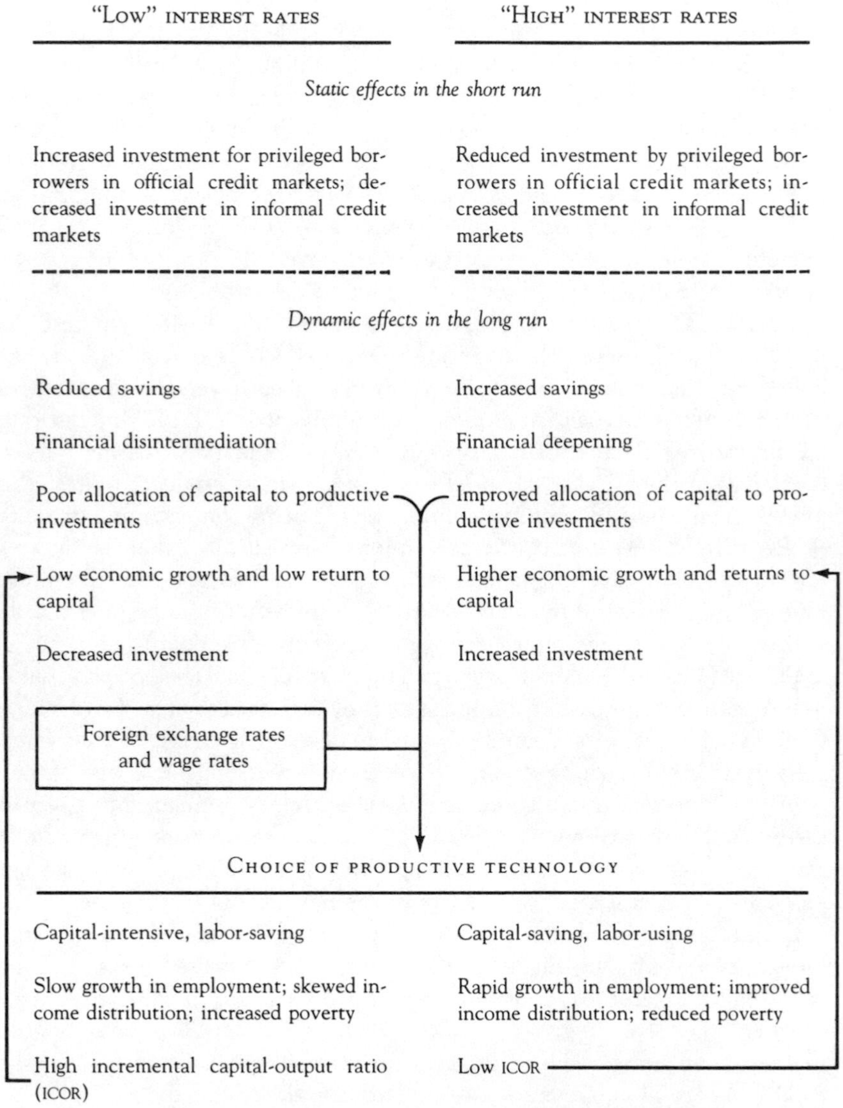

"Low" INTEREST RATES	"High" INTEREST RATES

Static effects in the short run

Increased investment for privileged borrowers in official credit markets; decreased investment in informal credit markets	Reduced investment by privileged borrowers in official credit markets; increased investment in informal credit markets

Dynamic effects in the long run

Reduced savings	Increased savings
Financial disintermediation	Financial deepening
Poor allocation of capital to productive investments	Improved allocation of capital to productive investments
Low economic growth and low return to capital	Higher economic growth and returns to capital
Decreased investment	Increased investment

Foreign exchange rates and wage rates

CHOICE OF PRODUCTIVE TECHNOLOGY

Capital-intensive, labor-saving	Capital-saving, labor-using
Slow growth in employment; skewed income distribution; increased poverty	Rapid growth in employment; improved income distribution; reduced poverty
High incremental capital-output ratio (ICOR)	Low ICOR

efficiency with which capital invested in one year is converted into new output the following year is crudely captured, after the fact, by the gross incremental capital-output ratio, or ICOR. In societies where disinvestment has occurred for many years and the economy needs major rehabilitation to function smoothly, the ICOR can drop as low as 2.0 or even lower. It was 2.1 in Indonesia between 1970 and 1973, when investment in spare parts and repair of bridges, roads, and rolling stock paid extremely high economic returns. More typically the ICOR is between 3 and 4 in developing countries, with 3.5 being an appropriate median. Table 5-1 shows a range of ICORs for a sample of sixty-six developing countries based on World Bank statistics.

Although the ICOR is not a very useful planning tool—it is difficult to measure accurately and is subject to a variety of influences on economic output not attributable to incremental investment—its wide range in developing countries illustrates an extremely important point. The productivity of an investment, or the efficiency with which capital is used in a society, is as important for growth and the alleviation of poverty as the investment rate itself.

Countries cannot simply assume a low ICOR for planning purposes and then have it happen, but they can attempt to create a policy environment that leads to the efficient use of capital. Positive real interest rates, increased domestic savings and financial deepening, and concentration on labor-intensive investments that create many jobs per unit of capital all contribute to a lower ICOR and more rapid growth in economic output. Equally important, because of the labor-intensive focus of such an investment strategy, the earned incomes will tend to be more equally distributed than is likely from a more capital-intensive strategy, even if equal growth were possible from both.

Growth-oriented financial policy requires that a government manage its macro policy to reduce inflation, set its nominal official interest rate higher than the rate of inflation so that the real official rate of interest is positive, and avoid imposing regulations that would unnecessarily constrain the growth of financial institutions. Such financial policy causes financial deepening as the services of financial institutions become more widespread. Financial deepening in turn results in (and is assisted by) more rapid economic development. Conversely, negative real rates of interest and excessive regulation cause financial repression. The outcome typically is financial disintermediation—

Table 5-1. Average Gross Incremental Capital-Output Ratios (ICORs) for Sixty-six Developing Countries, 1968–73

Gross capital-output ratio (ICOR)	Number of countries	Illustrative countries
1.5–1.99	6	Singapore, Indonesia
2.0–2.49	5	Korea, Mali
2.5–2.99	10	Gabon, Ecuador
3.0–3.49	9	Kenya, Colombia, Pakistan
3.5–3.99	9	Thailand, Mauritius, Zaire
4.0–4.5	5	Jamaica, Tanzania
Above 4.5	22	India, Gambia, Guinea, Chile, Guyana, Zambia

Source: World Bank, World Tables, 2d ed. (Baltimore, Md.: Johns Hopkins University Press, 1980).

a smaller role for financial institutions—and stagnant or even negative economic growth. The rural sector in particular benefits from an expansion of financial institutions that gradually replace higher-cost, informal sources of credit. Inversely, financial repression and financial disintermediation place a heavy burden on development of the rural sector.

Wage Rates

Returns to labor are the primary source of personal income for the vast majority of the world's households. Incomes generated by the other primary factors of production—capital, land, entrepreneurship and managerial skills—tend to be skewed toward the upper third of the income distribution in most countries. Since the creation of productive new jobs that pay a living wage is the only long-run solution to poverty and hunger, the ability of a government to raise wages above a subsistence floor and to keep them there for the entire population should be a key concern of food policy. As noted earlier, however, the mechanisms by which wage rates are actually set are quite complicated, and the scope for successful government intervention to raise real wage rates in the short run is surprisingly limited. Attempts to set minimum wages often cause repercussions on decisions about investment, technology choice, and job creation which have the opposite effect from those intended. Just as interest rate policy can have perverse dynamic effects which swamp any desirable short-run results, so wage rate policy has the potential to cause serious distortions to the development of the economy and to exacerbate poverty.

FORMATION OF WAGE RATES. Except where labor unions introduce an element of collective bargaining into the process, wage rate formation in most countries takes place in a context of informal markets conditioned by tradition, social norms, and labor supply and demand factors where employers tend to have much more negotiating power than individual workers. Separate but connected markets exist for various skill levels and occupations. In most poor countries the important questions for policy analysts concern the formation of wage rates for workers who perform unskilled tasks. For workers who have no assets other than their own physical capacity, the wages in this market determine how close to survival they will be. When governments are actively concerned about poverty and income distribution, the pressures to legislate a minimum wage for these workers may be great. Understanding how these wages are formed without government policy provides the insight needed to judge the efficacy of minimum wage legislation.

Labor markets tend to be more segmented than capital markets, even for the basic grade of unskilled workers. Part of the segmentation arises from the lower mobility of labor compared with capital. Workers are limited in their willingness and ability to move from one region to another in search of job opportunities, and employers frequently are unwilling to hire workers from other regions or because of their race, religion, or sex. Knowledge about labor availability and job opportunities is spotty and uneven. Because of these labor market imperfections, an equilibrium wage in the absence of government intervention is hard to determine even in urban labor markets.

In rural labor markets wage rate formation is even more complicated than in urban markets. Many labor agreements for rural workers involve land tenure relationships and conditional access to land, payment in kind for specific agricultural tasks, and highly regimented division of labor by sex with wages bearing little relation to actual physical productivity. Even in regions with substantially more workers available than can be used productively for the available rural tasks, wage rates do not drop to an equilibrium that is below a subsistence level. Access to the jobs available tends to be by rationing, luck, or the establishment of patron-client relationships that bind landless workers to individual landowners or to merchants and small-scale rural manufacturers.

MINIMUM WAGE LEGISLATION. Governments have found it virtually impossible to intervene successfully in such complicated rural labor arrangements without drastic restructuring of tenure relationships and rural asset ownership. Even indirect mechanisms, such as helping to organize unskilled landless laborers into trade unions, have had little effect on changing the real access of such workers to regular, productive jobs in the countryside. To create such jobs, the structure and dynamism of agriculture itself must change, which is a long-run task for development policy, not a short-run task for minimum wage legislation. Direct rural job creation through food-for-work projects or labor-intensive rural works projects have the potential to guarantee jobs at a minimum wage if local management is effective, if engineering design has made the projects useful and productive, and if government finances enable a continuing commitment to the program.

In urban labor markets, attempts to legislate minimum wages and improved working conditions have been much more successful. In large-scale industrial firms, in modern banks and service organizations, and in government employment itself, legislated minimum wages for unskilled employees are enforced relatively easily. Foreign enterprises in particular, not wanting to be charged with exploitation of cheap local labor, usually pay wages at or above the legal minimum and above the rates prevailing in nearby informal labor markets unaffected by government legislation.

The effects of minimum wage legislation on urban labor markets are quite controversial. Almost everyone agrees it has little impact on rural wages, except very indirectly. For workers able to obtain jobs at the higher wage, the result is clearly beneficial. Their incomes are higher than in the absence of the legislation, and their families are likely to be better housed, clothed, educated, and fed. As part of an urban "working-class elite," these workers are likely to be very strong and vocal supporters of the government program and of efforts to keep intact the real purchasing power of the minimum wage if inflation is tending to erode it. Since many of these workers may actually be part of the government itself, pressures are great to implement and maintain in real terms a minimum wage that provides a comfortable standard of living.

As figure 5-4 illustrates, however, such a wage policy causes several untoward effects. In the absence of minimum wage legislation, the urban labor market clears at an equilibrium wage of W_e and workers employed number L_e. An effective legislated minimum wage raises wages to W_m, which reduces employment to L_m^d, while it increases the number of workers willing to work at W_m to L_m^s. Consequently, the result is unemployment equal to $L_m^s - L_m^d$ workers.

Figure 5-4. Illustration of the Effect of a Minimum Wage on the Urban Labor Market in the Formal Sector

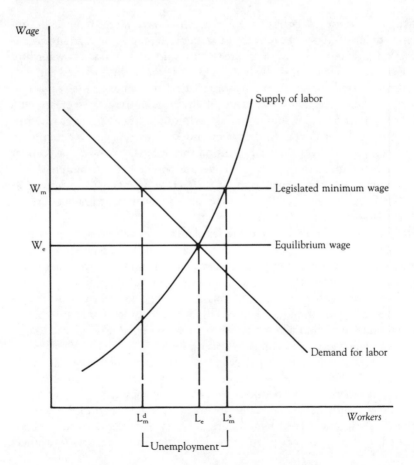

In most poor countries these unemployed workers cannot survive without some type of job, and they seek work in an informal urban sector while awaiting the lucky break that secures them a formal job at the minimum wage. Hence a greater segmentation of the urban labor market exists than before the legislation. Frequently the benefits from official jobs are so great that it is worth spending the entire educational process, including college if necessary, collecting the qualifying credentials and then waiting for years in the informal urban sector until the opportunity comes along. Although the worst manifestations of this queuing occur for civil service sinecures, the problem is pervasive all the way down the hiring range to janitors in a branch bank.

Figure 5-5 illustrates wage formation in the informal urban sector. In the simplest case, the demand and supply of labor for the formal sector are

Figure 5-5. Illustration of Wage Formation in the Informal Sector of the Urban Labor Market after a Minimum Wage Is Legislated in the Formal Sector

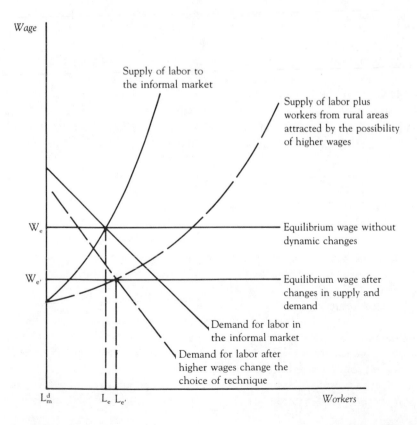

subtracted from the total labor demand and supply curves, and the previous overall equilibrium wage W_e is established as the equilibrium wage in the informal sector, with employment equal to $L_e - L_m^d$. Thus workers fortunate enough to have a job in the formal sector are paid W_m (the minimum wage shown in figure 5-4), and all other workers who were willing to work at W_e actually have jobs at that wage in the informal sector. This presumes, of course, that the government does not try to enforce minimum wages in the informal sector by police crackdowns or closing of establishments. If it does, then the previous equilibrium shown in figure 5-4, with its open unemployment, is the actual outcome.

Two dynamic effects prevent the outcome in the informal market from being quite so positive as initially shown in figure 5-5. First, decisions about choice of technique in investment alter the consequent creation of productive jobs. High wages induce firms to substitute capital (especially when subsidized) for labor, no matter how many workers may actually be available in the economy. Labor absorption can proceed more rapidly where entrepreneurs are encouraged, not discouraged, from using the relatively abundant resource. The reduced demand for labor is shown in figure 5-5 by a shifted demand curve, although part of the choice-of-technique effect would show up in the informal labor market as additional supplies of workers in search of jobs.

The second factor also affects the potential supply of urban workers looking for jobs in the formal sector but pushed into the informal sector until they are successful. If the possibility of obtaining a high-paying job in the formal sector attracts additional migrants from rural areas beyond the number that would come at the lower equilibrium wage, then the labor supply curve for the informal market is shifted out. In combination with the shifted labor demand curve, the new equilibrium wage in the informal market falls to $W_{e'}$, well below even the W_e level that would have prevailed in the absence of legislation.

The equilibrium real urban wages that accurately reflect labor abundance may be very low and may leave many families in poverty. The alternative, however, is a badly segmented labor market with many families left destitute by unemployment or low-productivity casual employment. While a targeted food policy can ease the short-run consumption problems of the productively employed poor, reaching the destitute requires relief efforts that are tangential and frequently competitive to the overall task of raising productivity and reducing poverty.

Because minimum wage legislation can be selectively enforced only for a few visible firms or in government enterprises, it tends to short-circuit the gradual process of poverty alleviation by jumping a few lucky workers directly into relative (but only relative) affluence. When the legislation has a meaningful impact on urban wages, and therefore on choice of technique in manufacturing and services, the result is to exclude many unskilled workers from these benefits and to generate a large, and frequently permanent, subclass of labor which must subsist on the fringes of formal economic activity. It is within these fringes that most urban food problems are found.

Rural-Urban Terms of Trade

The rural-urban terms of trade, or the food parity price discussed in chapter 4, are determined by the interaction of four separate sectoral price elements—output prices for agriculture, input prices for agriculture, output prices for the urban-industrial sector, and input prices for the urban-industrial sector. Governments can and do influence all four of these sectoral prices, usually with very specific objectives. Tariffs on rubber tires make the domestic tire industry more profitable, subsidies on steel make bicycle factories more profitable, subsidized fertilizer makes grain production more profitable, and subsidized grain imports make consumers better-off.

When combined, these separate price interventions make up the terms of trade for the rural sector relative to the urban or industrial sector. These are then a direct indicator of the profitability of agriculture and of the purchasing power in goods and services of agricultural income. The terms of trade will find their own market-determined level in the absence of government intervention. But since all governments intervene, the issue is how domestic and international markets condition what governments can do and should want to do to structure the profitability of agriculture relative to industry.

Macro Policies and the Rural Sector

The social profitability analysis in chapter 3 and the price policy analysis in chapter 4 present tools to help address this issue of appropriate government involvement in specific sectoral pricing questions. However, the emphasis here is on the macro economy. How do macro prices and macroeconomic policy influence the rural-urban terms of trade, and how is that influence transmitted to and felt in the rural sector?

Budget policy, fiscal and monetary policy, and macro price policy have a far stronger effect on the rural-urban terms of trade than is often realized. In many circumstances, sectoral efforts to design incentive price policies for particular commodities are partly or even totally vitiated by contrary pressures from the foreign exchange rate, alternative subsidy policies, or high internal inflation. Understanding the incentives facing rural producers is impossible without tracing both the impact of commodity-specific price policies and the broader influence of the macro economy on agriculture.

RURAL-URBAN BALANCE. Most industrial sectors in the developing world are protected by high tariff barriers or direct controls over competitive im-

ports. Agricultural producers receive little protection and frequently are actively discriminated against by subsidies on competitive imports and by taxes
on their exports. As a consequence, the rural-urban terms of trade are skewed
quite directly by government policy in favor of the urban-industrial sector
and against the rural sector.

Such a direct policy has an important indirect effect on the terms of trade
as well. The higher the level of protection against imports, the more overvalued the foreign exchange rate will be. The agricultural sector produces a
much higher proportion of tradable goods—whose prices are directly connected to international prices—than does the urban-industrial sector. An
overvalued exchange rate, even when direct controls are not needed to
enforce it because of supporting trade and protection policies, discriminates
significantly against agriculture by reducing the rural-urban terms of trade.

The discrimination has consequences for both agricultural production and
income distribution. A slower growth in output, reduced incomes in rural
areas relative to urban areas, and less job creation in agriculture and the rural
nonfarm service economy all result from unfavorable rural-urban terms of
trade. Specific commodity price policy can overcome this discrimination to
some extent. A high rice price, for example, will directly alter the profitability
of growing rice, and the wide variation in domestic rice prices in various
countries in Asia is evidence of the substantial scope to use trade and subsidy
policy to separate internal commodity price policy from international market
prices.

But the vitality of the rural economy depends on more than a single
commodity. The influence of the macro economy—the foreign exchange
rate, industrial policies that alter costs and prices of important urban goods,
and fiscal and monetary policies that generate internal inflationary rates
higher than those among the major trading partners—extends into the rural
economy and affects its vitality in indirect but powerful ways. The clearest
example in recent years of the macro economy's role in altering the profitability of agriculture occurred when oil prices were pushed up on two occasions
in the 1970s. The agricultural sectors of oil-exporting countries suffered a
sharp decline in their rural-urban terms of trade, while the terms of trade for
agriculture in oil-importing countries improved dramatically.

The mechanisms by which oil price shocks were converted into significant
changes in the rural-urban terms of trade are instructive for food policy
analysts, for they help identify the important connections between macro
policy and food sector performance. The first connection is through the
foreign exchange rate directly. Oil exporters tend to run balance of payments
surpluses when oil prices rise sharply, and thus their domestic currencies
appreciate relative to trading partners who are oil importers. Mirroring this
effect, the currencies of oil importers tend to depreciate when oil prices rise.

Actual changes in nominal exchange rates are not necessary for these shifts to take place because differential inflation rates can accomplish the same changes in real terms. Thus Indonesia maintained an exchange rate of Rp 415 per U.S. dollar from 1972 to 1978, although its domestic inflation rate averaged 5 to 10 percentage points higher per year than the U.S. inflation rate over this period. The rupiah appreciated relative to the dollar by perhaps 50 percent during this time, although no macro policymaker decided to make a change in the real exchange rate. The rural-urban terms of trade were hit hard by this real appreciation of the exchange rate, and rural productivity and incomes suffered. The 50 percent devaluation of the rupiah in November 1978, a conscious macro policy decision, sharply reversed this rural decline. At least during the late 1970s and the early 1980s, Indonesia was the only oil exporter with a large rural population that was able to maintain a healthy rural economy. This was accomplished by macro policy designed, at least partly, with rural interests in mind.

The second major impact of oil prices on the rural-urban terms of trade is less direct. When oil prices rise, oil-importing countries must find a way to spur exports if the flow of oil is to be maintained. Governments can stimulate exports by providing incentives through a devaluation and also by more specific government actions. If a developing country's local industry is not competitive in export markets because of high protective barriers (at both ends—high costs in its industry and poor access to markets in developed countries), policymakers inevitably look to the rural areas for increased exports. To spur rural exports, greater incentives and increased competitiveness are needed. These come through cost-reducing measures, increased availability of yield-increasing inputs such as fertilizer, removal of export taxes, better attention to infrastructure and marketing facilities, and a commitment to new research and technology for agriculture. The evidence is quite clear that pressures to pay for oil imports force macro policymakers to improve the terms of trade for agriculture.

INCOME DISTRIBUTION AND PRODUCTIVE INVESTMENT. The importance of the rural-urban terms of trade extends beyond structuring incentives to increase output or to earn more foreign exchange to pay for oil imports. Rural-urban income distribution is also to a large extent a function of these terms of trade. Differentials between rural and urban incomes are the source of much of the rural poverty and hunger that food policy analysts are attempting to understand. Through migration decisions made by rural households, many problems of urban poverty are also connected to these differentials. In nearly all countries, average per capita incomes in rural areas are lower than per capita incomes in urban areas. In a few industrialized countries the disparities are only 10 or 20 percent, but in some African and Latin American countries urban residents earn ten times and more the income of the average rural inhabitant. Apart from its obvious impact on human welfare, the distribution of national income between urban and rural areas is important to food policy analysts because it is linked to the macro economy through the structure of aggregate demand.

Rural consumers have different spending patterns from those of their urban cousins. At any given income level they consume more food and fewer imported goods and services. Rural demand for domestic manufactures emphasizes clothing, cookware and dishes, tiles, bricks, and other home construction materials, lanterns, and eventually bicycles, radios, and sewing machines. By comparison, urban demand patterns usually have relatively less domestically produced starchy staples, more meat and fish, more imported food (both basic grain and processed luxury foods), and manufactured goods with a heavy import content, such as automobiles, motorcycles, television sets, and refrigerators.

In addition, rural households have a higher savings rate at all income levels, reflecting the dual role of many households as both producers and consumers. A significant share of rural household income is reinvested in productive inputs. Some, such as fertilizer or seeds, are only short-run investments, although usually with very high annual rates of return, while others, such as investments in farm implements, irrigation and drainage facilities, and livestock, may have a significant long-term payoff. A diminished flow of income to rural areas usually means a sharply diminished rate of rural investment and a consequent slackening in demand for rural labor.

Extensive research by John Mellor and his colleagues, especially in an Indian context, has shown the important second-round effects of the different consumption patterns in urban and rural households. Each rupee spent by a household creates additional spending as the recipients add these rupees to their incomes and then pass them on through their own expenditure patterns, thus multiplying the effect of any new purchasing power. In terms of employment created and further economic activity in total, the multiplier effects of the extra rupee spent by a rural household are larger than those of the marginal rupee spent by an urban household in the same income class. Some evidence suggests that the multiplier effects are larger for rural lower-income households than for higher-income households in either rural or urban areas if their additional food demand is met from domestic production rather than from imports. Otherwise, as Mellor points out, poverty-oriented development strategies are self-defeating: food price increases or balance of payments problems eliminate the income gains of the poor.

The discussion of the impact of macro policy on the rural-urban terms of trade has now come full circle. A failure of the rural sector to increase productivity is the primary bottleneck for any strategy attempting to raise the incomes and reduce the hunger of the poor. To eliminate the bottleneck, additional incentives to agricultural producers are likely to be needed, but these may well lower the real incomes and increase the hunger of the poor. The food price dilemma has reasserted itself, this time with the added macro dimension. It is important to understand the implications of this new connection, for it narrows the options for policymakers striving to generate a healthy rural economy in the long run, while it reemphasizes the need to find short-run food interventions to reach the poor.

Rural Growth and Long-run Economic Efficiency

The elements of a strategy for dynamic growth in the rural sector include a modern technology base, an infrastructure capable of moving inputs and output efficiently, an institutional support system that provides farmers and merchants with reliable and current information and that sets and enforces fair "rules of the game," and a set of positive incentives to farmers to increase output. In the context of the available technology and all the other infrastructural investments and institutional support, these incentives are heavily influenced by the rural-urban terms of trade, which are the outcome of a host of interacting sectoral and macro policy decisions.

It is fair to say that much of the environment for rural decisionmaking is dictated by macro policy and the macro prices. Rapid rural growth over long periods can occur only when this macro environment encourages the efficient allocation of resources. Short bursts of growth are possible from any of the other elements in the decisionmaking environment—a new seed technology, subsidized fertilizer, or a more effective extension service. But for the long haul, rural growth will falter in the absence of an overall economic environment that encourages and ultimately forces the allocation of land, labor, and capital into their most productive uses. Good macro policy facilitates rural growth.

Precisely the same statement holds for the rest of the economy. The overwhelming lesson of development experience over the past few decades is that the efficiency with which resources are allocated determines how rapid the growth path will be. This experience is contrary to the expectations of many economists and planners in past years, who noted that static economic losses to allocative inefficiencies were small, typically less than 2 percent of national income even for severe distortions, and hence could easily be dominated by more rapid growth. Just the opposite has happened.

The dynamic efficiency losses are compounded, not eliminated, in the face of macro policy that distorts the allocation of economic factors, diverting them from their most productive uses. The distortions usually found—overvalued exchange rates, subsidized interest rates, minimum wage legislation, depressed agricultural incentives, and low food prices—arise from attempts to control inflation and the distribution of output in the short run. But economic growth, including growth in rural areas, is ultimately inhibited by such a set of macro signals. At the same time, the short-run distributional and welfare concerns remain and, indeed, are exacerbated if attempts are made to bring the macro prices and macro policy into alignment with the underlying scarcity value of resources.

The tension between productive efficiency and economic growth in the long run and the short-run consumption consequences of the macro environment needed to generate such growth is one of the core topics of this book. A fairly direct link exists between efficient growth in the rural sector and efficient growth in the rest of the economy because both are conditioned by the same set of macro prices and macro policies.

This means that the food price dilemma, which has been treated so far as primarily a sectoral problem, is in fact part of a larger macro price dilemma. This larger dilemma is the basic choice all societies must make between equity and efficiency. To show the nature of the tradeoffs involved in making this choice, it is convenient to focus the discussion on the food sector itself. Even here quantification is not easy, but it is easier to deal with the tradeoffs in the food sector alone than to juggle those in the entire economy.

Figure 5-6 illustrates the basic issues. The core of the figure is the curve showing the "welfare-efficiency frontier," or the short-run choices available between food intake of the poor and efficient allocation of productive resources in the rural sector. There is, of course, much more to the distributional and welfare aspects of the food price dilemma than the food intake levels of the poor. Similarly, there is much more to efficient growth than static allocation of resources and total factor productivity. However, these two axes capture the essence of the dilemma while still permitting some concrete sense of what is at stake.

Figure 5-6. The Food Price Dilemma Illustrated

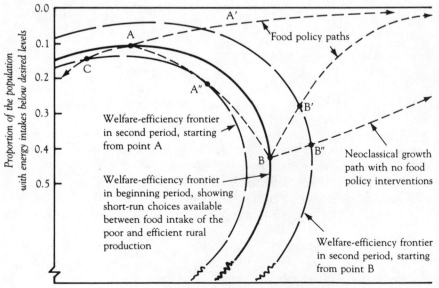

Total factor productivity of rural resources

The curve depicting the current choices available between "efficiency" and "welfare" is drawn in such a way that only part of the range involves a tradeoff. For both low welfare levels and low efficiency levels, raising one also raises the other. In many countries whose present situations fall within these boundaries, greater efficiency in production will improve welfare, not decrease it. For some countries greater welfare would lead to improved efficiency. In contrast, countries currently between A and B on the choices frontier have to make very difficult tradeoffs with respect to food price policy and other food sector interventions, and these countries face the food price dilemma directly.

A healthy rural sector with appropriate incentives will grow in total output and in productive efficiency over time. This is shown by a widened frontier in the second period if society starts at point B, which maximizes the efficiency of resource use. As the productive capacity per capita grows, the society's potential to eliminate food energy deficits also improves.

By contrast, if the society starts at point A, where food intake of the poor is maximized at the expense of efficient use of rural resources, the future capacity either to produce or feed people is reduced—to the inner frontier shown in figure 5-6. The growth path available to society is a function of the actual starting point on the short-run curve of available choices. A high welfare, low efficiency starting point, such as A, is not stable in the long run because the welfare potential declines either toward C, with negative growth, or through A″ toward B, with greater growth but reduced welfare. Alternatively, a high efficiency, medium welfare starting point, such as B, puts a country on a path of rapid growth in output via B″ but slow progress in reducing hunger.

Starting point B is generated by a macro policy environment that provides efficient incentives to the rural sector but with no food policy interventions on the consumption side. A continuation of such a policy approach would lead society out path BB″. The result is rapidly increasing rural productivity and a gradual reduction in the proportion of the population with food energy deficits. In the absence of any consumption interventions, such as the food stamp programs or fair-price shops described in chapters 2 and 4, such a neoclassical growth path eliminates energy deficits slowly and asymptotically. Even wealthy countries without food interventions have hungry people.

The alternative to the neoclassical growth path BB″ is a food policy path BB′ that involves more active government intervention in the food system. Some growth in efficiency and output is sacrificed for a much more rapid elimination of hunger, but economic growth remains a major objective of overall food policy. How to reach and stay on BB′ is practically a definition of the food price dilemma. The resolution requires a combination of policies that provide farmers with adequate incentives while poor consumers are protected from high food prices by targeted food interventions. By now the analyst can begin to see the various pieces needed to complete this puzzle.

Some countries have attempted to use their macro food policies and budgetary allocations to favor short-run welfare. Those that have succeeded find themselves at point A, facing production stagnation and some difficult choices over what policies will best provide for continued short-run protection of existing welfare levels and yet guarantee that future welfare levels can be maintained. As T. W. Schultz's book (see Bibliographical Note to chapter 1 above) on distortions of agricultural incentives indicates, many countries that have followed such a welfare policy are actually at point C, where greater productive efficiency would help welfare even in the very short run.

Ideally, a country starting at point A (or even at point C) could find a set of policies and programs that would permit rapid growth in productive efficiency in the rural sector without sacrificing welfare. Path AA' (or CAA') would then permit the small remaining food energy gap to be closed in the context of rapid and efficient growth.

Most rural growth strategies as now understood by the economic development profession do not permit a direct transition from A to A'. In fact, most of the welfare policies that have produced starting point A are inimical to rapid and efficient growth because they suppress incentives to farmers as a way of keeping food prices low to all consumers or financing direct food subsidies for urban consumers. Implementing a rural growth strategy that reverses this low food price bias and provides new price incentives to the rural sector will cause the growth path to be from A via A" to B, and then along B".

For policymakers in countries starting between C and A, a growth path of AA" to BB" must look distressing indeed. Taking that route requires a significant increase in the degree of perceived hunger among the population, which gives rise both to legitimate welfare concern and to strong political pressures to dismantle the growth policies that use incentive prices. Are there any alternatives?

This book attempts to outline the framework for a set of food policies that open path AA' and BB' to governments with a significant desire to alleviate chronic hunger among their people. Reaching such paths requires active government intervention in food systems in a way that encourages private incentives. Simultaneously, consumption interventions that reach the target population of individuals and families with food deficits must be designed in a way that maintains fiscal integrity and does not destroy farm incentives. Achieving these multiple and conflicting objectives is the task of a macro food policy, whose elements are assembled in chapter 6.

The Macro Perspective

Macroeconomic issues are abstract and frequently counterintuitive. What seems at first glance like good policy turns out to have negative consequences. In addition, the familiar decisions of everyday life are not paralleled in macroeconomic decisionmaking. To be sure, there are macroeconomic decisionmakers, but they are public officials who must respond to a wide variety of pressures and constraints, not simple economic criteria, in designing and implementing macroeconomic policy.

Macroeconomic policy also performs in a subtle and frequently irreversible fashion. Economists are accustomed to being able to operate policy levers equally well in either direction and expect decisionmakers to respond at the margin. Supply and demand elasticities work both ways, but response to macroeconomic policy changes is not so direct. Expectations and a sense of the future are inherent components of that response, for the role of macro policy is to keep a nation's economy on an even keel, headed in the right direction, and actually making progress. In short, macro policy fosters the environment in which economic development takes place.

This environment is not merely a succession of short-term policy settings, but is more properly conceived of as part of a historical evolution, where decisionmakers have memories as well as expectations. The memories cause a sharp dichotomy in what macroeconomic policy can accomplish. It can be very effective in creating an environment of distrust, high risk to investments, and extremely short time horizons for decisionmakers. It can, in fact, bring the economic growth process to a halt almost overnight.

Macro policy cannot, however, easily recreate the environment for growth once its fragile structure has been undermined. Regaining the confidence of investors large and small, foreign and domestic, requires a lengthy commitment to investment incentives which have few short-term payoffs. Policymakers often cannot withstand the pressures to show immediate results. They respond with actions that threaten further the very confidence they must win.

The food system has a major stake in this process. Macroeconomics *is* far removed from the problems caused by a delayed shipload of grain, but solving those problems in a sustainable manner comes with the structural transformation of the food system itself. This transformation is intimately tied in with the development of the rest of the economy, which depends on the continuity and skillful design of macroeconomic policy.

Bibliographical Note

The literature on macroeconomics is vast, but it virtually ignores food and agriculture. Similarly, most of the literature on food and agricultural policy has a micro focus which does not examine the macro environment in which the food sector must develop. The references here note the exceptions, but provide mainly a guide to the macroeconomic policy literature that is relevant to the food policy issues discussed in this chapter and to the literature on food and agriculture that raises macroeconomic issues.

The four basic areas of macro policy—budget policy, fiscal and monetary policy, macro price policy, and the rural-urban terms of trade—are placed in an economic development context in a textbook sponsored by the Harvard Institute for International Development, S. Malcolm Gillis, Dwight H. Perkins, Michael Roemer, and Donald R. Snodgrass, *Economics of Development* (New York: Norton, 1983). Many of the theoretical issues connecting the macro topics discussed here are dealt with in detail in a textbook by Rudiger Dornbusch, *Open Economy Macroeconomics* (New York: Basic Books, 1980). A helpful review of the formal models available to macro policy analysts is Lance Taylor, *Macro Models for Developing Countries* (New York: McGraw-Hill, 1980). Chapter 5 of Taylor's book contains a model called "price policy and the food that people consume" and concludes: "The best way to summarize . . . is to observe that like many macro interventions, changes in food price policy cut with more than one edge. . . . This conclusion . . . does point to an important corollary: attempts to 'get the prices right' may indeed have positive effects on output or economic efficiency, but their negative distributional consequences for some groups in the population may be large." Taylor's book tends to build from Ricardian and Keynesian bases rather than from a neoclassical market-equilibrium approach, but it provides a powerful insight, available in no other volume, into how to think clearly about macro problems, including food and agricultural problems, in a development context.

Budget policies and their relationship with fiscal and monetary policies are summarized in W. M. Corden, *Trade Policy and Economic Welfare* (Oxford: Clarendon Press, 1974), especially pp. 58–87, and are treated at greater length in John F. Due and Ann F. Friedlaender, *Government Finance: Economics of the Public Sector* (Homewood, Ill.: Richard D. Irwin, 1973), and in John F. Due, *Indirect Taxation in Developing Countries* (Baltimore, Md.: Johns Hopkins University Press, 1970).

The term "macro prices" was first used in a paper by C. Peter Timmer, "Public Policy for Improving Technology Choice," Discussion Paper no. 84 (Cambridge, Mass.: Harvard Institute for International Development, March 1980), where their impact on the rural sector and on appropriate development strategies was treated in the context of a continuum of decisionmaking between micro and macro levels. The literature on each individual macro price is extensive. A theoretical approach to exchange rate policy is fully developed in W. M. Corden, *Inflation, Exchange Rates and the World Economy* (Oxford: Oxford University Press, 1977). Complementary textbooks include Richard E. Caves and Ronald W. Jones, *World Trade and Payments: An Introduction* (Boston: Little, Brown, 1981); and Charles P. Kindleberger and Peter H. Lindert, *International Economics* (Homewood, Ill.: Richard D. Irwin, 1978). Empirical evidence on the purchasing power parity theory is contained in Ronald I. McKinnon, *Money in International Exchange: The Convertible Currency System* (New York: Oxford University Press, 1979); on the effects of a devaluation in Richard N. Cooper, "Currency Devaluation in Developing Countries," *Essays in International Finance*, no. 86 (Princeton, N.J.: Princeton University, June 1971); and on the implicit tax on agriculture fostered by an overvalued exchange rate in Ian Little, Tibor Scitovsky, and Maurice FG. Scott, *Industry and Trade in Some Developing Countries* (London: Oxford University Press, 1970).

The approach followed here to analyze interest rate policy is based largely on two seminal books, Ronald I. McKinnon, *Money and Capital in Economic Development* (Washington, D.C.: Brookings Institution, 1973), and Edward S. Shaw, *Financial Deepening in Economic Development* (New York: Oxford University Press, 1973). Empirical evidence of the links between positive real interest rates, financial deepening, and economic growth is presented in Hang-Sheng Cheng, "Financial Deepening in Pacific Basin Countries," *San Francisco Federal Reserve Economic Review* (Summer 1980).

A particularly useful review of financial policies is contained in a special issue, "National and International Aspects of Financial Policies in LDCs," *World Development*, vol. 10, no. 9 (September 1982). The paper by John Williamson in this volume, "On the Characterization of Good Economic Policy: Is There a Consensus?" suggests four policy rules which appear to be consistent with the main themes of this chapter: "(1) the pursuit of micro-economic efficiency, to place the economy on the frontier; (2) maintenance of an effective, though not necessarily rigid, anti-inflationary stance; (3) continuous maintenance of internal balance [between aggregate demand and aggregate supply]; and (4) medium-term pursuit of a current balance [of payments] target guided by thrift and productivity" (p. 695).

The discussion of the formation of wage rates draws on a literature as vast as the economic development literature itself, based as it is on labor surplus models and the availability of rural labor at subsistence wages. A recent review places this entire topic in historical and analytical perspective and emphasizes the enormous complexity of rural wage determination: Hans P. Binswanger and Mark R. Rosenzweig, *Contractual Arrangements, Employment and Wages in Rural Labor Markets: A Critical Review* (New York: Agricultural Development Council, 1981). A book by John Connell and Michael Lipton, *Assessing Village Labor Structures in Developing Countries* (New Delhi: Oxford University Press, 1977), discusses the implications of rural labor markets on rural-to-urban migration. Two books provide very helpful insights into the overall effects of macro policy (and macro prices) on choice of technique, employment generation, and the ultimate impact on alleviation of poverty. A. K. Sen, *Employment, Technology and Development* (London: Oxford University Press, 1975), presents an integrated theoretical perspective on the topic, while Gary S. Fields, *Poverty, Inequality, and Development* (Cambridge: Cambridge University Press, 1980), is the best available review of empirical evidence on the impact of macro policy on the distribution of income and on alleviation of poverty.

For over two decades the works of Bruce F. Johnston and John W. Mellor have provided insight and evidence on the connections between agriculture and development of the rest of the economy. Their joint article in 1961, "The Role of Agriculture in Economic Development," *American Economic Review*, vol. 51 (September 1961), pp. 566–95, began the long process of thinking about the agricultural sector as a potentially positive factor in development rather than as a repository of resources to be tapped at the pleasure of national planners interested in industrialization. Mellor's text, *The Economics of Agricultural Development* (Ithaca, N.Y.: Cornell University Press, 1966), developed many of these themes empirically and analytically. Chapters on "Agriculture and Capital Formation," "Agriculture and Foreign Exchange," and "Increasing Rural Welfare" still speak directly to the macro issues discussed here. A book that synthesizes much of Johnston's thought, done jointly with Peter Kilby, an industrial economist, is *Agriculture and Structural Transformation: Economic Strategies in Late-Developing Countries* (New York: Oxford University Press, 1975). The Johnston-Kilby volume is particularly concerned with the issue of technology choice discussed here and with appropriate policies to generate efficient use of resources. A similar book by Mellor, *The New Economics of Growth* (Ithaca, N.Y.: Cornell University Press, 1976), identifies both conceptually and empirically the important linkages between agricultural performance and overall macroeconomic growth. A paper by Graciela Chilchilnisky and Lance Taylor, "Agriculture and the Rest of the Economy: Macro Connections and Policy Restraints," *American Journal of Agricultural Economics*, vol. 62, no. 2 (May 1980), pp. 303–09, presents a comparative statics framework for addressing these issues, primarily in a Latin American context.

The model of macro-micro connections and the empirical evidence that provided an understanding of the impact of oil prices on the rural-urban terms of trade are presented in C. Peter Timmer, "Energy and Structural Change in the Asia-Pacific Region: The Agricultural Sector," Discussion Paper no. 140 (Cambridge, Mass.: Harvard Institute for International Development, December 1982).

The consequences of macroeconomic distortions and of a macro reform are beginning to be documented in a rapidly growing literature. An analysis of the comparative empirical evidence on the important relationships between macroeconomic policies and development is in two volumes published in the series "Foreign Trade Regimes and Economic Development," for the National Bureau of Economic Research (Cambridge, Mass.: Ballinger Press): Anne O. Krueger, *Liberalization Attempts and Consequences*, vol. 10 (1978), and Jagdish Bhagwati, *Anatomy and Consequences of Exchange Control Regimes*, vol. 11 (1978). The results of these books and of other recent work on this topic are reviewed and extended in Ronald I. McKinnon, "Foreign Trade Regimes and Economic Development: A Review Article," *Journal of International Economics*, vol. 9 (1979), pp. 429–52. A lively debate on the actual effects on developing economies of stringent macro reforms occasioned by external debt crises, as well as a more general discussion of economic stabilization theory and comparative policy experience, is contained in William R. Cline and Sidney Weintraub, eds., *Economic Stabilization in Developing Countries* (Washington, D.C.: Brookings Institution, 1981).

6

Macro Food Policy

Public policy is the major factor in solving the problem of hunger. This potential for policy to influence the lives and well-being of vast numbers of people explains much of the dominance of ideas and ideology, rather than experience and empirical result, in attempts to improve global food security and in the efforts of individual countries to reduce the number of hungry people. A better understanding of the world food system and the potential for domestic food policy can help bridge this wide gap between ideas and actual results.

This book is about the formation of domestic food policy. Although the international economic environment conditions the options and influences the performance of a nation's own economy, the most immediate potential to improve the lives of the poor in a sustainable fashion lies in effective domestic food policies. Chapters 2, 3, and 4 assembled the sectoral components of those policies; chapter 5 placed them in a macroeconomic context. With these pieces and this perspective in hand, food policy analysts should be able to form a consistent picture of the country's food policy as it stands, as well as the effects of policies and programs with other objectives that impinge on this policy. The goal is to understand how all the strands of national policies and programs affect the food system—food production, consumption, marketing, and especially food prices for farmers and consumers.

Food systems are made up of highly diverse producers and consumers connected by a network of markets that function in a macro and international context. The diversity of producers and consumers is important to the design of effective food policies. Much of the micro-level analysis done by food policy analysts is intended to discover how differently situated decisionmakers react to changes in their economic environments, particularly the poor who have greater sensitivity to changes in their incomes and the prices they face. The food consumption patterns of the poor usually include large proportions of cheap starchy staples. These people are forced by economic circumstances to be more flexible in their choices as market signals reflect varying degrees of commodity scarcity and as prices rise or fall.

Similarly, food producers are also remarkably diverse. They include rural households with less than one-tenth of a hectare of cultivated land who must earn most of their incomes from off-farm jobs. These households purchase a significant proportion of their food from rural markets, and it is a mistake to think that all small farmers are benefited by incentive price policies that raise the market cost of food. Most food available in rural markets comes from larger farmers who do profit from greater incentives and who typically respond enthusiastically to them with greater output.

The link between these two types of farmers, who represent points along a continuum, is often the rural labor market. Price incentives for agricultural output raise demand for labor in these markets directly through additional wage labor demanded on farms that produce marketed surpluses. At the same time, the labor market is affected indirectly because less labor is supplied from small-farm households that find it profitable to use more household labor on their small plots. In a roundabout way demand for labor is increased by the higher farm incomes because rural household expenditure patterns usually reflect a demand for labor-intensive goods and services. This positive effect of price incentives on job creation and rural wages causes a major dilemma, however, for the incentives also mean higher food prices.

The solution to poverty and hunger is jobs and access to food. Many of the productive jobs will be in the rural areas, and access to food is a function of its price as well as household incomes, especially in the short run. Rural labor markets and food markets are the primary connecting mechanisms between employment and food prices in market economies, and even socialist countries must find some mechanisms to connect workers with jobs and to signal producers and consumers about the opportunity cost of growing and consuming food.

When the actual signals convey misleading information in either kind of economy, the resulting decisions distort resource allocation and lower economic welfare on average. Distorted macro prices may protect the interests of the poor in the short run to some extent, but the future welfare of a society, especially the welfare of its poorest members, depends on the efficient use of resources, including human resources. Policies in the agricultural sector—for example, prices for fertilizer, charges for irrigation water, or the commitment of resources to agricultural research—directly affect the efficiency of resource use. These are all important elements in how rapidly agricultural output grows and who benefits when it does.

At the same time, many of the factors influencing the efficiency of resource use in agriculture and the distribution of benefits are reflections of the macro economy and the various policies and programs that affect it. Consequently, food policy analysis includes the connections between the food system and the rest of the macro economy. Ignoring the macro aspect of food policy virtually guarantees partial and simplistic solutions that can be sustained only at high economic and political cost. A "macro food policy" approach is required for a society to find a satisfactory reconciliation of its producer and consumer interests.

The Macro Food Policy Perspective

At this stage in the analysis of a country's food policy, the budding analyst no doubt feels a bit like a juggler, with many pieces to keep in the air all at once. Some are more important than others, depending on the circumstance, but that is precisely the problem. How does the analyst know at the beginning what will be important in order to find a shortcut through the complex maze of data, issues, and connections?

There is no substitute for an empirical understanding, however rough, of how the food system works. For this task certain key data provide much insight and do not require that the analyst spend years in village surveys and model building: simple disaggregated food balance sheets; a few representative farming system tableaux; local prices relative to international prices; and the size of and reasons for various marketing margins for important commodities as they travel from farm to consumer. Prices in world markets keep the concept of opportunity costs to alternative policies squarely in the picture, but they also raise important macroeconomic questions. Food policy analysts even in the provinces and regions become increasingly aware that foreign exchange rates, inflation rates, and real interest rates condition how the food system works and where it is headed.

Where the food system is headed, of course, is the key question. Developing an intuitive understanding of the critical pressures on the system at any particular time is the artistic part of analysis, but having a framework of how issues are connected is the starting point for the craft. This framework begins with a disaggregated knowledge of how producers and consumers make their decisions and is built on an appreciation of the coordinating role of markets— in both socialist and capitalist economies. With an understanding of how markets are actually working, analysts recognize that producers, consumers, and government agencies all have at least part of their fate linked through markets. Policy decisions, whether motivated by analytical insight or political pressures, can change both the signals transmitted through markets and the rules of the game within which markets operate.

The central theme of this book has been the need to think about the problem of hunger as susceptible to domestic food policy interventions, while simultaneously recognizing its macro and international context. This perspective has created two policy dilemmas: a micro-level food price dilemma that recognizes the tradeoffs between producer and consumer interests in the short run; and a macro price dilemma that reflects how strongly the macro economy conditions the scope for food policy. An important link between the two dilemmas is budget policy. Targeted food subsidies are one mechanism for dealing with the food price dilemma, but only if the macro economy is generating both expanding budget revenues and more jobs for poor people. Too large a budget drain for subsidies almost always results in fiscal deficits, inflation, an overvalued exchange rate, slow economic growth, low labor absorption, and an exacerbation of the policy dilemma rather than a solution to it.

When macro and international economies create a hostile environment for food policy, finding effective policies is even more difficult. Progress can be made in some areas. Sectoral strategies and efficient infrastructural investment programs can be developed to maintain some growth in agricultural output. Targeted food subsidy programs can be tried in various field settings to discover workable interventions under different circumstances. Agricultural research can build a responsive productivity base.

In one sense, however, these are all essential preparations for the time when a major macro reform must be instituted either to satisfy foreign creditors or simply to revitalize the country's growth prospects. When the crunch comes, it is often too late for food policy analysis, except for the roughest, back-of-the-envelope kind. At this stage, it is enormously valuable to a country to have a few analysts who have done their homework, who understand the food system, and whose intuition can provide policy direction in the pressured give and take over the nature and content of the reforms.

Macro reforms are often triggered by unexpected events in world markets. Export prices for primary goods may collapse, the cost of imported grain may skyrocket, or a global credit squeeze may prevent the rollover of short-run loans and thus precipitate a crisis of confidence in a country's ability to service its debts. One response to this exposure to the vicissitudes of international markets is not to play the game. But autarky has turned out to be enormously costly to economic growth and, eventually, to the well-being of the poor as well. Food security does not depend on food production strategies alone, and the use of world markets to offset domestic instability can bring substantial gains in consumer welfare.

The question for food policy analysts is how to link a domestic economy, and especially its food system, to the international economy. Countries have two primary decisions to make about this link: the appropriate level of domestic prices relative to international price levels; and the extent to which global price instability will be transmitted to domestic producers and consumers, whatever the long-run relative price levels. The mechanisms for implementing a domestic price policy relative to international prices—buffer stocks, foreign exchange contingency funds, futures markets, and skilled market analysis—are an important component of managing a food policy, to be discussed in this chapter. First, a better sense of the international context itself is needed.

The International Context

Food is simultaneously an economic commodity and a biological necessity. More than any other commodity in the world economy, food is torn by a contradiction between its value in exchange and its value in human use. In economic terms, food can be produced, purchased, stored, and speculated on, just like steel, cement, tin, or gold. Unlike any of these other economic commodities, however, food must be provided on a regular basis in adequate amounts to all individuals if they are to survive, grow, and thrive.

One of the most pervasive forces in the economic history of modern societies has been an apparently irresistible and irreversible trend toward the commoditization of food. Modern processing and transportation techniques have converted food from a local product for home and regional consumption to an interchangeable commodity moved from one part of the globe to another. As food becomes ever more like other economic commodities in regional and world trade, its biological uniqueness endures. An inevitable consequence is that the adequacy of food intake for millions of people hinges increasingly on the ebb and flow of the world economy and on the response of their own local economies to it.

The international economy limits what policymakers can accomplish, but simultaneously it offers opportunities for improving the design and implementation of food policy. A healthy and competitive relationship between the domestic and the international economy has characterized most successes in economic development for the past two decades. An openness to the world economy, at least to the extent of judging domestic policies in terms of their international opportunity costs, is a major ingredient in domestic food policy formation.

Food policy is constrained by the international economy through its impact on the balance of payments and the foreign exchange rate. The exchange rate fundamentally conditions the environment in which public and private food sector decisions are made. Food policy deliberations taken in isolation from the exchange rate and the balance of payments miss one of the major building blocks of the structure of rural incentives.

The international economy impinges on domestic food policy in a second way. Instability in world grain prices can upset development plans to allocate foreign exchange to capital investment and social infrastructure. Being small in world markets is an advantage in this context, but it does not alter the reality that import price fluctuations require great flexibility in foreign exchange allocations for grain imports. Direct transmittal of the food price fluctuations into the domestic economy entails large burdens of adjustment for producers or consumers.

Most countries try to protect their domestic economies from such shocks. Government intervention to buffer the effects of large price fluctuations is easier from day to day than it is from year to year. The costs of short-run insulation from the world economy are not large, and the benefits are substantial. To implement such policies successfully, a country needs the analytical capacity to interpret international commodity price trends, the budgetary resources to finance short-term stabilization policies, and the administrative capacity to carry them out.

The benefits from international trade come in the medium to long run when specialization and efficient resource allocation permit both trading partners to gain. To help a country participate effectively in this trade, analysts need to recognize that underneath all the global instability is a world economy undergoing major structural changes. These long-run changes are of particular importance to a poor country; they dictate the nature of the goods and services that can be traded and at what opportunity costs to the country's own economy.

Structural Changes in the World Economy

The world economy is vastly different from what it was just a decade ago. Sharply higher real energy prices have induced much of the change, bringing a significant redistribution of world incomes and very different expenditure patterns as a result. The indirect and long-term ramifications of this change continue to be worked out, and the full extent of the structural adjustments is still unknown. The slowdown in the world's economy, the mounting debt of the developing world, and the delayed prospects for rapid growth of the poorer countries are apparent even now, however.

Mostly as a result of long-term changes in the balance of economic power in the world, the Bretton Woods system of fixed foreign exchange rates broke down in 1971. Interest rates and exchange rates became much more volatile and interdependent when the need to finance oil imports and to recycle "petrodollars" back into the world economy was piled on top of the new floating exchange rate system. The monetary and fiscal policies of the major industrial countries and the overall health of their economies became linked into more synchronous patterns than had existed before 1970. At the same time, the economies of the oil-exporting nations seemed to fluctuate in countercyclical fashion to those of the industrialized countries, mostly because of the petroleum price link and its macroeconomic effects on buyers and sellers.

Both the petroleum price and the international macroeconomic environment influence world commodity markets. When real interest rates fluctuate in the Eurodollar market, price formation in world markets is affected by the altered costs of carrying inventories of food commodities. In a more roundabout way, the structural changes affect supply and demand in individual countries, and the cumulative effects gradually spill over into world commodity markets and affect their structure and price behavior.

PETROLEUM PRICES. Rising petroleum prices in the 1970s had both direct and indirect effects on domestic agricultural systems throughout the world. The direct effects of higher oil prices were to raise the costs of pumping irrigation water, the costs of fuel used in tractors, the energy costs of food processing and distribution, and, though the correlation was far from perfect, fertilizer costs. Higher input costs caused farmers to use energy-related inputs less intensively. The resulting lower output caused grain prices to rise; higher input costs were then covered by the higher grain prices. Through such equilibrating market mechanisms, higher input costs translate into higher output prices. Similarly, as market forces and continued investments bring input prices back down, especially fertilizer prices, then grain prices also work their way down in real terms.

As chapter 5 explained, higher petroleum prices also had important indirect effects. Many food-importing countries import oil as well, and they faced a double balance of payments problem after 1973–74. Some countries reduced petroleum imports and slowed their economic growth, some reduced food imports and pushed domestic food prices higher, and nearly all food- and oil-importing countries borrowed heavily from world credit markets. The large and growing international debt of developing countries is a potential source of disruption to world trade because the international financial system is a key factor in the smooth functioning of trade movements.

An even more roundabout impact of higher petroleum prices may turn out to be the most important of all. The oil-exporting countries experienced extremely rapid increases in their incomes while the industrial economies showed slow growth or declines. This redistribution of world incomes is important for several reasons. For the world food system it meant income shifted from relatively rich populations in the United States and Western Europe, where income elasticities of demand for food are nearly zero, to populations in the Middle East, Nigeria, Mexico, Venezuela, and Indonesia, where food income elasticities are significantly positive. Consequently, the 1970s saw a sharp increase in demand for food from a given dollar increase in average world incomes.

In the framework of price formation in the world grain market shown in figures 4-6 and 4-7, the redistribution of incomes caused demand curves for food grains in international markets to shift out faster in the 1970s than in previous periods. The decade also saw several years of poor production and slow growth in supplies available to international markets. As a consequence, real prices for wheat and rice, the two primary food grains, were higher in the 1970s than in the 1960s.

THE LIVESTOCK ECONOMY. The structure of the food demand itself has also shifted in response to the size and location of the income growth. A consequence of the redistribution of incomes has been a sharp increase in demand for livestock products. In market economies normal demand forces cause this shift to increased meat consumption when incomes rise rapidly, but even in socialist oil-exporting countries such as the U.S.S.R. and China, providing additional meat supplies has a very high priority in the economic plan. Much of the increased supply to meet the demand is produced by feeding grain—especially corn and other coarse grains, but also low-quality wheat—to livestock. In periods of rapid income growth, this demand for feed grains can push up the prices of all grains, not just corn or sorghum.

Considerable concern has been expressed that the indirect demand for feed grain to produce meat for the affluent has the potential to "bid food off the plates of the poor." Certainly in an environment of static supply response, the added grain demand will raise market prices. One of the most persistent trends in modern economic history, however, has been the elastic response of commercial farmers to even modest improvements in the real price of grain. Demand pressures may yet outrun supply response and reverse the long-run decline in real grain prices. But lagging income growth in the early 1980s in the industrial countries along with weaker oil prices have relieved much of the demand pressure in world grain markets in the mid-1970s. Supplies have continued to be responsive to higher incentives. As developing countries attempt to implement a food price policy consistent with international opportunity costs, their primary problem is not likely to be a sharply higher long-run level of grain prices in world markets, but rather their sharp instability.

The growing world livestock economy plays a somewhat surprising role in conditioning this grain price instability. Grain price fluctuations are likely to be dampened by the increased use of grain to feed livestock. Although demand for grain for direct human consumption is normally very price inelastic, the demand for feed grain for livestock is quite price elastic in the medium run—about twelve to twenty-four months. With 40 percent of world grain production now destined to be consumed by livestock, the buffering opportunities against extreme price fluctuations are quite substantial. This buffering does not work very effectively in the short run—up to twelve months or so—and price fluctuations can still be very large in the face of significant production shortfalls or new sources of demand for international supplies.

The potential of the livestock sector to stabilize international prices is diminished, moreover, if countries cut off their producers and consumers from international price signals for long periods. Farmers then do not adjust feed use in response to changing grain prices because domestic production and consumption decisions are not influenced by international prices. Protectionist policies of countries in pursuit of domestic price stability can thus increase international price volatility.

For example, in response to sharply higher grain prices in 1973 and 1974, the amount of grain fed to livestock in the United States fell below 1972 levels by 6.0 million metric tons and declined further in 1974 and 1975 by 38.7 million and 28.6 million tons, respectively. The total drop in feed use for the three years amounted to 73.3 million tons. By contrast, during the same period, feed use in Japan and the U.S.S.R. actually rose because feeding decisions were isolated from the opportunity costs of the feed. When producers and consumers are completely protected from price changes, they cannot be part of the adjustment process that price changes are intended to call forth.

INDIRECT EFFECTS ON FOOD DEMAND. In addition to changes in food expenditure patterns caused by the redistribution of global income, petroleum wealth created a new demand for industrial goods, many of which were supplied by the newly industrializing economies, such as Brazil, Taiwan, and the Republic of Korea. Their incomes too became linked to rising incomes in oil-exporting countries and further extended the income redistribution effects of the oil price increase. The food consumption consequences of this indirect redistribution were similar to the direct effects noted above.

An even less direct effect of petroleum wealth on food demand has come from the remittances of foreign workers. The Middle Eastern oil exporters have hired many immigrant workers from poorer countries in the region and from countries as far away as Bangladesh and Korea. The foreign exchange remittances from these workers are a significant factor in the balance of payments of several countries, including Pakistan, India, Bangladesh, and Sri Lanka, permitting somewhat freer imports of food than would otherwise have been possible under the dual burden of higher prices for petroleum and grain.

MACROECONOMIC EFFECTS. The indirect and roundabout impact of higher oil prices on agricultural systems and the price of grains traded in international markets are mediated mostly through macroeconomic mechanisms. Those specifically connected to the redistribution of income were noted above, but several operate more through financial changes and exchange rates than through demand patterns for food.

The most obvious result of the "new international financial order" and the use of high interest rates to control inflation is the almost universal slowdown in the economies of industrial countries. The effect on developing countries is twofold: the slower growth reduces the demand for their primary exports used as inputs to industrial processes while increasing competition for their manufactured exports; and the high interest rates raise the cost of storing commodities and depress their prices further. Such economic mechanisms work both ways. When interest rates decline, economies should be revitalized. Storage costs fall and induce greater storage and higher commodity prices in international markets. The interactive leveraging of these effects is one of the main reasons for the dramatic swings in the expectations of market participants and in commodity prices. For countries dependent on exports of a few primary commodities for both their foreign exchange earnings and domestic incomes in rural areas, these price swings play havoc with macro plans and the costs of providing food security to poor households.

The most important structural change under way in the world economy at the moment, and the one for which the least statistical evidence is available, is the gradual adjustment, through exchange rate realignments, in the overall terms of trade for agriculture in oil-importing countries (and in oil-exporting countries wise enough to recognize the importance of their rural sectors for long-run growth and more equal distribution of incomes). As chapter 5 explained, high-priced oil imports put pressure on the balance of payments and cause a gradual depreciation of a country's currency. This depreciation raises the opportunity cost of food imports (or the incentives to export) and thus stimulates a country's rural economy. The gradual, but cumulative, effect is to add new food supplies to world markets and to reduce demand in those markets.

These trends of added supplies and reduced demand clearly complicate efforts to predict future directions for world grain prices, for the trends run counter to pressures from increasing population and the redistribution of income to countries with higher income elasticities of demand for food. It is inappropriate here to predict which direction future prices will take. The goal has been more limited—to identify several new elements that will influence those trends and that analysts can follow in their own efforts to track historic trends and discern directions for the future.

Managing a Food Policy

Countries have only limited experience with managing a food policy that is internally consistent and designed around the framework and perspective developed in this book. Pieces of the approach have been tried in various places, for example, targeted ration shops in parts of India, incentive price schemes in the Republic of Korea, and a macroeconomic environment conducive to agriculture in Indonesia. No country has put the pieces together, largely because the need to have an integrated food policy has not been fully appreciated, nor has the knowledge been available to do it. Consequently, this discussion of managing a food policy focuses less on evaluating what works and what does not than on emphasizing several important issues for implementation.

Administrative capacity is the first of these, for any program, no matter how beautifully designed, is only as good as the ability to make it work in the field. Many of these administrative issues are important to managing the food price dilemma successfully and to creating effective institutional structures and financial arrangements for setting domestic food prices relative to international market prices. Buffer stocks and foreign exchange contingency funds are mechanisms for implementing a food policy and managing the inherent instability of agricultural systems. These mechanisms help cope with this instability as it spills over into the macro economy through budgetary, fiscal, and monetary effects, the balance of payments, and the availability of foreign exchange. Managing a food policy means first of all understanding these issues and then being prepared to deal with them day by day. Some of the understanding can be provided here, but the day-to-day lessons will be learned on the job.

Administrative Capacity

Traditionally, two separate and unconnected efforts have gone into public policy formation. The analytical or design effort has focused on policy objectives and on financial and technical constraints. From the juxtaposition of objectives and constraints emerged an optimal policy, which was then handed over to the civil service for the second part of the effort—implementation and administration. A long-standing complaint in developing countries has been the relative ease of getting "good" policy advice, but the subsequent difficulties in implementing the recommended policies. Separating policy analysis in this way from policy implementation is simply wrong. Policy analysis must evaluate the capacity to implement and manage the policy on a daily basis. That need has complicated the analytical approaches in each chapter. The analysis is not complete without a specific concern for political and bureaucratic capacity to implement the results of the analysis.

Limited capacity to do this analysis is a major constraint in all countries. More troubling, the capacity to train analysts with appropriate tools, perspective, and sensitivity is also extremely limited. This book is a bare beginning toward an understanding of the type of analytical capacity required and toward the development of the skills needed to make that analytical capacity effective.

The importance of administrative capacity in implementing policies and programs is apparent when analysts consider the tradeoffs between a desirable policy, its administrative intensity, and the capacity to implement it. As a general rule, price policies implemented by appropriate trade instruments at the international border do not require complicated bureaucratic management. But as the domestic price diverges more and more from the international opportunity cost in either direction, the administrative task of keeping the country's cheap grain at home or keeping out the international market's cheap grain becomes much more difficult, even more so if the coastline is long and open.

A food price policy that permits free trade of basic food grains in either direction requires almost no effort to implement, but it might not be very satisfactory in furthering the government's objectives because of the extreme instability that would be transmitted into the domestic economy. The more vigorous the objectives relative to the international price standard, the more administratively intensive the policy will be. An administratively intensive food price policy, without the bureaucratic resources to implement it, will be circumvented and ultimately frustrated by market forces. Consequently, for food price policy an assessment of administrative capacity is a necessary component of the planning.

The capacity to implement a fair means test to limit access to a targeted consumer food subsidy scheme clearly conditions the entire tenor of all food planning discussions. If the government plans to provide adequate incentives to farmers to grow more grain, it needs some mechanism to protect the poor from higher food prices during the transition to rapid and equitable agricultural growth. An incentives-led growth strategy requires sufficient administrative capacity to locate the very poor suffering from food deficits and to design mechanisms to reach them with food without bankrupting the treasury or having serious spillover effects on farmer incentives.

Food stamp programs or a network of fair-price shops restricted to poor consumers appeal to economists because they target food subsidies efficiently. But if the programs cannot be restricted to the target population, the budget costs mushroom and the efficiency disappears. If the bureaucracy cannot implement a fair and efficient means test, then *administrative targeting* of programs directly to the poor is not feasible, and other targeting mechanisms must be found.

An incentives-based food price policy in itself will require significant administrative capacity to implement. Few countries leave food price determination entirely in private hands. Most evidence suggests that private food marketing agents tend to be competitive and do not exert significant influence on seasonal or spatial price formation. However, a public role still exists for smoothing out year-to-year variations through import-export policies and a well-managed buffer stock program.

The major goal of such a program will usually be to ensure that incentive prices actually reach the farmers during the weeks immediately following the harvest and that price ceilings for urban consumers are not exceeded during brief, preharvest shortages. A price policy that leaves most of this task to the private sector is no doubt the least costly in terms of government resources and administrative capacity, but it might not accomplish the objectives the government desires of its food price policy. A more active role for government in influencing price formation, perhaps with some subsidization of marketing margins, is likely to be part of the management of food price policy.

The importance of food price policy has been a persistent theme from the beginning of this book. The inverse impact of food prices on producers and consumers creates a significant dilemma for policy by separating the short-run interests of the poor from their long-run interests. Managing this dilemma while trying to achieve all four food policy objectives, rather than just one or two, is the essence of a successful food policy. That success requires an understanding of the political economy of food prices as well as more specific tools for managing a country's border price through buffer stocks and greater financial flexibility and control.

Food Prices and Consumer Pressure

In virtually all poor countries the strongest and most visible constraint on choosing among food policy alternatives is consumer pressure in urban areas to keep basic food prices cheap. The less developed the country, the more acute the problem. Figure 6-1 shows the relationship in 1975 between the prices of calories from staple foods—cereals and pulses—relative to per capita incomes in a sample of seven diverse countries. Both axes are drawn in logarithms to capture the proportional relationship better. For every 10 percent difference in per capita income, the staple calorie price varies roughly half as much. At India's 1975 per capita income of $140 (converted at the nominal exchange rate for the year), prices for staple foods were only 5.95 cents per 1,000 calories. In Mexico, with a per capita income of $1,335, prices for staples were 16.0 cents per 1,000 calories, while in the United States the price was 33.8 cents and per capita income was nearly $7,150. The other countries in this sample are smoothly distributed in between. The evidence is fairly clear that poor countries feel pressure to keep their basic cereal prices low to consumers and thus forgo the gains in productivity that might come from offering their farmers better incentives.

Politicians and most bureaucrats in the developing world are susceptible to this pressure because food forms a large share of the budgets of all but the most privileged, and urban populations must buy all their food. High food prices hurt with an intensity which varies from a pinprick for wealthy merchants, to the disappointment of a movie missed or a radio not purchased for students or factory workers, to the dull, chronic pain of continuous hunger for the unemployed. Raising food prices sends many of these people clamoring in the streets. Although the urban pressure for low food prices is usually exerted by consumers who are relatively well-off by nutritional standards, this does not dismiss the importance of that cheap food grain to the truly malnourished and hungry—the urban unemployed, the rural landless, or disadvantaged infants and children.

The mirror image of urban pressure for cheap food is production stagnation or unsatisfactory performance in the agricultural sector. Much of the production stagnation is *caused* by a cheap food policy, or so the available economic evidence would indicate. Whatever the cause, the result is slow growth in food and feed grain output relative to effective demand and especially to nutritional requirements. Stagnation leads to rising food prices, which are resisted by urban consumers, or to growing imports from the world market. Many countries have resorted to imports to satisfy the rapid growth in food demand fueled by growth in population and incomes. Resort to international supplies is not a bad thing in isolation. Only if the imports are used to support a strongly urban-biased development strategy do they create a significant problem for domestic food policy.

Precisely because the urban pressure for low food prices is so strong, however, a disproportionate amount of government policy attention and budgetary resources has been devoted to nonprice policy issues. Priority attention to the neglected price issue should pay very high returns in both short-run and long-run productivity growth. At the same time, mechanisms can be designed to deal with the short-run consumption consequences of providing better incentives to farmers. In the longer run, efficient job creation is a

Figure 6-1. Relationship between Staple Food Prices and per Capita Incomes in a Diverse Sample of Countries, 1975

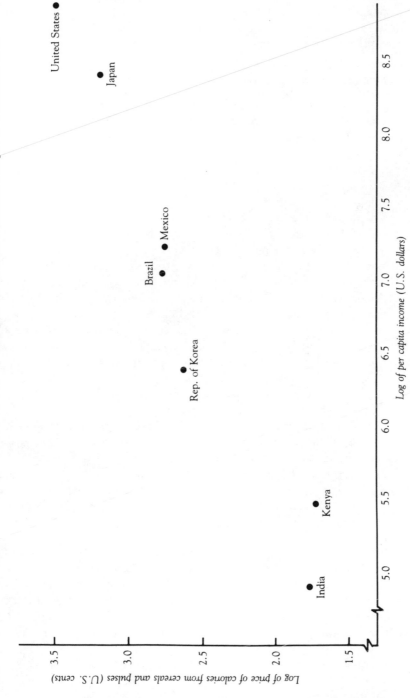

concomitant of a dynamic agriculture, and rapidly growing employment contributes to more equal income distribution in poor countries and improves the welfare of food consumers.

Domestic Food Price Policy

Managing domestic food price policy requires setting and maintaining a border price relative to international market prices. As chapter 4 explained, this task has essentially three time horizons. The first focuses on the day-to-day and month-to-month fluctuations in domestic import needs relative to international market prices and on management of a buffer stock operation to achieve the lowest cost possible for imported grain (or the highest price for exports).

The internal price range set for domestic producers and consumers reflects a second time horizon, for this price is most effective if maintained for a year or two at a time. This provides reasonably stable signals to domestic decisionmakers about the opportunity costs of their production and consumption allocations. Such stability improves the efficiency of resource allocation if it does not lock in misleading signals about the long-run opportunity costs of producing and using resources. These long-run opportunity costs are read from international market price trends, and they represent the third time horizon important for domestic food price policy. Investment decisions with a payoff several years in the future should depend on these long-run opportunity costs and not on short-run prices.

It is the inherent instability of both domestic agricultural production and international market prices that complicates the management of food price policy. Otherwise, prices in the three time horizons would correspond, and borders could simply be open even in the very short run to free trade in agricultural commodities. Price instability is a problem in the case of both food imports where foreign exchange is needed and agricultural exports where foreign exchange is earned. In both cases the important management issues revolve around fluctuations in foreign exchange available to the entire economy, not just for the implementation of food policy.

FLUCTUATIONS IN FOOD IMPORT BILLS. The balance between domestic food production, imports (or exports) of food, and food consumption is often quite delicate. Variations in domestic food output of 20 percent occur on occasion, and to maintain stable levels of food consumption, imports must fluctuate substantially. They frequently do not adjust enough to prevent serious shortfalls in consumption. As table 6-1 shows, for several low-income countries, the total value of food imports averaged more than 10 percent of the total of exports. But the average value for food imports is not the primary issue. Committing 10 or even 20 percent of export earnings to food imports can be entirely appropriate if other socially profitable activities can pay the bill.

Table 6-1. Measures of Food Insecurity in Developing Countries, 1961–76

Country	Probability of consumption falling below 95% of trend	Probability of domestic production falling below 95% of trend	Average ratio of cost of food imports to total export revenue	Variability of food import bill (percent)	
				Because of quantity variations	Because of price variations
Algeria	42	43	6.0	88	12
Bangladesh	26	22	88.4	84	16
Brazil	20	17	3.9	85	15
Chile	36	33	5.3	88	12
Colombia	14	13	2.8	83	17
Egypt	34	13	14.0	69	31
Ghana	21	20	3.7	65	35
Guatemala	24	22	2.4	55	45
India	17	22	22.2	96	4
Indonesia	21	18	9.5	92	8
Jordan	40	47	10.6	79	21
Korea, Rep. of	22	24	13.5	80	20
Libya	38	43	1.4	57	43
Mexico	17	36	0.4	100	0
Morocco	40	43	7.0	93	7
Nigeria	19	19	1.9	62	38
Peru	10	30	6.6	45	55
Philippines	6	19	4.9	68	32
Senegal	37	39	12.2	55	45
Sri Lanka	27	29	27.2	40	60
Syria	39	45	5.7	100	0
Tanzania	37	35	5.5	96	4
Upper Volta	30	30	7.4	85	15
Zaire	11	15	3.1	40	60

Source: Alberto Valdés and Panos Konandreas, "Assessing Food Insecurity," in Alberto Valdés, ed., Food Security for Developing Countries (Boulder, Colo.: Westview Press, 1981).

The main issue is the variability in imports and the foreign exchange needed to pay for them. A sudden jump of the food bill from 10 to 50 percent of export earnings is highly disruptive to the rest of the macro economy. The unexpected need for foreign exchange can put serious strains on the balance of payments and the ability of the central bank to defend its foreign exchange rate. Fluctuating domestic food production causes most of this problem, but volatility in international commodity markets also plays a role, for the cost of those food imports may increase suddenly. Managing these price fluctuations is a function of border price policies and the design and implementation of buffer stock operations.

AGRICULTURAL EXPORTS. Fluctuations in food imports primarily affect the demand for foreign exchange. Since the agricultural sector is often an important supplier of foreign exchange, normal variations in the production of export crops can also create difficult problems for macro management and alter the availability of foreign exchange. The proportional changes can be quite dramatic when a country is dependent on only a few agricultural exports and there are large variations in crop yields. A crop failure can sharply reduce foreign exchange availability as well as rural incomes.

Even without any variations in agricultural production, variations in international market prices for food and cash crops can cause similar problems for countries that rely on exports of cash crops to earn foreign exchange to import both food and capital goods. The prospects for stabilizing markets for basic grains and cash crops, such as coffee, sugar, cocoa, and tea, are not very bright, and most macro policymakers will have to continue to cope with significant fluctuations in the demand for and supply of foreign exchange arising from the food and agricultural system.

Part of the effort to cope will require better estimates of likely export earnings by commodity. In addition, when large shortfalls occur because of poor international prices or domestic crop failures, the International Monetary Fund (IMF) offers compensatory financing at preferential interest rates. In the long run, governments can make investments in research on disease resistance and in irrigation and crop diversification that will result in greater stability of crop production. Internationally, greater price stability for primary products seems a remote hope without a significant lessening of protectionist policies in both developed and developing countries.

The food policy analyst can help in each of these areas, especially by focusing attention on the reality and likelihood of large fluctuations in the demand for and supply of foreign exchange from the agricultural sector. Plans made on the basis of the most optimistic assumptions, rather than realistic estimates, are likely to go awry, with important consequences for the rest of the economy as well as for agriculture.

FOOD AID. In some circumstances the foreign exchange needed to import food can be provided by food aid through grants or long-term loans. Such food aid is attractive to recipient countries, for it reduces the import bill, ensures supplies especially for urban food markets, and generates domestic currency revenues for the government treasury when the food is sold. The attractiveness of food aid to donors depends very much on the commercial outlook for grain sales. When international markets are weak, as in the early 1960s and early 1980s, the opportunity cost of grain provided as food aid is quite low, especially if it can be delivered in a manner that adds to effective global demand. Then food aid is a very attractive way for the United States and the European Economic Community to provide foreign assistance. It is doing well by doing good.

Despite the appeal of food aid to both donors and recipients, the disincentive effects on domestic producers and the problems of implementing food aid agreements are so serious that they vitiate much of the usefulness of food aid. Especially as a way to cope with fluctuations in grain import needs in countries with serious foreign exchange shortages, food aid is simply not available with sufficiently flexible timing to be helpful. Emergency food aid for famine relief is a separate story, but routine food aid—Title I in the U.S. PL-480 program, for example—is not an instrument for dampening macro fluctuations caused by instability in food import needs.

Food aid provided under longer-term arrangements might be useful in providing temporary outside resources to assist a country in transition to a balanced macro food policy. This typically means moving from a consumer-based price policy and producer-based projects orientation to a mirror image— the incentives-based price policy and food subsidy programs targeted to poor consumers that form the policy focus of this book. In this sense, food aid will be much more important as a bridge between short-run problems and long-run solutions than as a mechanism for coping with short-run instability directly.

Managing Instability

Even in periods of scarcity in world markets, higher prices have stimulated increased exports from food-exporting countries where commodities had alternative domestic end uses. Food-importing countries are generally less concerned with the physical availability of grain in world markets than with budget costs and amounts of foreign exchange needed to pay for the grain the country needs. The fundamental need of most importing countries is for mechanisms to deal with budgetary and balance of payments problems caused by unexpected variations in domestic production or international prices.

Since the basic problem is price and not export supplies, financial schemes have been designed at the international level to help low-income importing countries solve food problems caused by variations in production or price. In 1981 the IMF expanded its compensatory finance scheme to cover balance of payments problems associated with rising costs of cereal imports. By adding grain import costs to previous provisions that had applied only to export shortfalls, the IMF recognized a basic international problem. For low-income countries with highly variable domestic food production and a weak balance of payments position, the buffer fund approach could be of considerable help.

BUFFER STOCKS. Another element in coping with fluctuating internal production and external prices is the maintenance of domestic grain reserves. Public storage capacity and emergency stocks are a sensible investment for several reasons, not the least of which is insurance for policymakers who otherwise would be exposed to the whims of international markets. Grain stocks can be used to buffer short-run fluctuations in import deliveries and prices, but they cannot smooth out major year-to-year movements in world market prices except at extremely high cost. Nor do such modest reserves insure a country against food price changes that come from fluctuating domestic production, except by providing several months' planning time to make decisions about import or export levels needed to defend domestic price policy.

A buffer stock program involving domestic price stabilization operated in conjunction with a public storage system can help increase the flexibility of low-income countries in using international markets to improve their own welfare. Having sufficient storage capacity allows a country to import grain when prices are relatively low, rather than during emergency conditions. In addition, the grain reserves permit more flexibility in coping with short-term lags in delivery, and the additional storage facilities increase the domestic marketing system's capacity to handle local surpluses. Especially if domestic production strategies are successful, an expanded storage and marketing system will be needed to help supply large cities from the hinterlands, rather than from imports. The location of new storage capacity should be determined by both potential sources of stocks. It is apparent that a buffer stock is most effective when used for implementing a domestic price policy that uses world markets effectively, not for isolating price policy from world markets.

A buffer stock program can be designed to defend floor prices to farmers and ceiling prices to consumers as well as to smooth year-to-year price fluctuations. For it to operate successfully, however, the government must stand ready to perform a variety of economic functions simultaneously. It must buy from farmers at the guaranteed price if private millers or middlemen find this transaction unprofitable. Grain must be injected into retail markets if private storage is exhausted or if there is any evidence of collusion among merchants to drive up prices. A buffer stock agency must carry stocks both to carry out these day-to-day logistical operations and to dampen price fluctuations from one year to the next caused by variations in the size of the harvest relative to domestic and international demand.

These tasks require administrative skills and budgetary resources. An efficient food logistics operation might cover most of its costs by purchasing at the floor price and selling at the ceiling price if adequate margins are permitted. But so would the private trade, which would then carry much of the burden. As the margin narrows under the pressure of keeping urban food prices low and farm prices high, the financial and administrative role of the government increases. If the government has defined its objectives clearly and understands the budgetary requirements, its enlarged role can pay social benefits. Conversely, the failure to plan and budget for government food logistics operations can result in reliance on fiat and coercion, actions which fragment markets and stifle the necessary signals between producers and consumers.

INCREASING DOMESTIC FLEXIBILITY. Although domestic buffer stock policies can cope with some of the instability in international markets, greater flexibility in planning and allocating budget resources and foreign exchange can also help. Financial and logistical flexibility in scheduling and contracting for imports or exports offers substantial opportunities to conserve foreign exchange if short-term market trends are read correctly. Many countries buy desperately in a rising market and thus push prices higher. Similarly, commodity exporters frequently sell aggressively into a soft market in the fear that it will fall further, which it does because of their cumulative actions.

Having the financial capacity to stand back from purchases or sales for a month or so until short-run market trends are clarified can pay very high financial returns in terms of lower average import costs or higher export receipts. Alternatively, the use of futures markets to establish rolling purchase or sale positions for either import or export commitments can, for relatively modest cost, insure a country against being caught in short-run market dislocations. The Peck paper cited in the bibliography introduces analysts to the workings of commodity futures markets in a food security context. More effective understanding and use of futures markets to buffer against short-run fluctuations will require investment in the education of managers who will be responsible for day-to-day operations and new bureaucratic procedures which maintain their financial accountability but give them freedom to take forward positions.

The efficient use of futures markets may require new operating skills and procedures in food logistics agencies, but the result frequently is greater financial flexibility in the use of domestic budget revenues and foreign exchange. This internal financial flexibility is an important component of the policies and programs that buffer a country's long-run food price environment from short-run import price fluctuations. Foreign exchange contingency funds can earn interest in international credit markets until needed to accommodate the times when international prices rise for imports or fall for exports or when domestic production is substantially less than expected. When such instability occurs in the face of planners' overly optimistic projections of production or prices, development plans must be curtailed or abandoned unless contingency funds are available to increase financial flexibility.

Budgetary, Fiscal, and Monetary Management

Most countries have agricultural sectors that can cause severe macroeconomic problems in the short run. Much of this impact stems from the inherent variability of both domestic agricultural production and international market prices for a country's agricultural imports and exports. This variability affects the balance of payments and the foreign exchange rate directly, but food price changes also work through the macro economy by altering demand patterns. In particular, a sharp increase in domestic food prices can force consumers to devote more of their incomes to maintaining food consumption levels. Their discretionary income for purchases of services and manufactured goods falls, and a Keynesian recession induced by inadequate demand can cause unemployment in the nonagricultural sector. The impact is mitigated if the country's manufactured goods are competitive in export markets or if import substitution is not complete and imports can be further restricted to protect the domestic industries. But several semi-industrialized countries such as Mexico, Brazil, and Egypt fall outside these provisos and find the link between food prices and industrial employment quite significant.

The level of food prices can also have macroeconomic effects through a variety of budgetary allocations, especially to consumer subsidies and programs for farmers. Much of the effect comes from the budgetary resources needed to stabilize food prices in the interest of overall price stability. Many countries judge their effectiveness in protecting personal welfare levels by the stability of their cost-of-living index. Food has a large weight in all such indices, and food price stabilization schemes are usually directed with an eye on the total index as well as on the specific component itself. If fiscal and monetary policies are causing a general inflation, one common response is to control food prices to slow the measured effects of those inflationary policies.

The consequences of food price stabilization policies can be quite burdensome for the budget. An effective buffer stock policy requires a government food logistics agency to purchase surplus supplies at harvest to guarantee a floor price for farmers and to sell in urban markets to hold a ceiling price for consumers. Unexpected bumper crops can then cause a massive flow of government revenues into the countryside. Financing this flow usually requires a sudden increase in the money supply beyond normal seasonal variations. How this money is spent in rural areas determines whether there is an inflationary spillover or a surge in import demand. If the government purchases are financed by diverting money from other budgeted areas, the inflation can be averted, but obvious tensions arise between government agencies when this happens. Consumer interests are frequently pitted against producer interests when the lines are drawn, and the easiest way out in the short run is to finance the added purchases out of a budget deficit.

Even without direct budget implications, variations in crop production can have significant macro effects. Unless the farmers are forced to hold a bumper crop themselves in storage, the demand for credit from the marketing sector to store and process the crop will increase sharply. Especially with segmented capital markets, this credit squeeze may put a severe strain on rural interest rates and on the availability of credit to farmers to finance the purchase of inputs for the next crop.

A credit squeeze also has a severe impact on industries that require large amounts of short-run working capital. These industries, especially construction and food processing, tend to be very labor-intensive relative to the amount of capital invested in plant and equipment. Tight money and high interest rates can nearly shut down these industries, creating substantial unemployment among unskilled workers.

Control over budget deficits is one of the basic tenets of sound macroeconomic management. Chapter 5 showed the relationships between budget deficits, an accommodating monetary policy, and chronic inflation. Such inflation often leads to overvalued exchange rates and to lower real food prices relative to other goods and services. Consequently, the rural-urban terms of trade are reduced along with incentives for agricultural production. Inflation frequently also puts heavy pressure on governments to use budget subsidies directly to keep food prices low in order to dampen the measured rise in the cost of living. Even when other prices are fairly stable, subsidies are sometimes used to stabilize food prices if they would otherwise rise rapidly.

THE TRADEOFF BETWEEN SUBSIDIES AND INVESTMENT. During budget crises fiscal expenditures must be reduced, and postponable or low-priority programs are the first to be cut. With the government's attention riveted on maintaining low food prices, many investment programs for agricultural development are vulnerable because they can be postponed with no immediate diminution of agricultural output. The building of feeder roads, irrigation dams and canals, improved port facilities, and better rail service all have payoffs well into the future, at some time when the budget crisis will be over or the responsibility of another administration. Cuts in subsidies for agricultural inputs, however, usually have a much more immediate impact on agricultural output.

An important tradeoff exists between cutting investment programs or cutting input subsidies. Investment programs require bids, contracts, and significant forward commitments. Canceling them, except when fraud can be demonstrated, can be quite expensive. Cutting input subsidy programs, however, usually garners the budget immediate (and often sizable) returns. Consequently, the treasury usually prefers a cut in input subsidies, whereas the food agency or ministry of agriculture typically prefers a reduction in the investment program.

From a broad policy viewpoint, a cut in input subsidies is preferable to reductions in investment programs. If a tight budget brings inflation under control, more potential may exist to raise farmer incentives directly through food prices rather than indirectly through input subsidies. Investment in long-run production potential then becomes doubly important to permit a more vigorous response on the part of farmers to the higher incentives. Adequate productive infrastructure in the form of dams and canals, for example, and low-cost, efficient marketing channels are essential for such a vigorous response.

A FOOD POLICY PERSPECTIVE ON BUDGET REFORMS. A budget crisis, or scarce budgetary resources in general, almost inevitably renews the debate over food price policy. Tight fiscal control, made possible at least partially by axing subsidies to agricultural inputs or other food production programs, permits less indirect agricultural incentives in the form of higher food prices. Because maintaining adequate production incentives is essential to sustaining adequate food production, farmers are protected somewhat even in the short run. Farmers can choose not to grow food for the market if the terms of trade become too unfavorable.

Consumers have no such option to withdraw from the market, and they usually get hurt in a budget crisis. Most countries have some form of consumer subsidy that requires budgetary resources to implement. (An exception is an export levy on the basic food grain that both reduces the domestic food price and generates budget revenues, though usually at the cost of lower export earnings and decreased economic efficiency.) The costs of consumer food subsidies become prohibitive in a budget crisis, unless they are carefully targeted.

Farmers' incomes are protected through higher food prices to consumers when budgetary integrity is reestablished. Initiatives to design short-term consumer subsidy programs to cushion temporarily the immediate impact of higher food prices have little chance of success in an atmosphere of severe fiscal restraint. But a reform of budgetary, fiscal, and monetary policies does increase basic food prices, and the short-run consequences for consumption remain significant. Failure to deal with them because of budget constraints means either greater hunger and malnutrition or mobs in the street (or both). It is no wonder that most governments seem paralyzed by macro economies out of control. Few of them have the analytical capacity to design or the short-run budget revenues to fund the food programs that would alleviate the difficult consumer adjustments associated with a macro reform.

MOVING FROM SHORT RUN TO LONG RUN. The food policy analyst is constantly facing such predicaments. It is hard to find feasible pathways from tightly constrained, short-run situations, where the objective is simply putting out the ever present brushfires, to the longer-run goals of reducing hunger and increasing productive efficiency. The short-run situation, however, is always the starting point for the search. A strategy for food self-sufficiency by the end of the decade does not help the food logistics agency at all in its concern over the delayed arrival of a critical shipload of grain. Fighting brushfires is an honorable calling, but food policy analysis has a long-run vision behind the short-run reality. With an understanding of what policy ought to be next year and in the next decade, it may be possible to plot a route from where it is today.

Experience with economic development efforts during the past few decades suggests that the route does not reveal itself day by day. Brushfires often seem to be fought in the same locations over the same issues with little apparent headway. The short-run problems assume overriding importance and fail to point the way to actions needed to reach longer-run objectives. This is partly because the longer-run vision itself has not been very clear, but part of the problem stems from offices churning out five- or ten-year plans which are isolated from the short-run concerns and thus are irrelevant to a policymaker's immediate needs. Food policy analysis is designed to bridge this gap. A good starting point is to understand how a country's basic food price policy compares with long-run international opportunity costs and how that policy affects agricultural production and food consumption. The food price is the key variable that links producers and consumers. Through its impact on investment decisions the food price also links the short run to the long run. A clear sense of the level and impact of food prices will help the food policy analyst identify realistic policy options and thereby gain access to the important policy debates.

An Effective Food Policy: Lessons and Perspectives

The recurring theme of this book is that policymakers face real and honest dilemmas with respect to basic food policy decisions. Policies that significantly improve production incentives for farmers often result in reduced food intake for many poor consumers. Broad strategies designed to keep food cheap for these poor consumers have negative production consequences and macroeconomic ramifications that can stifle the economic development process.

A political-economic perspective that reconciles objectives and constraints in the process of policy formation has been used here to evaluate and determine the elements of a successful food policy. What follows are some personal judgments on those elements. Ideal policies are discussed first, not to dismiss them but rather to be sure that analysts understand fully the appeal of theoretical solutions and the nature of the constraints that cause implementation problems. For the government charting its policies, many of these constraints are like icebergs. At a distance they do not seem dangerous; their full cost can be assessed only after they have been struck. Even bold planning in this area usually means investments to loosen constraints over time rather than frontal assaults to break constraints.

A number of popular food policy instruments simply do not work most of the time. Comparative experience has revealed fundamental forces operating in a food system that lead to almost inevitable failure for certain kinds of interventions. An analyst who understands the nature of these failures is prepared to consider the elements of a successful food policy summarized at the end of the chapter. This final perspective grows out of the same empirical experience and analytical approach that were drawn on in developing the book.

The Ideal Answers

Most economic models are driven by optimization principles. Producers maximize profits, consumers maximize satisfaction, and market traders shift products to their optimal time, place, and form by capturing all income-generating opportunities induced by price differences among markets. Such economic models, when applied to food policy problems, frequently identify ideal solutions that depend critically on the assumptions that allow the models to abstract from the full complexity of reality. The assumption of competitive behavior of all market participants and access to market information is particularly relevant to food policy analysts. In addition, the institutional and social costs that must be paid when policymakers attempt to implement an ideal intervention cannot be ignored. The reality of the assumptions and the costs of implementation are both of paramount relevance. The existence of these issues does not mean that economists' ideal solutions should be dismissed out of hand, but that policy analysis has an added and difficult dimension. The ideal answers to food policy problems have very desirable characteristics. If ways can be found to implement them, the payoff to both producers and consumers will be very high.

REDISTRIBUTION OF ASSETS. In many countries with highly unequal ownership of assets, especially land, food production and consumption goals could be significantly furthered by a more equal distribution of those assets. The most successful examples of agricultural development coupled with the reduction of poverty-induced hunger have all emerged from war-based and almost revolutionary land redistributions, as in Japan, the Republic of Korea, and China. The importance of land reform, especially in Latin America, has been recognized for some time, and many countries, including Mexico, Peru, Iran, and India, have made attempts at reform. The dynamic effects of breaking up large landholdings, by shifting the attitudes and mobility of peasants, are potentially as important as the static effects of providing smallholders and the landless with viable farms. In some settings these dynamic effects might be achievable by other policies, including village-level education, organization, and cooperative mobilization. But in some societies, for both static and dynamic reasons, no other food policy initiative seems to make sense without a significant restructuring of landholdings.

Experience with land reform programs since the 1930s has shown that land tenure patterns are not a simple question of economic ownership. Large-scale landownership conveys great power in rural communities. Such power is not relinquished lightly and almost certainly not cheaply. Hence, in most cases expropriation is to some degree the only financially feasible way to implement land reform. This action directly threatens the vital interests of the most powerful citizens in the countryside. It is no surprise that meaningful land reform has been a policy instrument available primarily to revolutionaries. In societies utterly dependent on land reform to open the door to effective food policies, analysts can identify the closed doors, but they do not have the key.

RAPID INCOME GROWTH FOR THE POOR. Aggregate economic growth since World War II in most developing countries has been remarkable by any historical standard. Even the very poor have shared in the benefits of this growth to some extent, for their life expectancy is higher, many of their children are literate, and they have greater opportunities than their parents would ever have imagined.

In some countries, however, the growth process has been feeble, in others the poor have participated to a very limited extent, and in virtually all countries a hard core of the "poorest of the poor" remains outside the formal economy and beyond the reach of government relief efforts. Finding ways to reach this population has galvanized the intellectual and emotional energies of many individuals in national and international communities. The obvious solution is to bring the poor into the mainstream of economic growth and to find policies that raise their incomes relative to the growth of the better-off segment of the population. One academic but typical calculation shows that if only half the increment in economic product could be directed to those in the bottom quarter of the income distribution, their incomes would rise above a "basic needs" poverty line in a decade.

How can this redistribution of growth be accomplished? The poor are poor because they do not own scarce factors of production that generate large income streams. The one asset they control, their labor, is not highly valued in their economies because there is so much of it relative to demand. It is not scarce compared with land (except in much of Africa, the frontiers in Latin America, and a few regions in Asia), capital, and skills.

As population pressures and the spread of market relationships remove traditional floors for subsistence wages, the average welfare and security of the very poor may decline. Growth strategies that tap this abundant resource offer hope of raising their real incomes. Such growth strategies require appropriate macroeconomic policies and agricultural incentives that together generate a healthy rural economy. These policies, however, provide solutions to poverty in the long run, not the short run. For the next decade the poor must be reached by bridging mechanisms that protect their food consumption intake while the growth strategies gradually open new opportunities for their productive employment.

LUMP-SUM INCOME TRANSFERS. Where redistribution of assets is blocked by political constraints and rapid increases in productive employment for the poor take too long to solve existing hunger problems, a third option favored by economists is to transfer money income to the poor from general tax revenues. If the taxes are raised from factor incomes in a nonregressive fashion and distributed without eliminating work incentives, the economy can function efficiently while the welfare problems are being treated.

The problems with such an ideal solution lie with the distortions to work incentives faced by both taxpayers and recipients, the administrative resources needed to raise and distribute tax revenues, and the political factors associated with taxing the middle- and upper-income groups. In addition, any revenues raised by taxation have multiple claimants. Irrigation investments, salaries of civil servants, and defense spending all compete with income supplements for the poor. In societies where the poor are a significant proportion of the total population (and the bottom 40 percent of the income distribution is frequently used as the target group in many countries), meaningful income transfers would be wildly inflationary. Lump-sum transfers usually are confronted by political, administrative, and budgetary constraints.

TECHNICAL CHANGE IN AGRICULTURAL PRODUCTION. Improved technology in food production during the past thirty years has benefited the poor significantly, primarily through cheaper food. Virtually all studies of the income distribution consequences of the seed-fertilizer revolution in the 1960s have shown that the major impact has been to lower food prices relative to what they would have been in the absence of new technology. The welfare benefits of lower food prices are captured predominantly by poor consumers. Even when new technology has been available primarily to large farmers and small farmers suffered as a result (and these circumstances are not the normal pattern), the overall distribution of benefits for the entire society is still heavily weighted to the poor because of the large role that food consumption plays in the total household budget.

Technical change has lowered the real price of basic cereal grains over the past century. Even though prices were high in the 1970s, real wheat prices declined to lower levels at the start of the 1980s than at the start of the 1950s. But despite this impressive record of beneficial effects, technical change cannot be considered the answer to the problems of hunger because of its long-run and evolutionary character. If higher food prices are needed to induce technical change, the dilemma is even sharper—as the problems in funding the international agricultural research centers in the early 1980s indicate. The poor must place their hopes on significant technical change in the long run while they seek their short-run survival in targeted interventions.

The Nonanswers

It is a mistake to think that governments do not feel the urgency of the hunger of their people. The pressures to do something are great, the time for analysis is short, and political priorities and constraints usually limit the scope for intervention. Many governments respond to this environment with programs that have great emotional and political appeal, especially if cast in a rhetoric that oversimplifies complex problems for mass consumption. Most of these programs do not work, and some make the problem worse. The leading candidates for nonanswers are discussed below.

ELIMINATING THE MIDDLEMAN. Most policymakers see the middleman as an unscrupulous rascal who buys food at low prices from disadvantaged small peasants and sells it to desperate consumers at prices so high they cannot afford bus fare to work. Surely the government can move food from farmers to consumers more fairly than that. The promise to do so, especially when food shortages are forcing food prices up, brings wild cheers from the urban population.

In its extreme form, in which the government takes over the entire food marketing function, the strategy almost never works. Consumers find that the government cannot provide food as cheaply as their corner market stall. Farmers discover that the government purchasing agent is missing when the crop needs to be sold or that payment will be delayed several months, even years. A furtive private trade springs up, reinforcing the government's view that the middlemen who conduct it are antisocial elements. Both producers and consumers, however, find they are better off dealing with them. Very quickly, the government's marketing program becomes a visibly empty shell.

There is too much truth in this caricature to ignore. Significant opportunities exist for government interventions to improve food grain marketing, to the benefit of both producers and consumers. Such interventions must take account of the productive roles played by marketing agents. If the private sector is not carrying out marketing functions efficiently, and most empirical evidence says it is, the government must understand why and how to intervene to improve matters. Simply attacking or supplanting the middleman will almost never be the answer.

CRASH PROGRAMS. Problems that have been allowed to develop into crises usually provoke a call for immediate and drastic action—a crash program. By definition, such programs are not built on an analytical understanding of the problem at hand, nor is there time to build one. The call for drastic action has political appeal precisely because of its hurried and makeshift aspect. The time is past for research, for analysis, for planning. Now is the time to act.

Food problems are extraordinarily complicated, and expedient short-run interventions frequently have devastating long-run consequences. Procuring grain at gunpoint, seizing private warehouse stocks, or placing embargoes on exports are examples of shortsighted policies. Food policy analysis attempts to identify the relationships between the short-run and the long-run effects of a policy. Failure to design interventions in the food sector consistent with long-run objectives eventually causes a policy fiasco. The greater the short-run pressures to implement a program—any program—the greater the probability that it will have effects just opposite to those intended. Crash programs tend to crash.

SUBSIDIZING FARM INPUTS. As the analysis in chapter 3 showed, for any output price, the incentive to increase production by more intensive use of an input can be improved by subsidizing the cost of the input. Using subsidies to lower fertilizer costs is an especially common technique for increasing the profitability of intensive agriculture while keeping food prices low. When total fertilizer use is low and the ratio of incremental grain yield to fertilizer application is high, such subsidies can be a highly cost-effective strategy relative to higher output prices or greater food imports with subsidies. Fertilizer subsidies can also speed the adoption of modern seed varieties. As fertilizer use becomes much more widespread, however, the costs of the program rise dramatically. The production impact per unit of fertilizer subsidy drops for two reasons: declining marginal response rates, and few nonusers of fertilizer remain to be converted to users.

Many governments subsidize other inputs as well. Irrigation water is provided to farmers well below cost, frequently at no cost, over much of the world. Subsidized credit is widely used to encourage the purchase and use of modern inputs despite poor repayment records and little apparent impact on output. Furthermore, no input subsidy program is able to encourage farmers to use more labor and provide better managerial care for the crops. All subsidies tend to distort the intensity of use of inputs from their economically optimal levels, and significant waste is a result. Since not all inputs can be equally subsidized, output price increases will have a greater impact on productivity than will input subsidies, especially in the long run. Consequently, input subsidies can keep farm profitability high and consumer prices low only for a particular stage of input use and for a short time. After that the short-run distortions significantly impede an efficient long-run growth strategy.

DIRECT DELIVERIES TO THE POOREST OF THE POOR. The basic needs movement has focused on the essential bundle of goods and services necessary to permit human dignity for the poor. In the absence of structural reforms that enable the poor to earn incomes that allow them to purchase these necessities, strategies have been proposed that would simply deliver a basic needs package directly to the needy. Some components of the package, especially clean water, education, and health care, can be provided as public goods. But housing and especially food tend to be supplied through private markets, and these two components of the basic needs package present major difficulties for delivery mechanisms. A direct delivery system must circumvent these private markets, with all the attendant difficulties just discussed. The alternative, to use private markets as the most efficient vehicle for delivering food, raises all the complexities and dilemmas discussed as the core of this book. Direct deliveries may well work for some components of the basic needs package, but getting more food to the poor will require much more sophisticated analysis of food policy mechanisms.

NUTRITION INTERVENTION PROJECTS. Traditional nutrition intervention projects, such as school lunch programs, iron fortification, amino acid supplementation of basic cereals, or milk distribution schemes, cannot solve the problem of chronic hunger caused by poverty. Such projects can be useful because of their demonstration effect, and some can be highly cost-effective in delivering important benefits to the poor. Their failure is relative to expectations—that somehow a marginal intervention to remedy a specific micronutritional problem will significantly alter the socioeconomic context of poor peoples' lives. Food policy analysts can be supportive of effective nutrition projects without mistaking them for answers to the basic food issues they are addressing.

FOOD AID. Food aid has had a very mixed record in reducing hunger. Its availability on short notice is critical for famine relief. In emergencies, tens of millions of people have been kept from starving by the speedy dispatch of food from donor countries, especially from the United States. But as a vehicle for more permanent improvement in the ability of poor people to feed themselves, food aid has been a failure. Countries that relied on food aid supplies to keep prices low created serious disincentives for their farmers. In countries where the food aid displaced imports, did not distort farm prices, and had a large enough flow to affect the level of macroeconomic resources available for development, its impact was entirely mediated by the efficacy and equity of the development strategy. When this was positive, as in Korea and Taiwan, food aid helped. When it was not, as in many other countries, it did not.

Food aid can provide both the macroeconomic resources and the food required for a country to switch from an urban-biased development strategy to an agricultural strategy based on incentives to farmers and designed to increase food production and the flow of income to rural areas. The short-run food consumption problems that make this switch difficult have been repeatedly stressed. Food aid can help by providing resources in the short run to soften the squeeze on the poor. But the overall volume of food aid available to poor countries is quite limited, and bridging strategies that use food aid as a support will be available to only a few. Even where it is available, the macro food policy context will dictate whether the food aid helps or not. Food aid is not a substitute for a sensible food policy. But it can provide useful assistance in putting one in place and speeding it on its way.

Elements of a Workable Food Policy

Food systems are complicated, and food policy is dependent on powerful macroeconomic policies and on the international economy. The chances of choosing the wrong path are great because no invisible hand guides policymakers, and good intentions are no guarantee of good results. Painful experience shows that uninformed policymaking usually makes matters worse. Analysis is needed to improve the poor performance of policymaking done blind—analysis that is done in the specific context of a country's own problems and resources. This book can show how to do that analysis, but it cannot show the specific results. The best the authors can offer as solutions at this stage is to reemphasize the basic themes of the book.

PRODUCTIVE JOBS. No practical and lasting resolution to the food policy dilemma is possible without the creation of vast numbers of productive jobs for relatively unskilled urban and rural workers. Such jobs provide two components of the answer: increased economic output to fuel economic growth, and greater earned income of the poor so that they are able to buy the essentials of a dignified life. Finding ways to create these jobs has occupied much of the development profession since serious concerns over the distribution of gains from economic growth emerged in the 1960s. One major lesson is that governments do not create these jobs very efficiently. Public sector or public enterprise approaches to unemployment cause massive overstaffing of bureaucracies and state-owned factories, stifling initiative and performance in both.

Efficient job creation is primarily a function of private or cooperative initiatives in conjunction with facilitative macroeconomic policy. Appropriate macro prices, fiscal control over budget balances, and careful attention to monetary growth foster an environment in which investment decisions create productive jobs. Macroeconomic policy is important to food policy in the direct ways outlined in chapter 5. For the long run it is even more important in determining the real productivity of the poor who are the primary concern of food policy.

PRICE INCENTIVES FOR FOOD PRODUCTION. There is no substitute for positive price incentives to the agricultural sector based on long-run opportunity costs. The pressures for such a price policy can be circumvented for a while through input subsidies and subsidized grain imports, but a poor country cannot long sustain the capacity to provide cheap food for everyone. Societies that insist on keeping it cheap will gradually distort their economies sufficiently to choke off the economic development process. The move to an incentives-oriented policy need not be immediate. Gradual increases over the course of a decade are reasonable if the government can maintain such a long time horizon.

Two critical variables that are subject to policy influence determine the level of rural price incentives compared with international opportunity costs: the foreign exchange rate and the domestic farm-gate price for food. If the government maintains an overvalued exchange rate, an additional and sometimes impossible burden is placed on domestic price policy. Discussions of domestic food price policy that do not include the role of an equilibrium exchange rate miss the most pervasive aspect of policies biased against agricultural production and rural income generation.

Removing the common biases against agricultural production in many developing countries would set the stage for a much more dynamic rural sector. For food-importing countries, however, a case can be made for going further and setting domestic food prices at a slight premium, perhaps 10 percent on average, over the opportunity cost of imports. Maintenance of such a price premium is justified by the second-round effects of the additional purchasing power in the countryside, where job creation for unskilled workers is most likely, by the further improvement in rural-urban income distribution, and by the added impetus to investment in future agricultural productivity. Private investment decisions are sometimes myopic, especially in the face of high and fluctuating interest rates. Agricultural investments in particular require long time horizons. A small premium on such investments in the interests of future generations can be produced with food price incentives somewhat above efficiency levels. The premium might vary by commodity, with preferred grains receiving a larger premium than staples consumed by the poor. Since the price premium will be reflected in market prices, such commodity discrimination would minimize the adverse consumption consequences for the poor.

PUBLIC INVESTMENT IN AGRICULTURAL PRODUCTIVITY. In no country does agriculture receive a share of public investment as large as its contribution to gross national product. Very few governments devote even half of agriculture's share in GNP to investment in the sector. While no economic law dictates that the shares be equal, public investment should be directed to projects with the largest social payoff. Following this rule would probably double agricultural investment if the projects could be prepared and administered. The bottleneck is in the preparation of sound agricultural projects.

Simply going this far would significantly improve the balance of public sector investments. But as with market prices to encourage private investment, it is desirable to go somewhat further. Because of its importance to the welfare of the poor, food can be treated as a merit good for purposes of public investment and valued at a small premium over its long-run opportunity cost via imports or exports. Placing such a premium on food also addresses the food security concerns of most countries by indicating their willingness to pay a positive but not infinite price for food self-sufficiency. A premium of perhaps 10 percent is a suitable starting point.

Since market prices for food grains in many countries tend to be below their long-run international opportunity costs, implementing a market premium is probably an issue for the future. The use of a premium in public benefit-cost analysis of investments, however, could be started immediately. For public investment analysis, the relative premiums by commodity might well be reversed: the inferior goods consumed primarily by the poor would receive additional credit in the project appraisal while the preferred staple could be valued at its (premium) market price.

TARGETED FOOD SUBSIDIES. A food price policy that provides farmers with positive price incentives relative to the opportunity cost of food from imports, when coupled with a favorable macroeconomic development policy, will gradually increase incomes of the poor and enable them to purchase their basic needs. The food price policy dilemma arises because the poor bear the brunt of the short-run adjustments needed to implement this long-run strategy. Historical experience suggests that only targeted food subsidies are likely to ease the nutritional burdens of these adjustments. Subsidies are critical because the poor do not have the resources to purchase adequate amounts of food from the market. Targeting is essential because society does not have the resources to subsidize food for the entire population. Much of this book has been devoted to understanding the likely efficiency of various targeting mechanisms in real-world circumstances. Since the ability of bureaucrats to administer a fair means test in most of the developing world seems questionable, much of food policy analysis involves a search for more effective self-targeting mechanisms for delivering food to the poor.

No single targeting mechanism seems adequate to the task. Some combination of intersecting mechanisms will probably prove essential to effective targeting and control over food subsidy budgets. One approach is to use fair-price shops in locations accessible primarily to poor people and to sell commodities that loom large in the budgets of the poor but not in those of the middle class. Distributing food stamps good only for certain commodities in particular government shops might be another. Whatever the specific mechanism or combination of mechanisms, only a clear understanding of the food consumption patterns of the poor can provide insight into its probable effectiveness.

A POLICY DEBATE FOCUSED ON FOOD PRICES. The emphasis throughout this book has been on the central role of food prices as the link between producers and consumers in the short run and as a significant determinant of investment decisions that connect the short run to the long run. A sensible price policy alone will not solve a society's food production problems. Price incentives exacerbate the consumption problems in the short run. However, an understanding of the positive and negative aspects of a country's food price policy illuminates most of the issues at the core of the food policy debate. With this understanding, government policymakers have gained a vantage point to survey the entire development process.

Food policy analysis can improve the quality of that debate by providing the best answers available to the tough questions that policymakers have every right to ask. How much will food production increase if food prices rise? When? Will the marketing sector be able to handle the additional supplies? Will traders siphon off all the gain? How badly will food consumers be hurt? How can they be helped? What are the implications for the budget? For the balance of payments? An analyst who can provide honest answers to these questions has learned all this book has tried to teach, and more.

Bibliographical Note

Visions of how to end hunger are a dime a dozen (in 1982 U.S. dollars). They range from the utopian schemes proposed by Frances Moore Lappé and Joseph Collins in Food First: Beyond the Myth of Scarcity, rev. ed. (New York: Ballantine, 1979), in which peoples' instincts for self-aggrandizement are set aside in the interests of more equal sharing of the earth's bounty, to the Panglossian treatment by Julian Simon in The Ultimate Resource (Princeton, N.J.: Princeton University Press, 1981), whose last sentence concludes: "[the] ultimate resource is people—skilled, spirited, and hopeful people who will exert their wills and imaginations for their own benefit, and so, inevitably, for the benefit of us all" (p. 348), to the frankly pessimistic, almost doomsday perspective of Lester R. Brown, with Erik P. Eckholm, By Bread Alone (New York and Washington, D.C.: Praeger, 1974), which sees the world food economy at a turning point in mankind's history.

Academic visions tend to be more balanced and hedged, and so they usually fail to gain the popular attention that the simplistic and alarmist treatments receive. Complex issues do not yield to such treatments, however, and a brief review of the academic research provides the pieces of a more complicated vision of solving the problem of hunger. As a starting point, a very extensive bibliography has been assembled by Nicole Ball, World Hunger: A Guide to the Economic and Political Dimensions (Santa Barbara, Calif.: ABC-Clio Press, 1981), which has over 3,000 entries. The commentary to this volume has a bit of the flavor of Food First, but the massive collection of references is extremely useful to a wide range of scholars.

Three relatively new books provide perspectives on the role of agricultural trade. Jimmye Hillman and others, *International Trade and Agriculture: Theory and Policy* (Boulder, Colo.: Westview Press, 1979), and the University of Minnesota Extension Service, *Speaking of Trade: Its Effect on Agriculture,* Special Report no. 72 (St. Paul, 1978), offer interesting blends of theory and agricultural trade policy viewed mainly from a U.S. perspective. T. K. Warley, *Agriculture in an Interdependent World: U.S. and Canadian Perspectives* (Washington, D.C.: National Planning Association, 1977), provides a clear sense of interdependence among East-West and North-South trading partners. An article by G. Edward Schuh, "The New Macroeconomics of Agriculture," A/D/C Reprint no. 29 (New York: Agricultural Development Council, 1977), presents a succinct review of productivity problems in U.S. agriculture in the 1970s, the macroeconomic implications for the United States, and the trade implications for the rest of the world. A similar article reviews the incentives-oriented food policy adopted in China in the late 1970s and examines potential trade repercussions for the world grain market: C. Peter Timmer, "China and the World Food System," in Ray A. Goldberg, ed., *Research in Domestic and International Agribusiness*, vol. 2 (Greenwich, Conn.: JAI Press, 1981), pp. 75–118.

The potential for international arrangements to improve the stability of commodity prices depends significantly on the structure of individual commodity markets. The world rice economy is summarized in Walter P. Falcon and Eric A. Monke, "International Trade in Rice," *Food Research Institute Studies*, vol. 17, no. 3 (1979–80), and the world wheat economy in International Maize and Wheat Improvement Center (CIMMYT), *World Wheat Facts and Trends* (Mexico City, 1981). Buffer stocks are assessed in Shlomo Reutlinger, "Evaluating Wheat Buffer Stocks," *American Journal of Agricultural Economics*, vol. 58, no. 1 (February 1976), and with quite different conclusions in Anne E. Peck, "Implications of Private Storage of Grains for Buffer Stock Schemes to Stabilize Prices," *Food Research Institute Studies*, vol. 16, no. 3 (1977–78). A proposal to build domestic buffer stocks to improve food security is in World Food Council of the United Nations, *World Food Security and Market Stability: A Developing Country–Owned Reserve* (Rome, March 1982). Serious doubts about the economic desirability or the workability of international (as opposed to national) buffer stocks are presented in both expository and mathematical terms in David M. G. Newbery and Joseph E. Stiglitz, *The Theory of Commodity Price Stabilization: A Study in the Economics of Risk* (Oxford: Clarendon Press, 1981).

The macroeconomic impact of food aid, its potential for building human capital, and its role in an overall national food policy are discussed in Gordon O. Nelson and others, *Food Aid and Development* (New York: Agricultural Development Council, 1981). Although food aid has often turned out to have negative consequences for agricultural development and ultimately on the ability of a country to feed its own citizens, project food aid, especially when managed by private volunteer assistance agencies such as OXFAM, was thought to have a much more successful record. However, a strong condemnation of the record of project food aid as a contribution to development is made by Tony Jackson with Deborah Eade, *Against the Grain: The Dilemma of Project Food Aid* (Oxford: Oxfam, 1982).

The book by Alberto Valdés, ed., *Food Security for Developing Countries* (Boulder, Colo.: Westview Press, 1981), deals with elements of instability as they affect domestic food security. This volume contains a discussion of the use of buffer funds to assist food importers by Louis M. Goreux, "Compensatory Finance for Fluctuations in the Cost of Cereal Imports," as well as an article by Alberto Valdés and Panos Konandreas, "Assessing Food Insecurity," which contains the data shown in table 6-1. The use of futures markets by importing countries is analyzed by Anne E. Peck, "Futures Markets, Food Imports and Food Security," AGREP Division Working Paper no. 43 (Washington, D.C.: World Bank, September 1982).

The literature on basic needs has grown rapidly in the wake of the food and oil crises of the mid-1970s. At that time sustained growth seemed to be impossible; much attention was devoted to finding new strategies to alleviate the misery of the poor in the context of a stagnant economy. The most eloquent outcome of this body of thought is Paul Streeten and others, *First Things First: Meeting Basic Human Needs* (London: Oxford University Press, 1982).

Index

The full range of World Bank publications, both free and for sale, is described in the *Catalog of World Bank Publications*; the continuing research program is outlined in *World Bank Research Program: Abstracts of Current Studies*. Both booklets are updated annually; the most recent edition of each is available without charge from the Publications Distribution Unit, Dept. B., World Bank, 1818 H Street, N.W., Washington, D.C. 20433, U.S.A.

C. Peter Timmer is John D. Black Professor of Agriculture and Business at the Harvard University Graduate School of Business Administration; Walter P. Falcon is Helen C. Farnsworth Professor of International Agricultural Policy and director of the Food Research Institute, Stanford University; and Scott R. Pearson is professor and associate director of the same institute. All three have been consultants to the World Bank.